# Even in the Darkness a Flower Can Grow

## by

## Arlington Andcis

EVEN IN THE DARKNESS
A FLOWER CAN GROW
by Arlington Andcis

Cover Concept, Book Design
and Layout by Arlington Andcis

©2013 Arlington Andcis. All Rights Reserved.

No part of this publication may be reproduced, stored in a retrieval system, or transmitted, in any form or by any means, electronic, mechanical, photocopying, recording, or otherwise, without the written prior permission of the author.

ISBN-13: 978-0615818351

# Chapter 1

It was a typical hot southern afternoon. It was so hot that the road in front of Sadie was bubbling like bacon in her momma's black, cast iron frying pan from the intensity of the heat.

Still Sadie didn't care.

Once again she had managed to slip away from the weekly Saturday family gathering to attend to maters closer to her own liking, and not even the melting road, rolling hills, or lonely hot walk would deter her in her pursuits.

She knew what they were saying about her amongst the family, but Sadie didn't care.

"Sticks and stones," was all Sadie said.

Several hours later, Sadie was greeted by a stranger - - a handsome stranger - - but still a stranger.

Wham!

Henry was dazed and confused. He staggered back and was miraculously caught by the double-decker, cast iron stove. Sadie's father had gotten the stove for her mother as part of an agreement not to kill a man who had crossed him and his family.

Henry was so stunned by Sadie's greeting that he didn't even check to see if the stove was hot. But at the moment that was the least of his concerns.

"Sadie!" Henry exclaimed.

She had this, 'go to hell look on her face.'

"Did you just hit me with that cast iron frying pan?"

Those were his last words.

From his seated perch on the usually hot stove top, he fell flat on his face.

Boom!

Henry's fall shook that little white house in more ways than one.

Sadie's parents, sitting under the stars on their little front porch, jumped and looked at each other with sheer fear written on both their faces. Her mother instantly stopping rocking and fanning, and her father stopped cleaning his gun.

Within seconds, they were on their feet and running into the house.

"Sadie! What have you done?" Her mother exclaimed.

Her father was already on his knees beside Henry.

Sadie was standing there still stunned and angry, and still holding the black, cast iron frying pan in her left hand.

"Is he dead Woodrow?"

"I don't think so Eleanor, but he is barely clinging on to life."

"We need to call the doctor."

"Eleanor, we can't afford a doctor."

"I got some money I was saving for a new dress." Sadie finally joined the conversation.

"No Sadie, I don't want you spending your money on me," said a voice nearly from the grave.

"Henry, boy you a'ight?" Woodrow asked.

'Henry let's get you on the sofa in the living room," Mrs. Eleanor said.

"Sadie bring me that pale of cool water from the well and some clean towels from the clothesline."

Sadie was frozen in her spot like a statute.

"Sadie, did you hear me child?"

Sadie knew that tone. It brought her back into the present. "Yes ma'am."

It didn't take Sadie long before she was back in the living room with her parents as they tended to the goose-egg-sized knot on the right side of Henry's face.

Mrs. Eleanor kept putting cold rags on Henry's neck and head to keep him awake and talking.

"Sadie what would possess you to do such a thing?" Her mother asked as she continued to tend to Henry.

"Sadie what's wrong with you? Your mother asked you a question. Cat gotcha your tongue?" Her father continued.

"Mr. and Mrs. Minwhite, it's not Sadie's fault. It's my fault."

Her parents were confused because Sadie looked confused.

"I don't understand," her mother said.

"I asked Sadie to marry me."

"And this was your answer?" Her father interjected.

"No. That is not why I hit him." Sadie said almost defiantly.

"Now I am really confused." Her mother said.

"Well I am getting damn angry about this game you are playing Sadie." Her father stated.

"I hit Henry because he had lipstick on his collar and perfume all over his clothes."

"What? That doesn't make sense." Her dad said.

"Woodrow, don't you see? Sadie was upset because Henry asked her to marry him just after he had been with another woman."

"Women," Sadie said.

"Damn boy you trying to marry a woman scorned?" Mr. Woodrow said moving from the couch to his favorite seat next to the wood-burning stove that took up most of the small living room. "Hell, you brave kid. Stupid but brave."

Henry starred at Mr. Woodrow as if he knew something the women in the room didn't know.

"Thank you Sadie, Mr. and Mrs. Minwhite. I need to get back to the city so I can get some rest. Again, thank ya'll for everything," Henry politely said as he tipped his never-leave-home-without-it brown fedora.

Sadie was completely disinterested at that point.

Henry slowly stood up. His legs were still wobbly.

"Henry are you sure you can drive home?"

"Yes ma'am Mrs. Eleanor. I'll be fine. And if I need some help Jackie can help."

"Who is Jackie?" Mrs. Eleanor asked before Sadie could, in a way that only a black woman could.

"Before you get too excited Eleanor Jackie is a guy. He's Henry traveling companion." Mr. Woodrow interjected.

"How do you know so much about Henry's comings and goings?" Mrs. Eleanor asked her husband.

Sadie was equally interested in her daddy's answer.

"On that note, I think I will leave."

"Yea boy, let me walk you to your car."

"Woodrow, you get back here. I want an answer."

"Yes dear," Mr. Woodrow answered his wife as he continued to walk Henry out the house and to his car.

"Listen son, you sure you can drive home? Now I am more than willing to take you home."

"Woodrow I'm just fine to drive and if I need any help, I'll just wake Jackie up from the backseat."

Mr. Minwhite looked into the backseat to make sure Jackie was there. As sure as it was Saturday night, Jackie was lying in the backseat sleeping off his usual stupor.

"Woodrow, I'll be fine. I got to go. Tell Sadie I will see her next week."

Henry took his time driving home that night. It just didn't seem to be much reason to hurry. Although he was going forward, he felt like his life was behind him.

"Man whoever you are talking to up there I wish ya'll would be quiet so I can get some sleep."

"Jackie go back to sleep."

"Too late for that," Jackie said as he sat up and leaned over the back seat.

"Damn man, you look like hell."

"You're one to talk." Henry replied.

"Shit man. Who beat the hell out of you?"

"Sadie hit me with a frying pan."

"Damn man that b____ is crazy."

Whap!

Henry backhanded Jackie with his right fist so hard that Jackie's head snapped like he had whiplash. But still that didn't stop Jackie's mouth.

"Don't you ever call Sadie that again or I'm gonna have to find a new best man."

"What! You mean to tell me that you gone marry this b…I mean this woman even after she tried to kill yo ass with a frying pan?" Jackie asked as he wiped the blood from his nose and mouth.

"You damn right. I'm gonna marry her as quick as I can."

"Man, Henry you've only known that b____, I mean you have only known Sadie a few weeks, and you telling me you gonna marry her?"

Henry kept trying to focus on the dark curvy country roads of Marvin as he kept blinking fast to try and focus. His headache was coming back.

"She must have some mighty plush pile," Jackie continued.

"I don't know," Henry replied.

"You mean to tell me you haven't even walked on her carpet?"

"Not even once," Henry replied. "And now I don't even care. I want to marry her because she is not like the rest of the women that spend all their time talkin' about marriage. Sadie has never once mentioned marriage to me."

"Then what makes you think she wants to get married and let alone to you?"

"Damn, I never even thought about that, but it don't change my mind. I still want to marry her."

By this time they were within the city limits and there were a few more lights to help guide Henry safely home.

Finally, they pulled into the long dirt driveway, in front of the brown house on the hill. Henry put the car in gear and then fell out right where he sat.

Jackie jumped out of the backseat of his chauffeured ride screaming, "Help, help!"

He ran up to the front porch and started banging on the door franticly. "Mr. Pottishear, Lucy, Martha Sue, Tommy Lee. Help!"

Tommy Lee jumped from his bed and came running in his long johns.

"Jackie what's wrong?"

"Henry done fell out in the car."

Tommy Lee rushes to his older brother's side. "Henry." Tommy Lee was shaking his brother and crying at the same time.

Lucy came out in her housecoat and shoes. She calmly felt Henry's neck for a pulse.

"Tommy Lee, you, Jackie, and George get him out of that car and carry Henry into the house. Put him on the sofa near the fire."

"Martha Sue get me some hot boiling water and a pale of cool water from the well."

"What the hell is going on around here," Mr. Pottishear was yelling as he came down the hall banging his cane on the floor.

Then he saw his eldest son lying on the couch. "What has he done? Spent all of his money as usual and now he has come home to pass out broke?"

"No Pa, Henry is sick," Martha Sue said.

Mr. Pottishear was quieted by Martha Sue's voice. She was the last and the youngest of his thirteen children, so she held a special spot in his heart none of her siblings could ever attain.

He walked over and put his old, care-worn hand on his son's forehead. Then he turned around and started to walk by down the hallway to his room. "There ain't nothing wrong with that boy except that he is drunk, in love, and somebody done gone and put a knot on his right temple the size of that big bird's egg."

Lucy knew exactly what to do. She started alternating between cold and warm presses on Henry's knot. She made Martha Sue keep it going while she went in the kitchen and fixed Henry a hangover concoction and some hot soup to sooth his bruised ego.

"Lucy, Lucy!" Tommy Lee screamed for his older sister.

"Tommy Lee what is all the screaming about?" Lucy said as she entered the room.

"Oh, so you are back from the dead?" Lucy was a short, but powerful woman. She was standing there with her arms crossed and patting her feet. The Indian side of their mother always came out in her when she was angry.

"Not now Lucy." Henry knew his older sister did not approve.

"Let me get this soup for you because I am sure that you haven't eaten all day."

"Henry what happened?" Tommy Lee wanted to know. He worshipped his older brother.

"On that note I better go. I can walk home. I'll talk to you later Henry."

"Okay Jackie."

Lucy brought the tray back into the living room where everyone was gathered.

"Okay, now are you going to tell us what happened?" Lucy was a little softer now and less accusatory.

Henry took a few sips of the soup. It brightened his countenance. "Thanks Lucy," he said as he reached out his hand of peace to his oldest sister.

"Okay, okay," Lucy said patting Henry's hand. "Forget the mushy stuff and tell us what or who tried to kill you tonight."

Henry started smiling.

"What's so funny?" Martha Sue asked.

"Well, first of all, nobody tried to kill me."

"What about the knot of your temple?" Tommy Lee asked.

There was banging in the back of the house.

"Pop you might as well come on down here so you can hear this too." Henry knew his dad wanted to hear but he would never let that be known.

"Come on Henry, what's going on?" Lucy insisted.

"I got this knot because I asked this new girl Sadie to marry me."

"Henry, that don't make no sense son." Their dad tried to sound concerned.

"When I asked Sadie to marry me she hit me side the head with a cast iron frying pan."

All of the air in the room was immediately sucked up when they all gasped at the same time.

"No wonder you have never been married," Martha Sue said.

"What does that mean?"

"It means how many frying pans have you been hit with before and we never knew."

"I have never been hit by a frying pan before, and I have never wanted to get married before."

"Get out of here," Tommy Lee chimed in.

"Henry you mean to tell me that all of those women you dated, you never wanted to marry any of them."

"Tommy Lee, Henry is not the marrying type. He is the love 'em and leave 'em type. Just like his papa," Lucy chimed in before anyone else could say anything.

"Just because I am old doesn't mean I can't beat your ass Lucy," their dad said shaking his cane at Lucy.

"Lucy, Sadie is not like any woman I have ever dated before. She is beautiful, kind, smart, independent…"

"And mean apparently," George interjected. Everyone turned and looked at him because George rarely said a word.

"What? Am I not a part of this family too?"

"Of course you are honey," Lucy said kissing her husband on his cheek.

"Okay so if you love Sadie and she loves you, then why did she hit you with a frying pan?" Martha Sue had to know.

Henry was silent for a long while as he rubbed his knot.

"Okay Henry what did you do?" Lucy said with her arms crossed again.

"I made a mistake."

"What kind of mistake Henry?" Tommy Lee inquired.

"I made the mistake of asking Sadie to marry me with a slight twist."

All eyes were glued on Henry and no one said a word.

"Okay Henry, what gives?" Martha Sue broke the silence.

"I made the mistake of asking Sadie to marry me after I had been out drinking with Jackie."

"You were drunk when you asked her?" Lucy was angry now.

"No, but I might have had a little alcohol on my breath."

"Then what Henry? Spit it out boy!" The senior Mr. Pottishear was banging his cane in agitation.

"Okay. Okay. I had lipstick on my collar and perfume on my clothes."

"Henry, you didn't!" Lucy walked over and smacked Henry on the back of his head.

"Lucy, I have enough knots for one night and on my head, please."

"Henry how could you be so insensitive?" Martha Sue was clearly disappointed.

"Martha Sue," Henry rubbed his little sister's face. "I had no idea that that girl's lipstick was on my collar or another girl's perfume was on my clothes."

"So who was it?" Tommy Lee was excited to know.

"Who what Tommy Lee?"

"Who was the woman?" Tommy Lee asked.

It was Tommy Lee's turn to get smacked by Lucy.

"You were with two women before you proposed to Sadie?" George asked in a slightly excited voice.

"George!" Lucy need not say any more than that.

"Boy you are a manwhore," his daddy said.

"He's a male slut is what he is." Lucy was firm.

"Good going boy," Mr. Pottishear said as he made his way back down to his room.

"Now that we've got to the end of this charade we don't have to worry about all this mess no more." It was their papa's parting shot.

"No Papa. I'm going to marry Sadie no matter how long it takes. I love her and want her to be my wife."

Their father turned around so fast that he almost fell. "You plan on doing what? I wish your mother was here to hear all of this."

"I wish she was here too papa. I wish she was here too."

"So Henry what makes you think Sadie wants to marry you after all of this?" Martha Sue asked. She knew her brother's heart was good and tender even when his brain was partially working.

"Martha Sue, I really believe she loves me. Why else would she be so mad about another woman?"

"Women," Tommy Lee said.

Silence.

"Have you had sex with her?" Tommy Lee asked, as it was Martha Sue's turn to smack him upside the head.

"No Tommy Lee I have not so much as touched Sadie. She's only let me kiss her one time in the last four weeks."

Although Henry was not accustomed to talking in this kind of detail to anyone, including Jackie, he decided he would answer Tommy Lee this time only because he had put his family through so much and because he really loved Sadie.

"What?" Lucy was stunned at what she was hearing from Henry. Henry would never pass up a piece of hot apple pie from any woman.

"So she refused your advances?" Lucy continued.

"I've never made any Lucy. What are you doing?"

Lucy was feeling Henry's head and she was holding his face tightly so that Henry could not move. "I am making sure that this is my brother Henry that I am talking to."

"Boy. Do you know what you are doing? What if she is only a missionary?"

"Papa I thought you had gone back to sleep?"

"How can I when my oldest son is losing his mind right before my very own eyes?"

"Papa I am not losing my mind. I'm turning into a man."

"How are you a man when you just turned nineteen years old?"

"Papa, I'm 20 years old."

"But your mind and your body are still childlike. So you can forget marriage and that's my final word."

"Henry are you sure?" Martha Sue's eyes were so innocent.

"Martha Sue I have never been more sure about anything in my life." Henry was looking directly into Martha Sue's eyes.

"Then we should give him some time and maybe Papa will change his mind."

"Martha Sue you know him. He will never change his mind."

"So then what are you going to do Henry?" Tommy Lee needed to know.

"I told you Tommy Lee I'm going to marry Sadie."

"But what about what Papa said?"

"Well one thing's for sure. We are not going to figure it all out tonight. So come on everyone it's time to go to bed." Mother hen Lucy had spoken.

It wasn't long before the previously busy house was completely quiet.

"Tommy Lee?"

No answer.

"Tommy Lee?"

"What Henry?" Tommy Lee said in a high-pitched, agitated tone.

"Never mind, we will talk about it later."

Henry rolled over on his pillow. "I just wanted to tell you that I'm gonna miss hanging out with you."

Tommy Lee's eyes popped open but he didn't dare move an inch because he didn't want to know what Henry meant.

A few days later…

Meanwhile back at Sadie's house, the mood was a little different.

"Sadie."

"Yes ma'am."

"You have been working harder in these fields than you have ever worked before."

"What are you talking about momma?"

"Listen child," Mrs. Eleanor said as she gently grabbed Sadie's chin and turned her daughter's face up to look in her eyes instead of at the ground.

"I'm your mother. You can fool a lot of people but you can never fool me. Now I know that you hate working in these cotton fields and so do I. But it is not important where you are as long as you are doing an honest day's work. What's important is that you don't let your dreams die in these fields."

"Momma, I don't know what you are talking about."

"Sadie, you have never worked as hard as you have worked since you and Henry had that little spat. Child it is written all over your face. You love that man and there is nothing you can do to tell me otherwise. And I know why you hit him too."

Sadie was speechless at the uncovering of her private thoughts. She was only used to getting undressed alone in the dark. She had never been undressed publicly before, and she didn't like it much – even if it was her mother.

"Sadie let me tell you a little bit about men. Even though they may wander the love that they have for you is always going to be real. But you have to be strong for them because they are weak enough for both of you."

"But momma he had another women's lipstick on his collar and someone else's perfume on him while he was asking me to marry him. Why did daddy have to bring Henry into my life?"

Sadie started crying.

"Sadie stop crying child," her momma said while whipping her tears. "It is going to be alright."

"You sure?"

"I promise. Now come on, let's get back to work before mister sees us sitting on this bale of hay having a family chat."

"But it has been a month since Henry has come around."

"It is going to be okay honey. Momma wouldn't tell you nothin' wrong."

Finally, the end of the work week arrived and not too soon because Sadie was exhausted emotionally and physically. Although the week was of no real interest to her, she was too disciplined to alter her normal routine of getting up early before the sun rose and start preparing breakfast for herself and her parents before they woke up. In fact it was the inviting aroma of Sadie's breakfast that often woke her parents up each morning.

"Sadie, honey."

"Good morning momma."

"Sadie, what are you doing up some early this morning?"

"I am making breakfast like I always do."

"Sadie, it's Saturday."

"Oh…oh," Sadie said as she turned around clearly out of sync.

"I'll get your daddy and we can all eat an early breakfast and go back to sleep for a little while longer."

It was 7:30 am, some four hours later, and Sadie's parents were up again.

"I just checked in on Sadie and she's still sleeping so that gives us time to talk a little."

"Sure Mrs. Minwhite, what's on that pretty mind of yours this morning?"

"I want you to tell me how you and Henry met and what possessed you to bring him home to our Sadie?"

As they sat there sharing a few cups of hot coffee, Mr. Minwhite pondered his options.

"Woodrow don't you dare try to conjure up some lie to tell me because I can see those little wheels in your head turning."

"Eleanor, you know I cannot lie to you."

"I am counting on that for Sadie's sake. She has fallen head over heels completely in love with Henry. Haven't you seen how she has been more dedicated to working in the fields lately?"

Woodrow had this blank look on his face.

"Of course you haven't noticed a thing."

"But Eleanor isn't it a good thing Sadie is in love. She is 18 years old. She is almost an old maid."

"Old maid? Sadie is not an old maid Woodrow she is a beautiful young teenager. She is strong, shapely, smart, independent, hard-working, and an excellent cook. Any man should be proud to have Sadie as his wife."

"That's just it Eleanor, Sadie has not been interested in any man a'tall. She has refused every boy at church, every single man her cousins have tried to introduce her to, and, she won't even talk to any of the men on Mr. Jack's farm."

"Good. Sadie is not going to settle for just any man and she shouldn't. Look at the men her cousins have married. None of them are worth a hoot. And I certainly don't want her marrying some field hand. I want her to marry someone who will take her away from these cotton fields."

"Then why did she try and kill Henry with that frying pan?"

"You tell me Woodrow?"

"What do you mean Eleanor?"

"We have come full circle back to my original question. How did you meet Henry and why did you bring him here to our Sadie?"

"I meet him at my little drinking spot in town."

"So you mean to tell me you and Henry are drinking buddies?"

"Not exactly. He came into the place about a month or two ago and I had to rescue him."

"Rescue him?"

"Yea he and his friend got into a fight not long after they came into the house."

"What house?"

"Ruby's place."

"Is this a new place?"

"The white men burned down Stiff's house because the white folk in town had started coming to him."

Eleanor just looked at Woodrow.

"Eleanor, Stiff was taking all of their money away so they burned him down."

"What about the police?"

"Eleanor, honey, how could Stiff call the police when he wasn't supposed to be selling liquor and especially not to white folk."

"So you met Henry in a juke joint?"

"Exactly."

Eleanor actually already knew the answer to her question but she wanted Woodrow to admit it.

"So anyway back to Henry."

"Right, so I had to rescue him the first night he came into Ruby's because all of the women jumped on him like he was honey and all of the men were ready to fight."

"And he you jumped in and started fighting too? Did you shoot anybody?"

"Didn't have to honey."

Eleanor knew her husband but she wasn't sure he didn't shoot someone.

"Eleanor, I promise you I didn't shoot no body. Anyhow, after I saved Henry's hide that night we started talking and we kept talking every time he came down."

Eleanor knew Woodrow was leaving something out but she wasn't sure she wanted to know exactly what that it was.

"Anyway I finally told Henry I wanted him to meet my daughter and he agreed."

"What made you decide to tell him about Sadie when you made me a promise."

"Because Eleanor, Henry is a good looking kid with a good job in the city, and I think he will be good to Sadie."

"How do you know?"

"Because I told him if he hurt my daughter I would kill him."

"Every father says that Woodrow."

"Not after they had just seen a father sh_____..."

Woodrow stopped short of a confession.

"Just trust me Eleanor when I tell you he knew that I meant it."

"But did you put him up to marrying Sadie."

Just then, Sadie's bedroom door opened directly into the kitchen.

"Good morning Sadie honey, again."

"So did you daddy?"

"Did I what honey?"

"Did you put Henry up to marrying me?"

Woodrow looked at his wife."

"Well Woodrow?"

"Listen, both of you. I had no idea he was going to ask Sadie to marry him. I just thought he would be a nice guy to get Sadie out of the house and help her start to see a new world."

Then Woodrow walked over to his daughter and looked her square in her eyes. "If I had known he was going to ask you to marry him I would have never let him come here with women's perfume on his clothes and lipstick on his collar."

"Daddy you knew too?"

"Sadie, baby, your daddy does know a few things."

"Yea like women," his wife replied.

Woodrow would not respond to his wife's comments because it would create more problems for him than it could solve.

"He also had alcohol on his breath," Sadie said.

"But Sadie honey Henry is a good looking man who has never been married before. He could have any woman he chooses."

"But daddy."

"But Sadie, he chose you, and that might just be a little scary for him. And sometimes alcohol can help strengthen a man in his weakness. It does not mean his intentions are not true."

"I didn't think about it that way. Besides it doesn't matter anyway, it has been more than four weeks since Henry has come around."

"Sadie, one thing you count on for sure if Henry comes around here again, he loves you despite the fact that you tried to kill him."

They all started laughing.

A few hours after their day was done they were all gathered on the front porch as usual enjoying the nice, cool, summer breeze, when an unexpected car pulled up the long gravel driveway.

Sadie's heart jumped with excitement inside her chest but she was not about to let it show.

"Good evening Mr. and Mrs. Minwhite," Henry politely said as he tipped his never-leave-home-without-it fedora.

No one immediately said a word.

Mrs. Minwhite kept on rocking and fanning herself with the fan her husband had made by hand. Unbeknownst to anyone Mr. Minwhite had been pilfering small amounts of corn from Old Man Jack's storage bins just so that he could make a fan for his wife. It was a beautifully crafted fan but Mrs. Minwhite loved it more because her husband made it just for her.

Meanwhile, while Sadie's heart was skipping beats like a love sick teenage girl, her mind told her that this man, who had just interrupted their Saturday evening, was slicker than a two-dollar Jezebel in a room full of men.

"How's that bump on your head Henry?"

"It's all healed now Mrs. Minwhite. Thank you for asking," Henry said while starring at Sadie the entire time.

Sadie's mother smiled a big smile that showed off her beautifully crafted mouth full of gold. Her dental work was beautifully detailed, with a natural look to it. Her mouth was the crowning piece to cap off her natural beauty. She had a beautiful, flawless, walnut toned skin, jet black curly hair with just touches of grey strategically placed that looked like God had painted them in her head personally. Although she was seated, she sat with such grace and finesse that it was easy to tell that she was tall, thin, perfectly shaped, and gorgeous to a fault.

The scene looked as if it was put together for a black and white photo shoot for Norman Rockwell. But it was not a picture. It was the face of true poverty – gracefully displayed, but still poverty nonetheless.

"Sadie." Henry forcefully said her name with such passion there was no way to hide it. He had this determined look on his face.

Mrs. Minwhite continued to gently rock in her rocking chair that had been in her family for almost a 100 years while proudly fanning herself with her handmade fan.

"Sadie." Henry called her name, took a deep breath, and said, "Will you marry me?"

Mrs. Minwhite stopped rocking like a car stops when braked. Mr. Minwhite looked squarely at Henry.

"Boy, you sure you know what you're doing?" Mr. Minwhite said.

Sadie sat there unfazed by the spectacle of it all. She was not one to be rushed into anything, no matter who or what was doing the rushing.

"Sadie why don't you and Henry go for a walk near the pond at the back of the house," her mother suggested.

Sadie's eyes questioned her mother's suggestion.

Go on, her mother motioned with her head.

Sadie followed her mother's command because she was never one to be disobedient to her mother, no matter what.

As they strolled down the path to the pond, Henry asked, "May I hold your hand?"

Sadie never said yes or no. But when Henry's strong hand touched her left hand, she jumped a little at first. Then she became comfortable with him touching her skin.

"You have really soft hands Sadie."

"You lie Henry."

"I'm not lying to you Sadie. You do have soft hands. And I don't want our relationships to be based on lies. Besides, you are far too critical of yourself."

"How do you know what I am?"

"Because you are always looking down so no one can look in your eyes."

"You've only seen me four times, how do you know what I do or don't do?"

"You are all I have thought about for the past month. But how could I think about anything else when my head was throbbing?" Henry chuckled.

"Then again, it was a good reminder of you, sort of."

"I'm sorry I hit you so hard. I never meant to hurt you."

"Sadie, why don't you look at me when you talk to me?"

Sadie was talking to Henry but she was looking at the forest to her right. The problem was that Henry was on her left.

"You've never had a boyfriend before have you?"

"Never needed one before."

"But who do you laugh and talk to, and tell your secrets to? Your dreams?"

"My baby dolls? Who do you think I talk to?"

"You still have baby dolls."

"Henry sometimes you are so dumb. I don't have any baby dolls. I have never had a baby doll in my life. I was just joshing you."

Henry wasn't paying any attention to Sadie's words because he was too busy focusing on her.

"Henry you aren't even listening to me. What are you starring at?"

"You Sadie. You."

"You haven't answered my question yet."

"What ques____"

Before Sadie could get the words out of her mouth, Henry kissed her and to his surprise she kissed him back.

For the remainder of the walk they just enjoyed each other. Words would have been an interruption into this most intimate time for both Henry and Sadie. As their walk started to come to a close Sadie's countenance changed.

"What's wrong Sadie?"

Sadie paused for a long time, and then she said, "I'm a little sad that our walk is over."

"But don't let that go to your head," she said pointing her finger at Henry.

Henry grabbed her finger and wrapped his hand around her index finger and kissed it. "This doesn't have to be the end of the walks or us."

As they got close to the porch, her parents were still sitting in their exact positions, which was not unusual, because they normally sat on their porch until extremely late into the evenings on Saturday anyway.

As soon as they reached her parents earshot, Sadie said "Yes."

"Yes?" Henry asked to be sure Sadie agreed.

"Yes, I will marry you."

Henry already had Sadie in his arms and was swinging her around just as her parents were jumping up to celebrate at the good news.

"Come on in the house and have a drink to celebrate this good news boi."

"Thanks Mr. Minwhite but I am going to go home now. I have had enough excitement to last for me a while. And driving from down here in the country back to the city is enough without being lit."

# Chapter 2

Over the next few months, Henry spent every single weekend with Sadie and her family. In fact that little white house on Marvin Highway became his second home.

"Henry would you like to go to church with us tomorrow?"

Henry hesitated.

"Sadie, it's been a really long time since I've been to church."

"So, no better time to start."

Henry still paused.

"You know what Henry, it's okay. I don't want to make you do something you don't want to do."

"Now I've gone and made you mad."

"No you haven't Henry. I'm not mad at you. How can I get mad at you about a decision that is between you and The Lord?"

"Are you sure Sadie?"

"I'm positive."

"Then give me a kiss."

Sadie reluctantly gave him a kiss. But she kept her eyes open to look at Henry.

"Why you looking at me like that?"

"You wouldn't know I was looking at you if you weren't looking at me."

"We're going to be two crossed-eyed, ugly people that nobody will marry if we don't stop."

They started laughing.

"Listen Henry. I know you have dated a lot of girls and I know you are used to all kinds of women falling all over you and jumping at you beck and call. But, I am not that kind of girl and I am not going to be hugged all up under you every time you make a move."

Henry was so moved by Sadie's words that Henry took her in his arms and kissed her like she was the last bite of the best ice cream he had ever eaten before in his life. Sadie's body went limp in his arms.

"I've got to go Sadie."

"Huh?"

"I've got to go. It's getting late."

"But the sun has barely gone down Henry."

"I've got a big day tomorrow."

"You've got to work tomorrow?"

"I didn't say that. I said I have a big day tomorrow."

"But tomorrow is Sunday."

"I know that honey and I have a big day tomorrow so I have to go early tonight."

He gave her a little peck on her pouty lips.

"Have a great day in church tomorrow."

Sadie was clearly disappointed.

She went into the house letting the screen door slam behind her.

"Sadie what's wrong with you girl?" Her daddy asked.

"Huh daddy?"

"What's wrong with you? You let the screen door slam behind you?"

She looked back at the door, still in a daze. "I'm sorry. I'm going to bed."

"Sadie honey do you feel okay?"

"Sure momma. Good night."

Her parents looked at each other in deep concern.

"She was pouting Woodrow. You know that girl can pout for a week."

Meanwhile back at Henry's home....

"Henry what are you doing home so early?"

"I came home to go to bed early tonight Tommy Lee."

Lucy came down the hall to check on her oldest brother. "Henry what's wrong with you? Are you sick?"

"No I'm not sick Lucy."

"Then why are you home so early on a Saturday night and why aren't you drunk?"

"I'm home because I have a big day tomorrow and I need to go to bed early so I can be ready for it. And I'm not drunk because I have been with Sadie and I don't have no reason to be drunk when I'm with her."

"You been where?" A graspy voice said as it rushed down the hallway.

"You heard me Pop. I've been with Sadie."

"I thought I told you not to see that girl no more."

"Sorry Pop I can't do that. I love Sadie."

"You look here Henry J. Pottishear as long as you are in my house, you will abide by my rules or…"

"Then Pop I guess I will have to find us somewhere else to live."

"Us?" Martha Sue asked as she jumped from bed and ran into her brothers' room where the action was.

"Yea Martha Sue." Henry's voice was a little less defiant now as it always was when it came to her. "I asked Sadie to marry me again and she said yes."

"Well I'll be a monkey's uncle," George said as he took his place beside his wife Lucy.

"When's the wedding?" Martha Sue was excited.

"Damn Martha Sue, I hadn't even thought about that."

Their father turned around and started walking back down the hall. Henry ran after his father.

"Pop listen. I don't know why you don't want me to marry Sadie, but I love her and the time has come for me to grow up and start my own family. Sadie has made me a better man just from being around her."

"She asked you to stop drinking and carousing with women?"

"That's just it Tommy Lee, she didn't have to ask. It just happened."

"Well I for one can't wait to meet this Sadie." Lucy said.

"Me too."

"Me too."

"Me too."

Lucy had set off some kind of chain reaction.

"So you see Papa, even if you won't be happy for me, I am going to marry Sadie and she is going to be part of this family, our family - - my family."

Their papa was mean like Ebenezer Scrooge and he sort of looked like him too. But even that was not enough to deter Henry's enthusiasm, much like Bob Cratchet.

"That man is going to be mean until the day he dies. But I can't worry about that. I got to do what is right for me." Henry was looking his Lucy squarely in her eyes, as best he could, because Lucy was only about 5'1" or 5'2" and Henry was 6'3".

"Okay mister dreamy." Lucy softened at her brother's confession. "What is so important that you are going to bed before the rooster comes out in the morning?"

"Sadie asked me to go to church with her tomorrow and I am going to go."

"What?" Their papa screamed from his room.

Every other mouth in the room also dropped open except for Henry's, and with that he went to bed.

No one in that room believed Henry would ever get up to go to church.

Sure enough 6:30 am came and Henry was up shaving and getting dressed. Shortly after that he had a small group of admirers watching him as he finished shaving.

"Do y'all mind, I need to take a bath."

"Well I'll be damned!"

SMACK!

Lucy hit Tommy Lee so hard his head jerked forward then back. And Tommy Lee wouldn't dare challenge Lucy.

Almost an hour later, Henry emerged from the bathroom and his audience was waiting to receive him.

"Henry, you are sharper than anything I have ever seen down at the general store," Tommy Lee shouted.

"Oh, Henry, you look so handsome."

"Thank you Martha Sue."

"Lucy, are you crying?" Henry asked with great concern.

"Don't worry about me. Go on get out of here before you be late."

As he was leaving their papa came out of his room banging his cane on the floor, "Lucy, where is my breakfast?"

Everyone knew that was just his excuse to see Henry in his Sunday gotomeetin' clothes.

The drive to Marvin seemed to last only minutes for Henry. When he pulled up in the driveway, he was met with great surprise.

Knock. Knock.

"Henry?"

"Good morning Mrs. Minwhite."

Sadie stepped into the small living room behind her mother. She was clearly stunned by their guest at the door.

"Henry?" Sadie was smiling.

"Good morning Sadie."

"What are you doing here?"

"I'm here to go to church with you."

"You are?"

Sadie was so excited that she actually hugged Henry right there on the spot.

But what came next was unexpected. When they arrived at the church, which was only about a mile down the road from the house, someone spotted the strange car as they pulled into the church's parking lot, primarily because there were so few cars at the church.

Before they could get out of the car, they were surrounded with eyes and faces and hands all over Henry's freshly polished car and cleaned glass.

But the amazing part was that Henry stayed cool about all the fingerprints all over his car.

"This scene never crossed my mind," Sadie's mother said.

"I'm embarrassed," Sadie said.

"Why Henry asked?"

"Because I can't believe my family is acting like they have never seen a car before."

"Sadie honey it's not the car they are interested in seeing. It's the driver," her father said.

Sure enough one of Sadie's cousins opened Henry's door before he could open it for himself.

"Hey good looking who are you?" These words came from a short, charcoal-colored, breasty woman. She did her best to push herself onto Henry.

Henry had to literally slide around to the other side of the car with his back pressed against the steel of the car in order to open Sadie's door.

Sadie shook her head in embarrassment. Then she spotted her grandpa.

"Henry come on I want you to meet someone."

The crowd surrounded them every step they took as they made their way up the steps to the church doors.

"Good morning Grandpa," Sadie said kissing her grandfather on the cheek.

"Good morning Sadie dear. How is my favorite girl this morning?"

"I'm good Papa. I want you to meet someone."

"Okay, who is this strapping young man?"

"Grandpa this is Henry."

"Henry this is my grandfather Mr. DeWitt Drasden."

"Good morning sir."

"Well good morning son. Welcome to our church home."

"Thank you for having me sir."

"Grandpa I have something to tell you."

Before Sadie could get the words out, the church bell began to ring.

"Good morning daddy." Sadie's mother stepped in behind her.

"Good morning Eleanor. How are you my dear? Morning Woodrow."

"Morning Mr. DeWitt."

"Papa I want you to come to the house for dinner this afternoon."

"Sure Eleanor."

Eleanor had to get it in early because she had fifteen brothers and sisters and it was hard to get her father alone on any day, especially on Sunday.

Church service seemed to last forever. Everyone was interested in everything but the preacher's message that morning.

When church did finally end, all attention was back on Sadie's side of the family, specifically her guest.

Once all of her grandpa's official duties were done, they were ready to leave. But it was no easy task waiting for her grandpa. They did not have a moment's peace while grandpa was overseeing the money count and recordation.

Normally after church everybody scattered for Sunday afternoon dinner. There was not a bad cook in Eleanor's family. But this Sunday you couldn't pull a single family member away with a tractor.

All of the women were mesmerized by Henry. The men were jealous of his debonair good looks. And all of the parents were just curious about what was going on.

Eleanor was huddled with her sisters and Woodrow was with the husbands. Sadie and Henry were trapped in a circle of on-looking cousins and their respective other halves.

Sadie's temper was starting to boil over and Henry could see it in Sadie's eyes but he didn't know what to do, so he just held on tightly to Sadie's hand and kept softly massaging it to let her know that he was with her.

Unexpectedly, their grandpa appeared at the top of the brick steps of the classic red brick church.

"Eleanor."

"I've got to go father is calling me y'all."

"Wait Eleanor. Daddy I thought it was my turn to have you for dinner."

"Emma Lee you didn't say anything to me about eating dinner with you today."

The truth is that some of Sadie's aunts were jealous of her mother. When they were smaller it use to bother Eleanor that her sisters were so mean to her, but as they have gotten older Eleanor does pay that any attention any more. However, it was clear to everyone that Eleanor was the beauty of the family and she had a gorgeous personality to match. So it didn't surprise her that her older sister Emma Lee was making a fuss about their father coming to dinner with her. The dinner wasn't the issue.

"Come on Eleanor let's go I'm hungry."

"Coming Papa. Okay girls I'll talk to y'all later."

Emma Lee had never forgiven Eleanor for being so beautiful and being her father's favorite. She was fuming. She tried to hide it but she was doing a piss poor job.

"Henry you sit here and talk to my daddy and grandpa. I'm going to help momma get dinner ready."

"So tell me son, what do you do for a living?"

"I'm a mechanic Mr. Drasden."

"Oh so you work on all kinds of cars?"

"Actually sir, I work on trucks. But I do work on cars for people I know."

"So you make a good living?"

"I do pretty good sir?"

"So you want to marry my Sadie?"

"How did you know sir?"

"Because you are the only man Sadie has ever brought to church."

"Sadie get away from that door eavesdropping on them and come over here and get these sweet potato pies out of the oven. And when you finish with that set the table and begin to put all of the vegetables in serving bowls."

"So Henry how did you meet our Sadie?"

Sadie was rushing to get her work done because she wanted to hear what her grandpapa was saying.

"Actually, Mr. DeWitt I introduced 'em."

"So you and Woodrow were drinking buddies?"

"Yes sir sort of."

"Explain that to me son."

"Well the first night I came to Marvin Mr. Woodrow saved me and my friend Jackie."

"So you brought a girl to your first trip to Marvin?"

"No sir," Henry chuckled. "Jackie is a guy."

Now it was Mr. DeWitt's turn to chuckle.

"Anyway some of the local fellas attacked me and Jackie the first night we walked into…"

"Let me guess. Stiff's place?"

"No, Mr. DeWitt. We was at Ruby's house."

"Oh," Mr. DeWitt said.

Henry held his head down. "Yes sir."

It was the first time ever that Henry was embarrassed about drinking and carousing.

"So Woodrow who did you shoot?"

Now it was Mrs. Eleanor's turn to listen at the door.

"Momma?" Sadie said in a funny but accusatory tone.

"Hush child."

"You know Henry, Woodrow has a temper but he loves my daughter. One time we was at a camp meeting and there was this incident right before the sermon was to be delivered."

"Please tell me sir."

"Well this gentleman was trying to come down the aisle beside Eleanor and Woodrow. The guy stepped all over Eleanor's foot. She screamed. Woodrow here stood up and told the man to apologize. The man refused. Lord, what did he do that for? Before I could make it over to where they were all sitting and mind you we were outside, Woodrow here had grabbed him by the collar and cut his throat from one side to the other. There was blood everywhere."

"You killed him?"

"No fortunately he didn't die, but he did apologize to Eleanor when he got out of the hospital," Mr. DeWitt continued.

"So was that the end of it?" Henry asked.

Mr. DeWitt deferred to Woodrow.

"No. I had to go to jail for about 45 days," Mr. Minwhite said.

"That's all?" Henry asked.

"That was enough mind you. But I didn't do any longer than that because Jackson refused to press charges against me. But now we are good friends."

"I told you all of this Henry because I expect you to take care of my Sadie the same way Woodrow takes care of my Eleanor. He isn't the best thing to look at and God's knows why my Eleanor married him and still loves him, but he does do a wonderful job of protecting her and I expect no less for my Sadie."

"Momma grandpa is putting pressure on Henry. He's not going to wanna marry me because he will be scared if he does something wrong, they will kill him."

"Come on y'all and let's have dinner." Mrs. Eleanor stopped them just in time enough to save Sadie's nerves.

After Mr. DeWitt blessed the table per Mr. Woodrow's deferment, they sat down to a lovely Sunday dinner. Actually it was more like a banquet because there was so much food beautifully prepared and equally presented.

Poverty didn't diminish Mrs. Eleanor's sense of elegance.

Sadie barely ate anything at all even though all of her favorites were laid out before her because she was too nervous. It was a beautiful spread. Everyone was clearly pleased.

This was yet another first of unfamiliar waters for Sadie.

Henry cleared his throat. "Does anyone mind if I step outside and smoke?"

"Come on," Woodrow said. "We'll smoke together."

Henry didn't say a word the entire time from dinner through his cigarette.

"Thank you all for this fabulous dinner and day. I never knew going to church would be like this. Mr. DeWitt thank you for the advice. Mrs. Eleanor thank you for the fine meal. And Mr. Woodrow thank you for introducing me to Sadie."

Everyone was holding their breath because it sounded like a but was on its way.

Henry turned to walk out the door. Sadie and her mother looked at each other.

"Oh I forgot, Sadie I hope you still want to marry me because I still want to marry you."

"Henry Pottishear, you cad," Sadie said.

With that Henry tipped his never-leave-home-without-it fedora, got into his car, and drove off.

She and her mother started screaming in shear excitement.

Over the course of the next few months the Minwhite house was overrun with family. Once the word got out that Sadie was getting married, all fifteen of Eleanor's brothers and sisters visited them more often than they already visited, which was often enough as it was.

The only time that Sadie and Henry had to themselves were a few hours on Saturday afternoons. But again Henry didn't care. He genuinely loved Sadie and that's all that mattered to him.

"You have a really large family Sadie and they are all so close and very nice."

"Henry, don't be so easily fooled."

"Whatcha mean Sadie?"

"I mean my family is nice and I love them, but lovely nice people all have ulterior motives at times depending on the circumstances."

"Sadie?" Henry asked in denial.

"Henry everyone in my family thinks I am an old maid because I didn't get married at fifteen or sixteen. So they are not coming around because they are happy for me. They are coming around to see if this is all true, and a few of my cousins have their eye on you for themselves."

"Sadie, do you think I haven't noticed all of that extra attention. I know women and I see what they are all doing, but none of that is of any interest to me."

"What do you mean you know women?"

"Sadie I can't change my past. But I have never asked another single soul to marry me. You can ask anyone who knows me and they will tell you the moment any women ever mentioned marriage to me, I dumped her on the spot."

"So then why are you wanting to marry me?"

"Because you are different Sadie. You could see through my bullshit from the very beginning. But you didn't let that stop you from seeing that my heart was good even if my all of my actions were not. But most of all, you are the most beautiful woman I have ever seen. And your brown skin is the beautiful wrapping that holds it all together."

Sadie was crying.

"Sadie baby what are you crying about?"

Sadie kept on crying.

"Sadie, please tell me what is wrong?"

Sadie slowly stopped crying. And through her whimpers Henry heard her say, "No one has ever told me that I was beautiful outside of my mother and grandpa. All of my aunts favored my cousins because they are much lighter than me. So I have been sort of the black sheep of the girls in my family for a long time."

"Well if I remember the Bible correctly, God always accepted the discarded before those who thought they were perfect."

"How do you know that Henry?"

"My mother taught all of us the Bible every day before she died. Some things stick better than others. So now I understand why you don't like me to stare at you. But you might as well get used to it because I'm going to keep on staring at you forever."

Sadie was tired of talking. But she didn't have to say it. Henry instinctively knew that Sadie was tired. So he just held her tightly while they sat quietly beside the pond. Sadie melted in Henry's arms.

"You've finally put your defenses down. I told you that I love you and nothing is going to change that."

Sadie sank her head deeper into Henry's chest, if that were possible.

"Let's just sit here and enjoy the sunset and shut the rest of the world out."

Sadie couldn't believe what she was seeing, hearing, and experiencing. This had to be a dream, a fairy tale for sure. And if anyone deserved a fairy tale love, it was Sadie.

"I keep waiting for someone to pinch me and wake me up."

"Ouch Henry."

They were both laughing.

"I love it when you laugh Sadie."

"Where did you come from Henry to treat me like this?"

Henry took a deep breath.

Sadie felt his heartbeat change. "What's wrong?"

"I am not perfect Sadie."

"Tell me Henry." Then she thought about it. "I changed my mind. Don't tell me. We agreed to stop talking. Let's stick to that agreement."

They were so at peace that they actually took a nap right where they lay. No tomorrow, no yesterday, it was just that moment.

"Sadie," She heard her mother calling her like Minnie Pearl.

"Coming momma. We're down here at the pond."

"Woodrow!" Mrs. Eleanor was frantic.

Mr. Woodrow jumped up from his napping spot on the front porch.

"What's wrong Eleanor?"

"You don't think that…"

"No Eleanor. No honey. Henry wouldn't, at least not with Sadie. And Sadie sho'nuf wouldn't."

Henry and Sadie appeared from around the corner.

"Sadie, you been crying. What's wrong?"

Then Mrs. Eleanor turned her attention to Henry.

"Henry Pottishear, if you hurt my…"

"Momma, Henry didn't do nothing. I was crying because…I was crying because.."

"She was crying Mrs. Eleanor because she doesn't think she is as pretty as you and she can't believe I want to marry her."

Mrs. Eleanor looked at Henry then Sadie, then Henry again.

"Sadie honey. Oh my lord, baby you got to let that old stuff they been saying about you go. You can't let what other people say about you rule your life. I've been through that baby and we already talked about all that."

"Who been sayin' things about you Sadie."

Mr. Woodrow was going to get his big gun, not the little pistol he carried on him everywhere he went except when he was working at Old Man Jack's place. If the foreman found a pistol on him at work, they would think he was trying to kill Old Man Jack and they would hang him.

"No Woodrow. You ain't going to shoot nobody."

"Why not Eleanor?"

"Because you would have to kill my own kinfolk."

"Oh," Mr. Woodrow said. "You sure Eleanor? This is my big chance."

"Woodrow you ain't going to use Sadie to settle your old scores."

"Thank you Henry. Come on in the house honey and let's get you some warm milk and get you into bed."

"Good night Sadie." Henry shouted.

"Good night Mr. Woodrow."

"Hold on a minute Henry."

"Yea Mr. Woodrow?"

Mr. Woodrow waited until the women-folk was out of earshot.

"Have you told Sadie what we talked about?"

"I started to tell her tonight but she didn't want to talk no more. So I didn't force it on her."

"But you are going to tell her before you walk her down that aisle."

"Yes sir, but…"

"But what?"

"Well sir Sadie don't want no wedding. She just wants to go to the justice of peace."

"You shittin' me boi."

"No sir. She didn't tell ya'll?"

"Hell nah she ain't told me."

"Well good night sir."

"Good night Henry. We gonna see you in the morning for church?"

"Wouldn't miss it sir. Wouldn't miss it." With that Henry climbed into his car and drove off.

It was the first Sunday in about six months that they were able to eat alone.

"Henry, why haven't we met your family yet?" Mrs. Eleanor asked.

Henry slowly put his fork down. All eyes were on him and getting bigger as the seconds of silence ticked away.

"Mrs. Eleanor, I come from a large family of thirteen children. And I love my brothers and sisters, but I haven't always been the best brother or son. In truth my family thinks Sadie is a figment of my imitation because they can't believe I want to settle down."

"But why haven't we met your family?"

Sadie looked at her mother rather strange. She didn't get it. But Henry did.

"Because my father, who is an extremely mean and angry man, told me that I couldn't marry Sadie."

You could see Mr. Woodrow was starting to steam at the thought of Henry's dad. But before he could completely blow his top Henry said, "The only reason I have been waiting so long to talk to Sadie about a date is because I have been saving money to find us a place of our own so that she doesn't have to come to my daddy's house with me."

Mrs. Eleanor burst into tears.

"Boi you done made my wife cry."

Henry started backing up from the table.

"Woodrow, you old fart, I'm not crying because Henry has done something wrong. I am crying because I just realized that my Sadie is going to be leaving us."

Then both she and Sadie were crying.

And that was the end of Sunday dinner ended.

## Chapter 3

"Henry J. why have we seen so little of you lately?"

"Lucy, I have to get to work."

"Henry J. what is going on?"

Henry knew he had to answer his older sister or she would never let up on him.

So he took a moment to sit down with her at the kitchen table while the house was quiet and the stars were still out.

"Lucy, this is just between me and you, you promise?"

"What are you involved in Henry?"

"Do you promise Lucy?"

"Okay, okay I promise."

"I have been working extra hours so that I can save up some money to find a place for me and Sadie."

"What! The hell you say."

"Lucy?"

"Henry what can I say. I have never heard you talk about saving money or being responsible about anything in your life. Where is the Henry who used to spend all his paycheck on strange women every weekend and come home broke and hungry?"

"I don't know."

"Where is the Henry J. that refused to help out around here that forced me to give up my every weekend to come down here just to make sure ya'll were alive and alright?"

"I don't know all the answers to that stuff Lucy. I just know that I met Sadie and she changed me."

Lucy was sitting there with her mouth wide open.

"Close your mouth sis before flies get in it."

"Have you told her about your little secret yet?"

"I tried to tell her a few weeks ago but it wasn't the right time."

"Well, if you are really turning over a new leaf you need to tell her about your past, the whole truth about your past."

Henry had a panic-stricken look on his face.

"If she still wants to marry you then she truly loves you too. Then you can bring her here so we can all meet her."

"And what about Pop?"

"I'll have Martha Sue talk to him. He softened up when she was born probably because she was his last child."

Henry still looked unsure.

"Trust me, it'll all be fine. Now go on and get out of here so you won't be late for work." Lucy kissed Henry on his forehead and handed him a breakfast sandwich in one hand and his lunch in the other.

"Thanks Lucy."

She looked up at her giant-sized brother and gave him a rare smile of approval.

Although Lucy had told Henry everything was going to be alright, he was very pensive around Sadie for the next few weeks.

Finally, after about three weeks of dodging the issue, Henry sat down to have a heart to heart with Sadie during their standing Saturday night date.

"Sadie I need to tell you something."

"You changed your mind."

"No and I hope you won' change yours."

Sadie stared at Henry without any emotions.

"Here goes. Sadie I have two kids by two different women."

"How old are they?"

"My daughter is two and my son is six months."

"What about their mommas?"

"One is engaged and the other lives with her mom."

"So is that why you are marrying me on the rebound?"

"No Sadie. I didn't want to marry either one of them. It was just sex."

"So what you gone do? Get me pregnant and leave me too?"

"No woman. I love you and I want to be with you until I die."

"No matter what?"

"No matter what."

"You know this isn't over right?"

"Whatever you say."

"Well for now I don't want those kids around my children."

"Done. So now you ready to meet my family?"

"You ain't hiding no more secrets are you?"

"Not a one Sadie. Not a one."

"Well okay then. I knew it had to happen sometime. But mind you Henry. This ain't over."

"So why aren't you upset and jumping up and down, and screaming all over the place?"

"What good is that going to do? The children are already here. You can't change that. So why act a fool? Doesn't mean I like it but I know you had a life before me and I know that included a lot of women. Actually, I am pretty surprised you don't have more children than that."

"I spilt it."

"Huh?" Sadie was confused.

"I spilt it outside when I didn't have any protection."

"Doesn't the Bible say you are not supposed to do that?"

"It also says no pre-marital sex, but if I tried to hold it in that long I would've exploded a long time ago."

They both laughed a little.

"Well come on. It's getting dark. Momma will be calling me soon."

"So you want to do it?"

"What!" Sadie exclaimed.

"When do you want to meet my family?"

"Oh," Sadie was embarrassed.

"Sadie." Henry said in that tone meant to embarrass Sadie some more.

"Henry J.!" Sadie thought about it for a while.

"You tellin' me that you ain't been with nobody?"

"Not a soul since I met you. I'm getting close to exploding."

"We might as well get it over with so why not next weekend?" Sadie said changing the conversation.

"Deal."

Sadie's stomach was in knots that whole week. Her mother and father both had to pick up her slack. But they didn't mind because they saw a better day ahead for their daughter. It was a long and short week for Sadie. She was a nervous wreck by the time Friday rolled around.

"Sadie, honey why are you so upset about meeting Henry's family?"

"Momma you heard everything Henry said. His daddy don't want him to marry me. His family thinks I been made up in Henry's mind. And don't forget his history and his kids."

"But Sadie, none of that has anything to do with you. And besides Henry has already prepared to find ya'll a place. So stop creating obstacles in your mind and worrying about every little thing."

"But momma…"

"No buts Sadie. Now let's move on and talk about your wedding."

"Oh that."

"What do you mean 'oh that'?"

Sadie took a deep breath.

"Momma I don't want a wedding."

Mrs. Eleanor fell back in the chair. Thank goodness it was there to catch her.

"Woodrow did you hear this?" Mrs. Eleanor screamed.

"Yes Eleanor dear. I already know."

"You told your father but you didn't tell me?" She was incensed and Mrs. Eleanor never got mad.

"Momma, I didn't tell daddy anything."

"Then how does he know? Woodrow, how do you know?"

Brief silence.

"Somebody better tell me something."

"Henry told me Eleanor. Calm down honey."

"Calm down. How can you tell me to calm down when my only daughter doesn't want a wedding, and she didn't tell me? Why would I be upset!"

"That's Sadie business to tell you Eleanor."

"Sadie you'd better tell your momma something."

Brief pause.

"Why don't you want a wedding?"

"Momma do you realize how much that would cost you and daddy?"

"Sadie you are my only daughter, my only child. You think I care about cost?"

"We are going to have a big wedding at the church and then a big dinner so your whole family can see you blossom into a beautiful woman right before their eyes."

"I just thought we would go to the justice of the peace and then have a big dinner afterwards."

"The answer is no. See you are trying to hide from everyone and it is time you stop hiding. So it is settled. We are having a wedding."

"Yes ma'am."

Henry pulled up just as the conversation was coming to an end.

"Out of the pot and into the frying pan," Sadie said.

"Sadie you are a beautiful woman. But it doesn't matter how many times I tell you that if you don't believe it yourself. Now that man has come here to show you off to his family. At least pretend like you are enjoying this. This is important to Henry so don't be selfish and blow it for him. Okay."

"Okay," Sadie said reluctantly.

"Good afternoon everyone. Sadie," Henry said tipping his never-leave-home-without-it fedora.

"Go on honey and have a good time."

Sadie kissed her parents bye. "I'll see y'all later."

"So how are you?"

"Nervous."

"Now you know how I felt when I first met your family."

"But you didn't know how my family felt about you like I know how they feel about me."

"I didn't want to tell you but I could not lie to your parents."

"I suppose."

Sadie was looking out the window and was clearly enjoying the ride.

"Sadie is this your first time ever leaving Marvin?"

"Yep," she said popping her lips on the letter p.

Henry wanted to talk with Sadie so badly the entire ride but he knew it would be a forced conversation so he was resigned to the fact that Sadie needed some personal time, although they were in the same car on the same seat, but they were miles apart. Nonetheless, Henry was determined that if they could make it through this car ride, they could make it through anything.

Back at home, Lucy was snapping her brothers and sisters, her husband, and her father into shape for this all important meeting.

"Lucy what made you change your mind about Henry's marriage idea?" Tommy Lee asked.

"Tommy Lee you don't have time to be asking all sorts of questions. You need to finish gettin' dressed. They will be here in just a little bit."

Henry had explained to Lucy in great detail how important Sunday dinners were at Sadie's house, although this was a Saturday. Still, Henry told Lucy, "I want Sadie to feel like she is at home – that there is no difference from her house and our house."

Lucy took those words to heart. Additionally, she prepared the best Sunday dinner she could think of, just like their momma used to do when she was cooking for all fifteen of them. She left no stone unturned.

"Martha Sue did you have that talk with daddy about his behavior?"

"Yes Lucy but he just sat there like he didn't hear a word I said."

"That's just his way of pretending not to hear you so that he can continue doing what he wants to do. He heard you loud and clear and that made him even madder. But he wouldn't dare let you see that, which is why I wanted you to talk to him."

"Well how do I look?"

"You look pretty as ever Martha Sue. That dress turned out very nice."

"Thank you for making it for me Lucy."

"Well this is an important day for Henry, and as much as we have ridden him about being a rebel rouser we need to support him when he is trying to get on that narrow road."

"Lucy, you look just like momma in her old apron, except on you it looks like a dress."

They both start laughing.

Then the door opened. To anyone outside, that laughter might have seemed planned, but they couldn't come today.

"Everybody, I want you to meet Sadie. Sadie this is my sister Lucy. This here is Martha Sue and that's Tommy Lee. And this is my brother-in-law George, Lucy's husband."

"How do ya'll do? Henry I thought you said there were thirteen?" As she went down the line and shook everybody's hand and looked them all directly in the eye.

"We have a sister in Miami, a few are in Detroit, one in the Army, and there are four more spread around the city."

"But they might come around later," Tommy Lee said.

"Go sit down boy," Henry said swinging his fedora at Tommy Lee. But Tommy Lee didn't budge.

"Please come on in Sadie." Lucy looked back and gave her brother the nod of approval.

"You don't plan on introducing your future Mrs. to your own father?" The senior Mr. Pottishear said turning the corner from the hallway.

"Sadie this is my father Mr. Herman Pottishear."

Sadie stepped boldly to Mr. Pottishear and took his hand. "How do you do sir?"

It was Martha Sue's turn to be impressed and a little jealous.

"Come on in here gal and let me talk to you."

"Sadie you and daddy go in the living room and sit for a moment while I finish getting the table ready.

"Martha Sue take that lemonade out of the box and take it into the living room."

"Ya'll sho do have a nice place here."

"Thank you little girl," Mr. Pottishear told Sadie.

"Okay," Mr. Pottishear continued. "Let's cut the chase. Why you want to marry this boy over here."

"Pop don't start?"

"That's okay Henry, your father has a right to know why we want to get married."

"Hmm." Martha Sue said.

"Mr. Pottishear, even though we got off to a rocky start, I love Henry."

"You mean to tell me you the one who precnear killed my son?"

"I'm ashamed to say yes sir I am."

"Well I'll be damned."

"Little woman you might survive this yet."

"Pop!"

"Hush up boi."

"Sadie I am surprised. I thought Henry was going to bring home some tight skirt philly, with big breasts and no brains. You know a Jezebel."

"Damn!" Henry said standing to his feet.

"Henry," Sadie exclaimed. "You apologize right now!"

Everybody in the room looked. Even Henry was surprised because he had never seen that side of Sadie before. He was captivated.

"Now. Mr. Pottishear I know Henry has a past and to tell you the truth I am not sure I will be able to satisfy him because of that past. But I am going to give it my best every day."

"Well you look like a strong young lady with nice hips. At least you will give him lots of children."

"But we don't have to start on that tomorrow do we since he already has a few?"

The whole family burst into a contagious laughter.

"Come on everyone let's eat," said Lucy.

"George will you bless the table?" Lucy asked of her husband.

"I ain't saying no damn prayers," and the senior Mr. Pottishear started eating.

"Amen." Mr. Pottishear was already ready for round two.

"Sadie you know this man ain't gonna be faithful to you."

Everybody started choking, except Sadie.

"Mr. Pottishear you might be right but everybody deserves to be loved. And even if he is unfaithful to me, I will always be true to him until the day I die."

Game. Set. Match. Sadie had won.

"Sadie go on and eat your dinner before it gets cold," Lucy said.

Henry was surprised by what he was seeing. Sadie was eating and she looked to be enjoying herself.

The remainder of dinner was uneventful…until.

"So have you guys set a date?" Martha Sue asked.

Sadie looked at Henry.

"Damn, Sadie we haven't even talked about a date."

"Watch your language at my table boi." Their papa shouted while biting into his fried chicken.

"Sadie do you have a dress yet?" Lucy asked.

"Not yet."

"I have a wonderful idea," Lucy jumped up from the table and ran into the bedroom she and her husband George shared when they came down on the weekends.

As Lucy started back down the hallway she heard screaming.

"Lucy! Not mama's dress."

"Why not? Sadie is her size and the dress hasn't been used except for that one time, and it has been in momma's trunk ever since she died.

Then screaming turned into tears. Martha Sue was crying, Tommy Lee was crying, and so was their father. But all for different reasons.

"Lucy, I wanted to get married in mama's dress."

"Martha Sue, you are too small to get married in mamma's dress."

"You could fix it."

"By the time I finished making all of the alterations to momma's dress Martha Sue there would barely be any dress left of its original beauty."

Martha Sue started crying again.

"Martha Sue stop crying. It makes perfect sense that Sadie would get married in momma's dress since he was her favorite."

Tommy Lee took offense at that statement. "Who told you that Lucy?"

Lucy ignored Tommy Lee because her answer would only make matters worse.

"That boi makes me sick," their papa said.

There was Tommy Lee's answer.

"Wait a minute everyone. I am not interested in causing any confusion in your family."

"Our family," Henry said.

"Huh?" Sadie said while looking at Henry.

"Our family." Henry said it a second time with more emphasis.

"Oh, yea, our family, just as we are starting out."

"Is this something that has to be decided today?" George asked.

"Then if not, let's just table it until everyone has a cooler head and is less emotional."

Without saying a word everyone deferred to George's direction. Henry smiled his approval at the brilliance of George's directions.

"Okay, Sadie come on so I can take you home before you daddy comes huntin' my head."

"My daddy ain't gone come lookin' for you."

"Yes he will too because you ain't my wife yet.

"Thank you all for a wonderful afternoon. This was the most fun I have had in a really long time."

"That gal don't get out much do she?" Their papa said matter-of-factly.

Sadie turns around and waves bye as they drive off.

"Henry I really had a good time."

"Sadie you don't have to pretend anymore there is no one here but me and you."

"I'm not pretending. I don't pretend. You of all people should know that."

"How could you have a good time with all that foolish going on and my papa being his normal charming self?"

"I had a good time because everybody was being here because they wanted to be and not because I wanted them to be. They were not putting on airs."

Henry looked at Sadie as if to verify what she was saying was true. "You really had a good time?"

"I did and Lucy's food was the best. It wasn't my momma's but it was still really good."

"Speaking of Lucy, I'm sorry she embarrassed you about wearing my momma's wedding dress. I didn't even know she still had it."

"Why would you know? That's women's business."

"You mean to tell me you're considering wearing it?"

"Sure why not? But only if Martha Sue agrees. That was a great idea George had to talk about it later. It gives me a chance to talk to momma about it."

"George is pretty smart to not be able to read or write."

"You are kidding."

"Not even."

"Wow, that's something I didn't see comin'."

"Yea, he has to write an X when signing his name at the bank."

"So what about a wedding date?"

"I was thinking before the cotton blooms like in May so that way we won't have to take too much time off from Mr. Jack's field and lose all that money."

"Sadie when we get married I don't expect you to work in the cotton field no more."

"Where am I going to work Henry? I ain't got no education. I quit school in the 9$^{th}$ grade to go work in the cotton field because we needed the money."

"You can get a job in the city doing housework."

"I never thought about that."

"Well honey you got to think about it because we are going to be living in the city."

"But we gone come see my family on the weekend?"

"I promise, every single weekend."

With that Sadie gave Henry a spontaneous kiss that caused Henry to almost run off the road.

Sadie rolled the window down and just enjoyed the rest of the ride home.

"Woodrow, Sadie's home."

"Mrs. Eleanor, I brought her home safe like I promised."

"Sadie, you're smiling honey. That mean you had a good time."

"I had a wonderful time momma."

"Come on in the house and let's talk about it."

"Good night everyone. I'll see y'all in the morning for church."

"Henry?" Sadie was confused.

"What's wrong Sadie?"

"You going to church with us tomorrow."

"My momma always told me don't start something you don't plan on finishing. Unless you don't want me to go."

"No. no."

"So you don't want me to go."

"No. I mean yes. I mean of course you can go."

"Good. I'm glad we got that cleared up. See y'all in the morning." Henry tipped his fedora.

"So how was your dinner honey?"

"Momma their family is just as crazy as our family and if not more."

"How so?"

"Well their father is really old and cranky, and he treats everybody like they are still little kids. And you can tell he does not want Henry to leave the nest, but he pretends like he can't wait to get rid of him."

"Was he mean to you?"

"He was trying to be, but he couldn't bring himself to be nasty. He did tell me the truth though."

"Like what?"

"He told me that Henry would never be faithful to me."

"What?"

"Yea. He actually said that."

"What did you say?"

"I told him that everybody needs to be loved and that I was going to be faithful to Henry no matter what he did until the day I died."

Her mother just kept brushing Sadie's hair.

"Sadie a parent knows their child."

"I know momma. I am sure Henry will get tired of me after I start having his children but I still want to marry him no matter what."

"Sadie that is a mature thing to say but are you sure you are not opening yourself up to unnecessary heartache? Because I can promise you honey, when your heart is broken and aching, it is not your mind that gets involved. It will be your emotions running things."

"Momma, Henry is the most exciting man I have ever been around. He is completely different from me. So I am willing to take that chance with him. I don't care that he has two kids already."

"What! Woodrow, get in here. Now Sadie tell your daddy what you just told me."

Sadie had this 'oh shit' I didn't mean to tell momma that yet look on her face.

"Speak up Sadie," her daddy said.

"I told momma that Henry had two little children."

Mr. Woodrow turned around to walk out.

"Woodrow where are you going?"

"Eleanor honey I have known that since before Henry proposed to Sadie."

"Why didn't you tell me?"

"Because Henry gave me his word that he would come clean before they got married."

"So what are we now a family that keeps secrets from each other?"

"Eleanor you and Sadie keep secrets from me all the time, and besides I had two children too when we met."

"That's different. "

"How so?"

"You were married before."

"Henry's never been married."

"But that's the point momma. He has been with a lot of women but he has never asked any of them to marry him. He has never been with me and he wants to marry me."

"I'm not sure I approve of this Sadie. We are going to have to talk with your grandpa."

Mrs. Eleanor was finding it hard to concentrate because she wondered if her husband knew her secret. But she couldn't leave without one more question.

"How old are these chaps?"

"Let me think. His daughter is two and his son is six months."

"I don't like the idea of you taking care of someone else's children."

"No momma they live with their mothers."

"Mothers? I have heard enough for tonight. Go to bed. We will finish this tomorrow."

Sadie didn't sleep all night thinking about what her mother said because Sadie knew her mother meant what she said. She just didn't know how her mother was going to carry out her plans. Therein was her fear.

But Mrs. Eleanor had a more pressing concern at that moment. She couldn't wait to get to bed.

"Finally," Mrs. Eleanor said.

"I thought you were never go to sleep," she whispered to herself as she ever so gently eased out of bed beside her husband.

Mr. Woodrow was such a light sleeper that Mrs. Eleanor knew this was a precarious situation because the slightest noise would have her husband shooting her head off as an unexpected intruder, although they did sleep with their doors and windows open quite often.

So to insure that her husband stayed in his exact spot on the right side of the bed, Mrs. Eleanor took a step and stopped. Took a step and stopped. Took a step and stopped. Took a step and stopped. It took her more than twenty minutes to go less than ten feet to the door and out of the house.

Mrs. Eleanor didn't take an oil lamp with her because she knew every square inch of their property like the back of her hand. She walked quietly in the dark, the complete dark, in the woods by herself to the spot.

In fact, she had to hurry because if her husband rolled over and she was not there, there would be hell to pay. So she picked up her pace.

It wasn't long before she was at her spot. It was mapped in her head. She dug up her treasure, gathered it into her arms, resealed her hole, and headed back to the house.

When she arrived back to the house she had to retrace her exact footprints in order to achieve her goal of not being detected.

Home free.

She was almost sleep.

"Your secret still there?"

"Woodrow," Mrs. Eleanor sat up in bed.

"How long you been awake?"

"Since you first got out of bed."

"You know about my sec...thing?" She smacked him on the arm.

"Since three years now Eleanor."

"How?"

"Eleanor I walk this land every day. You don't think I know when something has been moved."

"Why didn't you say something?"

"Because it was important to you to keep your secret. So I let you keep you secret."

"Did you count it?"

"Nah I didn't."

"It's a little over $10,000."

"What did you think I would do with it if you told me?"

Mrs. Eleanor shrugged her shoulders. "I guess I was just proud of doing something by myself for a change since you take care of everything else."

Mr. Woodrow kissed his wife.

"You want to know what it is for?"

"Sadie's wedding," he answered.

"How did you know?"

"I've known every since her cousins started calling her an old maid about three years ago."

"You want to know why?"

"Because you wanted Sadie to have a good running start when she got married; and, you wanted to rub it in your sisters' faces a little bit."

"Hell! I want to rub it in their faces a lot!"

"Eleanor!"

"You think you know me don't you."

"I do and I want to get to know you a little bit better right now."

The next morning, Sunday morning, the Minwhites were full of energy, although it took them a little bit more time to get going than on most Sundays. Regardless, Sadie had breakfast waiting for them when they did get up.

Henry showed up a little earlier than expected.

"Henry what are you doing here so early?"

"I was just sittin' around the house doing nothing so I decided to come on down."

"Did I do something wrong?"

"No…" Before Sadie could finish her sentence, her mother interrupted them.

"Henry Pottishear I want to talk with you."

"Uh oh?"

"What uh oh?" Henry said.

"Henry?" Mrs. Eleanor called his name a second time.

"Go go," Sadie told Henry.

"Yes ma'am." Too late. They were caught.

"You too Sadie. Come in here."

"Now when Sadie first told me about your two babies last night I was furious and I had decided right then and there that you could not marry my daughter."

"Why?" Henry exclaimed.

"Sit down son." Henry had jumped to his feet.

"I was furious that you guys would hide such important information from me." Then she paused.

"But after Woodrow and I talked I understand why. That is a decision that you and Sadie have to be willing to make and move forward with. I realize that I must let Sadie grow up so she can become her own woman; and, I don't want to be a mother-in-law that interferes."

Henry was so elated that he was smiling bigger than a Cheshire cat.

"Thank you momma." Sadie was on her knees looking directly into her mother's beautiful golden brown eyes.

Her mother kissed her forehead. "Okay let's go to church."

"Before we go momma, I have something I want to tell you."

Mrs. Eleanor sat back down.

"Okay Sadie."

Sadie looked at Henry for moral support. Then she took a deep breath.

"Henry's oldest sister Lucy offered me their mother's wedding dress to get married in."

Mrs. Eleanor looked. It was not a look that anyone in that room had ever seen before.

"Oh my lord," Mrs. Eleanor was crying.

"Momma that's okay. I don't have to use the dress."

"No. No."

Henry was a little disappointed but he accepted Mrs. Eleanor's decision.

"Okay then its settled we won't use the dress."

"No. no. I think its wonderful."

"What?" Sadie exclaimed.

"Yes, I think it is wonderful because it means you have been truly accepted into their family. That is a wonderful sign."

Mrs. Eleanor started screaming. She and Sadie were hugging and dancing around in the living room. Henry and Mr. Woodrow just stood there watching.

A few weeks later it was a far different scene.

"Momma, I'm nervous."

"Why honey?"

"Because if Henry's father comes, daddy may shoot him. They are both so stubborn."

"I'll take care of your father. Don't you worry about that one bit. Now come on let's go check on dinner."

After that there was no time for worry. There was too much left to be done in the kitchen. All you could hear was pots, pans, and dishes banging in the kitchen.

"Come on y'all here comes Henry and his people."

They all gathered on the front porch. It was truly a Kodak moment. It just so happened that Mrs. Eleanor was standing tall in the middle looking regal as a queen wearing a simple white dress and a flowered apron that was clean or as clean as her dress. The dress and the apron looked seamlessly as one piece. The dress ended mid-calf, which left just enough room to see her beautiful and flawless carmel colored legs.

To her left was her husband Woodrow, who was her constant companion for more than 25 years. He was almost hidden or overshadowed by his wife's beauty, but he didn't care. He was proud of his beautiful wife. And he served at her pleasure and dared anyone to say otherwise.

Sadie was standing to her mother's right. Sadie was not as tall as her mother, nor was she as beautiful, however that was not to say that Sadie was not goodlooking. If there was a pecking order, Sadie's mother was gorgeous and Sadie was pretty. But she was the apple of Henry's eye and that made her mother stand even taller.

"Oh my gosh Henry who is that tall gorgeous woman who the porch with Sadie?" Martha Sue asked.

"That's her mother Martha Sue. Oh my goodness, I wish I was tall and beautiful like that. Look at her, her hair is flawless - all pulled back, rolled up, and crimped around the edges. I don't see any gray in her hair."

Martha Sue had every one focusing on Sadie's mother.

"How old is she Henry?" Tommy Lee asked.

"About 50 or so I think."

"Damn," George said under his breath.

Lucy just sat there with a beautiful box on her lap. She pretended not to hear her husband's comments, but she heard.

"I can't get over how beautiful her mother is," Martha Sue stated again.

"Where is her pa?" Tommy Lee asked.

"You don't see that dark skinned man standing on the other side over there?" Henry responded.

"You mean to tell me that beautiful woman is married to that short, black man."

"That ugly duckling is married to that beautiful swan?" Lucy said as she started to laugh.

The whole car shortly burst out into laughter too.

As Henry pulled into the driveway all the Minwhites heard was laughter. They took it as a good sign.

"Welcome to our home." Mrs. Eleanor spoke up for her clan.

Mr. Woodrow stepped up. "Howdy."

"Martha Sue close your mouth," Tommy Lee said.

"Be quiet you two," Lucy said.

"Hello Mrs. Eleanor, Mr. Woodrow, Sadie. This is my family. Part of them anyway. This is my oldest sister Lucy, her husband George, my youngest sister Martha Sue, and my youngest brother Tommy Lee."

"Well hello everyone. I am so glad to meet each one of you. I am Eleanor, this is my husband Woodrow, and of course you know our Sadie."

"Hey everybody." Sadie finally said.

"Mrs. Eleanor you sho' is beautiful."

"Why thank you…"

"Martha Sue," Henry said completing Mrs. Eleanor's sentence.

"Why thank you Martha Sue." Mrs. Eleanor repeated.

"Martha Sue is right Mrs. Eleanor. Look!" Tommy Lee was excited.

"What Tommy Lee?" Henry asked.

"Sadie's momma got more gold in her mouth than I have ever seen in my life."

"And it sho' is beautiful Mrs. Eleanor," Martha Sue said.

Martha Sue continued, "You are more beautiful than our mother was and I have never seen a woman more beautiful than her."

"I must agree with Martha Sue. But here is the most important reason we are here," Lucy said as she handed a beautiful gift box to Sadie.

Mr. Woodrow was beaming from ear to ear because he was so proud of his wife.

Sadie's eyes were big with excitement.

"Really?" Sadie asked.

"Really," Martha Sue said.

"Everybody is in total agreement? Because you know I cannot take this if one of you has any doubts."

"We are in total agreement," Henry said.

"Where's your father? And what about him?"

"He refused to come," George said.

Sadie and her mother looked at each other.

"That don't mean a thing Sadie. You know our father doesn't care about anything," Lucy said.

"But he did tell me to tell you that he liked you and you could have the dress," Martha Sue said.

Her brothers and sisters looked at her.

"Did he really say that?" Tommy Lee asked.

"He called me in his room and told me last night," Martha Sue continued.

"Why didn't you tell us this before now Martha Sue?" Lucy asked.

"Because papa made me promise I wouldn't tell until we were all together in front of Sadie."

With all of that the ladies ran in the house to look at the dress.

The men stayed on the porch to get to know each other a little better.

"Try it on Sadie," her mother said.

When Sadie came back into the room they all started crying.

"It is a perfect fit," Lucy said.

"You will be a beautiful bride," Martha Sue said.

The remainder of the visit was uneventful, until Tommy Lee said, "So is this the room where you tried to kill Henry?"

Everyone dropped their forks in their plates.

Before another word could be spoken, Henry jumped to his feet and was dragging Tommy Lee by his collar out of the back door and down the long flight of concrete stairs.

SMACK! Henry backhanded Tommy Lee.

It was on.

They were rolling around in the dirt. Tommy Lee was younger than Henry, but he was a definite scrapper.

Meanwhile inside the house, no one moved.

Mr. Woodrow wanted to join in the scramble but Mrs. Eleanor shook her head no without even looking up at him. He eased back into his chair.

"We normally let them finish," Lucy said.

"How do you know when they are finished?" Sadie asked.

"They start laughing," Martha Sue said.

Sadie jumped up and ran outside.

"Henry don't you hit him again."

You could hear brakes screeching to a halt.

Henry stopped his blistering punch in mid-air.

That gave Tommy Lee an opening to get Henry back for that first sucker punch.

"Tommy Lee you better not!" Sadie said.

"Now listen you two. I don't care what you are used to doing, but you are not going to be fighting like that around me. Look at you both. Dirty as rag dolls."

"Momma would you get me some wet rags please," Sadie asked.

"Come here Tommy Lee. We need to put some cold presses on your nose and eye so they won't bruise too bad."

"What about me? I'm gonna be your husband," Henry said.

"You sit down right there on the porch until I can get to you, and don't you move a muscle."

Henry was Sadie's puppy.

Henry's sisters marveled at the sight.

"I'll get you Henry J," Martha Sue suggested.

"That's okay Martha Sue. I want Sadie to tend to me."

"Excuse me."

"Cut it out Martha Sue. Can't you see the boys in love?" Lucy said.

"Tommy Lee you have every right to ask that question. And Henry should have never hit you. I'm sorry he did that. But let me explain." Sadie continued talking as she tended to Tommy Lee's wounds.

"You ain't got to explain nothing to that boy," Henry shouted.

"Henry Pottishear you best not say another word," Sadie replied.

Henry smiled.

"Tommy Lee I didn't mean to try to kill Henry. I love him. I loved him from the first time I saw him. But I couldn't let him come into our house and disrespect me and my family by being drunk and having women's perfume all over him."

"Don't forget the lipstick on the collar," Martha Sue shouted.

"She don't need no help remembering Martha Sue," Henry said.

"So anyway Tommy Lee I just picked up the first thing I could grab and I hit him, although I didn't mean to hit him so hard. But I was just so mad. And for that I am sorry. I am truly sorry. Actually, I thought I would never see him again, but when he came back I knew he was the man for me. Can you ever understand that?"

Sadie was gently applying the cold press to Tommy Lee's left side of his face.

"You alright with me Sadie Minwhite," Tommy Lee said as he gave her a big hug.

"Thank you Tommy Lee."

"Now as for you Henry." Sadie walked over to her man and gently caressed his face and rubbed his handsome masculine brow with the back of her hand.

Henry could not help but kiss the hand that rubbed the dirt off his face.

"I love you Sadie. I really do love you."

"I love you too Henry and I don't want you fighting your family over me."

"Aw shucks Sadie, that won't no fight. We been in some real fights before and besides you are part of our family now."

"Well from now on if you need to fight, I don't want y'all fightin' each other."

"Yes ma'am Mrs. Pottishear," Henry was happy to say it out loud.

Sadie was blushing.

"Don't think you can get out of this that easy." Sadie was still smiling.

They were staring at each other with an obvious look.

"Okay, maybe this time. But don't do it again."

"Yes ma'am," Henry said.

"Look at the time. We've got to get back to town to check on daddy," Lucy said.

As everyone was making their way back into the house, Henry stole a long kiss from Sadie. "I can't wait until you are all mine."

They all said their so longs and see you laters.

"Oh wait," Sadie said. "I prepared this plate for y'alls daddy all special just for him."

"Thank you Mrs. Sadie," Henry said tipping his hat.

"Go on get out of here Henry," Sadie said. She was blushing again.

"I'll see y'all in the morning."

"Good night Henry," they all said.

The next few months passed relatively quickly and before you knew it they were all gathered for the final meeting before the wedding. The Minwhite house was completely overrun with people.

All of Henry's brothers and sisters came in for the wedding. And all of Mrs. Eleanor's brothers and sisters were there too. There were more people there than at the church's annual picnic. There was tremendous laughter coming from inside the house where all of the women were cooking every kind of country food you could imagine.

Outside, all of the men were building tents, telling bullshit stories, and keeping fires going in huge barrels, in between answering to their wives' cat calls and sneaking a sip of white lightenin' whenever possible.

Sadie wanted to be locked away in bedroom because she had gotten a sudden case of the nerves, but the women would not allow her to do so. And tomorrow was going to be worse because all of her cousins would be there at the wedding.

Henry, meanwhile, was trying to make his way to Sadie but every time he got near the house, somebody was blocking his viewsite of Sadie.

"Boy don't you know it's bad luck to see the bride before the wedding. Y'all already got enough going against you. So you don't need no mo'," Sadie's Aunt Emma Lee said to Henry. She was a short fat woman who dipped snuff and she was strong as an ox. Henry knew he would get a shellacking by her, so he resigned himself to being stranded outside with all the other men of his family.

But nothing could stop Sadie from starring out the kitchen window every chance she got to steal a glance or two from Henry.

It was a long night. A really long night.

The menfolk slept outside in the tents, the women slept throughout the whole house, like at an all girls sleepover.

Finally, the next morning came.

Henry and Sadie were both up early, even if they could not see each other. But even though they were up early, still they were not the first ones up. Sadie's mother was up and when she got up so did her husband, who was outside with the other menfolk, and there in started the domino effect.

The wedding was not until 1 pm but the entire house was abuzz with activity and it was barely 6:30 am. With each passing half hour, the activity increased more and more until the house started to thin out as individual family members either went to the church or made their way back home to get the rest of the family.

The time came for Henry, Mr. Woodrow, and the rest of the wedding party men to get dressed and head out to church. Mrs. Eleanor would not even let Sadie begin to start getting dressed until all of the men were gone.

Now it was time for Mrs. Eleanor and all of the other ladies to get dressed. Mrs. Eleanor had managed to find time to make herself a brand new dress.

"Momma, that is a beautiful dress. You look absolutely gorgeous,"

"Thank you Sadie dear. But today is about you not about me."

"No momma it is about both of us. For far too long I have brought shame on you and daddy because I was the laughing stock of the family for being an old maid. But today you can hold your head high because your only daughter is getting married to a handsome man who is not a sharecropper."

Her mother started to cry.

"No momma don't you start crying because that will make me cry and then we will both have to redo our makeup which means we could mess up our dresses and our hair dos."

Sadie was standing in front of the mirror as her deceased mother-in-law's dress was slipped over her head onto her untouched womanhood.

"Sadie you really are a catch for Henry. You will make a wonderful wife just as beautiful as you are right now."

They were standing there together looking in the mirror. Her mother's beautiful flowerprint dress looked like a field of red, yellow, and orange lilies against the back drop of Sadie's pure white dress.

"Don't we make a pair?" Her mother said.

"This is only the beginning momma."

"But Sadie honey you could not get off to a better running start."

"I know momma. It is like a dream come true. Don't pinch me because I don't want to wake up."

"This ain't no dream dear," her mother said, putting her left hand on her daughter's shoulder.

Sadie looked. She couldn't believe what she was seeing.

"Momma, where is your wedding ring?"

Her mother jerked her hand down and tried to move on to a different conversation.

"Momma, you have never taken you ring off since the day you got married. So where is your ring?"

Her mother was hesitant to answer.

But Sadie was not going to be deterred until she had an answer.

"Sadie," her mother cradled Sadie's hands inside of hers, "I took my ring off because there was a need that was greater than my own that I could do something about."

"So you took your ring off to give it to Henry because he couldn't afford a ring."

Her mother's eyes told the story of agreement.

"But momma, I don't want you doing that. We can get a ring later. The most important thing is that I am getting married to Henry."

"In front of a church full of people who want something to talk about so you have got to have a ring to put on your finger."

"What about a ring for Henry?"

"Black folk don't care about no ring for men. In my day all we cared about was jumpin' the broom."

"Why aren't we jumpin' the broom?"

"Because your grandpa says it is not important because it reminds him of everything we were denied as slaves. So he said he didn't want to see no broom at the wedding."

"So why can't Henry have a ring?"

"Sadie most black folk can only afford one ring and that is usually for the bride."

"Yea momma, but remember what Henry's pa said."

"What did he say honey?"

"He said that Henry was not going to be faithful to me."

Her mother still didn't get it.

"If Henry decides to cheat, I want any women he sleeps with to know that he is sleeping with a married man."

"And you still want to marry him?"

"Momma, if that is the worst thing Henry can do to me, I still would marry him."

A car pulled up in the driveway.

"Well maybe it's too late to talk about it. Your carriage has just pulled up to take you to your big day."

"What?"

"Your grandpa arranged for your Uncle Herbert to come and take you and me to the church."

"How did grandpa do that and why?"

"Your Uncle Herbert loves you very much and your grandpa never asks him to do anything. So when he asked him your Uncle Herbert knew it was important. So he kept his mouth closed and here he is."

"Aunt Emma Lee."

"You got it honey. Your aunt has bullied all of us since she was born. And your grandpa knew that, which is why Uncle Herb kept his mouth shut."

"Ellie, come on gal. We gone be late and papa will be yelling at me."

"Uncle Herbert thank you for doing this for me."

"Sadie baby, don't you know your old unc will do anything he can for you?"

She gives him a big kiss on the cheek.

"Now enough of this mushy stuff. Come on y'all let's go."

As they were getting into the car, Sadie asked her mother, "Why don't Uncle Herb have any kids of his own?"

"Sadie honey that is a really long story and it has to do with a whole lot more than I can explain right now. So let's just say Uncle Herbert can't have kids. Now come on let's get in the car, we have a wedding to get to."

As they pulled into the church's gravel parking lot, there was barely room for Herbert to maneuver his car up to the front door. But nothing was going to stop him from getting that car next to those red brick steps like his papa had told him to do. It was the first time in forever that their father had asked him to do anything and Herb was not about to mess this up.

Sadie looked up to see her daddy waiting for her at the top of the steps.

They smiled at each other a look of approval.

"Okay Sadie don't you start up those stairs until I have time to get around to the back of the church and get in my spot so I can see everything."

As soon as Mrs. Eleanor was in her spot the music started. It was an old piano playing the wedding march but it was the most beautiful music Mrs. Eleanor had ever heard. On cue the doors of the church opened.

It was a small church and everyone could see clean outside, but there was no Sadie or her father standing there. Then slowly and methodically this beautiful young bride started to appear in everyone's eyesight, one step at a time as she ascended the red brick stairs she had climbed so many times before.

When Sadie finally reached the top, the church did a collective gasp. Sadie was gorgeous.

"That dress really shows off her figure doesn't it Lucy?" Martha Sue said.

"That's momma's dress," Henry heard his sister from Detroit say.

"It's Sadie's dress now," the sister from Miami said with pride.

"Maybe she will pass it on to their daughter," Martha Sue said.

"It would be nice to keep it going as long as we can," Lucy said.

"It's like momma is here with us," Tommy Lee said.

Everybody looked at him.

No one could believe he would say something so profound.

"Did you have to make any alterations to it?" The missionary sister from Detroit asked.

"Not a one," Lucy said.

"Uncanny," Sister Missionary said.

"Why so?" Tommy Lee asked.

"Welcome back Tommy Lee," Martha Sue said.

"Because Henry used to always tell me that he was going to marry a woman like momma," Sister Missionary said.

Martha Sue, Lucy, Tommy Lee, and Lucy's husband George all looked at each other like they had seen a ghost.

Meanwhile, Sadie was taking extremely slow steps as she took her time to take in everybody and every facial expression from both sides of the family. Her family was on the left and Henry's was on the right. And there were people lined all around the church. Sadie couldn't tell who they belonged to.

"Daddy, I am no longer an old maid," she whispered to her father.

"You never were he replied."

"Look at them all seething with hatred and jealousy."

"Why not? Look at you. You are the cat's meow."

"It only took 18 years right."

They started laughing.

"I thought you would be nervous."

"No papa, it's way too late for that now. Besides I know what I am getting myself into."

Everybody was either crying, smiling, or frowning.

But to Sadie it was all poetic justice for years of abuse and back-stabbing.

They finally reached the front of the church where she saw her husband for the first time.

"You didn't look at me once coming down that aisle," Henry said.

"I have the rest of my life to look at you, but I am going to only have this one wedding so I wanted to enjoy every single minute of it."

"Well I couldn't take my eyes of you and neither could everybody else."

And the ceremony began.

The pastor read from I Corinthians 13 about the power of love.

When it came time to exchange rings…

"With this ring I thee wed," Harry slipped Sadie's mother's ring on her finger. She started to cry.

When Sadie's turn came, she said, "Excuse me."

Sadie turnaround and everyone immediately assumed she was walking out of the church. Her cousins almost broke out into cheers.

Sadie walked over to her father and said, "Give me your ring."

"What?"

"Give me your ring daddy."

Her father looked at her mother for her approval. It was gladly given.

Then she walked back over to her position in front of her husband.

"Okay pastor."

"With this ring I thee wed," and with that Sadie slipped her father's ring on Henry's finger.

"I now pronounce you man and wife. You may kiss your bride."

The sentence was barely completed before Henry was kissing Sadie with passion never before seen by those church folk.

Then everyone burst into clapping and rushed Henry and Sadie at the altar.

It took quite a while before everyone had hugged Sadie and shook Henry's hand but they eventually greeted every single person that came to their wedding, not by choice but by force. Nonetheless they did it.

"Sadie I have had enough of this."

"No Henry we must. It is the polite thing to do and we are probably never going to see some of these people ever again."

"Only for you Sadie."

"Thank you Henry. I promise it will be worth your while."

It was nearly three hours after the wedding before Henry and Sadie left the church.

"Can we go home now?"

"Wow."

"What?"

"It just hit me that I will not be sleeping in my old bed anymore in my old room at my parent's house."

"So is that a no?"

"Of course we can't go home yet. We have to go to the dinner at my parent's first."

"Please promise me we won't stay all night."

"I promise."

That little white house was still overrun with people everywhere. Everybody had just shifted locations from the church to the house. Actually it looked like more people had showed up at the house than at the church. It all looked just like last night, except today the menfolk were not trying to hide their white lightenin'.

"You know black folk?"

"What Henry?"

"They ain't gone miss no free food."

"That's okay Henry we have more than enough."

"Look a there. You see that?"

"What Henry?"

"They are already carrying plates to their cars before we can even get here to get our first plate."

"Henry don't be concerned about no food. Today is our wedding day, let's just enjoy it. All of it."

No sooner had they been spotted was the car surrounded by folk. You would have thought they were movie stars. But today Sadie didn't mind it one bit.

Sadie's grandfather stepped into the doorway. "Give them some room to get into the house."

The crowd parted like it was all scripted in a movie or something.

"Come on in here you two and get something to eat and open your gifts."

"Gifts?" Sadie was not expecting that.

"I'm not hungry papa," Sadie continued.

"I can believe that," her grandfather responded.

"Still you need to open your gifts," he continued.

And they had plenty of them to open.

Finally Sadie was down to her parent's gift.

Her mother handed her a dirty box.

"Do not open this until you and Henry are at home alone."

"Momma you and daddy have done so much for us. You don't need to give us anything else."

Her mother ignored her words. "Did you hear what I said?"

"Yes ma'am."

It wasn't long after that that Sadie and Henry were on their way to their new home.

"They didn't even cut the cake," one of Sadie's cousins shouted.

"Then we will just have to wait until they cut it tomorrow after church."

# Chapter 4

"Excited?" Henry asked.

"Excited and a little sad."

Sadie couldn't tell Henry she was excited about doing her wifely duties. Not yet anyway because she didn't know if she would like it or not.

"So why sad?"

"I told you why."

"Oh, right."

But it was hard to keep her excitement a secret with the dirty box that her mother had gave her sitting on her lap, on top of a handkerchief because Sadie still had on her wedding gown. Her knees were shaking a little bit.

"Well I promise you it is going to be alright."

"I trust you Henry."

Henry speeded up a little more and before you knew it they were almost home.

"Henry this is the way to your family's house."

"Yea."

"But you said you were saving up for our own house."

"Yea."

Henry kept on driving. As he got closer to his family's house, he slowed down a little to see his papa sittin' on the front porch. Henry had to make sure his daddy saw him in his new seat with his new wife.

His papa smiled. "That damn boy," he said.

Then Henry just kept on driving up the hill a little piece. Then he pulled in front of this small cottage, couldn't have been more than three rooms in the whole house.

"Welcome home Mrs. Pottishear."

Sadie smiled and took her time getting out of the car.

As she started to walk up the steps, Henry swopped her up and carried her up the steps, across the threshold, and into the house. He didn't put her down until they got into the bedroom.

"Wow Henry did you do all of this?"

"No. Lucy and everybody else helped."

He closed the door and before you knew it all you heard were screams and moans coming from inside of that little house. The sounds carried everywhere because there was no furniture in the house except for the bedroom they were in.

Four hours later they emerged from the bedroom. Sadie was a woman now.

"Okay."

"Just okay?" Henry asked.

"What are you talking about Henry?"

"What are you talking about Sadie?"

"I was answering my own question."

"What was the question?" Henry asked.

"If you must know I was wondering if I was going to like doing my wifely duties."

"Do you?"

"Very much Henry, very much."

Henry threw his new suit on the floor and took Sadie again. Actually Sadie gave herself to him. Either way they were very much engaged.

A few more hours later Sadie said, "I could get used to this so don't you start something you don't plan on finishing."

"Don't you spend one moment worrying your pretty little head about that now." Henry replied.

"So why is there no furniture in here or in the kitchen Henry?"

"For two reasons Sadie. First I don't know how to decorate nothin'. And two, I ran out of money with getting this house …"

Sadie put her finger on his soft red lips.

"You ain't got to explain nothin' to me Henry. I know what all you have done for us and I thank you for every bit of it."

"It is bound to be something we can use in all those gifts."

"Gifts!" Sadie exclaimed.

"Sadie what's wrong?"

"I forgot momma's gift." Sadie jumped up and ran into the bedroom, bare rump and all; and, Henry was right behind her.

Sadie grabbed the dirty box and jumped in the middle of the bed. Henry was already there waiting for her.

"Wonder what it could be?" Sadie said.

"What I want to know is why it's so dirty?"

"Let's open it."

"No you open it. Your mother gave it to you."

"She gave it to us!"

"Well us says you should open it."

"You sure?"

"Yea. Now open it."

Sadie slowly lifted the cover off the box. Inside the box was a handcrafted tin can.

"I remember this can. It used to be my grandmother's before she died."

"So how did it get in the box?"

"My grandpa snuck and gave it to my mother at my grandma's funeral."

"Why did he give it to her?"

"Probably because my mother was the only one who didn't ask for anything when my grandmother died and my grandfather knew my mother would cherish it."

"So then she is passing it on to you so you can pass it on to one of our daughters."

"It feels heavy. Feel it."

Henry lifted the little tin can. "It does feel heavy."

"How do you open this thing?"

"I thought you said I could open it."

"You're taking too long and now I want to know what's in it."

Henry tried everything he could but he couldn't get the top open.

"Henry that's not how you open it."

With one small twist, Sadie twisted the bottom and all of those money started falling out of it.

"Henry!"

"Sadie!"

They were screaming and hollering and rolling around in money. They were kissing and cuddling and playing in money like they were on a haystack back at Old Man Jack's place.

Suddenly Sadie stopped screaming.

"Henry we can't take this money. This has to be my mother's and father's life savings."

Henry saw the sadness in Sadie's eyes.

"I would like to keep honey. I would be lying if I said I didn't. But if you want to give it back, then we will give it back."

"I'll tell you what, let's count it. Then we can put in back in the box and take it with us in the morning so we can have a long talk about it with them in the morning before we go to church."

"No don't count it. Let's just put in back in the box and take it with us in the morning."

"Okay. Thank you so much Henry for doing this for me."

"I don't want to but I will for you."

"We'll find another way to get by."

"I'll go out first thing Monday morning and find me a job keeping house for some white folks. It'll be alright."

"What?" Henry said in a comical fashion. "No honeyman."

"You better come and get it honey before I go to sleep. Oh and look there's your full moon."

And so ended their first night of marital bliss.

"You still feel like exploding?" Sadie said to Henry, while smiling.

"I'm all exploded out for now."

Sleep came easy for both of them.

CLING, CLANG!

The noise was so loud it woke Sadie up. As she got out of bed, she instinctively grabbed for her morning robe.

"Oh no," she said out loud.

Then she put on the first thing she could find. It was Henry's big white shirt. It swallowed her.

As she went out into the small hallway she heard doors slamming, and drawers opening and closing. Then Sadie sniffed.

"Henry what are you doing?"

"Good morning Mrs. Pottishear."

The sound of that name brought a smile to Sadie's face.

"Good morning to you Mr. Pottishear."

She forgot why she came into the kitchen.

Then she saw smoke coming from the oven.

"Henry somethin's burnin'."

"Damn," Henry said

"Henry!" Sadie exclaimed.

Henry pulled out a pan of black and crispy miniature tires.

"Well I hope you didn't want no bread this morning."

"That's okay. It just nice you thought of it anyway."

Then Sadie jumped up without notice and ran to the bathroom. Henry ran after her.

"Sadie, what's wrong?" Henry's heart was beating fast in his chest.

Sadie was face down in the toilet boil. She stayed there for a while.

"Sadie, what's wrong?" Henry was frantic now.

"I don't know Henry. When I saw those burnt biscuits I started gettin' sick."

"Those weren't biscuits. They were sweet rolls."

Sadie tried to laugh a little but her stomach was too upset.

"Let me get you some water." Henry rushed to the kitchen to get Sadie a glass of water.

"Here, rinse your mouth out with this honey."

Sadie did as she was told.

Then she looked at the bowl and back at Henry and then at the bowl again.

"Oh you want to flush it," Henry said.

"I want to do what to it?" Sadie asked.

"Flush it Sadie." Henry pushed a silver knob on the side.

"You know this is all new to me. I am used to going in our pot in the house and taking it out in the woods and throwing it away and then rinsing the pale out at the pump outside."

"Well honey this toilet does all that for you now."

"You sure we not trying to be uppity with this whatchamecallit."

"I'm positive we are not Sadie. Everybody in the city has a toilet in their house."

Sadie wasn't sure she was buying what her husband was selling, and she got ready to say so when she got a second whiff of his biscuits.

"Yea that's what I wanted to talk with you about."

"What is that?"

"What you doin' tryin' to cook so early in the morning for anyhow?"

"I was trying to cook you breakfast before we left for church. I know how you are used to having a good breakfast every morning."

"That's it!"

"What's it Sadie?"

"My clothes."

"What about your clothes?"

"Henry we forgot all about my clothes and left all of them at my momma's house."

"Oh shit!"

"Henry. It's the Lord's day." Sadie exclaimed.

"Come on. There has got to be something you can wear to your parents so we can get your clothes."

"And don't forget we still got to get to church on time," Sadie insisted.

"Well come on let's get cleaned up so we can go," Henry said.

"Where we gon' bath Henry? I didn't see no wash tub."

"It's right here Sadie."

"Where? I don't see no wash tub."

"It's right here Sadie."

"Where Henry?"

"Right here." Henry took off his clothes and stepped over into the tub. "Come on get in."

Sadie dropped Henry's shirt and tacitly stepped into the big white open coffin based on her husband's word.

"Where does the water come from?" Sadie asked.

"It comes from here Sadie." Henry turned on the water.

"Henry my hair!" Sadie screamed.

"Oh shit Sadie. I'm sorry."

"Henry." Sadie was still screaming his name while trying to decide whether to cover her hair or body.

Sadie had made Henry nervous and he couldn't get the shower turned off fast enough.

"Henry that's hotter than before," Sadie was screaming like a little girl.

Henry finally got the water off and jumped out of the tub to get Sadie a towel.

Sadie stated laughing. "Henry you okay?"

Henry had slipped and fallen on the bathroom floor. But he didn't have time to stay there. He still had to get Sadie a towel.

"I'm sorry. I didn't mean to mess up your hair." Henry said as he gently caressed Sadie's Coke bottle figure.

"I like you Henry Pottishear."

"I like you to Sadie Pottishear."

"You wanna take a bath with me instead of a shower?"

"Sure. I don't think I like showers Mr. Pottishear."

"Come on. Let me run you some nice warm bath water and see if I can help you enjoy taking a bath."

"I don't know Henry that is going to be pretty hard to do."

"Why so?"

"Because I ain't never took a bath in a fancy tub like this before, let alone with another person."

"Let me show you how easy it is." Henry extended his big hand to help Sadie get into the tub safely.

"Now come one and ease down into the water." Then Henry sat down at the other end.

Pretty soon they were laughing and playing like two teenagers in love.

Shortly after that they were splashing around in the water like two fish. This time Sadie wasn't concerned about her hair.

It took a while before they were ready to get dressed. But neither of them had a reason to complain.

Sadie put on a pair of Henry's boxer shorts and a pair of his paints. She had to use a piece of rope to tie the pants to hold them up because Henry's belt was too big to hold the pants up on Sadie's tiny waist. Then she threw on one of Henry's shirts and tied a do-rag around her hair.

"Don't forget the box Henry."

And off they went.

An hour or so later.

"Momma. Hey daddy."

"Hey gal."

Sadie ran up on the porch to hug her parents who had come out to greet her and Henry.

"Sadie child you been gone one day and you already wearing pants and dressing like a man."

Sadie and Henry both started laughing.

"No momma. In all our planning you know what we forgot?"

"We didn't forget nothin'."

"Yes we did momma. We forgot to get my clothes packed up."

They all started laughing. Mr. Woodrow was shaking his head as he took a puff off his cigarette.

"Come on in this house girl and let momma do your hair and get you in some decent clothes."

"We gone miss church y'all," Mr. Woodrow said.

"It's a special occasion Woodrow."

"Good I didn't want to go this morning anyway."

"Tired Mr. Woodrow?"

"Late night son."

"Me too sir. Me too."

"That's my daughter you talking about."

The thought had never crossed Henry's mind.

"I apologize sir. I didn't mean no disrespect."

"You'll learn this when you have your own daughter. While we fathers want our daughters to get married. We don't want to know they are married if you know what I mean."

"I think I do sir."

"Woodrow come quick!" Came the scream from inside the house.

Sadie was lying on the floor.

"What happened Eleanor?" Mr. Woodrow swooped down and picked up his daughter in one clean swoop.

"We were talking and I was doing her hair and she fell out."

"Interesting."

"What Henry?"

"Sadie woke up sick this morning."

Mrs. Eleanor kept applying presses on her daughter's forehead. "Tell me what happened."

"Nothing much. I was trying to make breakfast for her, she came in the kitchen, smelt the breakfast, and ran in the bathroom and threw up."

Mr. Woodrow and Mrs. Eleanor looked at each other.

"Henry was there anything unusual when you two did your duties last night?"

"Duties?" Henry asked.

Mr. Woodrow elbowed Henry in the side.

"Ohhhhhh, duties."

"Not that I can recall," Henry said.

"Yes momma," Sadie said as she started to come around.

"Baby, you alright?"

"Yes ma'am. I'm fine."

"Was you bleeding last night Sadie?"

"A little bit."

"Why didn't you tell me Sadie. I would have stopped."

"Boy what you do to my daughter?" Mr. Woodrow was getting steamed.

"Woodrow hush."

Mr. Woodrow walked over to a corner chair and took a seat. Not his preferred option. "I don't want to hear this," was his parting shot.

"Sit down and be quiet old man," his wife told him.

"Sadie why didn't you tell me?"

"Because I didn't want to stop and I didn't want you to be worried that something was wrong."

"Sadie honey can you sit up and look at momma?"

Sadie sat up on the bed and looked at her momma.

"You're pregnant."

"Pregnant!" Mr. Woodrow and Henry said the word in tandem.

Henry sat down on the bed beside Sadie.

"What's wrong Henry?"

"I'm happy honey. But we can't afford no baby yet."

"We'll make a way honey."

"What you mean you can't afford no baby?"

"What about the $10,000 I gave y'all yesterday? Surely you ain't had no time to spend it yet."

"Sadie said we had to give it back."

"Give it back?"

"I'll take it." Mr. Woodrow was lively again.

"Sit down Woodrow. You ain't takin' nothin' because ain't nobody givin' nothin'."

"Sadie you listen to me. I have been saving that money for about three years or more in that very back yard near the pond. And I saved it up because I wanted you and your husband to have it and you ain't givin' it back. You are going to use that money to start a new family and give us some grandchildren."

"Momma you sure?"

"I'm positive."

"Well momma we are at least going to buy you and daddy some new marriage rings since we have y'alls old ones."

Mrs. Eleanor looked at her husband. He nodded his approval.

"Deal," Mrs. Eleanor said.

They had a wonderful time the remainder of that Sunday, packing, laughing, and moving.

"Come on honey. We got to get home so I can go to bed and be up early for work in the morning."

"Who's going to stay with you tomorrow while Henry works?"

"I'll get Martha Sue to stay with her and Tommy Lee too."

Sure enough it was just as Henry said. Martha Sue and Tommy Lee stayed with Sadie for the next few months until Sadie was stabilized. Once Henry's good news traveled to the rest of the family, Henry's sister from Miami, Dottie, came up and stayed with him and Sadie until the baby was born.

Dottie and Sadie became the best of friends.

"Dottie tell me something."

"Sure Sadie."

"Why does everyone hate your papa so?"

"Oh Sadie you ask things that are painful to the heart to remember, and even harder on the mouth to speak."

"I only ask because he is so kind and gentle to me. I cannot imagine how it is so that he is so hated of his own children."

Dottie put her head in her hands and started to whimper.

"Dottie I'm sorry. I won't ask again."

"Sadie our father was a mean old drunk who used to come home after drinking all day and night with his buddies and beat us for no reason."

"Dottie tell me no more."

"Sadie he used to beat the men twice as hard and he beat Henry the worst."

"That is why Henry's back is full of scars and whelps."

"He used to drag Henry out of bed half asleep and make him take his clothes off just so he could beat him until he bleed. He would only stop when mother would cover Henry with her own body."

"Sadie was full out crying now."

"Sometimes he even hit momma."

"Why did he hate Henry so?"

"Because momma loved him so. He reminded her of papa when he was younger."

"And because I took everybody else's whooping so he wouldn't beat on them," Henry said as he walked through the door.

Henry sat down beside his sister.

"Dottie…"

"No Henry it's my fault. I forced Dottie to tell me. It's not her fault."

Henry looked at Sadie with a look she had never seen before.

"That man was so mean that he purposely wouldn't buy us any soap to wash with."

Dottie finished Henry's thoughts. "Momma had to go out and collect bags of little pieces of used soap from other people just so we could take baths."

"I've never told that story to a single soul."

"Me either Dottie.

But Sadie smiled at Henry, a smile of love and approval, not a word was required. Still when Sadie smiled at Henry, his world was alright and he had no defense against her beauty or gentle soul.

Then he bear hugged his sister Dottie. "You always were the prettiest girl in town."

"Oh boy put me down yo silly self."

"I'm so glad you are here."

"So am I Henry. So am I."

Over the next few months Dottie's, Henry's and Sadie's bonds all became stronger.

"Henry you know it is almost time for me to have the baby."

"I know honey."

"I think I want to go home and have the baby with my mother."

"Is there anything wrong?"

"I'm getting nervous."

"There is nothing to be nervous about."

"How do you know Henry Pottishear? Have you ever given birth to a child befo'?"

"You got me there."

"Where are you going Henry?"

"I am going to pack your things so I can take you home."

"I'm going to miss you Henry."

"Sadie you won't have time to miss me because I am going to be down there every Friday night after work and stay until Sunday."

When Henry and Sadie broke the news to his family, who only lived a little walk down the hill from them, they too were saddened by it.

Lucy said, "We thought you were going to have the baby with us."

Sadie said "You all are welcome to come home with Henry every weekend until the baby is born."

Sure enough every weekend was like a big family reunion. But they wouldn't have many of them.

Three weeks in, on a late Friday night after Henry had come home to his beautiful pregnant wife, he awoke in a puddle of water.

"Sadie, you're wet honey."

"Henry call momma."

"Mrs. Eleanor!" Henry screamed.

She came running. So too did Henry's sisters, Tommy Lee, and Mr. Woodrow.

"Her water's broke Henry," her mother said.

"Okay all y'all men get out of here," Lucy said.

"What are we supposed to do just wait?"

"Go chop some wood," Martha Sue said.

"Martha Sue its pitch dark outside. Then go collect some wood because we need hot water and we need this house to be heated up very quickly."

So everyone had their marching orders.

One hour. Two hours. Three hours. Four hours. Four turned to five, then six, then seven, then eight, then nine.

Then there was a lot of commotion and screaming heard in Sadie's old bedroom.

"Push Sadie."

"I don't know how to push."

"Stop everyone." Henry heard Mrs. Eleanor say on the other side of the closed door.

Henry was trying not to panic. But he was not doing a very good job.

"Sadie listen to me. Now you remember when you first learned how to go to the pottie and momma told you that you had to push the booboo out of you?"

"Yes ma'am."

"Well I need you to push like that again now, but even harder. Okay." Sadie was resting on her mother's breast for support.

"Okay everyone here we go."

Henry was really beginning to panic because he did not hear anything happening in the room.

"Okay Sadie. When I count to three I want you to push as hard as you can. One. Two. Three. Pushhhhhhhhh!"

Suddenly Henry heard Sadie straining. Then silence. Then Sadie let out a piercing scream.

"AGGGGGGGGGGGGGHGHGGGGGGGGGGGG!"

Then he heard a SMACK. Then baby crying.

The men were yelling on the other side. While the women were cleaning up Sadie and the baby.

"Meet your new baby girl," her mother said handing Sadie her new baby girl wrapped in clothing Lucy had made from her father's old shirts.

Henry could be patient no longer. He burst into the room.

Martha Sue hit him like she always did when he burst in on her.

"Come see your new daughter Mr. Pottishear."

Henry was standing at the doorway frozen in his stance except for his eyes. They were locked in on his daughter.

"Don't be scared." Tommy Lee pushed his brother.

Henry's feet finally started moving. It was obvious that Henry thought he was walking fast. But Henry was walking like he had lead in his pants.

"Sadie. She is beautiful. Looks like you got your first real baby doll." He kissed Sadie's sweaty forehead.

"And who better to give her to me than you."

With that Sadie was exhausted.

"You hair is wet honey."

Sadie and Henry started laughing. Everyone else was confused.

"Sadie she looks just like a miniature version of…"

"Momma." Dottie said, finishing her brother's sentence.

Henry was absolutely glowing with proud and awe. He could not take his eyes off his daughter. He cradled her as the precious commodity she was. Nobody else could hold her. He even took a nap with her still in his arms. That went on like that every weekend. And every week Henry was at home alone, working and missing his family.

One Friday evening, about four weeks after RuthAnn was born, Henry had just turned the corner to go home and get ready to go see his family, when Tommy Lee ran out to the car.

"Martha Sue wants to see you Henry."

Henry kept on walking.

"Come on Henry. You heard me."

Henry knew he could never refuse Martha Sue.

"Okay. Tell her I will be there as soon as I get my stuff packed to go see Sadie and RuthAnn."

"Okay Martha Sue whadda u want?"

"Martha Sue didn't want to see you. I wanted to see you."

Henry turned to walk away. When he moved out his daddy's house, he was finally done with that old man.

"Henry, at least hear him out." Martha Sue asked.

"What you want papa?"

"I want to see that child of yours."

"You're crazy old man."

"Henry she is his grandchild," Tommy Lee said.

"Besides Henry what is it gonna hurt for him to see her?" Martha Sue asked.

"Okay. Okay. You can come down with everybody else tomorrow when they come visit. But the only reason I am doing this is because Sadie loves you and only God knows why."

With that said Henry turned around and walked out the door.

Henry was rushing to get to Sadie, RuthAnn, and the rest of his family.

He pulled up in that familiar driveway, barely put the car in park, and jumped up on the porch and into the house.

"Knock. Knock."

"Henry."

"Hey Mrs. Eleanor. Hey honey. Where's my favorite girl?"

"I thought I was your favorite girl Henry."

"Can you share me for a little while?"

"As long as I get you back," Sadie was smiling.

"I promise you I ain't going nowhere."

Henry was kissing all over RuthAnn's face and head. He even kissed her little feet that she kept kicking outside of her blanket.

"She still hasn't opened her eyes Sadie."

"She opens them a little bit but then she closes them right back."

"But I want her to see me and know me."

"Momma made Doc Glain come out here and check on her on Wednesday and he said she was fine. That she would open her eyes when she gets ready."

"Which reminds me. My papa wants to come see her tomorrow."

"You better had told him yes."

"I didn't want to but I did."

"Good. It'll be great to see him."

Henry wasn't paying any more attention to conversations about his daddy.

That night Henry was exhausted and he went to bed early. And so did the rest of the family. Henry accidentally rolled over and kicked Sadie.

Sadie woke Henry up.

"Really Sadie right here in your momma's house?"

"You kicked me so I figured that's what you wanted."

"We make too much noise."

"We'll just have to be quiet."

They both started laughing at that crazy idea. But it didn't deter either one of them.

Sadie was ready to scream out when Henry kissed her and took all of her scream in his mouth. Now Henry really was tired.

"Is Henry not coming to breakfast?"

"He is as absolutely exhausted momma."

"I understand honey."

"Where is daddy this morning?"

"He's a little tired too this morning."

"Well you go back to bed. I'll go ahead and get dinner started."

"No child. I'll help you."

"So they set out and started to make dinner for their in-laws."

A few hours later Sadie said, "I haven't heard RuthAnn crying for anything to eat. Let me go check on her."

She opened the door to her old bedroom and clutched her chest at the beauty of what she saw.

"Momma," Sadie whispered. She motioned for her mother to come over.

"Oh my goodness. I wish we had a camera."

Henry had gotten out of bed and gotten RuthAnn and put her on his big manly chest. She looked like a baby doll on his big chest.

They were breathing in unison, and RuthAnn was clutching the hairs on her daddy's chest with her little fist.

"Come on let's not disturb them."

So Sadie and her mother went back to preparing dinner while the menfolk slept.

A few hours later Henry relinquished RuthAnn long enough for her to get cleaned up for their guest. This also gave

Henry time to take a bath in the wash tub, which was a long process.

Several hours later, the cars started arriving.

From the front porch it looked like a caravan of cars had come. "Oh Woodrow I hope we cooked enough food," Mrs. Eleanor said.

Henry walked outside to greet his family. "Damn!" He said. "Excuse me Mrs. Eleanor. I didn't know everybody was coming."

"That's okay Henry," Mrs. Eleanor tried to calm him.

"I'm not sure Mrs. Eleanor. They have never been interested in anything I did since we were little except for Tommy Lee, Martha Sue, Lucy, Dottie, and a couple of my older brothers."

"Well Henry they see a change in you and you know people. They want to know if it's real or not."

Sure enough by the time they were finished counting there were 10 people in all.

"So who's missing Henry?"

"My two sisters and youngest brother from Michigan and my brother Duke who ran away from home to join the Army when he was 16 years old. That was about the time my momma died."

Before they could continue their conversation, they were greeted by the crowd carrying bowls, bags, and boxes.

"What is all this Mrs. Eleanor asked?"

"We couldn't come here empty handed for papa's first grandchild."

Henry wasn't buying any of it yet.

"Henry stop being so suspicious," Lucy said.

He looked at her to determine where Lucy really was. His instinct told him his sister was telling the truth.

"Sorry Lucy."

Henry greeted everyone and invited them all in the house to see his doll-baby. Both of them.

Hell, he even held the door open for his daddy to enter.

"Pop." He said greeting his old man.

As usual his father ignored him and walked on into the house.

The senior Mr. Pottishear was not necessarily a patient man. "Be quiet y'all he said to his children."

"Now that all that cacklin' has stopped, let me see this baby," he demanded.

Mr. Woodrow was not taking too kindly to where this thing was going. Mrs. Eleanor really had to hold his hand tightly because he was quick and fast when he was mad. And he was mad.

"Sadie let me see this baby."

"Look here now," Mr. Woodrow said.

"It's okay daddy." She shook her head that it was really okay. "Senior don't mean no harm."

Sadie laid RuthAnn in his arms and her grandpa just starred at her examining every inch of her being. A single tear fell from his eye onto RuthAnn's forehard. She fully opened her eyes and looked right into her grandfather's eyes.

"Well I'll be!"

"A monkey's uncle," Martha Sue said to her brother Tommy Lee.

The whole room was a gasp by what was happening.

But Dottie hated her father and nothing was going to change that, at least not today.

Then RuthAnn started kicking and coming alive right before their very eyes.

"Come on Dottie. I know how you feel. But let's just forget it for today. Okay," Henry pleaded.

Dottie was not moved.

"Besides look at my baby girl. She is happy as a lark and so is our pistol of a father."

Dottie smiled.

"That's my beautiful sister."

"I love you Henry."

"I love you too Dottie more than words can ever say."

"She is the spitting image of her grandmother. Long beautiful jet black hair. Beautiful olive-colored skin tone. Ruby red lips. Yep my baby you are definitely a child of a full bloodied Cherokee Indian, just like your grandma," Senior whispered in RuthAnn's ear.

RuthAnn either loved it or agreed because she was laughing, giggling, and kicking.

It was the most touching thing any of them had heard or seen from their father since he last spoke to them the night before they were to bury their mother.

"You did good boi. Sadie you did real good."

"Thank you papa," Sadie said while kissing her father-in-law on his forehead.

He was smiling.

He stayed in that spot the rest of the visit. And so too did RuthAnn except for diaper changes. No matter how many times they tried to convince him otherwise.

And when it came time to leave, RuthAnn cried all night long. There was no rest for anyone in the house that night.

None.

"We are going to go home tomorrow momma."

"Are you sure?"

"Yea. I can let RuthAnn visit with Senior as much as she wants during the day and maybe she will sleep at night."

"Okay. That's a good idea."

So RuthAnn had a built-in babysitter who didn't mind sitting with her all day long. And Sadie had time to turn their house into a home.

This went on uninterrupted for four months or so.

"Sadie, let's go out on a date this weekend."

"Henry, not this weekend RuthAnn has a slight cold and I want to stay home and keep her comfortable this weekend."

"Just one night honey. Please?"

"Okay I'll see who's available to babysit this weekend."

A few days later.

"Henry everyone has plans for this weekend."

"Everyone?"

"Everyone."

"What about one of your cousins? They have all been asking to spend time with RuthAnn."

"Henry I am not going to be one of those parents who lugs their child off on anybody they can find just so they can go out and party."

"Sadie you are not going out to party. You are going on a simple date with your husband for the first time in more than a year. And I won't keep you out all night long, just a couple of hours."

"Well…"

"You can make me pay for it when we get home."

"You promise?"

"Sure. As a matter of fact we can start right now."

The next day, Sadie was motivated to find almost anyone to help her accommodate her husband's request.

Friday night came.

"So are we on?"

Reluctantly Sadie said, "Yes. My cousin Josephine is going to watch her for us."

"Who is she?"

"She is my Uncle Herb's daughter. You know, my Uncle Herb is the one who drove me to our wedding."

"I thought he didn't have no children."

"He doesn't claim her. He says her mother was a whore."

"Hey Josephine."

"Hey Sadie. Hey Henry."

"Back up off my husband gurl."

"Just being hospitable. Now give me that baby?"

"Sadie she looks just like a porcelain baby doll."

"Now listen Josephine. RuthAnn has a slight cold so I have put a little rub on her chest. Make sure she stays wrapped up and warm. We are only going to be gone about a couple hours and then we will be back to get her."

"Sadie get out of here. I know how to take care of children. Who you think raised all these children around here?"

"Come on Sadie honey. RuthAnn is going to be just fine."

A few hours later.

"Sadie you can't even enjoy yourself."

"I'm trying Henry. I'm really trying."

"It's okay honey. Let's go. It's my fault for insisting you go out on this date tonight. Let's go get RuthAnn and go home."

Sadie already had her coat on and headed for the door.

"Josephine."

"Hey you two. How was your date night?"

"Where's RuthAnn?"

"She's lying down."

Sadie opened the door and flipped the light switch.

"Blood!" Sadie screamed.

"RuthAnn!" They were all screaming.

"She's dead. My baby's dead." Sadie was hysterical and sobbing from the depths of her soul.

"Oh God. No. No. No. Lord! Oh God No." She was screaming.

She could not be consoled.

"Go get her parents," Henry said. Henry wanted to cry but he was too scared and too busy trying to console Sadie.

Sadie was cradling RuthAnn's limp, cold, and bloody body to her chest. "RuthAnn wake up honey. RuthAnn!" Sadie fell on her knees holding RuthAnn." She started screaming even louder and harder as if she was in physical pain.

A few miles down the street there was a knock on the door.

"Aunt Eleanor. Aunt Eleanor!"

Mrs. Eleanor and her husband rushed to the door.

"What's wrong?"

"Come quick it's Sadie."

"Oh Lord. What's wrong?"

"There ain't no time. Come on we gotta go."

They shut the door and jumped in the car in their night clothes, but not before Mr. Woodrow grabbed his pistol.

They rushed back up the street a couple of miles. Mrs. Eleanor jumped out of the car when she heard Sadie screaming. She ran into the house to see Sadie covered in blood.

"Sadie!"

She rushed to her side.

"RuthAnn's dead momma. She's dead."

Sadie started screaming all over again. This time her mother joined her.

"Henry what happened boy?"

Henry recanted the story about the date.

"Why is this room so cold?" Mr. Woodrow asked.

Josephine was standing back in the corner scared to answer. She didn't know if Henry or Uncle Woodrow was going to kill her.

Before anyone knew it, the house was overrun with family.

Mr. Woodrow was looking around. Then he walked over to the window just over the bed. "This window's broken Josephine! You mean to tell me you put RuthAnn in this room last night and didn't even check on her?"

Josephine was even more scared now.

"I ought to beat your ass like the child you are."

Just about that time, Sadie's grandfather walked in.

"You stupid child." Their grandfather walked over and smacked Josephine. "I knew there was a reason I didn't like you."

All of those people in the house, but the house was mouse-quiet. No one knew what to do.

Mr. Woodrow came over and whispered something in Mrs. Eleanor's ear.

"Sadie, honey we are going to have to give RuthAnn's body to the funeral home folk so they can prepare her for burial," her mother said.

"No momma I can't let her sleep alone tonight."

"Sadie honey let me take RuthAnn while you get cleaned up."

"Don't you touch me Henry! This is all your fault. If you hadn't insisted on that damn date my child would be alive."

"Sadie honey. You don't mean that. This is not Henry's fault," her grandfather told her.

"What am I going to do papa my baby's gone?"

"Come on let's go home and we will all figure it out together," her grandfather said to her.

Sadie refused to let go of RuthAnn. So no one said another word to her about letting the baby go.

As they were leaving out the house, Josephine said, "Sadie I am so sorry."

"Josephine I never want to see you again as long as I live." And Sadie meant it.

Her Uncle Herb got there just as they were leaving. "Sadie, Sadie."

"Oh Uncle Herb."

"Herb we're going back to the house. We can talk there," his sister said to him.

By the time they got back to the Minwhite's place, Henry's family was waiting for them. Even Henry's father was there.

"Sadie can I hold RuthAnn?" Senior Pottishear asked.

Sadie didn't say a word, but she did slowly let Mr. Pottishear hold RuthAnn.

He put her little cold face next to his and held his face to hers as tight as he could. He kissed her on the lips. Then he handed the body over to the funeral home men.

"Don't cut her little body please," Sadie said.

Then the funeral home man whispered to Mr. Woodrow, "This means we will need to bury her in two days if we can't properly embalm her."

"We will get everything ready for Sunday," Sadie's father responded.

"I need to get in the house and start making RuthAnn's burial outfit," Sadie said.

"We'll all help," Lucy said.

"Henry I want to talk to you boi."

"Not now papa."

"Now boi!" He demanded and banged his cane.

"Come on y'all let's all go in the house," Mr. Woodrow said.

"How could you let this happen Henry?" Mr. Pottishear slapped Henry not once but twice.

Mr. Pottishear was crying.

Henry started crying too.

"I don't know what to do. I just wanted us to have a little bit of fun."

"Fun. Fun. That is all you ever think about boi is fun. When are you ever going to start getting serious about life? About taking care of your family?"

Henry was sobbing like a kid in his baseball glove.

His father went in the house and left Henry outside.

Mrs. Eleanor went outside. "Henry come on inside."

"Don't no one want me in there Mrs. Eleanor."

"Henry come in the house you are part of this family and we all need to find a way to get through this."

"But Sadie hates me. She blames me for RuthAnn being gone and I think she is right."

"Henry it is going to be alright. Come on. Sadie needs you even if she doesn't know she needs you."

Henry slowly walked in the house and looked at everybody in the house looking back at him with accusatory eyes.

"Go on in there with Sadie, Henry," Mrs. Eleanor said.

She was lying in the bed still wearing those bloody clothes.

Henry got in bed behind her. Sadie didn't move. She looked like she was in a trance. Henry put his arm around her and held her. They fell asleep. They were both so exhausted from crying.

The next few days were a blur. Nothing much mattered except that RuthAnn have the most beautiful funeral dress they could make. Without asking anyone, Sadie took the bottom part of her wedding dress and made it into a funeral dress for RuthAnn.

"Sadie, that's your wedding dress," Henry said.

"Don't much matter. My daughter ain't gone never get to wear it at her wedding."

Sadie, with the help of Henry's sisters, had sewn little colored porcelain dolls all over RuthAnn's dress. It was an even more beautiful dress now than it was when Sadie wore it except that is for RuthAnn's burial. The lacy collar and lacy fringe at the edge of the dress were beyond reproach. It was better than anything that could be store bought.

The dress was later delivered to the funeral home late that Saturday night for that dreaded day tomorrow.

"Sunday came so fast it don't seem like we even had time to sleep," Henry said.

It was a beautifully sunny spring day outside. But inside, there was no happiness to be found.

"What!" Henry was stunned at what he was hearing.

"Sadie how can you say that you don't want to go to RuthAnn's funeral?"

"I've had enough pain from this Henry. I can't handle no more."

Henry did not attempt to talk with Sadie anymore about it. He needed big guns. He went looking for Mrs. Eleanor. She was sitting outside on the front porch in her rocking chair.

Henry just blurted it out. "Mrs. Eleanor, Sadie said she is not going to the funeral."

"What?" She jumped to her feet.

Sadie was sitting on the bed nearly naked.

"Sadie child what's wrong with you? Did you tell Henry you weren't going to RuthAnn's funeral?"

Sadie was full out crying. She looked horrible.

Nobody knows what was said to Sadie by her mother that day, but whatever she said it caused Sadie to get up, clean herself up and get ready for the funeral. All anyone knew was that Sadie and her mother stayed in that room for a very long talking quietly.

It was a slow procession to the church. And when they got to the church and Sadie saw that hearse with the small mahogany casket inside of it, Sadie went berserk. As they opened the door to pull out the casket, Sadie jumped out of the moving car and ran up to the hearse and threw her body on the casket such that the men could not remove the casket from the hearse.

Henry had to lift Sadie up and carry her into the church. And it took almost every other man in the family to hold Henry up because Sadie wasn't going with him willingly. Finally, they made it up the stairs and into the small church. The congregation stood up when they heard Sadie's piercing cries come into the church.

Josephine was so distraught that she ran out the back of the church. Sadie had to be held down by her mother and Henry as RuthAnn's casket was carried into the church. It was gut-wrenching and beyond belief. There was not a dry eye to be found in that congregation that day. Even the pastors in the pulpit were crying.

Sadie's Uncle Herb went outside to talk to Josephine after they got Sadie settled down.

"Josephine I need you to tell me exactly what happened that night."

Josephine's eyes were as big and wide as black pearls. If only they were as beautiful. Still Herb needed to know.

"Tell me Josephine and you better not lie to me because I know when you are lying to me just like your momma."

"Daddy." Josephine was weeping.

Herbert stood there emotionless.

"I rocked RuthAnn in the living room until she was completely asleep. Then I took her in the bedroom and laid her down in her blanket."

"And?"

"And what. That's what happened."

"So are you telling me that you never went back in that room to check on that baby!" Herb was furious.

"Answer me!" He screamed at her. Although there was still sobbing inside the church, everyone could hear Herb screaming outside.

"Papa, you better go get Herb before he kills Josephine on the church grounds." Aunt Emma Lee said.

Slowly but surely their papa, Sadie's grandfather, went outside and made his way over to where his son Herb was interrogating his granddaughter Josephine.

"Herb!" His father tried to calm him down.

Herb would not be so easily assuaged.

"What about the broken window?"

"I forgot."

"YOU FORGOT!" That was the wrong thing to say.

Before anyone knew it. Herb had taken off his belt and was beating Josephine like a child. He was talking, screaming, crying, yelling, and swinging all at the same time. Josephine was writhing on the dirt in her black dress that was sliding up enough to show all of the fat parts of her that no one wanted to see.

"Help!" Josephine yelled.

His father hit Herb over the head with the cane. "Stop beating that girl. We will not have two murders in this family this day."

Herb spit on Josephine! "I hate you and your momma."

"Somebody come help me get this big girl off the ground," their papa yelled out.

While a few of the deacons were going outside to help, Herb was coming in the church like a lion. He walked straight down to the first pew and fell on his knees in front of Sadie.

He was crying.

"Sadie I am so sorry. I know that don't mean much but I am truly sorry."

Sadie looked at her Uncle Herb whom she loved very much, and the for the first time she saw someone else's pain for RuthAnn that was greater than her own. And a little part of her started to heal at that very moment.

"Uncle Herb I love you so much. I am sorry too. Maybe someday this won't hurt so much."

Herb hugged Sadie like he was saying goodbye. Then he hugged his sister Eleanor just as tightly.

They say Herb walked out of that church that day and was never seen again.

Herb's pain gave Sadie a little peace, at least enough to get through the funeral and RuthAnn's burial. They buried RuthAnn on top of her great grandmother – the love of Sadie's grandfather's life, even though he had two more wives after her. Azalee was her name.

The next few months were difficult. Although their lives had a routine attached to them, there was nothing routine about it all. RuthAnn was all Sadie could think about.

It took her a while before she could start giving herself to Henry again, and even when she did it was not the same. And on top of that, Sadie made him spill his seed outside of her.

"You should know how to do that," Sadie said.

"Sadie we can have more children."

She slapped him.

"What did I do?"

"You said it like more children will just make RuthAnn go away."

"That's not what I meant."

Henry started crying. Sadie's heart broke.

"What are you crying for?"

"Because I miss her too, and no one has ever thought about all my pain in the midst of this whole thing."

Sadie sat down on the bed. Her husband was right. No one, including her, had ever given any consideration to the pain Henry was feeling.

Sadie grabbed her husband and caressed him in her arms. He suckled on her beautiful breast just like a babe.

"Henry you are so right." She rubbed his head as he suckled.

"I'm so sorry. I never meant to forget you. I love you." She clung tight to him. "I don't ever want to lose you."

At that point, it had been more than a year before they truly made love to each other like they used to do. But tonight was different. They wrapped themselves in each other's pain and promise of a new life, a better life. They washed each other's kisses with tears of joy and longing for each other.

Things started to get a little bit better for them. Sadie got a job doing day work and Henry got a promotion that put him on third shift.

Henry also formed a band that sang gospel music. The group was named the Golden Crowns. They even cut several albums that were a big hit.

Then it happened.

Henry didn't spill his seed outside of Sadie one night, and low and behold, Sadie was pregnant. Everyone was overjoyed but Sadie. It had been two years since RuthAnn died but Sadie's arms still ached for her.

Just before Christmas, 1955, Henry Junior was born. Two years later about that same time Sadie gave Henry a second son named Claude. They were happy boys who spent most of their time at Sadie's parents' house riding ponies and running around the sprawling farm that Sadie's parent owned. Sadie wouldn't let anyone keep these boys, not even Henry's family. And Henry dared not object. Even Sadie was a little scared to keep them herself.

About three years later Sadie gave Henry a third son name, during the height of the civil rights movement. His name was Jacob. And three years after that she gave him one more son. His name was Matthew.

## Chapter 5

"I didn't know you two were still trying to have more children," Lucy said.

"We weren't Lucy. But we also were not trying. He just sort of showed up," Henry said.

"Look at him. He is the spittin' image of RuthAnn," Sadie's father said.

"I thought so too, but I was too scared to say so," Sadie responded.

"Why?" Her mother asked.

"Because I didn't want to jinx him and something happen to him."

"Stop thinking like that," Henry said.

"I agree," her mother said.

Within a few months, Matthew was crawling around and getting into everything imaginable. As he grew more and more, things only became worse.

"Sadie come here. Look."

"Momma, I'm getting' ready to go outside and beat those boys."

"Stop child and look."

They stood there and watched while Matthew's older brothers pushed him into the dirt.

"Why did they push him down in the dirt?"

"Because he was trying to follow them into the woods to play and no one wanted to watch him," her mother said.

"Let me go get that boy. I swannee."

"Don't you sware in this house. Leave him alone. Just watch."

"He looks like he is enjoying himself."

"Exactly. No matter what they do to him that boy is just so happy that it is simply amazing."

"Momma he is filthy rolling around in that dirt."

"Leave him alone. Boys will be boys."

"But…"

"But nothing."

"Let Matthew be himself. Besides look at him. He doesn't need anyone or anything to entertain him. He knows how to entertain himself. That is a gift from God. And besides he ain't got nothing that a little soap and water won't clean."

At the end of the day Matthew was still playing but in his bath water this time in the kitchen sink.

Sadie remembered what her mother showed her earlier that morning and she couldn't help but laugh as she washed her dirty son. As always before she was done washing him, he was fast asleep.

"Henry come get this heavy boy and put him in bed."

That was their regular schedule.

As Matthew grew older not much changed. Even though he wasn't able to go to school yet, he knew when it came time to go to their grandparents early every Saturday morning. He would be up in bed wide awake and kicking long before it was time to get up.

"Matthew be still and go back to sleep," his bed partner Jacob would always say.

Their mother would hear Jacob complaining and she knew that meant her baby was up and at 'em.

"Come on Matthew." Sadie would come and get him and put him in the middle of her and Henry in the small two-bedroom apartment they had moved into after RuthAnn died. Sure enough that was what Matthew wanted because he would snuggle up underneath his daddy and go right back to sleep.

"Damn."

"Come on Matthew. You've wet the bed again."

"Why is it he only pisses on me?"

Sadie was laughing. Henry' wasn't so humored by it all.

Sadie knew it was time for everybody to get up because that damn meant Henry was soaked.

"Okay, y'all get up and start gettin' your things ready."

Before long, they were all piled up in Henry's car to take that long drive down to their grandparent's house in the country, way back in the woods.

Matthew had gotten big enough that he was able to sit up in the backseat with his older brothers. It didn't even bother him that they ganged up on him in the backseat during the ride because he was the smallest of the quartet.

"Momma, this boy done fell asleep again and he's all over me."

"Get off me Matthew."

That's all her mother heard most of the way down to her parent's house.

"Hand him to me." It took all three of his brothers to lift Matthew over the backseat into their mother's arms.

But, as soon as the car turned down the street to their grandparent's house, Matthew would pop up like a jack-in-the-box. It was the prize in his Cracker Jack's.

Mathew loved being at his grandparent's place like he loved nothing else. When they arrived he was free to roam the woods, wade in the water, slop around in the pig pen, and chase his grandma's cats. The brothers didn't see much of each other from the time they arrived until the time they left, except for bedtime and church.

But Matthew also knew how to make his grandmother mad. He messed with her cats on a regular basis, which Matthew did not know at the time. Matthew just hated cats for some unknown reason and so his grandmother had given him enough automatic play dates every time he saw her cats near him. That won Matthew a lot of extra attention from his grandmother - - on his rear end that is.

But Matthew didn't care, he was free. It took him a good little while to figure out that she was watching him from the kitchen window. But once he figured it out, he learned how to get the cats without getting caught. But when his grandmother would catch him, she would fire up his rear end with her hand. Matthew would cry, but nobody came to his rescue.

While he was busy crying his grandmother would take a wet cloth and wash his dirty face and hands. Then she would fix Matthew a hot, homemade biscuit with honey. They would sit on the back porch together while Matthew ate his biscuit and his grandma told him stories about their family.

Matthew loved sitting on the porch looking at his grandmother's face. She was so pretty and she had a mouth that shined in the sun. Heck, her mouth shined even when it was raining.

Matthew was almost five years old before he realized that his grandmother had a mouth full of gold teeth. They were not gaudy like you see today. His grandmother was regal looking and she carried herself like a true lady. And everyone treated her like a queen. In fact, their grandmother's mouth was so expensive that she could make a down payment on a house today if she had to. And she didn't even mind Matthew putting his dirty sticky fingers in her mouth to touch her gold teeth, like his daddy did, except that he didn't have no gold in his mouth.

They would sit there until Matthew was finished eating, no matter how long it took. When he was finished she would wash his hands and face again and then Matthew was free to start all over again, until his turn came.

Back then there were no neighbors around their grandparent's house for more than four or five miles. So Matthew just roamed as free as a bird for as long as he wanted to, not like back home where his parents would not let him out of their sight. Being at their grandparents was sort of like a vacation for Matthew's parents too. Boy did they need it after he was born. Their grandmother and mother would be in the house cooking together, like old times. Meanwhile, their father and grandfather would be on the front porch sitting, talking, and spitting or in the woods shooting at targets.

They, the Minwhites were so poor that they didn't have a television, bathroom, or running water in the house. But for Matty, as he was affectionately known, it didn't matter. He was having more fun than he could have imagined. Oftentimes they would all get together and play target practice with all of their granddaddy's guns and rifles.

They looked like they had just stepped out of a *Norman Rockwell* picture except they were black. But if you didn't know them you couldn't be too sure about that because Mr. Woodrow, their granddaddy, was the only chocolate one in the bunch. He was dark roasted chocolate. The rest of them were fairly bright.

But that dark roasted man could shoot, chop wood, and scrap like no other. One weekend while they were all having fun, Matty saw something strange on the ground. The older folks were shooting off their guns and the women were watching the men. So Matty, as usual, wondered off.

"Matty!" His momma screamed. Her heart sank.

"Henry!" Sadie screamed.

"Matty!" His daddy was frantic as he ran towards Matty.

Matty's grandfather was right behind his daddy with his pistol ready.

Matty had wondered right up to big black snake.

Without a thought of concern for themselves, Henry grabbed Matty in the nick of time, and his grandpa grabbed the snake with his left hand by the head and squeezed it until the snake was dead.

Matty was unfazed. He was starring in his daddy's face with those big beautiful brown eyes, smiling. It was contagious. His daddy and his granddaddy started smiling back at him.

Matty stuck his dirty fingers in his daddy's mouth. Then he hugged his neck real tight.

"Oh RuthAnn," His daddy uttered without a thought.

"What'd you say Henry?" Mr. Woodrow asked.

Henry caught himself.

"I know Henry. I know. I was thinking it too," Mr. Woodrow said.

A few weeks later it was Claude's turn.

Against everything they had been told not to do, Claude and Jacob were climbing up the ladder on the back of the caddyshack garage their granddaddy had made for his nice new-old car.

"AAGGGHHHH." Claude let out a scream.

Before anyone knew what was happening everybody was running out of the house past Matty toward the garage. Matty had been knocked on the ground so he just sat there and watched everybody else run.

Their granddaddy shimmied up that ladder behind Claude and told him not to move. Claude had come face to face with a big poisonous snake lying on the roof waiting for him. They were starring each other in the face.

Their granddaddy reached around Claude and threw him down to Henry, and shot the snake right in the mouth. Matty jumped at the unexpected gunshot but he would not move.

Their grandpa had saved Claude's life from that poisonous snake that day. Needless to say Claude never climbed up the back of that garage ever again.

As always was the plan, about the time the sun started to go down on Saturday evening, it was to pump the well for water.

The Pottishear quartet got so dirty that they had to take a bath every night before they went to bed, especially on Saturday nights. When Matty saw his grandma getting the big, shiny, metal tub that was hanging over the back porch, he knew bath time was almost upon them.

The three older brothers would always go first because they could bathe themselves and because by the time Matty was finished they all would be ready for bed.

Matty was always last because that meant grandma would have to heat less water on her black, cast iron, double-decker, wood-burning stove to put in the silver, metal tub to cover his little fat body. But Matty didn't mind, it gave him a little extra pussycat chasing time without fear of getting caught. Being last also meant that grandma would not have to use as much wood to keep the stove burning while Matty took his bath in her big open kitchen, near that big beautiful wood-burning stove. The kitchen would already be nice and warm like a steam room from his brothers taking their baths.

"Matty," his grandma would call his name like she was yodeling or something.

Matty would come running immediately as fast as his little legs would carry him. But before he could get his prize he had to climb up the back porch.

It took a lot of effort for a five-year old to climb up that porch because Matty was only about 4.5 tall, if that tall.

The porch was five Mattys stacked high at its tallest point. It was made of cinder brick and they were all painted starch white. The back of the house was on a big hill that slopped down to the creek that ran through the back of the property. So the porch had to be extra tall to reach the back of the house.

The house had this big open space underneath that Matty played under all day even though it was a little scary because it was dark under there, really dark. That was not enough to stop Matty.

But those stairs, Matty had to get on his knees in order to crawl up these high steps. But he didn't care because it was a fitting end to the first day of his weekend adventure. His grandmother stood at the top of the stairs smiling down at him the whole time with her beautiful, expensive smile. She never moved. She was Matty's prize for finishing his climb.

And Matty made it his business every time to get to the top of those stairs, knees scrapped up and all, just to be able to hug his grandma around her apron covered knee caps, which was the extent of his reach.

She would escort him through the outside, screened-in porch and into the warm and toasty kitchen. In one quick swoop, she would have him naked and dipping his fat toes into the warm metal tub.

Matty didn't have a rubber ducky, his father and grandfather would not allow it. But they did let him have a battleship, a big battleship for a little guy like Matty. It stayed at his grandparent's house so they wouldn't forget it at home when bath time came.

His grandmother was busy scrubbing everything; I do mean everything on Matty. He didn't care; he was too busy enjoying his battleship and his grandma. When she was done Matty was done. Matty was already falling asleep before his grandmother could finish drying him off.

There was just enough awake time left for Matty to see his daddy's face carrying his little piggy to bed through the slits in his eyes that were quickly going shut to meet the sandman.

The only thing that used to wake Matty up at night was when he heard water hitting metal. That meant that one of his brothers or somebody else was using the night bucket that they brought inside because they could not go to the outhouse at night. Actually Matty never went to the outhouse, since the accident.

One Saturday afternoon they were all sitting around and the house was quiet, too quiet.

"Where is Matty?" Sadie asked.

Her sons ignored her. She stomped her feet.

"Where is your brother?"

They knew that tone. They would not dare ignore her now.

"We don't know."

"Get up and go look for him!"

They all fanned out over the house and property.

"Wait. What was that?" Mrs. Eleanor said,

"That sounds like water splashing." Henry said.

So they all took off toward the pond.

Matty was nowhere to be found.

"That's coming from the outhouse," Henry Jr. said.

Sure enough. Matty had gotten into the outhouse and had fallen in the hole.

"Who left this damn door open?" Mrs. Sadie asked. She knew one of her sons did it.

"I'll get him," Henry said.

"Don't y'all realize that boy could have drowned?"

The thought of it made his brothers gag.

"Boy you smell just like that shithole you been in."

"Henry!"

"What Sadie. He does smell like…"

"You don't need to say it again."

Everybody was laughing. Henry was holding his son with outstretched arms like he was a plague because he was all tangled up in toilet paper, shit, and piss.

"Let him put his hands in your mouth daddy," Claude said.

"Shut up boy."

It took five baths before Matty was clean. After that Matty was not allowed to even be in the area of the outhouse, which was a little distance further behind their granddaddy's garage.

"If Matty even gets so much as near that outhouse again, I am going to cut all three of y'alls asses when we get home," their mother said.

Their grandmother tried to intervene to save them, but the boys knew their mother didn't make idle threats. So every time they wanted to go somewhere they had to make sure Matty was in the house of somewhere where he could be seen by their parents or grandparents.

After that, every time Matty had to go to the bathroom somebody would have to come and hold his little wee-wee while he peed in the bucket in the house. And if he needed to do a number two, there was a little piece of wood they would put over the bucket with a hole in it so Matty could balance himself.

But at night, when the water stopped hitting the metal, Matty would grab his bunny rabbit tighter and go back to sleep.

Jacob hated having to sleep with Matty at home and at their grandparents because that rabbit was so old and so worn that it had wire sticking out in the back just where it met Jacob's spine. They tried to take the rabbit several times, but Matty knew and it was never a success. So oh well, Jacob had to suffer for the room necessary for Mr. Jangles. And suffer he did.

It never dawned on Matty that his grandmother worked harder taking care of them on the weekends then she did washing clothes and cleaning up for all those white folks, after she left Old Man Jack's plantation.

Matty walked into the kitchen one time when he heard one his grandmother's sisters say, "I hear those white folk you work fo' scared to ask you to do too much because Woodrow told them if they mistreated you there would be hell to pay."

They all started laughing.

Matty just stood there looking and waiting.

"Grandma's baby wants a hot honey biscuit," she said as she swooped him up.

On Sunday mornings the family would get up extra early and eat a big breakfast their mother and grandmother had already prepared long before the kids were out of bed. Then Matty's brothers would wash up real good and put on their Sunday clothes their mother had laid out for them the night before. Matty had a little extra time to eat because their mother or grandmother would always dress him after they got almost dressed.

When everyone was ready they would hop into both cars, half in their daddy's car and half in their granddaddy's car. Matty would always ride with his grandparents because his granddaddy would let him stand up in his lap and steer the car.

Everybody in their family went to this church, except for his daddy's people so Sunday mornings were a true family reunion every single Sunday. And, everybody in their mother's family loved Henry.

He was the quintessential tall, dark, and handsome man, a regular knight in shining armor. Actually he was more of a sandy beach color. But when you saw all of them standing together, the parents, their four sons, and their grandparents, it was damn-near picture perfect. Matty's parents had good genes, and their parents had good genes, and so on and so on, so much so that they all came together to produce those boys.

And Matty was as dearly as loved as his father. They would take turns passing him around so they could look at his pudgy face and beautiful hair that was a long as any girl at church. So long in fact that Matty had been wearing a pony tail every since he was one. And all of his girl cousins used to chase him around the church yard to take turns playing in his hair.

As the adults stood around chattering about anything and everything, Matty used to try to get away from his mother but he wasn't nearly as successful most of the time because his mother knew that his suit would be dirty before church started. Therefore, expecting doom for Matty's clothes his mother held his hand very tightly. But that did not deter his female cousins from wanting to play in his hair, which only irritated him more, at least to the point where he would shout, "STOP!"

"Go on girls leave Matty alone," his grandma would say. And she didn't care if it offended any of her sisters. That left Matty free to pout as he tugged at this mother's skirt which covered most of her legs. But it did give him some cover when they pesky girls would come back around.

Compared to his brothers, Matty was a miniature sized Santa, unlike his brothers who were all tall and skinny like their dad.

Just as escape from his mother's grasp seemed imminent, the big steeple bell above the small red brick church would start to ring. That was the single that morning service was about to begin and that everyone needed to come on in and take their seats.

Matty used to look up to heaven wondering if God was against him, but he enjoyed the singing. Then there would be a lot of different people talking between the singing and the time the preacher actually started preaching. Even though Matty really didn't understand what they were talking about, he had to sit there like everybody else in his obligatory spot beside his mother at the front of the church because back in the late 60's there was no such thing as children's church.

There was one church and one service and everybody sat there together from beginning to end. Matty couldn't wait for church to end, but it didn't come that easily.

That boy used to get so bored and it would be so hot in that little brick church that he could not help but fall asleep. But his mother was Johnny-on-the-spot. As soon as he started to nod off she would pinch him so hard that he had no choice but to wake up and pay attention.

And cry, Matty had better not even think about crying in church or making a scene because that was a guaranteed ass-cuttin'. And Matty's mother was the kind of woman you did not want to cross. If she told you you were going to get a whoppin' when they got home, she meant just that.

But as soon as church was over, Matty would be out of there so fast that even he had to laugh as he past his granddaddy and his daddy, who always sat at the back of the church with the other men, except for his great grandpa. He sat at the front of the church because he was somebody important and because he helped found the church.

The reason Matty couldn't wait for church to be over was because their family always served food after Sunday service, or so it seemed. So Matty wanted to rush to the desert table so he could get a piece of sweet potato pie. He would run past everybody and rush to that table non-stop. When he got to the table, his grandma's sister Emma Lee was always there. She was one of the three sisters, including Matty's grandma that was left.

Aunt Emma Lee used to always ask Matty, "Boy what are you doing?"

Before he could even formulate an answer she would say, "Don't eat that."

No matter whether it was cake or pie, she would take it from him. Then she would hand him a piece of sweet potato pie or something else from her special stash and just like that it would be gone.

Then Matty would have to run and catch up with the family because they had to get back home. His mother and grandmother would always finish preparing the Sunday dinner they started early that morning while they were fixing breakfast before they came to church.

Matty was relegated to sitting on the porch with the men and his brothers until dinner was ready. They would all eat and then they would sit on the porch together until late in the evening before the time came for them to take the ride back to the city. It was the perfect ending to a perfect weekend, every weekend without fail.

Early one Monday morning before they were all barely out of bed, the phone rang. It was so early that it was still dark outside. It was early September.

Matty heard his daddy say, "Hold on." Then he handed the telephone to his wife.

Their mother screamed, "What!" It was a shrilling sound that sent chills up Matty's spine. Matty was standing in the living room of their two bedroom apartment staring into his parent's bedroom too scared to move. Then he heard his mother start crying. Matty had never seen her cry before.

His daddy was holding his mother, trying to calm her down but nothing was working. Matty could tell his mother was in pain but what he didn't understand was why. The next thing they knew was that they were all being packed up and put in the car without any indication of what was going on or where they were headed.

That car ride was the longest car ride. Matty was so scared that he didn't even go to sleep. There wasn't a word spoken the entire ride and the radio was silent. The only sounds that were heard beside the car's engine were the sobs that came from their mother the entire ride. There was no clue where they were going until their father made that distinctive turn. Immediately Matty knew exactly where they were going. But he didn't understand why.

"Why we going back to grandma's house? We was here yesterday."

Nobody said a word to Matty.

Everybody walked in the house real slow except for Matty. He pounced out of the car and ran into the house wanting to see his grandma again. Then everybody broke out into loud sobs. All of his grandmother's sisters were there with their husbands, and a whole lot more people that Matty didn't know.

Matty was running through the house, "Grandma. Grandma."

People started crying louder.

Matty couldn't find his grandma. He ran to his daddy. "Daddy, daddy where is grandma?"

Matty saw water rolling down his daddy's cheeks. He had never seen water roll down his daddy's cheeks before. He put his fat fingers on the water to try and make it stop.

Then he looked and saw these strange men in suits coming in the house with a bed on wheels.

They went into his grandma's bedroom.

Before Henry knew it, Matty had already jumped out of his arms and was through the door before it closed. No one could stop him.

His granddaddy picked him up and gave him to his daddy.

Matty started crying. He didn't understand what was going on.

Those men stayed in there a really long time, along with their mother and grandpa. Then the door opened and out came the men with somebody under the sheet and Matty's mother and grandpa behind them.

Matty started screaming. "I want to see my grandma. I want to see my grandma."

He was violently screaming. Until his daddy had to put him down and the men had to stop and let Matty see his grandma.

When they pulled back the sheet to let him see her face, Matty was not scared. He stood there looking at her. He touched her face. He started crying.

"Grandma please wake up."

When she didn't open her eyes, he kissed her and hugged her. "Grandma, I love you. When I gone see you again."

The house was tore up by what they were witnessing.

The men slowly covered Matty's grandma back up, put her in a black car, and took her away.

As they took her away Matty just stood in the door looking at the car drive away. Matty was emotionless at that point. He went over in the corner and sat down by himself.

It took a while for Matty to understand that his grandma died in her sleep that Sunday night after they left.

Their grandpa went to wake her up the next morning and noticed that she wasn't moving and that she was cold. That's when he called momma so that they could come down. That's when Matty realized that it was his grandpa on the phone early that morning.

And the reason the men took so long in the bedroom is that they had to clean grandma up before they brought her out.

Matty just sat in the corner crying.

Shortly after that, their daddy and granddaddy brought the mattress out of the bedroom and took it down to the woodshed to air out. Matty was trying to figure out what they were doing. He never found out the answer why until he was in Mr. Brevard's high school biology class. There were people in and out of his grandparents' house the remainder of that whole day.

Matty stood there looking around at all the faces but none of them were as beautiful as his grandma's face.

"There ain't nobody just for me no more," he said.

Then he went outside and sat on the steps in the back house. It was as close as he could get to his grandma. That's where they found him when it was starting to get dark and their father was gathering up his kids to get ready to leave.

"Daddy where is momma?"

Their father didn't answer.

Matty started crying because he wanted to stay with his momma but they wouldn't let him stay.

When they pulled up in the driveway of their two bedroom apartment Matty just sat in the car. He looked like the loneliest child in the world.

The ride home was as quick as it was painful. That was the first time Matty had seen his oldest brother, Henry junior, sit in the front seat beside their daddy. The rest of them sat in the backseat with Matty in the middle. It just didn't feel right. When they finally pulled into the small, tight parking lot right outside their apartment, Matty didn't want to get out of the car.

"Daddy why can't it go back the way it was yesterday?"

Henry just looked at his son in amazement.

"If I had known grandma was going to be leaving I would have given her an extra hug and kissed two more times."

They all went into the house and got ready for bed.

Matty slept with his daddy for the first time that night, him and his torn rabbit with the wire hanging out. It should have been a treat, but it didn't feel like a treat. Matty snuggled up to his father as tightly as he could that night.

"Daddy?"

"Yea Matty."

"You ain't going nowhere are you?"

"No son. Daddy ain't going nowhere."

"I love you daddy."

"I love you too son."

The next morning before their daddy made breakfast, he called their mother to check on her.

Matty heard his daddy say, "That boy slapped me in my face all night long and his fat feet kept kicking me in the chest."

Then it happened. Matty heard his daddy say, "We got to get rid of that rabbit."

Matty jumped up and ran into the bedroom he shared with his brothers and hid under the bed along with his rabbit.

They were supposed to go to school that day but they didn't go. As soon as they had breakfast, they were all being loaded up again along with all kinds of stuff that Matty had never seen his daddy pack let along touch before. Just like that they were back in the car with lots of suitcases, including ones for their mother.

There was no reconciliation of the drive back down to their grandparents' house, but that had to be the shortest drive his daddy ever made down to their house. Yet, there was no excitement in this drive. It was more trepidation if anything.

They spent the remainder of that week at that little white house. In Matty's mind that house was no longer grandma's place. There was no running around, no cats to chase, nobody to wash the dirt off his face, and no hot honey biscuits.

But Matty could do without all of that if he could just have her skirt to hug again.

All that was left were strangers, big smiles, and lots of food that Matty didn't want to eat. The house was overrun with people inside and outside. The women were all gathered inside the house and the men were gathered outside around big barrels of fire. Matty didn't fit in either group.

This happy playground, his playground was gone. "What did I do to make God angry at me so that He would take my grandma?" Matty asked out loud.

Matty just kept walking around in circles kicking an old soda can somebody had thrown down on the ground. This went on for several days.

Then on Tuesday, as if things couldn't get any worse, a big brown limousine pulled up. This big black man, who looked like Lurch from the *Adam's Family* got out of the car and walked up to the door and hung this big white flower on the door. Matty fell out in the yard right where he stood and started crying. It took both his mother and father to calm him down, but it took all evening.

Matty stayed in bed the whole next day. He only got up to use the pot and then he went back to bed, he and Mr. Jangles.

The next few days were pretty much more of the same until Friday night came. Matty had never seen a hearse before that pretty, brown, high-top car pulled up in their grandma's yard. Then three men got out of the front of that fancy car, walked around back, and opened this large door.

Matty was more than intrigued.

He stood there and watched them pull this beautiful brown box out of the back of the high-top car. He wanted to run away and never come back, but he didn't know where to go.

Instead, he followed the men in the house. They had put the pretty box on this big silver thing with wheels and rolled it into the house.

The entire family stood up when the box came in.

Then the men rolled the box into grandma's bedroom.

No one saw Matty.

He was right behind the last man who was pushing the box.

"Where is grandpa going to sleep?" Matty said.

But still he followed the men into grandma's room, sat down, and watched as the men meticulously opened the box, set up the lights, and made other preparations Matty didn't understand.

Matty had had enough. He wanted to see what was in the box.

"Grandma," Matty exclaimed.

He just stood there at her hear looking at her.

The rest of the family came in and joined him.

Matty would not move from his grandma's side.

Matty didn't sleep at all that night and maybe no one else did either. It was the same thing on Saturday night. He kept going into the room waiting for his grandma to get up.

Their grandma was home. Her body was home but it wasn't the same thing. Matty wanted his grandma back so bad but their momma had explained to him earlier that, "God don't make no mistakes and that his decisions in this case are final, and we just had to find a way to accept His wisdom."

"Momma I don't like this. I might have to accept it because I know what the Bible says in Genesis after Adam ate the fruit of the forbidden tree. I have never experienced death before but it just don't seem right."

It was the last day before the funeral.

His mother kissed him on the forehead but it wasn't like his grandma's kisses.

Grandma's body lay in state at Matty's former playground for two days and two nights. Then Sunday morning came.

It was a strange feeling, people running around, chatting, talking, and drinking.

The night before the funeral Matty said his prayers just like his grandma taught him to. He asked God to let him wake up from this horrible nightmare and wake up to his regular Sunday routine like he loved so much.

"And whatever I did to make you mad, please forgive me and give me my grandma back."

His momma, daddy, and grandpa were all standing at the door listening to his prayer. It brought tears to all their eyes.

Matty got up extra early the next morning.

"I guess God didn't hear my prayer," Matty said.

So he went into his grandparent's bedroom and watched the men as they prepared to close his grandma's beautiful bronze box and take her body to the church down the road. He was standing there in his pajamas but this was no Christmas morning present.

After they took her casket out of the house, Matty looked over and saw his mother sitting on the bed. He walked over and sat on the bed next to her. The sun was shining down on both of them.

"Momma, look. God is shining down on us. What is He saying to us momma?"

She kissed Matty on the forehead and got up to start making sure everybody was ready.

Everybody was ready when daddy came in and said it was time to go. It was a horrible feeling.

The whole family climbed into this brand new polished, beaming in the sun limousine. It was Matty's first ride in one.

"If this is the reason for being in a limousine I never want to ride in one again," Matty said as he lifted one little leg than the other to get in the limousine.

As the limousine started out the driveway, Matty jumped up and plastered his face against the spotless glass. He had to look at that house once again because the next time he saw it it would not be the same.

As he looked around at the faces of his family inside that limousine during that slow ride to the church Matty realized that his family looked beautifully broken.

When the limousine pulled onto the church's yard, it was overrun with people. There were cars everywhere on both sides of the street, behind the church, and in the open fields on both sides of the road. There was also a green tent in the field to the left of the church.

"I don't remember seeing that tent there before," Matty said.

It was a long funeral, but their mother had done a beautiful job making all the arrangements. Their grandpa had left everything up to her. He told her that she could do anything she wanted and he would pay the bill.

It was the first time the whole family sat together on the first pew of the church.

"I don't want to sit up here no more," Matty said.

Matty was sitting beside his daddy who was crying like a baby. He had never seen his daddy cry before.

Matty didn't cry at the funeral.

Matty crawled up onto his daddy's lap and gave him a big hug. He thought that would keep his daddy from crying. It didn't work.

As the time came for the family to walk out of the church behind the casket, Matty couldn't help but look at all of those faces that were staring at them in pity.

Matty paused for a second. Every Pottishear in the country had taken up the whole left side of the church.

"I didn't know there was so many of them."

Then, they walked down those steep stairs behind her casket for the last time and over to that green tent that was in the field. Those men lowered her casket in the ground and they all just sat there. The funeral home men walked them back to the car after they sat there for another half hour. Their daddy and grandpa had to practically carry their mother back to the limousine. The funeral home people would not let them watch them cover her grave. They almost had to push Matty away from the gravesite.

After that Sunday, the family kept its standing weekend appointment with their grandpa every Saturday and Sunday like they always did but it was never the same.

Their mother would work all week cleaning that big mansion and then she would spend all weekend cleaning and cooking for everybody at grandpa's house. She always cooked enough so that he had food to eat all week until the next weekend.

"Matty go outside and play son there ain't nothing for you to do in here."

"That's okay momma. I don't want to go outside. I feel closer to grandma if I stay here in the kitchen."

There was an obvious silence around the old place that no one could fill, not that anyone wanted to but they just could not shake the heaviness of grandma being gone.

"This is worse than when RuthAnn passed," their grandpa said.

Matty ran outside.

"Who is RuthAnn?"

His daddy and granddaddy looked at each other. But no one answered him.

Matty turned to go back in the house to ask his momma.

Again his daddy and granddaddy looked at each other.

"You better go get that boy," his grandfather said.

Before Matty could get his question out, his daddy scooped him up and carried him back outside.

"Matty, listen. RuthAnn was your older sister."

His father proceeded to tell him everything Matty wanted to know about his sister – how he reminded everybody of her; how his grandma loved RuthAnn; how beautiful she was; and, unfortunately how she died.

What Henry didn't know is that his wife was standing just inside the door way listening to his every word. It was bittersweet.

"I will never forget your sister just like I will never forget your grandmother. They were both angels taken away from us much too soon."

Although their grandmother may have died peacefully in her sleep, there was no peace for those left behind. And it was even worse at church. Matty still fell asleep in service, but his desire for pies was gone. And because their entire family attended that same church, everywhere Matty looked was a reminder of something that his grandma did for somebody else.

"Matty." The way his grandmother called his name never sounded so sweet, and he would never let her voice die inside his soul.

Life sort of got back to normal after his grandmother's death, if you can call it that.

For the first time ever on a Saturday morning, the Pottishears did not go visit their grandfather. Matty was trying to figure out what to do with himself when he found himself standing at his father's knees with his head strained back looking up at him shaving with this green powdery mix that he had to make like a paste. It smelled terrible but Matty was intrigued.

He watched his daddy pull out this big knife, which Matty learned years later was a razor, and he started to scratch himself with it. It looked like a strange thing to do so Matty observed the ritual.

"Why doesn't momma do this daddy?"

No response.

Then his mother turned the corner and walked past the bathroom door, and put her hands in Matty's hair. Matty was rockin' a jumbo afro that lay down in some places because his hair was so fine that it would not stand up stiff, and it was kinky and curly at the same time.

Matty's hair was so kinky that it was tender to the touch and Matty had refused to let anyone comb it since his grandma died, which had been just about a year. When he used to see his mother going for a comb, his little fat legs would take off running, and if she caught him he would scream so loud and so long that he would win every time. But that particular day she had him hemmed in, and Matty wasn't thinking about his hair.

"I want you to take him to get his hair cut," his momma said.

Henry did not move a muscle or say a word. He just kept on doing what he was doing, and so Matty kept on watching him doing what he was doing. Matty was so caught up in him that he didn't even realize his mother's hand was in his hair.

When his father finished scraping his face, he washed up, put on a clean shirt, picked Matty up, and headed for the car, all before Matty knew what was going on. They didn't ride very far, but when they arrived Matty immediately knew this place was not the usual place his dad brought him to when he needed to keep Matty from getting in trouble.

You see, that familiar place had this big parking lot and there were always lots of cars out front, and the building looked like a house, not a very big house, but still it was a house.

Matty would be standing up in the seat waiting for his dad to step out of the car and take a big breath. He would always take a big breath before he picked Matty up. By the time Matty was five years old he was fat and round like a miniature *Fat Albert*.

Anyway, his father would carry Matty to the door of the house because he walked to slow for his dad. His daddy was a tall, thin man and either Matty had to walk on his tiptoes or his dad had to slump down a little to reach Matty's hand. So it was easier for him to just carry him.

But Matty didn't mind because it gave him a chance to look in his daddy's face. Matty would just stare at him for hours – his eyes, his nose, his mouth, and his teeth, like he was trying to etch his face in his memory.

Sometimes Matty would take his hand, without knowing what he was doing, and accidentally slap his daddy in the mouth. He would yell, "Boy!"

Matty was trying to touch his teeth but he didn't realize his little fat hands were so heavy. But after his dad would yell boy, then Matty would be focused on the hair above his eyes because now they were crunched together with nothing separating them but all these wrinkles. So then Matty had a new focus. Just about the time he would reach his hand up to trace his daddy's wrinkles, like a coloring book only better, he would put Matty down. They would be at the door to the house.

As soon as Henry opened the door, people would start calling his name.

"Hey man," was all you could hear from all around the diner.

The little house was a diner, although it took Matty quite a while to put those two together. Matty's daddy was the most popular person in that diner.

He would show Matty off like he was his pride and joy. Matty saw his daddy standing tall with his chest out and Matty would be standing right there beside him, standing as tall as he could with his stomach out. Matty was proud to be with his daddy.

When they would finally make their way through the crowd over to the row of stools, Henry would take another one of those obligatory breaths before he reached down and picked Matty up and sat him on a stool next to him.

Matty couldn't see much over the top of the counter but he didn't care as long as he could see his daddy's face the world was alright with him.

That little house diner had become their place because his dad took him there when he would come home after working third shift and Matty had so much energy that his daddy could not sleep. He would be too busy trying to keep Matty out of trouble. That became their routine after Matty got into his mother's powders one time and powdered their entire apartment including himself.

When his daddy got up that day and came in the living room to see a little fat *Casper* standing in the middle of the living room, completely covered in white powders smelling like perfume, Matty swore he saw steam coming out of his daddy's ears.

Meanwhile, Matty was standing there with one of those doggy looks. You know the look when dogs turn their heads from side to side trying to figure out what they are seeing.

So to his dad Matty must have looked liked a cute cuddly puppy because he started laughing.

Then he stripped Matty down, changed his clothes, and off they went. It took Sadie forever to clean up all those powders. She never used powders again.

After they would leave the diner, they would always come back home and take a nap. Henry kept Matty in his arms the whole time, probably because that was the only way he knew where Matty was.

Without fail, they would wake up just in time for Sadie to come home and change Matty's clothes because he always peed on his daddy's chest.

He would have just enough time to take a shower before he had to leave for work.

But that place was not the house with the big parking lot - - their place.

This place was a different building that was stuck in the middle of two other buildings on either side. This was a new place that Matty had never been to before.

There was no parking lot and this wasn't a house. Matty noticed his daddy had to park on the street and carry Matty across the road to the other side where this building was.

When they walked in these people knew his daddy too.

Matty didn't have time to look in his father's face because he was too busy trying to take in the sights and sounds that were going on.

There were lots of strangers sitting in chairs to their right. To the left were these men standing behind some more chairs, but these chairs would turn around back and forth. There was a lot of laughter, chattering, and Matty kept hearing this strange buzzing sound. And there were all these mirrors. Matty had never seen his own reflection before.

Anyway, Henry carried Matty over to a chair near the middle of the room, and they both sat down. Actually Henry sat down in the chair, and Matty sat in his lap. Matty sat there and watched his daddy talk to all of those strangers, and how they responded to his father's every word. That's when Matty realized that his father was a smooth operator.

As they sat there the place slowly cleared out and more people came in.

After sitting there for a little while, one of the guys behind those chairs that turned around called them over. The guy put some kind of board down over the chair and Henry hoisted Matty up onto the board. Then the other guy wrapped Matty up.

Matty called it a plastic blanket.

"Cut it all," Matty heard his father say.

Then there was this buzzing noise around his head.

The next thing Matty knew his hair was falling down around him. He picked it up and looked at it. The more of it that fell, the more of it he picked up and held in his hands. He even put some in his mouth.

Matty stopped when he heard this other kid screaming and crying a few chairs down, but it didn't dawn on Matty that he needed to scream and cry. It didn't seem to be helping that kid, so Matty didn't see a reason to do it. Within a few minutes it was all over and they were back in the car headed home.

It didn't really hit Matty that his hair was gone until they got back home and he saw his mother start yelling at his daddy.

"Why did you let him cut all of his hair off?" She was furious.

Then it hit Matty, and he started crying.

That was the first time Matty had ever heard his mother raise her voice to his father. No matter what happened Matty had to start going to the barbershop on a regular basis.

Now that Matty had had his first haircut, he was a big boy now, and it was time for him to go to school.

Matty protested at the idea of being a big kid.

His protests fell on death ears.

Shortly after that he started going to nursery school.

"Everything is changing now that grandma is gone."

Matty was sitting on the edge of the bed by himself.

Again, it didn't matter, Matty's protest. His mother had decided and that was that. Matty cried every morning the entire time his mother walked him to nursery school and he continued to cry even after she left. Some days his crying was so bad that his mother would have to turn around and come back to get him and take him home. Other times, she would call from work to see how he was doing and she could still hear him crying in the background.

Then one day Matty wasn't crying. He was just sitting there in his chair not doing anything.

All of a sudden there was a smell.

Then there was something weird against Matty's butt, but he couldn't move.

Pretty soon, everyone else in the nursery started to smell the smell too. The ladies went around checking all of the kids.

When they got to Matty, he refused to stand up. He was pretty heavy and strong enough that no one could lift him out of the chair.

The ladies had no choice but to call his mother.

"What!" Matty could hear his mother yell clean across the room.

He sat up straighter.

When his mother arrived she was furious that she had to lose a day's pay to come and get Matty from the nursery school once again.

She walked straight over to him, grabbed him by the hand, and dragged him out of that chair.

But Matty was not trying to walk because he had an extra load in his pants swooshing in his underwear.

But Sadie didn't care. She kept on walking as fast as she could. She refused to carry Matty.

Sadie was so mad that Matty had to break into a trot to keep up with his mother, even though she was tightly holding his hand. Normally, she would carry him. But that was not about to happen that day.

Sadie was walking so fast it just seemed impossible to keep up with her, particularly, with the extra load Matty was carrying in the seat of his pants.

Thank the Lord it wasn't the runny kind.

Matty must have looked like a miniature Dr. Frankenstein monster trying to run, if that was possible, like on the cartoons.

But without even trying Matty had won.

The nursery threw that chair away and Matty didn't have to go back ever again.

Everything that happened in Matty's life kept taking him back to his grandma's death for years. Matty went through the motions but he had no emotional attachment to anything or anyone.

Slowly Matty started hating being outside playing either in the city or in the country.

Then he developed some kind of allergy that made his eyes itch so bad that he would scratch to the point his mother thought he was going to scratch his eyes out.

His eyes would be all gooey and full of so much yellow yucky stuff that they would stick together like they had been glued together over night.

Dr. Walker made a lot of money off Matty's parents during time. Sadie and Henry thought Matty had hay fever but Dr. Walker called it something else. Whatever it was, it made Matty's life miserable, which was pretty hard to do considering his circumstances.

When Matty did go outside, his best friend at the time, JPH only wanted to play house with Matty and a few girls in the neighborhood.

"I'm going home," Matty said.

"Why?" JPH asked.

"Cause I ain't no girl and I don't like playing house."

"Come on man. What you scared of?"

"I'm not scared of anything. You just don't know how to have fun except play with girls and do girly things."

Matty's protest went unheeded.

Then JPH graduated to touching, not the girls but Matty. And it got worse as time went on to the point that JPH was openly trying to touch Matty in front of the girls. Matty would run into the house and look at television or play with his army men by himself.

Then one day it happened. "Matty why don't you like to go outside and play anymore?" His mother asked.

Matty didn't have an answer.

"Henry something's wrong with Matty. He hates being outside now."

A few weeks went by of Matty being cooped up in the house.

"Matty," his daddy called him into the living room.

"Daddy, whose bike is that?"

"It's yours."

"I don't know how to ride a bike."

"I'm going to teach you."

"Yea."

Matty was so excited that he started putting the bicycle together right there by himself. His parents were stunned by what they were seeing.

Matty's brothers all had bicycles and had been ridding for years so it was finally his turn to learn how to ride.

The only thing was that his father didn't have time to teach him how to ride and his brothers were not interested in the task, even though they were told to do it.

So Matty taught himself how to ride his own bicycle and within days he was begging his daddy to take the training wheels off. It took his daddy about another week or so but he did it. Matty was fully prepared for when he did.

There was this huge hill behind their small apartment, huge. Matty wanted to ride that hill every since he first saw it but it was not possible because of the training wheels. So when his father took them off, Matty was free to pursue this quest.

"It's not as good as chasing cats at grandma's house, but it will have to do."

It didn't take Matty long to realize that he had forgotten one very important part of his training.

"If grandma was here she would have never let me forget."

Matty had forgotten to teach himself how to stop. But that didn't stop Matty from riding that hill.

The first couple of times he came barreling down that hill he ran right smack into the apartments at the bottom of the hill. But Matty didn't care. At least he had learned how to stop.

It was so thrilling that he kept pushing his bike up the hill just so that he could ride down the hill again. And when he wasn't riding that hill he was riding around the whole neighborhood.

When he got ready to stop he would just run into a pole and fall off. Matty was having fun again.

Maybe the most fun he had had since his grandma died.

But Matty's stopping techniques also cost his parents a lot of money to repair and buy new bikes. Matty probably went through three new bikes in less than two months but he was out of the house and back outside playing.

But his happiness was short lived.

Suddenly JPH became interested in bike riding and wanted to hang out with Matty.

Matty detested the thought and boom, no longer was bike riding fun for him.

JPH was like that one gnat or that one fly that just would not go away, the one that nagged you every time you tried to enjoy a nice piece of watermelon in the sun.

Matty was back in the house.

"What did you say Matty?" His mother asked.

"Nothing momma."

"Are you talking to yourself?"

"Of course who else can I tell?" Matty said under his breath.

Matty was at his wits end and he didn't know what to do. It didn't dawn on him to tell anyone and he hated the fact that he was running away, but he did.

JPH had a hold over Matty, but Matty didn't know why. JPH was forcing Matty into the shadows slowly but surely, inch by miserable inch. Matty was powerless to push back.

So Matty became an irritated, finicky kid who used to be happy go lucky. He stopped eating and he even started acting up to some extent.

Once their mother had cooked a pot of pinto beans and corn bread but Matty refused to eat.

"Matty what is wrong with you?"

Matty just sat there staring across the table at his mother while she and his brothers all ate their food.

When they were finished eating, Matty was still sitting at the table with his full plate in front of him. Then the sun started to go down and Matty was ready to eat.

"Momma, can you warm my food so I can eat?"

"No. You should have eaten your food like everyone else. You don't have no special food privileges," Matty continued to sit there.

It got later and later until finally his mother turned off the lights and left him sitting in the kitchen in the dark by himself. Finally, after about an hour of Matty sitting in the dark his mother came and got him. She wrapped his food up and put it in the refrigerator.

"You can have this for breakfast." Then she put Matty in the bed.

It didn't take Matty long to figure out that he was not going to win that battle so he didn't try that ever again. And the next morning he was so grateful that he ate his full plate of food, no questions asked.

The time had now come for Matty to go to big boy's school.

Matty was in the third grade now. At this new school they did everything as a class. They marched everywhere in single file from one class to another. They were a disciplined bunch and the students were under the complete control of the teachers.

One day Matty saw this new girl in school.

He asked everybody about her but no one knew anything about her. He watched her for weeks on end trying to get her attention when they filed past each other's class in the hall, on the playground, and in the cafeteria.

But new girl just would not give Matty the time of day.

"Dang. I feel like a clown. She has no interest in me."

Matty was mad.

He decided to write her a note.

They were sitting in English class and Matty started writing this note to her except the note went from being happy to very angry, very quickly; and, instead of writing the note to her, Matty wrote the note about her to JPH.

He wrapped the note like a paper football. Then as they filed past each other to change class in the hallway, Matty passed the note to this goof ball kid that had class with his perverted best friend, JPH, the very next period.

That idiot read the note and then gave it to his teacher, who in turn gave it to the principal.

The next thing Matty knew, the principal, Mrs. Carver, was coming to get him out of class. Matty's heart was in his feet.

They quietly walked back to Mrs. Carver's office.

As they passed the secretary's desk, she gave Matty this disapproving look.

Then Mrs. Carver closed the door. She proceeded to give Matty a stern lecture on so many levels.

"Matty I know you have had a difficult time dealing with your grandmother's death. But I cannot excuse this."

She pulled out Matty's letter.

Matty was stunned. His eyes were big. His mouth was wide open. And his little body pushed back as far as possible in that chair.

Then she walked around to her desk where she kept her paddle.

But instead it was much worse.

She made Matty sit there in her office while she left.

When she came back in she had Matty's winter coat and books in her hands. She calmly helped Matty put his coat on and then they walked outside. She opened the rear door on the passenger side of her car and told Matty to get in. Then she walked around the car and got in the driver's seat and drove off.

It was a good day for a drive, Matty thought to himself. He was enjoying the ride. He was quite comfortable.

Then it hit him.

Matty's body turned into complete stone when he realized that they were pulling up in the parking lot of their apartment complex off Remus Road. Matty rushed to the left side of the car to open the door and get out. But he wasn't quick enough.

"No Matty. You stay in here while I talk with your father."

Matty sat back down, terrified - - beyond terrified.

It just so happened that Matty's dad was outside working on his engine, which he did more often now that

Matty was in school full time and didn't require his constant attention.

When Henry looked up and saw that white woman walking up to him he didn't say a word. Then he looked around her to see Matty in the backseat. Now he was more interested in what this white woman could possibly have to say.

He and she stood outside for a good twenty minutes talking in the cold air. Matty pressed his face up against the glass trying to hear what they were saying, but he could not make out a single word.

When they were finished, Henry opened the door and calmly said, "Come on Matty." Everything seemed cool.

He closed the hood on his car and threw his arm around Matty's left shoulder and escorted him back into the apartment.

They crossed the threshold, his dad closed the door, and then he told Matty to go into his room. No sooner was Matty just inside the bedroom door, his father stepped around the corner and pounced on Matty.

He started beating that boy with a belt like no one had ever seen Henry do before except there was no one there but Matty and his dad.

Matty was hollerin', screamin', and cryin' all the while his daddy was muttering some kind of gibberish no one could have understood.

He was kicking and screaming trying to get his coat off because it felt like he was drowning or smothering but he couldn't get it off for trying to protect himself.

Henry was madder then Matty had ever seen his dad because Matty could feel his daddy's licks through that thick grey overcoat. Henry had never whopped Matty before. What a way to get broke in?

Whoppin' was Sadie's job when it came to the boys. She was the disciplinarian in their family.

Henry beat Matty until they both were exhausted. Matty cried the rest of that afternoon. And that boy had one sore ass to boot.

Sadie called later that day and Matty answered the telephone. She was stunned to hear his voice as he was stunned to hear hers.

"What are you doing home? You sick?"

"No ma'am."

"Then what are you doing home?"

"I got in trouble at school."

"You were in a fight?"

"No ma'am."

"Okay Matty stop playing games with me and tell me what happened."

Matty told his mother the whole story from liking the girl to the note to Mrs. Carver bringing him home."

"Matty I am going to beat your ass when I get home. You know better than that."

"Momma I already had one whopping today."

"Your daddy beat you?"

"Yes ma'am."

"Did he give you a good whoopin'?" she asked.

"Yes ma'am," was Matty's response a second time.

"Good because if he didn't you know you would get one when I got home." That was the gospel truth if Matty ever heard it.

"Let me speak to your daddy." That was the end of my days of writing notes and chasing girls.

When Matty went back to school after his three-day suspension everyone knew what he had done. It was beyond embarrassing for Matty and his parents who had to escort him back to school his first day. But Matty handled it like a trooper. He kept his mouth closed and never spoke of the incident again; and, he kept his head high because he had made that bed, so to speak.

After that Matty was again content to stay in the apartment every day after school.

Knock. Knock.

Matty normally would not answer door because he was under strict instructions, and his mother had the neighbors spying on him to make sure he did not go outside until she got home.

"You can't come in here JPH because my momma ain't home," Matty closed the door.

But that didn't stop JPH.

As soon as Matty's mother was home he was back on their door step.

"Mrs. Pottishear can Matty come out and play?"

"That's up to Matty."

Matty looked at him for a moment then he closed the door.

But that only made JPH more determined. He kept coming back until Matty finally gave in to his request.

"Come go with me Matty."

"Where?"

"To see Boston."

Matty knew of him but he didn't know him, know him.

Matty reluctantly agreed to JPH's request. Although they all lived in the same apartment complex, Matty had never been in that part of the apartments before that day, even during his bike riding days. Actually, after that day, Matty never went back again either.

Anyway, they took that short walk down the street.

"JPH this doesn't feel right."

Matty knew he should have turned around, but he didn't. Reluctantly Matty kept on walking. When they finally got to the apartment Matty started grabbing his chest.

"You okay man?" Boston asked.

Matty didn't respond to Boston's question but that strange feeling in his chest increased exponentially. Matty was now sweating.

"Run Matty, Run," his brain told him. But Matty was glued to the spot where he was standing. Matty should have left right then and there, but he didn't have the courage to leave.

Then he looked around the room. "They planned this. I just know it," Matty said to himself.

On top of that, there was nobody at home, and they wanted to play in Boston's room - - his bedroom. All of these things were clear violations of Matty's mother's play policy. But still he let JPH bully him into staying.

Without notice they were all three in the dark bedroom closet with their pants and underwear down to their ankles. Matty was sandwiched in between JPH and Boston.

JPH was in front of Matty with his back against Matty's front and Boston was behind Matty.

Matty kept telling himself, "Don't remember this. Don't remember this."

Matty tried to forget everything so that he could never recall it. He tried to bury the rest of it too, but it wouldn't go away, which is exactly why Matty has never told a single living soul all of the details of that day.

And worse, the only thing that saved Matty from that closet was the older brother of Boston, the stranger Matty had just met for the first time that day.

The door burst opened. The sun shined into that closet upon Matty's shame.

"What the hell are y'all doing?"

They were all rushing to pull up their underwear and pants. Matty was trying to get out of the apartment.

"It was all his idea," JPH said pointing to Matty.

Boston said, "Yea."

As Matty made his way out of the apartment and started walking home alone, he kept thinking, "If it was my idea, why would they agree to it if it was so bad?"

That just didn't make any sense to Matty.

"Momma always said, 'What's done in the dark will always come to light.'" But Matty didn't have the courage enough to be the one to bring it out.

Later on the older fat brother tried to corner Matty on the street and have his way with Matty also. But by then Matty had gotten the courage to fight back, so that didn't go anywhere. Matty didn't think the fat brother was exactly what his mother was taking about but he did save Matty for that moment.

After that day Matty spent even less time with JPH, to the point where Matty was even ignoring JPH at school, and he had convinced his parents to take him to school and pick him up every day. Everyone kept asking what was going on between Matty and JPH but Matty just couldn't bring himself to say those awful words. So he lived in silence - - loud, blaring silence.

Matty went to school and he came home. Although he hated being in that apartment by himself, he did it. Matty's dad had just enough time to drop him off at home and get to work. So then Matty was the first one home every day.

So Matty used to come home every day and look at *Dark Shadows. Barnabas Collins* scared him but not as much as JPH did. So he chose the lesser of two evils.

After that life just sort of rolled along for Matty. The sun rose and the sun set. That went on for about another two or three years.

Matty just stayed in the bedroom he shared with his brothers every day after school and every weekend they were not in the country.

So one day he was staring out the window when he heard his daddy getting ready to leave for work. Matty instinctively jumped up and ran to catch him.

Matty caught him right before he was getting ready to walk out the front door. His dad didn't have a chance to do anything else but catch him because Matty leaped across the room and into his daddy's arms.

His daddy caught him like a wide receiver stretched out for the most amazing catch at the one yard line.

He kept trying to put Matty down but Matty wouldn't let him. He had a grip lock around his father's neck.

"Okay, come on Matty, I have to go to work."

Matty lifted his head from around his daddy's neck to look him square in the face. He gave Matty one of his rare, rare smiles. Not a word was said between them. Matty just hugged his neck even harder.

"I've really got to go son."

"I love you daddy."

"I love you too."

Then his daddy said, "Goodbye."

That word lingered in Matty's spirit the remainder of that day. It was a Friday night, so their mother let them stay up a little late so that the boys, especially Matty, could see his daddy when he came home. It was just about time for him to come home.

*The Late Show with Johnny Carson* was on when the telephone rang. Matty sat there and listened to the whole conversation, at least his mother's side of it anyway.

"Hello."

"What?"

"Okay."

Then their mother hung up the telephone and called her husband's favorite brother, Tommy Lee, who also lived in the same neighborhood.

Without hesitation, Uncle Tommy came immediately and took their mother away. They were gone all night long. Their momma came home just before sunrise.

"Momma, when is daddy coming home?"

Matty was so bold and independent.

Sadie smiled at her youngest son.

"Matty honey I'm not sure. Your daddy had a blood clot in his leg at work, so they rushed him to the hospital to do emergency surgery."

"That's where you been all night?" Matty asked.

"Yea honey."

"So what does that mean?" Jacob asked.

"I don't know. I am going to get a little bit of rest and then go back over with your uncle. Then maybe we will know something."

One day turned into two, turned into three, turned into a week, then two weeks. And every day Matty asked his mother when was their daddy coming home.

Then finally Sadie got the news that he was coming home on the 4th of July.

When she told the boys they were excited and yelling all throughout that little apartment. Sadie had even agreed to throw the first party ever for Henry's homecoming.

So the next morning their mother and Uncle Tommy went to the hospital early that morning to pick up their daddy. They ended up staying all day. So there was no party and no momma and daddy. When she did finally get home, she said that daddy was having a slight problem and that he couldn't come home today, maybe tomorrow or the next day.

The day after that, there was no one at home but Matty and his mother. Jacob had spent the night with Aunt Martha Sue and her family. Henry Jr. and Claude were up and out of the house right after breakfast.

Sadie was in the living room ironing and Matty was on the living room floor pretending to play but he was really watching his mother.

The phone rang.

Matty and Sadie both jumped.

It was the hospital calling, Matty could tell by his mother's body language. Matty's suspicions were confirmed when his mother quickly hung up the telephone and called their Uncle Tommy. He came right up and they left for the hospital. Matty had to go down to JPH's house to stay until she came home.

Matty tried to play but he was not interested even though JPH had every kind of toy imaginable. Matty didn't mind being there so much that day because his parents and brother were there so he knew he would be safe, miserably safe.

He was wrong.

Matty spent the entire time fighting JPH off of him.

They were in JPH's bedroom playing with the door open, which his bedroom was like a toy chest, literally. But Matty's heart was just not into it. Hell, he didn't have a chance to get comfortable for fighting off JPH.

The moment he got calm enough to pretend to be interested in playing, a car door closed outside.

Matty bolted out of that apartment and headed home so fast it was not even funny. He ran down the stairs from JPH's apartment and up the stairs to their apartment within seconds of each other. He rushed to open the door and there was Sadie sitting in his father's chair. She turned and looked at Matty.

Matty knew.

He fell to his knees in front of her and they started crying together. Matty cried into his mother's chest for an hour or so while she was crying in the top of his head. They were completely lost in each other.

"Momma what are we going to do?"

"I don't know Matty."

"My heart hurts."

"So does mine."

"Why is God so mad at us?"

"What do you mean Matty?"

"He took RuthAnn, grandma, and now daddy. Why is he so mad at us?"

"God's not mad at you Matty."

"Then what's going on?"

"I know I should have a good answer but I don't Matty. All I can tell you is that God works in mysterious ways."

"Momma this wouldn't hurt so bad except that the hospital wouldn't let me see him because they said I was too young. I'm not too young."

"I know Matty. I know."

"All of my brothers got a chance to see him a couple of times before he died. It just feels like that hug I gave him was not enough and he just slipped through my fingers."

They started crying some more.

"The last thing daddy said to me was goodbye. That is the saddest word in the world to me."

They sat there crying alone together for another hour or so. It was like time stood still but it just seemed a little too late.

They cried until they were all cried out. Then somehow they pulled it together and Sadie started calling the family.

Sadie became Matty's best friend that day and he committed himself to her well being for the rest of his natural life. Their father was the last remaining piece of support system for Matty and now he was gone too.

Within hours, that small apartment was overrun with people.

It was July 5, 1972, and they were having a party but it wasn't the homecoming party they had planned. And the guest of honor could not even attend.

Matty knew his daddy was popular, but he didn't know he was that popular and loved by this family. But what was clear to Matty was that this handsome playboy was the most popular child of the whole clan of thirteen, even if he wasn't the most responsible of them all.

"Hey Matty."

Matty stood there looking at those strangers.

"Come here."

Matty didn't move.

"I'm your sister Caroline and this is your brother Curtis."

Matty wasn't buying it.

"RuthAnn is dead," Matty said.

"That's right. I was born after RuthAnn."

Matty refused to shake their hands.

That was only the beginning. That went on for three or four more days because Sadie wanted to wait to bury Henry. His family was so spread out that she wanted to wait until they all could get in town before she laid him to rest. But there was no rest for Matty.

Matty tossed and turned in the bed, no matter which one it was. He vacillated between his mother's bed and sleeping with Jacob. Suddenly their two bedroom apartment that had been the only home the six of them had ever known for so long was now crowded.

Matty loved seeing his family but not under those circumstances. He tried to smile and be polite but Matty didn't know how to fake it.

All people kept saying was, "I understand how you feel," or "He's in a better place," or "Your daddy wouldn't want you to be sad."

"How do you know how I feel hell I don't even know how I feel?" Matty said back.

Matty was standing alone in the kitchen, when he heard one of his daddy's snooty sisters say, "Henry loved Sadie, women, cars, and drinking, in that order."

Matty was furious at the suggestion and he wanted to respond, but his mother would never forgive him.

Instead Matty snapped on one of his cousins.

"Momma said your daddy's in a better place."

"How could he be in a better place than being here with his family you dumbass?" Matty responded.

"Momma, Matty called me a dumbass," his cousin said as he ran off crying.

Matty knew that the Bible said to be absent from the body was to be present with the Lord. But he didn't know that meant his daddy had to leave them behind. He especially didn't know what that meant that day.

Somewhere in Matty's mind he got the idea stuck in his head that his daddy walked out on them that day and he never looked back. He told his mother that very same thing.

"Matty what would make you think your daddy would walk out on us?"

"He didn't even insist that they let me see him while he was in the hospital. So if he didn't want me to be sad, he should have never walked out on me - - on us!"

Matty stormed off to his bed and his bunny rabbit.

Then the time for the wake came. All of Henry's people, some who Matty never knew, had finally arrived.

It was  more of them this time then there were when his grandma died.

Matty just kept standing at the front door waiting for a hearse to pull up with his daddy's casket. But it never came.

Instead a couple of big black limousines did pull up in the parking lot. Matty looked at his mother.

She said, "Come on Matty it's time to go."

I'm sure Matty thought, "Where the heck are we going?"

The limousines slowly strolled through downtown Charlotte, a city that Matty had never seen before and no reason to see it.

Matty was holding on to Sadie as closely and as tightly as he possibly could. The driver drove around for a little while making slow turns in and out of traffic until they finally came to a stop in front of this huge white antebellum house. There were crowds of people standing around everywhere, on the porch, on the grounds, on the sidewalk. It looked like they were either at a concert, a garden party, or waiting for some superstar to show up. But the reality was they weren't.

They were all standing around with their long faces full of pity waiting for Henry Pottishear's family to arrive. That reminded Matty of his grandmother's funeral. Then the finality of it all hit Matty – again and in less than three years they were both gone. Matty stood there frozen on the steps.

His refusal to move forward was an unexpected jolt that caused Sadie to jerk backward.

"Come on Matty."

Matty shook his head no.

As they reached the top of the stairs, these huge giant men stepped in beside Sadie. So Matty was left there standing alone. Then the same thing happened to each of his older brothers. These men were assigned to each one of them to escort them into the house, in order of their birth.

When Matty's turn came it wasn't that simple.

Matty was looking down at the porch trying to decide what to do. As the porch light dimmed from some sort of shadow, Matty looked up to see these big black men staring down on him like he was there dinner.

Matty looked. He was stunned. Then without notice Matty took off running into the house. And he didn't stop until he was standing right up there next to his father's casket.

Matty was looking out at the gathering and they were all staring at him. Matty hadn't even realized that he was standing next to his father's casket.

Then he turned around and saw where he was standing. But instead of being scared, Matty just sort of matter-of-factly walked down to the other end and stood on his tiptoes to peer inside.

There he was. "Daddy," Matty said.

Matty stayed there. Pretty soon his mother had joined him, and then his brothers.

Quietly they all slowly moved to the left front pew of the chapel. Matty's grandfather escorted their mother, which seemed appropriate because they had both lost their spouses, but their mother had the double loss.

When Matty finally got his bearings he looked out over the crowded chapel. The crowd inside was larger than the crowd outside and the sun was starting to go down. Matty sat there and watched as it took more than two hours for everyone to file down those aisles like they were marching down the aisle in a wedding or something. Matty looked at every single face that stepped up to his daddy's casket, like he wanted to catalog every one of them.

When they finally left, Matty spent the entire long walk looking back at his daddy's casket until it was out of sight. But it wasn't that easy to get it out of his mind. If Matty wasn't sleeping before, he definitely couldn't sleep that night. And he definitely didn't want to sleep in the bed with his mother because that meant he had to sleep in his father's spot which was the right side of the bed.

The next day, it was the exact same thing at the church. But this time the limousines were following behind the hearse that carried their father's body. Matty didn't want to go but what choice did he have. This time their grandpa had Matty sit beside him, but that didn't last too long because Matty wanted to sit by his mother, and sit by her he did.

As the limousines made their way out of the complex that Sunday morning, everybody was standing on their front porch. The limousines even passed by Boston's apartment. Matty was looking out the window and saw him standing on the porch. Matty became even sadder, but he didn't know if it was for him or his father. He went to sit back down, not beside his grandfather, but beside his mother.

When they arrived at the church, it was more people there than there was the night before. Everything seemed like it was moving in slow motion. The hearse was moving slowly and the limousines were moving even slower. But Matty was strangely happy about that because it gave him a better opportunity to take it all in.

He stood up and leaned over the front seat and perched himself. There he watched the men take this silver stand out of the hearse that looked sort of like an accordion. They brought it to the back of the hearse and pulled it open. It went from short to long. Matty was confused.

Then they opened the hearse. There was his daddy - - shut up in that box. It was a pretty box but it still was a box.

"I've seen that box before," Matty whispered.

He chased the thought down in his mind. Then he realized.

"Grandma."

Matty tried to shake it off but he couldn't.

"So grandma and daddy are on the other side and we are over here. Why can't we all be together on the same side?"

"Matty what you talkin' about?" Henry Jr. said.

Matty ignored him. Like he always did.

The men pulled his daddy's casket from the hearse. It was really long. But somehow those men made the casket fit on top of that silver accordion stand.

Then they carefully rolled the casket over the gravel yard to the edge of the brick steps. There, six men were standing – waiting, but for what. Then, almost in military-like precision, they picked up the casket and started up the stairs. The casket tilted upward but the guys didn't seem to mind it.

They carefully carried the casket to the top landing and sat it back down on the silver accordion stand.

After that the doors opened on the limousine. Everybody filed out. Matty was still in his spot. Then he spotted the green tent. Matty started crying. His grandfather grabbed him.

They started walking over to the stairs, then up the stairs. Matty didn't know they were supposed to be getting into position. But whatever they were supposed to be doing, it started.

The choir started to sing, the congregation stood up, the casket started rolling, and they started that long walk - - again.

Matty remembered how it felt when they had to do this about three years ago. But somehow, these faces looked more pitiful now than then.

As they got in their customary seat, a seat that Matty would gladly give up, then everyone took a seat. The choir sang some more, people spoke, and the preacher preached. Matty jumped up. He was ready to go. But it wasn't time.

He stood there.

Then the men opened up his daddy's casket. Every action and every moment they made was exact. Matty kept on standing and watching. Then the crowd started to file in one last time. All those people who could not fit inside the church came in first. They were in no hurry. Matty kept standing. The line never seemed to end. Then the people inside the church started to move. First it was the ones on the right, then on the left. Finally everyone was done.

Then those big men came over and got Henry Jr., then Claude, then Jacob. Then they came to get Matty. But this time, he refused to go up to that casket.

Those giants kept asking him, "Don't you want to see your father one more time?"

Matty kept shaking his head no while looking down at the floor.

"That man in that casket is not my father."

Matty put his head down. The church cry became louder after Matty's words.

"My father was a tall, lively, fun-loving man." Matty said to the floor.

Then it was their mother's turn. She was wearing this black lace thing over her face. She lifted it for the first time that day, leaned over into the casket, and kissed Henry one last time.

Then she shouted in an agonizing cry "What am I supposed to do now? Who's going to help me raise these boys?"

Their mother was sobbing to the point where she couldn't catch her breath like Matty had never seen anyone cry before and never wanted to again. His mother was crying from the depths of her soul. Matty knew this because his soul was hurting too. It was in this pain that Matty truly realized that his mother loved his father, even with all his faults. Somewhere Matty and his mother's tears were meeting to bind them more tightly to each other than ever before.

Matty had had enough of the whole thing.

But no sooner had they closed that casket and started to roll it out down the aisle, did Matty want to get up and make them stop so that he could see him once again.

But he didn't.

He did, however, run up to the casket and walked his daddy down the aisle with his little hand on the casket. They rolled his daddy's casket to the stairs. They were all lined up behind him and the rest of the church was behind them. There was such heaviness over that church that you could see it, despite the fact that the sun was shining beautifully outside.

Strange, the day their daddy died it rained cats and dogs all day, all night, and half way into the next day. It was like God was washing away their sorrow. So why would he bring that sorrow back even heavier a few days later.

Matty remembered somebody saying, 'The rain that comes on the day a person dies is God shedding tears over a good one fallen.'

When they came outside and down those long steep stairs at the same church their beautiful picture perfect family had always attended, the hearse was gone.

It took six men to carry their father's coffin down those stairs, but the hearse was gone.

"Where's the hearse?" Matty whispered.

Suddenly Matty noticed all of these women in front of his daddy's casket carrying a big flower in each of their hands. The women walked over to that field to the right of the church. There was this big hole dug right beside where their grandmother was buried.

Matty was in a total fog. All he heard was "Ashes to ashes and dust to dust."

Then his daddy's casket started to go down in that hole. Matty wanted to jump in with him but his grandpa was holding him tightly by the hand. This time though, Sadie would not leave until they started to cover his casket with dirt.

"Daddy, what happened to your promise?" Matty said as they left the gravesite.

The ride back to their little apartment was heated. The sun was shining so bright that it was scorching hot. Matty knew they had to rebuild their lives, but he was just a kid, so he didn't know how. What he did know is that God had taken another little piece of his heart.

## Chapter 6

A few months past and life went on, but Matty couldn't call it normal because there was no longer a normal for them, for him.

Out of the clear blue their mother came to them one day, sat them all down and said, "The time has come for us to move."

Matty's brothers were all excited but Matty's enthusiasm was muted to say the least. Matty knew the answer was in the details so he wanted to hear the rest of the offer before he said anything. Their mother gave them two options.

"We can move to a nice neighborhood in the city or we can build a house in the country down near your granddaddy."

As usual Matty and his brothers were on the opposite of the spectrum. His brothers all wanted to stay in the city. Matty didn't say anything. Then his mother turned to him and said, "So Matty what do you want to do honey?"

Matty looked at her, then his brothers and said, "I want to build a house in the country."

His brothers all scrawled at the idea, which Matty didn't understand because before he came along they all had horses to ride, go carts, and all that stuff. Matty never had any of that because one of those dufuses got kicked in the head by the horse and almost died. So their mother and grandmother made their grandpa get rid of the horses over his and their daddy's objections. The city won and Matty lost.

Not long before the time came for them to move, JPH and his mom were visiting with Matty's mother. Matty was just there. He clearly didn't have much to say to JPH.

It was a Friday night, and their mother was going out for the first time since their father died. All of their daddy's people were encouraging their mom to get out and do something. So she decided to get out and hang out with adults for a little bit.

Matty wasn't sure why his mother was going. She didn't drink, she didn't smoke. So Matty just wasn't sure what his mother was going to do. Someone must have really been praying because it took heaven and earth to move their mother to do anything after their dad died but this one time she agreed.

This was okay with the brothers because there was a big horror fest going to be on television that night and they were going to stay home to watch it all. But that included babysitting Matty.

Matty hated horror movies because real life was horrible enough, but he was willing to tolerate them this one time.

Anyway, during JPH's visit that day, he begged his mother, right there in front of Matty, to beg his mother to let him spend the night with Matty. Matty could not believe what he was seeing, but it was really happening. It was too true to make up.

As JPH continued with his urgings to his mother Matty just stood there silent as a street lamp and let him and his momma make all of these plans without uttering so much as a word. Sadie kept saying no.

"Pat no. The boys will be babysitting Matty and that is going to be enough."

But JPH's mother was begging because her son was begging. Right before their very eyes.

Finally their mother agreed to their ridiculous pleading probably because she figured they were moving and wouldn't be seeing each other again. Sadie had no other reason to refuse their requests because Matty had never told her about everything that had gone on before. It was an incredulous spectacle that Matty was witnessing. He wanted to scream but instead he stood there not saying a word.

Nightfall came. Sadie left. And Matty's older brothers were so engrossed in the horror movies that they didn't even notice that JPH's sneaky ass had dragged Matty off to their mother's bedroom and pushed the bedroom door closed.

And to silence Matty, "If you tell anybody about this I tell your brothers you made me do it."

Matty thought to himself, "That shit shouldn't work a second time."

But Matty's own thoughts were drowned out by the threats coming out of JPH's mouth. Threats that included lies about shit he had never done, including the closet incident where Matty was set up to be the crème in the middle of their Oreo.

To add insult to injury, they were in Matty's parents' bed. And Matty was in his father's spot.

This time, JPH was more aggressive than ever.

In the midst of all of Matty's protest, JPH pulled Matty's underwear down and then his own.

Matty protested.

"Shut up!"

Then he did something to Matty that made his little wee-wee get big. He put his mouth on Matty like a lollipop.

After Matty's wee-wee was big then JPH turned over and put Matty's wee-wee inside of him several times.

"JPH this is not right."

"I told you to shut up before your brothers get up and come in here."

Matty wanted to scream but his voice was muted like someone had pushed a button and turned it off.

It didn't help that Matty's body was betraying his mind the more JPH did to him.

"I'm tired JPH. I'm ready to go to sleep."

JPH was relentless. He wouldn't let it go. He kept putting his mouth on Matty until Matty just fell asleep.

The next morning Matty woke up excited about moving and didn't care where it was as long as it was away from JPH. But he was also angry that his brothers paid him or his friends absolutely no attention to what was going on.

A few more weeks passed without notice for Matty.

Then one Thursday night, late that night, their mother snuck into their room and grabbed Matty without notice.

She took him out of his warm bed where he was sleeping against the wall behind his brother Jacob. Matty and Mr. Jangles. Then she rushed out of the house with Matty in her arms.

Sadie stole that boy that night and whisked his off to this unfamiliar place, in his pajamas – him and Mr. Jangles, Matty's torn up bunny rabbit. If Matty didn't know any better, he would have sworn his own mother was kidnapping him. But he was too sleepy to care because it was the best night's rest he had had in months, if not years, three years to be exact.

The last thing Matty remembered his momma saying was, "You remember how to get back here tomorrow?"

Although Matty was still half asleep, he remembered saying, "Yes ma'am."

The decision had been made. The house was purchased, and there was nothing else to be done but go along with the plan, albeit begrudgingly.

The first day Matty arrived in the Park was an overcast Friday afternoon. The only thing that was on his mind the entire day was that bus ride home – to his new home. He couldn't concentrate on anything else that entire day, and the whole day just seemed to fly by, which just made matters worse.

The bell rang and it was time to get on the buses to go home. Instinctively, Matty headed to his normal bus. But his bus driver stopped him and told him that he was riding on a new bus.

Matty honestly had forgotten just that fast. He walked over to the new bus with his head down the whole time.

That little boy was so lonely that he sat on the bus paralyzed hoping something would happen so that he would not have to go through with it. But he couldn't go back. There was nothing to go back to; and, going forward was even more scary than that.

No matter. His prayers went unanswered anyway.

The wheels on the bus just kept churning forward and forward, sloshing through rain and mud.

"Where was God when I needed him?" Matty muttered to himself with his face plastered against the cold window.

In the midst of his prayer, the driver pulled up to the stop and shouted Matty's name.

"Matty," she yelled out over the noise of the crowded bus.

Surely he wasn't the only Matty on the bus, but no one else moved.

It took everything within Matty to muster up enough courage to stand up. Then he had to find even more courage to walk down that long black aisle. And even more to step off that bus.

When he stepped outside he took a long deep breath.

Then he stood on that corner looking around at his surroundings.

Then the rain started, heavier.

Nothing looked familiar. But then again why would it.

After a few more minutes of wishing things were different, he accepted the reality of the situation. He went ahead and bundled up his jacket and then he took his first step, then a second step, and a few more.

But the fact never escaped Matty that he was alone, truly alone.

He was more alone than when he lost his grandmother or his daddy.

Matty was really alone. There was no one for him to lean on, snuggle up to, or hold their hand. There was no honey biscuit or anyone to tell him that everything was going to be alright. It was all on Matty now.

But he knew that once he took that first step there would be no turning back. It was an all or nothing deal.

If he stopped for one moment at any time during that montage of events he would have never left that corner.

But when Matty stepped off that bus and started the long walk, he might as well have been walking in the woods, in the dark woods, because the loneliness this time was a dark place. And being alone was as scary as being in the woods in the dark. Every sound, every crick, every snap of a twig held hidden danger.

All of the houses looked like they had come alive, laughing at him, and were waiting for just the right moment to grab him, like he was in a haunted forest.

"When did I go from real life to the enchanted forest?" Matty was used to having conversations with himself by now.

He put his head down and kept on walking, trying to pretend not to notice his strange surroundings. But how could he not notice. He had to pay attention in order to know where he was going.

"Lions, and tigers, and bears." The thought kept running through Matty's overworked mind over and over again. And Matty was so busy thinking that he was walking all erratic. On top of that he didn't want to step on a single crack in the sidewalk.

After a while Matty was able to stop looking at his surroundings and instead turned his attention inward, as he struggled to hear his mother's voice giving him directions.

But he couldn't hear her voice.

He looked to his left, then his right.

Suddenly, his feet started moving as if they knew which way to go, without needing any help from his brain.

The more he walked, the more he started to hear mother's instructions a little louder. These were the instructions that she had given him last night when she stole him out of bed.

But this was a different walk from the walk that day from the nursery after he did the number two in his pants.

After Matty returned from his mental escapade back in time, which was only about four or five years ago, he noticed there was this huge hill in front of him. He stopped for a moment and looked back to see how far he had come.

His mind had wandered so far away from the present that he did not realize that he had actually walked around this huge curve that prevented him from seeing the corner where his trip began. And he didn't have any idea how much further he had to go.

Then he turned back around and looked at that big hill in front of him. He had barely made it as far as he had come, and he had doubts that his short fat legs could carry him any further. Matty was already tired, and he did not want to climb that hill. But what choice did he have? His mother didn't leave him any options. His father hadn't left them any options.

Matty's mind was overrun with thoughts. He wanted to panic, but that wouldn't do any good. Besides, Matty learned how not to panic on that horrible day in his mother's bedroom.

So he just stood there for a moment, thoughts running through his head, trying to remember that hill. His mind drew a blank.

With no other options left, Matty kept moving forward. It was the most logical thing to do. So Matty started walking faster to pick up speed so that the force would help him get up the hill. And so he did. Matty made it over the top of the hill.

"Home free," Matty said.

But now he was facing a different kind of obstacle. There were cars zooming back and forth, like on a race track.

"I don't remember no race track," Matty said.

There were not that many cars in the projects where they came from. It dawned on Matty that he had been living a very limited existence.

"So, if all that stuff hadn't happened would I ever be forced out into the world like this?" Matty asked, rain falling in his open mouth as he was breathing heavy to take in more air.

Betrayal, hatred, friendship, death, loneliness, and emptiness were all too familiar companions of Matty.

"Now is not the time to think about all that Matty. You have got to focus," he told himself.

But Matty had enough since to know he was in trouble. He was lost, and more importantly, no one knew he was lost. So that meant that no one was looking for him.

"This is all daddy's fault," Matty said.

"How can I forgive him for what he has done to us?"

Then it hit Matty like a baseball bat.

"My mother really trust and believes in me!" Matty was excited at the revelation.

But maybe she had to believe in him. Their father did not exactly leave them any options.

The only thing that was completely clear to Matty was that last night was the last night in his warm bed surrounded by the only world he had ever known. A world that no one ever knew could change literally, in the twinkling of eye.

One minute he was hugging his father's neck and telling him bye as he went to work. The next moment they were loading up all of their belongings.

Matty tried to fight off any thoughts of comfort as he struggled to stay warm in the cold weather that he had not really paid attention to during that arduous journey.

He had just enough energy to take one more right turn, which was a good thing because there was no other way to go.

Then he saw it. He picked up his pace.

Then he broke into a slight jog. Finally, he ran up the long concrete driveway, took the three steps all at once, and pounced on the doorbell quicker than a Baptist minister's wife at a pie eating contest at the county fair.

Matty had already started unfastening his jacket, when he looked up and saw this strange old man staring down at him.

Immediately, Matty burst into tears. And he wasn't just crying. He was screaming at the top of his lungs because of all the pain he felt inside but could not express.

Matty was crying so hard that snoots were coming out of his nose running down into his mouth. He was screaming so loud that he didn't even notice that it had started to rain again. This wet snooty mixture was building up in his mouth, but he was too busy crying to care.

This old man just stood there patiently looking at him, like he was crazy.

'Why did this little fat kid pick my front porch to come up and start crying on?' Is what the stranger probably was thinking.

But to Matty's surprise he did not move.

He just stood there and let Matty completely cry until he was done, which incidentally didn't take very long because he was already out of breath. Fat kids don't cry very long. It takes too much energy.

What a way to start a Christmas vacation?

If Matty was lost before, he was completely lost now.

Everything he thought he had remembered, he clearly had not.

Finally, Matty caught his breath long enough to stop crying, and to ask this old man, "Do you know where my momma is?"

This heavy voice replied, "No son, I don't know your people."

Matty started crying all over again. He didn't even give that man a chance to say anything else.

He turned around and took a slow walk back down the brick steps, the same steps he was so happy to jump up a few moments ago. Then he walked back down that long concrete driveway.

When he reached the end of the driveway, he looked back hoping he was wrong. Nothing had changed.

This was far beyond Matty's worst dream.

There he was a lost 9-year-old kid in a strange place, alone and in the cold rain.

The hill was gone, the curve was gone, the bus was gone – Matty had nowhere else to turn. He was still crying.

He just stood there looking up and down the street not knowing what to do.

Then, he slowly started walking to the house next door to ring that doorbell only because he did not know what else to do.

He was so upset and whimpering with each step that it took him 20 minutes to walk roughly twelve yards.

When he did take that final step onto the porch, he dreaded the thought of ringing the doorbell. He got a sinking feeling in his stomach.

Could it be any worse than what he had just experienced?

While his mind was rushing around in his head like a race car on a fast track, his arm reached out and rang the doorbell.

Then he stepped back to wait and to see who would answer.

It was worse!

No one answered.

As he turned to walk away, he heard the door open and then he saw a silhouette. It took a moment for his mind to register that it was his momma standing before his very eyes.

Matty almost broke the screen door down trying to get to her.

He hugged her so tightly that she could not budge one inch. And his ugly snooty cry started all over again on her beautiful white apron. It reminded him of grandma. He never wanted to move from that spot.

As ugly as he must have looked, it was the most beautiful place in the world to Matty.

He was crying so hard that he was heaving and could not catch his breath. He had never appreciated his mother as much as he did at that moment, but then again, he never had a chance to because he spent all his time with his father and grandmother.

Matty's tears were not just about being lost that day. They were about everything that he had lost - - period. It flashed through Matty's mind that his father would not be around to teach him about a good handshake, how to stand tall, and how to hang out with the fellas – in short, his daddy was not going to be there to teach him how to be a man.

Matty's tears turned to an all out water facet.

Sadie was standing there frantic.

"Matty, what's wrong?"

She said it over and over again.

She thought something had happened to her son, but he couldn't tell her because he was too busy crying.

"Here boy."

His granddaddy came in and put a bag over his mouth.

"Breath Matty," his granddaddy said.

It took a good fifteen minutes before Matty stopped crying.

Finally he was able to tell his mother the entire story about the bus stop, the hill, the rain, the old man next door, and being lost. But he refused to take his face out of the safety of his mother's dress.

After Sadie heard the whole story she started laughing.

Matty was so relieved that he started laughing too. Matty then knew the world was alright – different, but alright.

"I knew you could do it honey," She said to him.

In the background, Matty heard his grandpa say, in his deep raspy voice, "Don't baby that boy."

That was their grandpa's way of reminding his daughter that she had denied Matty the opportunity to become a man. Riding horses was a rite of passage to manhood per their grandpa. He had not quite gotten over the fact that Sadie would not let him teach Matty how to ride a horse after one of the older boys was kicked in the head. They say he almost died, but hell Matty wasn't even born yet.

Matty agreed with his grandpa. They messed up his life before he was ever born.

As they settled into their new house, Matty did what he was told to do, for the most part, although he openly hated that middle class, predominantly black neighborhood regardless of the idea of moving on up, economically anyway.

It took Matty a good two or three years before he started to get to know anybody in the neighborhood. In the meantime, most of his entertainment consisted of his three older brothers serenading him with their musical talents. His brothers did have excellent voices like their dad, and they loved showing them off as a trio.

"Too bad these dumb asses don't know how to make money off of their talents," Matty used to always tell his brothers.

One reason it took so long is that their mother refused to put Matty in a different school until the school board forced her to, even though all of his brothers changed schools right after Christmas vacation the year they moved.

So for the first couple of years Matty had to make that same walk every morning and every afternoon. He had to retrace those same painful steps he made when he first arrived in the neighborhood every day. He walked that same path like a mailman - - in the sun, in the rain, in the dark, and in the cold.

And when the school board finally forced his mother to change him to the new school, things only got worse.

Matty went to a school he hated and he came back to a house he hated even more. No one even noticed him except for the few times he was being bullied, or he was trying to fit in by imitating some other goofy kid. That too was a miserable experiment. Matty was a bona fide misfit.

Then one day Matty made a fascinating discovery.

Matty looked in the dictionary and discovered the word outcast.

Matty knew he wasn't liked and that he didn't like very much in return. But then he discovered that he was an outcast, he became an even worse reclose.

In Matty's mind, he didn't have a place where he belonged, either at home or at school. Things were changing and Matty didn't know what to do about it. Or maybe the way things were was the way things had always been which meant that things were the same as they had always been, but Matty just refused to see it until now.

After about the third year in the Park without a single friend, Matty realized that no matter how much life he had inside of him, it was meaningless if he hid himself away from the world.

"Hey y'all it's snowing."

They were on winter vacation and it was the first time Matty had ever seen snow, let alone snow in their new back yard.

"It's beautiful," Matty said. "Let's go outside and play football."

"Boy, I don't want to play no football with you." That was the same answer Matty heard from each of his three brothers, Henry Jr., Claude, and Jacob.

"You know that boy ain't gonna go away," Henry Jr. told Claude.

Sure enough, fifteen minutes later, Matty was back in their room pleading with snow covered boots and shoes. And he was laughing.

"Come on, let's go play football."

"If we go play will you leave us alone?" Jacob asked

Then the three stooges looked at each other and agreed to…

"Humph."

"Oh."

"Ouch."

It didn't matter how many times his brothers knocked him down in the snow, Matty got back up and started playing again.

"Waaaaaaaa." Matty ran in the house crying.

"Matty what's wrong with you?"

"They keep hitting me hard and pushing me in the snow."

"They who?"

"Henry Jr., Claude, and Jacob."

"Then go in the room and take your clothes off and watch tv."

Matty was stubborn.

He bundled himself back up and went back outside. It was the first time that he had ever enjoyed his brothers since he was born, outside of the singing. So it took him twelve years to get to this point, he was not going to give it up that easily.

Matty would come back in the house three more times that day before he finally relented to their punishment.

Although it didn't happen instantly, Matty started to get to know people in the neighborhood slowly but surely.

But just as he was starting to come out of his shell and forget the past, guess who showed up, JPH.

Without any notice or forewarning, JPH, his parents, and his younger brother all showed up on their doorstep. Matty was stunned. He honestly thought he would never see them again. It was JPH's mother that gave Matty the nickname butterball.

Matty resented that and her too although he never said anything.

"I hate that name. That just pisses me off that she thinks she can call me whatever she wants to when her own son is big as a pig," Matty murmured to himself as he stormed down the hall into his bedroom.

But that didn't matter. They were still there sitting in Matty's family's new living room laughing and chatting like nothing had happened.

"I guess they would act as if nothing was going on because I am sure that son of theirs would have never let on to his parents who he really was underneath all those fake smiles and shit." Matty was having another one of those private conversations again.

"If they only knew that their son was a bonafide pervert and I am his main prey."

"Matty what are you doing in your room? You have company. Come down here and go outside and play with JPH."

Against his better judgment, Matty honored his mother's request and came down so he could go outside and play outside with JPH.

"Okay I'll do this because they will be gone in a little while, and I hope they never come back."

The idea of their leaving freed Matty and suddenly he started having a pretty good time.

As JPH's mother called him and his brother to leave, Matty stated smiling even more.

"Hey mom can we spend the night?"

Matty was horrified. And there was no hiding it.

"Oh my. Who's running things in that family?" Matty heard his mother say.

"Maybe next time," Sadie continued.

Matty looked up to heaven and said, "Thank You Lord."

He was so relieved they were gone that he went back outside and enjoyed playing in the backyard the rest of that day all by himself. It was a pervert free zone.

But the next time came quicker than Matty could have imagined.

A few short weeks later, there was a knock at the door.

"Momma," Matty screamed.

Sadie came running.

"My dumbass, I honestly thought they would not come back again – ever."

But sure enough, they were back. And this time they brought a suitcase. After they stayed for what seemed like forever, Matty was ready to scream again, but they finally got up to leave.

As they prepared to leave, JPH's mother said, "Well, Sadie here's JPH's bag. This boy has not given us a moment's peace until we came back over here so he could spend the night."

"What about the whole weekend," JPH shouted out.

Sadie said, "JPH you can only stay tonight."

She didn't offer any further explanations. It was just that simple and she didn't care if his parents liked it or not. Sadie was not one to coddle people.

"Lord, I wish I had your strength momma," Matty said.

Then his younger brother started crying that he wanted to stay too. Matty thought he was being setup for the closet thing again but it was much too late to protest now.

Since it was going to be only one night, Sadie agreed.

Wouldn't you know that JPH's parents had Vincent's things packed in the same suitcase?

When Sadie opened that suitcase Matty could tell by her face that there would be no more overnight visits.

She looked at Matty, "Now all we have to do is get through tonight."

Matty looked back at his momma and said under his breath, "That is much easier said than done."

It started off okay, as sleepovers went, not that Matty had any experience because he had never had any sleepovers before JPH.

JPH didn't know it but since they had moved Matty had quite a few toys of his own to play with this time and he had a room to go along with them. But despite the toys, Matty still didn't have many words for JPH. And if he did, they would not be words that the Bible would approve of it. So Matty considered his best option was to keep his mouth closed.

But in the time it took Matty to decide not to speak, JPH changed, just like a light switch. Within seconds, JPH was forcing himself on Matty and in front of his brother, Vincent.

And he told his brother, "If you tell anybody I am going to kick your ass."

To ensure his brother's silence, JPH made his brother take his clothes off and they jumped on Matty together. Vincent held Matty down, and JPH ripped Matty's underwear off his small body, that is compared to JPH.

Vincent did not look like he was enjoying it any more than Matty was, but JPH was a big guy to be his age. Therefore, it was JPH's way or not at all. Besides that, JPH was the chosen one in his family so if Vincent had gone against him it would have been his doom.

If Matty was a butterball turkey, then JPH had to be a hog. And that boss hog assaulted Matty and his own brother all night long.

The next morning when they got up for breakfast, Matty went straight to his mother and asked her, "When are they going home?" right there in front of them. Finally Matty had gained the courage to speak up.

Sadie gave Matty this strange look like she knew something was wrong.

Vincent was sitting at the kitchen table directly across from Matty with eyes that seemed to say I'm sorry, but in Matty's mind that was too little too late.

JPH was fuming mad but what could he do?

"Pat. I think you need to come on over and get JPH and Vincent right now."

That was the end of Matty's sleepover days and JPH.

Back in his shell Matty went.

"Matty why don't you go outside and play." His mother told him. It was more of a statement than a question.

Matty kept reading his book.

"Matty it's a beautiful day. Go outside and play."

Matty's ears heard not a word his mother said. Matty loved his mother but it was going to take more than mere words for him to go outside.

A couple more years passed. Matty was now about in the 8$^{th}$ grade.

It was a warm Friday night, Spring was ending, and the true summer heat had not yet begun. Matty was sitting on the front porch alone. His mother was in the house resting from her long work week and his brothers were all spread out throughout the neighborhood.

Matty was trying to figure out how he or how they got there.

"Where did we go wrong?" Matty uttered before the blanket of stars that enveloped him. He was empty inside. He had no feelings for anything or anybody. So he sat there some more taking in the nightness of his neighborhood. Then he started to hear some music.

*Jump in the ride.*

*Oouou,*

*It's Friday night.*

*Yea, yea, yea.*

*Living it up, living it up oh yea.*

*Friday night.*

It was like the *Pied Piper* was playing music to specifically attract Matty. And Matty was powerless to stop it. So he started following the music that was being piped throughout the neighborhood. And before he realized what was happening, he was already on his feet and mindlessly headed toward the music.

Matty knew the house and he knew of the family because of his brothers, but he had never met any of the family himself. When his footsteps stopped he was standing on the patio of the designated neighborhood funhouse.

There was a whole group of kids hanging out on the patio dancing, singing, and laughing that Friday night. It was a veritable who's who of the neighborhood. The boom box was playing and everybody was dancing, and Matty just jumped right on in and started dancing. And he was received with open arms.

"'Bout time," someone shouted toward Matty.

The most popular dance back then was the bump. So Matty jumped in dancing, bumping, and laughing just like they did on *Soul Train*, including the clothing, hair, and platform shoes. Underneath the bright lights of the patio, afros were swaying, hands were waving, and bodies were moving. Again, it was just like being on stage.

Then the lights went out.

Matty was having such a good time. It was the first time he truly felt like he belonged in the neighborhood. Actually it was the first time Matty had felt alive in about five or six years. But he was so happy, he just kept dancing and bumping.

Suddenly Matty felt something very stiff behind him. He turned around to look who was bumping, more like grinding on his butt. It was the brother, who lived in the funhouse.

Matty was simply mortified!

"What the?"

The brother, who was much older than Matty, stood there looking directly into Matty's eyes. Matty had seen that look before.

Matty stopped immediately and went home.

On his short walk back home, Matty asked himself, "What is wrong with me that I keep attracting these perverts? I hope and pray that this is not a new JPH in my life."

Matty never put the two together, but about the same time Shaun started making advances toward Matty, Matty started acting up in school. He became a true terror.

"Matty what is wrong with you? I have been to Carmel more times this week than I have ever been to school for all of you kids in my whole life."

Matty was quiet the entire ride home. Sadie had just learned how to drive only weeks before although Henry left her a practically brand new car when he died in 1972. Sadie let the car sit in the driveway at their new house for a good five years.

Although Matty's mouth was motionless, his brain was the absolute opposite. He started smiling as his mind wondered back to happier times.

"There's nothing funny about this situation Matty," Sadie said to her youngest son.

Matty was completely oblivious to his mother's words. He was tuned in on his grandmother's voice.

"I remember once right after your mother and father married and moved away that they had an argument."

Matty was sitting happily by his grandmother's side on the high steps of the back porch. He was eating a honey biscuit and his grandmother was trying to clean him up while he ate. But he didn't care, she was right there beside him.

"Anyway, you and Jacob hadn't been born yet. So it was just your momma, daddy, Henry Jr., and Claude."

Matty was happily chewing and happily staring at his grandmother's grand golden mouth. It glistened in the sun like God, Himself approved.

Present day.

Matty was paying no attention to the fact that his mother was driving considerably slower than all those around them. But that didn't much matter to Matty. He was happy being stuck in the past.

His mind jumped back to his grandmother's voice.

"So your father made your mother really mad and your mother, being the stubborn woman she is, set a trap for your daddy."

"What's trap grandma?"

"In this case, it's setting something up that gets someone in trouble by surprise."

"Momma got daddy in trouble?"

"Well you see Matty, your momma waited until your daddy was fast asleep. Then she gathered up your brothers and their things, along with her things, and loaded everything up in the car."

Matty was almost done with his biscuit but he was in no hurry to leave his grandmother's side. So he took a break in chewing so he could listen better.

"Then your mother knew just enough about driving to back the car out of the driveway and then she drove all the way down here by herself in the middle of the day."

His grandmother was laughing. She had such a wonderful laugh that was both contagious and inviting. Matty started laughing too.

"Matty stop laughing. There is nothing funny about you being suspended from school again."

Again, Matty was absolutely not present in his mother's conversation.

"But when your Uncle Tommy Lee was finally able to bring your daddy down here to get your momma and your brothers, he was furious. And when your daddy gets mad.."

"His face and his ears turn red, and his eyes bug out." Matty finished his grandmother's sentence for her.

"That's right Matty. But he wasn't mad at her for leaving. He was mad at her for driving his car all the way down here in first gear. Your daddy worked on that car every day for three weeks after that; and, he learned not to go bed with your momma being mad."

Matty jumped up on her neck and hugged her tight.

"Love you grandma."

"I love you too Matty."

"Matty!" His mother shouted at him.

Matty was mentally back in the car with his mother. They were almost home.

"Matty now that I have your attention. You are an excellent student, smarter than me and all your brothers. But beyond that you are a terrible child. You are constantly getting into fights. You have been to the principal's office five times since school started two months ago, and this is your second suspension of the year."

But Matty did not know how to tell his mother all that he was up against, the most urgent being the fact that he would ride the bus home and be bullied most of the time by Roy, who bullied almost everyone.

But now that he had been suspended again, he had three days plus the weekend to try and figure it out.

"You do realize what this means don't you?"

They had finally pulled into the driveway and were sitting in the car discussing the situation.

Matty looked at his mother with his eyes wide.

"Punishing you by saying you cannot go outside is not going to do anything because you don't go outside anyway, which I don't understand. So instead, I am taking all of your books and the television for the next week."

"Momma," Matty exclaimed. "What am I going to do?"

"You are going to do your homework. At least the principal did allow you to keep up with that. After you finish your homework, you are going to sit and think of ways to combat your problems, whatever they may be, that are forcing you to act up in school every day."

That house, the new one they had moved into, the one that Matty hated so much, *that beautiful prison* - - had actually become Matty's safety place, his sanctuary, at least for the next three days.

Although the punishment didn't mean anything to Matty, it was not lost on him that he was gaining a stress free weekend, the first in a while. But more importantly Matty was getting a readymade reason to stay in without being interrogated by anyone, especially his mother, because she was the jailer this time.

So while his brothers were on their regular strict weekly schedule, Matty was free to roam, even if there was nowhere to roam. So he laid in the bed, up all night long staring at the ceiling, which was easy to do because he slept in the top bunk of the bedroom he shared with his brother Jacob. That was no easy transition either because Matty had enjoyed the security of Jacob protecting him and Mr. Jangles since he could remember. But Matty had a problem.

"Momma!" Jacob would scream her name in the middle of the night.

The scream would startle their momma as she looked at the clock.

"3 am?" She would say.

"Momma, Matty done peed in the bed again!"

Matty knew what that meant. Within seconds he would be getting his ass whopped - -screaming, jumping, hollerin', and cryin' as he tried to avoid momma and her punishment strap.

"I'm tired of you pissing in my bed," she would yell as she hit me unmercifully with her strap while I was still wearing my pissy pajamas.

Wap. Wap. Wap. Wap. Was the sound of the belt.

"You are going to stop pissing in my beds because I am going to whop your ass every time you do until it stops." Wap. Wap. Wap. Wap. More licks.

Claude and Henry Jr. would be so terrified they wouldn't dare come out of their room.

"Don't be trying to hide behind me," Jacob would say.

"Momma, you whopping me," Jacob would scream.

"Get out of my way," Momma would respond.

After her anger would subside so would the licks. Then she would meticulously strip down our bed.

"Matty take those pissy clothes off and get in the tub."

I would be whimpering the whole time because my feelings and my ass would be so hurt. But momma didn't care about that.

So while I took a hot, steamy bath to wash the stench of piss from my body and sooth the wounds of my spirit, momma would take the time to meticulously layer our bed with a few towels, plastic, new sheets, and covers, so that by the time I was finished taking my bath we would have a fresh new, cozy bed to get into, like I was a VIP.

"But I never knew that being a VIP required such hard work."

Shortly after me and Mr. Jangels were comfortably snuggled under the fresh, new covers, Jacob would join us again, after he too had taken a quick shower to wash my piss from his back.

Matty was laughing as he reminiscenced about his bed-wetting days, which were not so far removed from his present. He had to cover his mouth to keep from waking his brother Jacob who was asleep in the bunk below.

"I don't' know why I hated getting up at night to go to the bathroom. But the one thing I clearly remembered was that every time I got a whoopin' I was mad at my daddy because if he had never left, I would have never had to sleep with Jacob and then I would have never gotten a whoppin'."

As Matty lay there in the dark room starring up at the ceiling, he felt some wetness on the side of his face.

He didn't move a muscle.

"Damn, I miss my daddy."

He laid there wide awake for most of the night thinking about his bed-wetting days, which was easy to do since he pissed in the bed about two or three times a week for the first couple of years after they moved into the new house.

"Hum, I wonder why I never peed in the bed on the weekends?"

But there was one saving grace during all those years - - no one outside of their family knew about Matty's peeing the bed.

And it was really quite simple. Their mother had a rule that "What happens in this house stays in this house."

That rule saved Matty from getting beat up at school and from several years of embarrassment because bad news traveled fast where they lived, even though none of his brothers went to school with him.

"Come to think of it, where are daddy's people?" Matty asked out loud.

Since they had moved they heard neither hide nor hair from the Pottishear clan except for Aunt Dot. She sent mother money several times a year from Florida because they were true friends.

"As for the rest of the clan, every since daddy died it seems that we have been shut out of the Pottishear family. I wonder why? It's like as soon as daddy's casket was closed, so too was the door closed, shutting us out of their family, but this time with no repercussions."

As Matty finally dozed off to sleep, the last thing he remembered saying was, "Damn I have been alone my whole life." Still it was okay because the next day was Friday.

So off to dreamland Matty happily went. There were no threats over there like there were where he regularly resided.

So Friday came and went. Matty fumbled around the house all day, doing much of nothing at all. In fact, it was quite surprising because he didn't even pick up a book that whole day.

As the sun barely started to set on that non-eventful Friday night, Matty had decided to take a seat out on the front porch, when guess who unexpectedly showed up for a visit.

"Jacob. Hey man? Whatcha up to tonight?"

Matty walked out of the hallway into the living room and stopped dead in his tracks.

Jacob stood there looking at his brother who was still standing there in the living room with his mouth wide open.

"Matty, what's wrong with you?"

Shaun locked eyes with Matty, and he had a sinister look on his face like the *Grinch* had in his movie when he was thinking about doing evil to the *Whos*.

"Matty," Jacob yelled his name a second time.

"What Jacob?" Matty still didn't move, except for his lips.

When his feet finally did start to move, Matty felt like he was in a cartoon. It felt like his feet turned around first, then his legs turned around, then his midsection, finally his head. It took a few minutes, but when Matty's entire body had turned around, he walked away as if nothing happened, although he wanted to run, he fought every instinct he had to run so that Shaun didn't know that he was beating Matty.

Now Matty wanted to go read a book, but instead he just crawled behind their bunk-beds and took a nap. By the time he woke up, he heard a lot of commotion going on outside, so he went outside to investigate.

They were all outside playing hide and go seek. Matty immediately joined in the game.

He ran around to the one place he had never been found before. There was this huge tree in the next door neighbor's yard that had the most beautiful flower bed surrounding it. No one dared hide in that flower bed, except for Matty.

No sooner was he settled into his hiding spot was he greeted by an unexpected visitor.

Shaun was on top of Matty with his weight on Matty's chest, his knees holding down Matty's arms, and his hands were covering Matty's mouth.

"If you scream I will knock the shit out of you."

Matty's eyes got big at the threat.

"Now don't you move an inch."

Matty did as he was told.

Shaun unzipped his pants and reached his right hand inside of his underwear and pulled out his black maleness.

"Open your mouth."

Matty refused.

Shaun smacked Matty.

When Matty opened his mouth to scream, Shaun put his maleness in Matty's mouth. Matty bit down.

Shaun smacked Matty harder.

"Do it again and the next one will be a punch in your mouth."

Matty relented.

"Now suck it."

Matty didn't know what Shaun was talking about.

"Suck it like a soda in a stray."

Matty closed his eyes and did as he was told. Then he started to cry.

"Stop crying boy. Ain't nobody hurting you. Anyway, you'd better get used to it because I ain't going nowhere."

"Why you botherin' me?" Matty managed to get out.

"I like you." Shaun said.

" Then why don't you suck my dick?" Matty asked.

"Are you crazy? I'm not sucking your dick."

This time Matty bit down harder until Shaun jumped. This gave Matty the opening to shift his weight and escape.

The remainder of that weekend was a blur. And then Monday came, so it was back to school because the suspension-vacation was over.

Matty stood at the bus stop alone, as he always did, waiting for the school bus. He was the last to get on in the morning and the first to get off in the afternoon. But still it didn't matter, in between coming and going, he was fodder for the older kids. Although they had been in the neighborhood about six years, Matty was still an outsider.

As usual, as he stood there on that dark corner waiting for the bus to arrive. And as usual, his heart started beating faster and faster the longer he stood there waiting for the bus to arrive. By the time bus arrived, Matty was generally ready to have a heart attack.

Actually Matty often prayed that God would strike him down right there at the bus stop, but God never answered Matty's prayer. So off to school he went.

Before he took that first step onto the bus, Matty would take a deep breath to gird up his loins before he stepped onto the bus, because once he was on the bus he was at the complete mercy of Roy and the other older kids that bullied him and a few others every single day. But Roy was the main culprit.

"Where you been Matty?" Roy screamed as soon as he saw Matty step on the bus.

"Yea Matty, where you been?" Another person said. Matty knew who it was but he refused to look his way.

'What's going on Matty? We missed you man."

Matty didn't say a single word to his tormentors. He just walked down the aisle and made his way to the first open seat he could find, which was a task in and of itself.

No sooner had he sat down was he being hit upside his head and pushed around by the older kids. Matty wanted to cry but he wouldn't dare let them see him crying otherwise things would get a thousand times worst.

"I'm in the eighth grade. I'm a big boy and big boys don't cry."

Then something unusual and weird happened, something Matty had never experienced before.

In the midst of the tussling and rough playing, not in Matty's mind, by the normal group of Matty bashers, Matty was groped - - once, then twice, and then a third time.

Matty had his head down and covered because he was trying to protect himself, but in the midst of protecting himself he left his backside open. It never dawned on Matty that another boy wanted to touch is butt. But he was sure that three different hands grabbed him right there on the bus.

Matty sat up in his seat, but he showed no emotions because he didn't want to call any extra attention to anything that had happened. But he was sure it happened. He just wasn't sure who done it.

When the bus pulled into the school parking lot, Matty sat there as the bus emptied out. He just couldn't figure it out.

"Why would someone want to touch my butt?"

"Matty, get off this bus and go to school," his bus driver yelled at him.

Matty knew he needed to go to school but he just didn't understand what was wrong with him. He couldn't focus in class all day long. He kept thinking about Shaun and what happened on the bus. The two incidents and all the hands threw Matty for a loop.

Between every class Matty found himself in the bathroom starring in the mirror.

"What is wrong with me?" Matty asked the mirror. "And even worse, there is no one around to help me figure this out. Grandma and daddy are both gone. I hate this life and I hate you." Matty told the mirror.

This went on for a couple of weeks.

"Matty be quiet."

Matty ignored Mr. Beyers directions.

"Matty I know your parents taught you better than you are acting."

Matty was fuming. He kept on talking.

Mr. Beyers walked down the aisle to Matty's desk.

Before Mr. Beyers could get his words out, Matty did something for the second time in his short education career.

He kicked Mr. Beyers directly on his shin.

Mr. Beyers jacked Matty up by his shirt collar and dragged him to the principal's office. By the time they reached the office Mr. Beyers' knee was as big as a grapefruit and he was limping.

While Matty was sitting there waiting on his punishment from Mr. Smith, he remembered the first time he kicked a teacher.

It was the first grade and Mrs. Turkeyfield was his teacher. She was a really, big, fat woman who scared everybody, even the principal.

"Matty put your hand out." She said to me.

I clinched my fist tighter.

"Matty put your hand out on the desk this very moment!" She shouted.

I refused again.

Then Mrs. Turkeyfield took my hand and forced it open. Then she smacked the inside of my hand with a ruler so hard that I screamed. As a reflex reaction, I kicked her so hard that she was out of school for three weeks.

I got two whoopins that day. I got one from the principal and one from my mother. My bottom was sore for two or three days. But I didn't get suspended.

"Matty, get in here," Mr. Smith yelled, interrupting Matty's trek down memory lane.

"Here we go again," Matty told himself.

Matty prepared to take a seat.

"No one told you to sit down son. You stand there," Mr. Smith barked.

He walked out of the office a few moments.

Matty heard a lot of commotion going on outside. He heard someone say ambulance. His legs became weak.

"Matty, I hope you are satisfied. Mr. Beyers has to be taken to the hospital to have his knee examined."

"Oh shit," Matty didn't mean to let that slip out.

"Bend over."

"Whack. Whack. Whack. Whack. Whack."

Matty refused to cry even though Mr. Smith's paddling stung his buttocks.

Then Mr. Smith called Matty's mother.

"Mr. Smith, I'm sorry. Please don't call my mother."

"Matty I have no choice. I must notify your mother."

When my mother arrived it was clear that she was not in the mood for any tomfoolery.

"Mrs. Pottishear I hate to have to call you but I had no choice."

"Matty tell your mother what happened."

"Matty what is Mr. Smith talking about?"

By this time Matty's mother was patting her foot.

"I'm waiting Matty," his mother said, patting her foot. "We don't have all day Matty."

"I kicked Mr. Beyers on the shin."

"Matty you did what?"

Matty was too scared to answer a second time.

"So tell me this. Why did you kick Mr. Beyers?"

Matty was still too scared to talk.

"Listen Matty. I know you. You may not say much, but I know you have a reason for doing everything you do. So tell me why did you kick Mr. Beyers?"

"Because he said something about daddy and I told him my daddy was dead. He said he didn't know. I called him a liar because it was in my school records. Then he said listen boy and jerked me by my arm."

Matty pulled up his shirt sleeve to show his bruises. Matty just saved himself from a serious ass-cuttin' when they got home and he knew it.

"Go wait outside Matty."

He did exactly what his mother said because she outranked Mr. Smith.

Once the door was closed behind her, Mrs. Pottishear turned her attention to Mr. Smith.

"Well?" She said.

Mr. Smith was silent.

"When were you going to tell me about the bruises your teacher put on my son?"

"Mrs. Pottishear, I did not know."

"Why is that Mr. Smith? Is it possible that you were too busy trying to convict my son that you failed to complete a proper investigation?"

"Mrs. Pottishear I don't know what to say?"

"Why not? Has the cat got your tongue?"

Mr. Smith stood there with a blank look.

"Well, Mr. Smith an apology would be nice place to start don't you think, because from where I am standing I have a clear lawsuit against the school, Mr. Beyers, and you as the chief administrator."

"Now wait a minute Mrs. Pottishear. Matty did kick Coach Beyers."

"Only after the Coach assaulted him," she replied.

"Matty will have to be suspended for six days."

"Try two and you better hope that is all I do."

With that Mrs. Pottishear opened the door, grabbed Matty by the ear, and lead him out of the school in front of the entire mall where everyone could see because they were changing classes.

"Matty you are becoming more than a handful. You are so much smarter than the way you have been acting. I think the time has come for me to consider putting you in military school."

Matty didn't utter a word, he just sat there lifeless, but inside his head the world was spinning. He just couldn't figure out why he was so attractive to men when he had done nothing to give them the indication that he was that way.

"You know what momma, maybe that is not a bad idea. I hate this school and I hate that neighborhood. So maybe I would do better if you sent me away."

"Matty you would be so willing to throw your family away that easily?"

"Momma what do you mean throw them away. Nobody cares about me but you."

"Matty that's not true."

"Momma it is true. My brothers don't care about me."

"Matty why would you say that?"

"Do you remember the time that I stayed in the front yard for three weeks straight?"

"You do that so often now how can I tell the difference?"

"Good point," Matty said.

"Well anyway, I had done something to one of Jacob's friends. I didn't mean to do it but I did."

"I'm listening."

"Well anyway, one day I was tired of being stuck in the yard. So Jacob was going down the street. I went with him. As soon as we got near Derrick's house, he came running outside and started punching me and asking me why I did what I did?"

"Go on."

"Well I was so shocked and stunned that I couldn't even answer him and that made him punched me even more."

"And."

"Well to my saving grace Uncle Tommy Lee saw Derrick punching me and he ran out of the house and he asked Derrick what was he doing. Derrick started trying to explain. Uncle Tommy Lee said he didn't want to hear it."

"Your Uncle Tommy Lee has always been there when we needed him."

"Anyway then he turned to Jacob and said have you lost your mind standing there while another boy beats up on your brother? Then Jacob started babbling and Uncle Tommy Lee told him he didn't want to hear it."

"So what happened?"

"Well Uncle Tommy Lee told Derrick he better not ever put his hand on me again. And then he turned to Jacob and told him that he better not ever stand around and watch somebody beat on his brother no matter what I had done."

"Is this the time you told that girl those lies about Derrick so that she would not be interested in him?"

"How did you know… I mean what you talking 'bout momma?"

"So why did you do it?"

"Do what?"

Matty knew exactly what she was talking about. But he just couldn't bring himself to admit that he was a failure in the eyes of every girl he ever knew or wanted to know.

The few attempts he had made to talk with girls were even worse experiments in heartbreak than what he had experienced at the hands of JPH and Shaun.

Matty's mother was still talking but Matty's internal conversation was louder than his mother's actual conversation.

Anyway, I know that I told her a great deal of lies about Derrick, Matty continued his internal conversation with himself, to try and knock him out of the running. I honestly don't know what possessed me but I did it anyway. I wanted to tell him so bad what I had done and how sorry I was but before I could do that he caught me in their yard one day.

He said, "Man I can't kick your ass like I want to today, but when I do catch you I am going to beat your ass." The emphasis was on beat.

Once again, I was confined to the house. I stayed there for a few weeks. I was scared. He had a right to do it, but I didn't think he would.

"Matty?" She said in that accusatory tone.

His mother's tone startled him back into the present.

"I don't know momma. I guess I liked her but I couldn't get her to like me back. And then she started telling me about how she liked Derrick and before I knew it - - it just all came out."

"But there is something good that came out of all that."

"What?"

"You found out that lying doesn't pay."

Matty turned and looked out the window.

"I know. You hate it when I'm always right," Sadie said to her youngest son.

"Anyway. My point is that my brothers don't care about me. And that is just one example."

"That beating and Jacob taught me a valuable lesson in lying, loyalties, and louses. You can figure out on your own which is which. And I don't know if I have forgiven Jacob or if I ever will."

Sadie knew her son and now was not the time to get Matty to see another point of view. It would only alienate him further. She let it slide.

A few hours later we were at home and the telephone rang.

"Mr. Smith," Matty heard his mother say. But the remainder of the conservation fell on death ears because Matty was too exhausted to stay awake any longer.

The school bus woke him up. It was his brother's arriving home. Matty didn't know this but by the time they got home from school, they had all heard the news. It did not even dawn on Matty to ask them how had they found out, all he knew was that they already knew. He knew this not because of their words but their actions.

When the bus let them off, not one of them came into the house. They were scared because they did not know what kind of mood their mother was in because of Matty. They most likely thought that Matty had gotten one of their mother's famous ass cuttins.

What they apparently didn't know was that Matty did not get any licks at school although he did get suspended for two days. And he didn't get any licks when they got home either because Sadie knew Matty was not over their father's death, so she gave him a pass - - one time only.

Matty had the bedroom window up, so he heard their oldest brother, Junior, say, "Damn, that boy is always getting into trouble."

"He's one to talk," Matty said.

When their mother realized what was going on, she went to the door to greet them. She opened the door and gave her three sons *that look*. They all ran into the house immediately!

After dinner, my brother Jacob finally got up the courage to ask me what happened, of course, out of their mother's earshot.

Matty whispered the entire story to him without adding or taking anything away.

Then Jacob did something that really threw Matty for a loop – he hugged Matty. That was no brotherly hug.

Matty's body went limp. He started crying.

"Why you crying Matty?"

"Because Jacob it felt like daddy stepped into your body, for that moment, just to comfort me."

But Matty didn't tell Jacob the bad news. His hug only made things worse because when it was over, their father still wasn't there to make sure everything would be alright.

That night Matty went straight to bed without doing homework or watching any television. He was exhausted.

The next day Matty got up to go to school as normal. He had a few bruises and some bandages, but he felt much better. Then he remembered he was suspended.

"Sit down Matty and finish your breakfast then I will tell you what you will be doing today while I'm at work."

"Damn," I said under my breath.

"I heard that," Sadie shouted from the hallway. "Shut up and eat your breakfast."

"Hurry up before ya'll miss the bus, and if you do everybody's gettin' a whoopin'."

His brothers jumped into warp speed and hurried out of the house.

Matty was still at the kitchen table, but he heard their mother making up his brother's beds and putting stuff away in their drawers.

Then it became eerily quiet. So he went down the hall to see what was going on. Their mother was standing there with a bag of reefer, a big plastic bag full, in her hand, and, her mouth was wide open.

"Oh, shit. Let me get out of here." So Matty rushed back down the hallway and sat down at the table.

Claude was in trouble but he had no idea or just how much trouble. But he was sho' going to find out when he got home.

"When I get home from work you will have washed all the clothes, scrubbed the floors, and cut the grass in the back yard."

"Momma. I'm not in military school yet."

"Are you talking back to me?"

"No ma'am."

"And you do understand that washing clothes means drying them, folding them, and putting them away?"

"Yea."

"What?"

"Yes ma'am."

"Very well then. Give me a kiss."

"See you later momma."

"Don't have nobody in my house either while I'm gone."

"Yes ma'am."

Matty set out to do his chores when the doorbell rang. Matty wasn't thinking, because he wouldn't normally answer the door. But for some reason he just walked to the door and opened it without even looking out the peep hole.

"Hey Matty."

Matty's mouth dropped to the floor.

"Open the door."

Matty was still trying to pick his mouth up off the floor.

"Open the door Matty or I'll make you regret it."

Matty reluctantly opened the door.

"How did you know I was home alone?"

"Don't you worry about that. Now we are going to finish that little visit we had a few weeks ago."

Shaun had not made three good steps into the living room before he had closed the door and he was naked.

He threw Matty down on the living room floor and had stripped Matty nude in a matter of seconds.

Then he forced Matty to finish what he had started when they were playing hide and go seek. Shortly after that, Shaun was breathing hard and thrusting even harder. Matty started wrestling to try and get up but Shaun had him solidly pent down this time.

Then Shaun let out this load moan.

"Swallow it."

Matty was holding it in his mouth while he was trying to get up at the same time.

"Swallow it!" Shaun held Matty's nose so that he had no choice but to swallow it just so that he could breath.

"Now that wasn't so bad was it?" Shaun kissed Matty on the cheek got dressed and left.

Matty rushed to lock the door, got dressed, and then brushed his teeth, gargled with Listerine, and he even tried to force himself to vomit. Nothing worked. He still had the smell of Shaun all over him and he had his salty taste in his mouth.

"I am not going to cry anymore," Matty said.

He gathered himself and finished his chores. In fact, he was so mad at himself, that he did a far better job than was required by his mother.

Once Matty finished his chores, he sat down and picked up a book. Then suddenly something started to happen. This strange tingling feeling started to go through his body, and he could not control it. It was a feeling Matty had never felt before.

He could not get the thoughts of what had happened that morning out of his head. Before he knew it, he was standing at attention, and it freaked him out.

Matty started running around the house screaming and hollering, trying to out run it, because he didn't know what it meant. He had never seen that thing before. Finally, he was so exhausted that he had to stop. That is when it dawned on him that that thing was attached to him.

Just then, his mother walked through the door, and Matty grabbed a pillow to try and hide that big thing, without being obvious.

"How was your day?" she said, and she was smiling.

Matty was scared. He blurted out, "I haven't done anything!"

Their mother looked at him smiling, and kept on walking.

Shortly after their mother walked in, his brothers came in behind her. And behind that was an immediate argument between Matty and Claude.

The next thing Sadie heard was "Shut up you pothead." Of course the words came out of Matty's mouth. She was not surprised.

"Man, you don't know what you are talking about."

Matty stared into their mother's eyes.

Claude was slow. So it took him a little longer to catch up to where the conversation was going.

Sadie looked at Claude. "You know when we are finished you are going to get it, right?"

It was clear from Matty's face that the only satisfaction he got out of that entire day was hearing his brother Claude screaming as he was getting a whoopin' for that little package their momma found earlier that morning.

Then Matty heard a shrilling scream come from Claude and immediately after that water flushing. That meant their mother was making him watch as she flushed his reefer down the toilet. That was satisfying enough to put Matty to sleep.

Matty had nothing to say at dinner or afterwards. He did what homework he had, and went to bed, but he didn't sleep at all that night. He tossed and turned so much that it woke up Jacob in the bottom bunk.

"What the hell are you doing up there?"

"Nothing," Matty said. "Go back to sleep."

Matty didn't move that much the rest of the night, but he was still wide awake.

Morning finally came. Everyone was rushing, trying to get ready to get out of the house. Matty just sat on the edge of

Jacob's bed looking lost. By the time he had realized it all of the commotion had stopped, everyone was gone.

Matty was alone again. He didn't even have the chance to ask his mother to stay home with him that day. It was too late.

He was so confused that he spent the entire day sitting in the living room, partly scared and partly intrigued by the previous day's events.

When his family started coming home, Matty didn't know if he was elated that he had no visitor or disappointed by the same fact.

The one thing Matty was sure of was that he was glad he was going back to school tomorrow.

He went to bed early that night because he wanted to be rested and refreshed for his first day back, even if he did have to endure bullying.

Wednesday morning came and sure enough so did the bullying. And so too did the groping, again.

But this time was different. The groping felt purposeful and exact.

Matty kept thinking how he could figure out who was doing the groping.

"I got it. I will start inspecting everybody's hands in that entire group."

"Did you say something Matty?" Mrs. Feaster, his advanced grammar teacher asked.

"No ma'am."

The bell rang.

Matty had forgotten all about gym class until the bell rang. He knew he had to face Mr. Beyers, but he had so many other things ahead of Mr. Beyers that he had not even thought about what had happened.

"Like grandma used to say, gird up your loins and do what you have to do. Whatever that means," Matty told himself.

As he headed into gym class, "Matty come here son."

Matty turned to see it was Coach Reid, a big muscular guy, who wore glasses. He looked like a nerd in a muscle suit.

"You are going to be in my classes now since Beyers is out on medical leave for a month or so. So go get dressed and you won't need a shirt because you will be on the skins today."

Matty was devastated.

While everyone was getting changed, Matty was sitting there with a new problem. Then he slowly started to get undressed. He heard the door open while he was standing there in his underwear.

"I also wanted to tell you one other thing. If you try that shit on me that you did on Beyers, you will have hell to pay."

Before Matty could even think of a response, Coach Reid smacked him on his ass with a grip that palmed his ass; and, as quickly as he came, he was gone.

Matty stood there in total shame. Until that moment he had never even considered coming out of the closet about his problem. But by his own unfortunate design, Matty had created this house of cards with one small retaliatory act - - "That damn kick was my own undoing."

He took his shirt off and started walking toward the exit door that went from the locker room to the outside world. But with each step the words of his brother Claude rang out in his head.

"Man cover that shit up. Don't nobody want to see that."

Matty had never gotten over those words from Claude.

Actually, until Claude uttered those words, Matty didn't think of himself as being different nor did he feel ashamed of being without a shirt.

There was only one thing left to do.

A few weeks later Claude was picking at Matty again, although not about his man tiddies.

They were standing in the kitchen and Claude continued to pick at Matty mercilessly, and without provocation.

In truth, Matty was a gentle soul but when he had had enough, then he had had enough.

Claude knew this about Matty and he also knew that Matty was unpredictable when he was angry. Still Claude insisted on continuing to tease Matty.

Just like that Matty snapped.

Before he or Claude knew what was happening, Matty had snapped.

"You stabbed me!"

Sadie heard the commotion and rushed into the kitchen to find Claude standing near the sink holding his side and breathing heavy.

"Come on Claude, let me get you to the hospital."

While they were gone, Matty replayed the scene in his mind over and over. And sure enough Matty had pulled out a kitchen knife and stabbed Claude in his left side.

Sadie came home a few hours later crying.

Matty sat there staring at her, but he didn't say a word.

Their mother was crying, and the greater the silence grew the more her tears flowed.

Matty started crying. His anger gave way to tears. Then he was mad that he was crying because of Claude.

"Your brother is in the hospital fighting for his life. I never thought I would see the day that one of my sons would try to kill the other one."

Matty was heaving. Then he managed to say, "Momma, I wasn't trying to kill Claude. I just wanted him to leave me alone."

"The knife that almost punctured your brother's lung don't know that."

Matty started crying again, but there was no anger this time.

It was several years later, many years later, when Sadie told Matty that the hospital wanted to have a warrant issued for his arrest.

The nurse at the hospital asked Claude, "Do you want me to call the police?"

Sadie answered for Claude, "No."

Then Claude too said no, maybe because he knew that everything that ensued was his own fault.

Claude spent that night in the hospital.

When he came home the next day things were still tense between he and Matty for quite some time.

Still they found a way to go on, which also meant that Matty had to go back to school.

A few days later Matty was in school and his brother's words reverberated through his head, although the stabbing crisis, at least in Matty's mind, was not yet over.

Matty pulled the door open and walked out into the gym. He walked over to his team the skins. Nobody said a word. They didn't have to. All eyes were on Matty's man tiddies.

Matty turned around and walked back into the locker room, got dressed, and went and sat on the bus for the long ride home. Thank God it was an uneventful ride home.

As soon as Matty got home, "Momma, I want to go see Dr. Walker to see if there is anything we can do about my man boobs." Then Matty stormed off.

His mother took him to the doctor the very next day.

"So Matty what's going on with you?" Dr. Walker asked.

"Dr. Walker I have man boobs and I want them cut off."

After he examined Matty, he sent him outside while he talked with his mother.

"Mrs. Pottishear, there is nothing medically wrong with Matty. He may not like the fact that his breasts are a little bigger than other men, but that does not necessitate a surgery, which could actually make the problem worse, by creating breast cancer."

"So what should I do Dr. Walker?"

"My suggestion is to not do anything. He should grow out of it and he will grow out of the attitudes about it."

As they were on their way to school, Sadie told Matty what Dr. Walker said.

"Momma let's go home."

Matty didn't say another word. When they got home he went straight to his room to work on a plan since Dr. Walker refused to cut his problem away.

But what Dr. Walker didn't know is that Matty couldn't see his future because his present was forever dark.

"If I am normal, how come I don't feel normal? Not only that but I practically had mother convinced that I needed to cut these things off until we went to see Dr. Walker. I did it to myself again."

After Claude's words Matty began to understand what shame meant even though he had never experienced it on that level before.

Matty devised an idea.

He decided to tape those boobs down. It was the only way that Matty could feel normal, although he used one abnormality to defeat another abnormality.

But no amount of tape could hide Matty's man boobs, and no amount of hiding would save him from gym or Coach Reid.

Matty was doomed to be a skin forever and even worse he was always the final pick every day for every team, in part because he had such low self-esteem that he could not even begin to focus on playing, especially since his man boobs jiggled like tiddies every time he ran.

"If my second secret is ever discovered to hide my first secret, I will drop out of school, period."

It was a tempting thought that Matty thought about often, but he could not figure out what he would do with the rest of his life. So he made it his life's mission to keep his secret identity hidden.

But keeping his secret hidden didn't just require tape, it required acting too. Every day right before gym, Matty learned how to fake an injury, catch a cold, hide away, or just plain skip class. He made a D in gym every year until he graduated.

It never dawned on Matty to have a talk with Coach Reid, until after the talk was no longer necessary. Matty never forgot that lesson.

Worst part of all is that Matty really wanted to be involved in gym, but it just seemed that gym class was yet another place that he did not belong.

So hiding his boobs to protect himself from additional abuse was Matty's only option. And hiding his boobs was a process that required time and privacy.

First he would layer his boobs with old gray duct tape to try and flatten out his boobs. The he would layer that old gray duct tape with white hospital tape to try and make him look normal. After all that layering, Matty would put on a white tee shirt to try and smooth out the look.

"Dr. Walker this don't feel normal, but what else can I do?"

Instead of easing his pressure, Matty had only added more pressure to his life. In addition to everything else he was already worrying about, he had to now worry about stuff like what if his tape popped off during school? Or worse, during gym?

And despite his best efforts, to keep his secret a secret, it did get out.

Although it was nice not to be alone, no matter how temporary, this was not the kind of notoriety that Matty sought. Still he had no choice. He was cornered. Either he shared his secret willingly or it would be revealed forcefully.

So reluctantly Matty revealed his prized hide-and-go-seek technique to one other buddy who, unbeknownst to Matty, shared this uncommon and unnatural bond.

"Matty tell me how you figured out how to hide these things man."

Matty did not immediately answer. In fact Matty just stood there as if he had no idea what fat boy was talking about.

"Matty come on man. I see you in gym class so I know you know what I am talking about."

Then it hit Matty that this was the fat boy running around during gym with all the fat jiggling. But his man tiddies could be excused because he was much bigger than Matty.

Nonetheless Matty was forced into revealing his girly secret not once but twice. He had to first own up to the fact that he had a woman's anatomy; and then, he had to own up to the fact that he was trying to have a breast augmentation without the surgery.

But again it was Matty's fault that his secret was being revealed because his mother had given him strict instructions to not let anyone in the house while he was waiting for the bus in the cold and dark.

But Matty thought he knew best, so when fat boy asked if he could come in and wait, then Matty agreed. And therein lay his downfall.

After his denial of the denial didn't work, Matty saw himself grabbing fat boy by his pants and throwing him out by the seat of his pants, but that option came with even more problems than his present options promised.

"Take your shirt off."

Then Matty meticulously explained and demonstrated how he learned how to hide his breasts from himself and others.

After Matty was finished taping off his second set of breasts that morning, then he said to fat boy, "There is one small problem with my concealment plan."

"What's that?"

"By the time you get home in the afternoon and get ready to take the tape off, the tape's thick plaster residue will show exactly where the tape had been plastered that day."

"That ain't no big deal man."

"Yea but the residue doesn't wash away with soap and water and you can't scrub it very hard because your skin will already be tender from the tape sticking to your bare skin so hard all day."

"Okay," Fat boy said.

Matty continued his explanation. "Some days when you get home in the afternoons your skin is going to be so tender that you are going to pull some of your skin off with the tape. So you need to be prepared for the pain of it and be prepared to do first aid on yourself."

Nevertheless, Matty followed his plan of disguise until it became too unbearable to continue. The tipping point for Matty came after about a month or so of wearing his disguise. Matty had noticed that the area underneath his arms was getting tender but it was not enough to stop or slow him down. As long as no one touched Matty's chest, he was good to go.

Anyway, one afternoon he came home and locked himself in the bathroom as he usually did to take off his masquerade costume.

When Matty snatched the tape off, a huge chunk of his skin came off along with the tape from both of his underarms.

"ARGHHHHHH!" Matty screamed.

Then he realized he was bleeding from where his raw meat was exposed. On top of that, Matty made the mistake of putting alcohol on his left side and he screamed even louder a second time.

"Matty what's wrong?"

"Nothing momma."

"Open this door right now."

Matty slowly opened the door.

His mother knew exactly what was going on.

She rushed into their bedroom and got an old tee shirt.

"Let's go."

"Where we going?"

"To the hospital. You have exposed skin and blood vessels. We can't afford for that to become infected."

Sadie and Matty rushed to the hospital with Matty grimacing the entire ride. But Sadie didn't ask any questions. But she really didn't have to anyway. The evidence was obvious.

But Matty had to be given credit for trying his best to gingerly work on saving his skin under his man tiddies. He didn't want to scream because the house was full but he had no choice. The pain was unimaginable.

After spending quite a bit of time attending to his wound and controlling the bleeding, he started working on the left tiddy. He was doing a pretty good removing the tape one quarter of an inch at a time. But when he got to the very end, the tape and his skin were inseparable. This tape was stuck in an even more vulnerable spot on his chest. It was stuck just underneath his tiddy, and when he pulled it, it took off more skin than the first one did, from his underarm and underneath his tiddy.

Not only did he have man boobs. Now he had bloody man boobs. And he had bloody man boobs that could not be taped. Each wound was as big around as a soda can, except that they were not perfectly round.

After an incessantly long wait in the emergency room, they finally got a chance to see the doctor.

The doctor looked at Matty and then his mother. They gave each other a nod of agreement.

"What's your name son?"

"Matty."

"The next time you want to cut yourself, you need to become a doctor before you try surgery on yourself again."

Matty smiled a half smile. But he was glad the doctor didn't mention the obvious.

Then he said something that almost made Matty jump off the exam table and into his arms.

"You know what this means Matty don't you?"

Matty shook his head no.

"This means that you are not going to be able to take gym class for about two months."

Matty wanted to do a happy dance but he figured that would be too obvious. But now he was willing to wear his pain proudly like a badge of honor. In fact, the news was so good to Matty that he no longer felt the pain and he didn't even need the pain pills the doctor gave his mother for him to take, at least not that day anyway.

Sure enough, Matty was bleeding into this tee shirt every day for about three months because the tears were in the folds of his skin underneath his arms. So Coach Reid made Matty write a different paper during gym class every day. But Matty didn't care. He figured it was harder on Coach Reid to come up with a topic than it was for him to right the paper.

Periodically, he did have to show Coach Reid the wounds, but if he needed to look at Matty's man boobs to keep him from playing, Matty was more than willing to have him gawk at his breasts for a few minutes.

Although, in a weird sort of way, Matty didn't mind Coach Reid seeing his tiddies and a couple of times when Coach Reid put his big, cold muscled hand on Matty's tiddies and caressed Matty's woman-like appearance, Matty had a strange reaction that he could not hide.

Needless to say Matty's taping days were over, but not his shame.

# Chapter 7

Despite Matty's injuries, nothing would stop Shaun from stalking Matty. In fact, Shaun's attacks increased because he knew that Matty was not able to defend himself. As Matty came to know Shaun's sisters and his mother more and more, Shaun's attacks became more prevalent.

And Shaun didn't care if there was anyone in the house or not. Whenever he felt like having Shaun he did. With each attack Shaun's resistance diminished a little more each time.

One Saturday night there was a special event at church and Matty was going with Shaun's sisters. Matty had on a brand new blue sweater. The house was crowded with people, but Shaun wanted Matty to perform fellatio on him before he (Shaun) went to the club. Matty refused.

Shaun threw Matty down on his parents' bed, and held Matty there while he ejaculated on Matty's sweater, without even touching himself. The house was completely full and not one person came into their parent's bedroom to see what was going on. Matty was stunned. Then he thought, 'Do they already know what is going on? Has Shaun done this before to someone else?'

When he was finished, Shaun said, "You can take a part of me to church with you."

Matty jumped up and tried to clean himself up. When he came back down the hall, Shaun's mother asked him, "Matty, how did you get that spot on your sweater?"

Matty was speechless.

"Come here. Let's see if we can get that spot out."

She tried to wash it out with a damp cloth but when it dried it was still there.

"You didn't have that spot on your sweater when you came here did you?"

"I don't think so."

It looked like a big oil stain. Matty had to sit in church that whole night with that big spot on his chest just like Hester Prynne in the *Scarlet Letter*.

When they got home from church that night, Matty threw that sweater away that very night.

The fighting, the bullying, the sex, the suspensions, and his momma's whoppings went on for the rest of that year and into the next.

Then one day their granddaddy was visiting, which was rare.

"Matty I want to talk with you son."

So his grandpa sat down on their front steps.

"Sit down beside me here."

Matty took a seat.

"Tell me about your new school."

"I hate it grandpa."

"Why?"

"The kids are mean. And I just don't feel like I belong anywhere or with anyone in the school."

"You know Matty at some point you are going to be alone in the world…"

"I'm already alone grandpa. How much more alone can I get?"

"Someday Matty you are going to have to go out into the world by yourself and you are going to have face some challenges. Some of those challenges are going to include being able to stand up like a man, even when you have done nothing wrong."

Matty was listening to his grandpa but he didn't quite understand what he was telling him.

"Sometimes you have to be willing to take an ass-cuttin' just so that people know they cannot push you around."

The light bulb went off over Matty's head.

That was a Saturday.

The very next Monday, the bus ride to school was unusually quiet for some reason. And the school day was equally as quiet. Matty just knew something was wrong somewhere but he couldn't put his finger on it.

The bell rang and it was time to head to the buses to go home.

No sooner were they pulling out of the school's parking lot did the bullying start. Grandpa's words rang in Matty's ears.

"Sometimes you have to be willing to take an ass-cutting so that people will know you are not scared of them." Those words stuck like glue.

Roy hit Matty upside the head one time as the bus turned onto Providence Road.

Matty immediately jumped up and said something like, "I ain't taking your shit no more. Don't hit me again. This next time you do that shit I'm going to beat your ass!"

Roy responded, "Man I was just playing."

Matty replied, "Well don't play with me like that," and he was starring Roy straight in his eyes so that he knew Matty meant exactly what he said.

Just like that the bullying ended.

From that point on Matty was willing to take an ass-cuttin' anytime from anyone as long as he stood up for himself. And everybody else knew it too.

Matty's defiance was a shot heard around the school. It won him a fan following, including one that he would have never suspected.

"Stephanie?"

"Hi Matty."

Matty had never noticed how beautiful Stephanie was primarily because he had sworn off girls after his last entanglement, at least until he got to high school anyway. But now that he had a chance to truly examine Stephanie up close, she was truly the most beautiful girl in school.

She had medium length brown hair that smelled like apricots. Her skin was flawless and smooth to the touch as he reached out to help her up.

"I'm sorry," Matty said. I didn't even see you there.

Stephanie was talking but Matty's ears were closed. His eyes were focused on the reddest lips he had ever seen, television-perfect lips. Sparkling white teeth, and humps and curves in all the right places, that was Stephanie Walker. She was freakin' irresistible.

As Matty reached out to help her up since he was the one to knock her down, even though he still didn't quite understand how, her tight brown skirt slide up her smooth thighs just enough to give him a glance at her white lace panties.

The brown skirt was a beautiful contrast to her beautiful alabaster thighs. The back side of Matty's left hand accidentally rubbed against her right thigh as he was helping her gather up her books. A shock went throughout Matty's entire body and then he felt that tingling again.

When Stephanie caught Matty staring at her personalness, he turned beet red, because he was a light caramel color, which was another thing the kids always teased him about. He was too light to be black and he was too dark to be white.

"You're blushing," Stephanie said.

It took Matty a minute before he could respond.

"Are you okay?" Matty asked trying to rush off. But Stephanie would not let him.

"Matty you've lost weight."

Matty was so busy running away from one problem to another that he hadn't even noticed that his body had started to change. Almost seemingly overnight, Matty had a mustache, his chest was sticking out, he could actually see his feet, and his fat turkey cheeks were gone.

But Matty was so focused on his man boobs, smaller though they were, he could not see anything else but.

And to top it all off, Matty had grown a few inches also, in more places than one. It was a complete metamorphosis that only took fifteen years or so.

"You look really good Matty," Stephanie said as she put her hand on Matty's chest.

Matty didn't even flinch, but his body did respond and Stephanie noticed that too.

"How would you like to go to lunch with me?"

Matty was caught in Stephanie's spell. He could only do what she wanted him to do.

"Okay," was all he could manage to get out.

A few days went by and Matty heard neither hide nor hair from Stephanie. A few more days went by and Matty decided he'd better drop it for his heart's sake. The whole thing brought back memories of his father, and that winter ass cuttin' he got that day Mrs. Carver brought him home from school.

"I will never forget the rejection I felt, nor will my butt."

And as Matty's luck would have it, no sooner had he made the decision to sign off from Stephanie that Stephanie showed up again.

"You ready to have that lunch with me?"

All Matty could do was say, "Yes."

"Okay, we are going to cut school tomorrow by pretending we are sick; and, you are going to come to my house in the morning. Here's my address. You got it?" Stephanie demanded.

"You dumbass." Matty said out loud. "You just agreed to go to Stephanie's house for lunch tomorrow morning. So why are we having lunch at 7 am in the morning?"

As Matty sat in Geometry class all he could think about was Stephanie's demand.

"How am I going to get to Stephanie's house across town by 7am in the morning? I ain't got no money."

Matty was nervous the rest of the day. Although he was flattered to be the former fat kid that was invited to the Walker mansion, he still didn't understand what Stephanie wanted with him.

But the fact remained that Matty could not refuse Stephanie Walker, but in his defense, who would refuse her if given the chance?

"Momma I don't feel well."

"You don't have a fever."

"My stomach's upset." And Matty wasn't lying his stomach was upset at the prospect of seeing Stephanie.

"Excuse me momma I gotta go."

Matty was on the toilet. In fact, he made so many trips to the toile that morning that his brothers almost missed the school bus, since the five of them shared one bathroom.

He was in there so long that his mother left for work without even saying anything to him or giving him any work instructions for the day.

It was the first time in Matty's educational career that he had ever played sick, but at the moment, it didn't feel much like play.

Matty didn't dare try to eat anything. Somehow he managed to stay out of the bathroom long enough to get dressed, jump on his bike, and start to ride.

This was a different ride from the walks he used to have to take to catch the bus for his old school, when he was a kid. There were no lights coming on to light his way or to protect him this time. And his mother did not bundle up his coat to see him off or kiss his forehead and tell him to have a good day in school.

It was just Matty and his bike. The only similarity this ride had to his past walks was the fact that he was alone, again. But this time alone did not feel so lonely. In fact, it felt sort of free. But even that thought could not deter Matty this time.

So he peddled across town as fast as he could, meandering in and out of traffic, horns blowing, tires screeching, and the morning air whisking past his face, but he didn't care.

It even looked like the sun was rising to meet him on his quest. It was the first time Matty had felt good about something, anything, in a long time. The only problem was that Matty didn't know exactly what the thing was he was feeling so good about.

After riding and thinking for almost 30 minutes, Matty had finally made it to the entrance of Stephanie's neighborhood. It was better and far different than he had imagined.

There was this man inside of a little house just looking at Matty as he rode his bike up to the gate. As Matty was preparing to go around him and the little house, he bolted out of the house, and grabbed the seat of Matty's bike.

"Whoa son, where do you think you are going?"

Matty was out of breath and tired from that long bike ride, especially since it was the first time he had ridden his bike since they had moved to the Park. Therefore, it took Matty a few seconds to answer him, besides the fact that he had grabbed Matty's bike and almost made him fall to the ground.

"I asked you a question."

"I am going to see the Walkers."

"They are out of the country. So where are you really going?"

"What business is it of yours who I am here to see?"

"How about we just call the police and you can tell them."

"Damn," Matty said under his breath. "That's all I need is more trouble."

"You are already in enough trouble I see."

"What," Matty exclaimed. "Were my words painted on my head like a neon sign flashing?"

"Okay, okay. I am going to see Stephanie Walker."

"Don't you move one inch," he said.

He went back into his little house, and picked up the telephone.

All I could hear him saying was, "Yes ma'am."

Then he finally stuck his head out of the door, and yelled, "Go ahead boy."

Matty had really gotten tired of people calling him boy or son.

Matty yelled back to him, "My name is Matty," as he rode off.

"Who cares?"

Matty finally reached the back of the city within the city, where the Walkers lived. He could not believe his eyes. The only thing he could compare it to was one of those huge plantation houses he saw when they went looking for their slave ancestors a few years back.

The trip wasn't a total loss. They did find some records that lead them to a few important markers on land now owned by the Charlotte/Douglas International Airport. It was hallowed ground, but how would anyone know it when there were no signs, no headstones with names, and no fence to border the site.

Matty had never seen his grandpa as emotional as he was when he saw those markers. But it wasn't the emotion Matty expected.

"They thought they could just put us in the ground in unmarked graves and that would clear their conscience. By not marking the grave there was no reminder of their sins. Secrets never stay secret forever." His grandpa's words rang in his head loudly that morning for some reason.

Matty thought about turning around, but it was too late. Maybe the house wasn't that big, but it was certainly larger than any house he had ever seen, in person that is.

And of course, it sat high up on a hill.

"What is it with these hills?"

Matty's legs were too tired to ride up the hill. He got off his bike and just left it at the bottom of the hill, and forced himself to start walking. Matty held his head down the entire time so as to gain a little momentum to help him get up the hill. When he reached the top, there she was standing in the door, beautiful as ever.

"You are late," she barked at Matty. But she was so beautiful, he didn't care.

"You didn't have to ride your bike twenty miles across town," Matty said.

She was laughing. Matty was panting, trying to catch his breath.

"Come on in, and don't touch anything. You are all sweaty."

Matty followed her down this long, really long hallway to this beautiful sunroom in the back of the house that looked out over a lake. Matty tried to pretend he wasn't impressed, but he was very impressed.

"Why are you going to a public school?" Matty just had to know. "Why aren't you in school today?"

"It's a long story, and we don't have time for that. Because I am here with you."

"Okay, what do we have time for?"

"First you need to go in that bathroom, take those sweaty clothes off, and take a shower."

"What?"

"You heard me," with her hands on her curvy hips.

"I thought. Actually I don't know why I came over here."

"Good because I do."

"You do what?"

"I do know why you came over here."

"But first, you need to clean up," as she stomped her right foot and pointed with her left hand. "Go take a shower!"

For some reason, Matty did exactly as he was told.

When he opened the door, the bathroom was twice as big as his bedroom at home – a bedroom that he shared with one of his three older brothers!

After Matty finished snooping around and admiring every inch of that room, he finally took off his clothes and stepped into a shower that had all kinds of sauna attachments and a seat. It was big enough for 12 grownups.

"Damn, I knew that they were rich, but I didn't know they were this rich!"

The door closed behind him.

"Stephanie."

Before Matty could get another word out of his mouth, Stephanie's lips were pressed against his. It was such an amazing feeling that Matty was just trying to savor the moment for as long as it could last.

Matty slowly lifted his hands to gently touch Stephanie's waist and pull her closer to him. It was like there was a different person occupying Matt's body.

He was so relaxed with Stephanie that he hadn't thought once about his man boobs, although that day they looked more like starter boobs.

When he pulled her closer to him that tingling feeling started again and Matty's soldier had an erect attention unlike anything Matty had ever experienced before. He started smiling.

"Why are you giggling?" Stephanie asked.

"I was thinking this is what Mr. McKenny was talking about when he taught sex ed last year before he was transferred to the main office downtown for teaching it to us."

"No one has ever giggled before when I kissed them."

"I'm not giggling about you."

"Whatever."

Stephanie tried to pull away, but Matty refused to let her go.

It all felt so natural and their bodies were so in touch that they melted into one. Those two kids were not moving like kids. Matty was moving, caressing, and touching Stephanie like a man and Stephanie was responding like a woman.

The funny thing was that Matty knew absolutely nothing about being a man in that way before that moment, but it all felt so natural, unforced, and unrehearsed that his body could not help but respond to Stephanie's body.

She was soft inside and out, and the more Matty thought about it, the deeper his thrusts came – from his soul. And the deeper his thrusts, the more Stephanie opened up and gave herself to him.

Within minutes Matty was screaming like a girl and his body was shaking uncontrollably, right after that so was Stephanie. But that did not stop them. Their eyes, brains, and bodies were all undeniably connected. They kept on going for several more hours because Matty's soldier would not go away, neither did their desire for each other.

Her breasts were so beautifully soft and round but firm, and when she held Matty's head to her breast, he could not help but slightly bite her – just enough to intensify her lustful desire for more but not enough to hurt or harm her - because she was after all a luscious fruit to be consumed.

Although Matty's brain said be gentle, his hips were violently thrusting and Stephanie stayed in unison with him the entire time. Her eyes told him that his hips were right. So Matty kept pounding, and pounding, and pounding. And Stephanie kept giving, and giving, and giving, until her fingernails were squarely clinched in his back like a cat. Matty didn't care. These were cat scars he would gladly wear.

He kissed her beautiful thighs all the way down and back up several times. When he kissed the inside of her thigh she would grab what was left of his beautiful locks of hair and hold his head there until they both were forced to come up for air.

It was a pure pleasure to be awashed in her juices, juices that brought out the complete animal in Matty. He could not help but to make sure she was completely satisfied. Stephanie had become Matty's most intoxicating drug of choice. He had no choice but to rub her thighs and hold her beautiful hips open in such a way that she could not resist his entry.

Their final releases met each other exactly four hours after they had started.

There they were two people, together, trying to find a connection in this world. And now that they had found it, they were both trying to fill that one space in time. It was the most amazing feeling in the world. But Matty didn't have anything to compare it to, nor did it need a comparison. Actually, there was nothing in Matty's life to compare it to.

They just laid there holding each other. But this was not one of those hugs that Matty's mother gave him.

Then as if nothing had happened, they were sitting in the kitchen, at the breakfast bar, having lunch.

Stephanie made them some kind of fancy sandwiches and some chips, as they sat and talked for a little while.

"I was a virgin until just a few hours ago."

"Why me," Matty asked her.

"Because I knew you were a virgin too."

Matty responded in his mind only, "That is true only if Shaun does not count."

"In truth I never really paid you any attention until I heard about your willingness to stand up to that bully. But after I heard the news, I knew you were the one."

"What one is that?"

"You ask too many questions."

Bong. Bong. The huge grandfather clock in the foyer struck 2 pm.

"I've got to go so I can beat my mother home," Matty offered.

And with that he jumped up, ran down the hill, and jumped on his bike. Then he realized that he had forgotten something.

So Matty jumped off his bike, ran back up the hill, and kissed Stephanie as long as he could.

Before either one of them knew anything, Stephanie's back was against the wall in the entry hallway for support. Her white lace, extremely delicate robe that teased Matty by showing him her erect nipples through the lace was on the floor as she held his neck with a determined grip.

She was some kind of gymnast because her legs were in the air at a 90 degree angle. Matty was holding her by her waist with his left hand, and with his right hand he was caressing her left breast.

Matty was mesmerized by how her body responded to his touch. Within minutes of entering her, his teeth were locked down on her nipple.

Stephanie's body was giving Matty her personal approval. And Matty was equally determined to show his appreciation. She bit down on his neck with furious pain and pure pleasure, giving Matty further assurance of her approval. Then their eyes locked. Her eyes were telling Matty something but he didn't know what.

By the look on Matty's face, he was begging Stephanie to tell him what she meant by that look. But his mind and body were otherwise occupied.

Matty knew they had achieved success when Stephanie's eyes widen and her mouth flung wide open.

Now Matty really had to rush home. With that, Matty finished what he had originally started and began his ride home.

The more Matty peddled toward home, the more he realized how truly exhausted he was, but he could not stop peddling for one second.

The entire ride home all Matty kept seeing was that look on Stephanie's face.

Matty knew he was going to get a beating when he got home, and he was not sure Stephanie was worth that much, no matter how much he enjoyed her. So he peddled even harder.

"Finally I made it!"

Matty beat his mother home by about two or three minutes. It was just enough time to put his bike away and jump into the shower.

While Matty was in the shower he noticed blood on his manhood.

"What are you doing taking shower in the middle of the day?" Their mother startled Matty just as he was coming out of the bathroom.

"I don't know," Matty responded while shrugging his shoulders.

While Matty was putting his clothes on the doorbell rang.

It was the next door neighbor, the same old stranger who met Matty on his very first day in the neighborhood. But now, he was no longer a stranger. Yet he was still watching Matty's every move just like he did that first day Matty stepped onto his front porch in the rain all those years ago.

"Mr. Grey," his momma said answering the door.

"Shit, I'm busted," Matty said from his hiding perch around the corner.

They talked for a few minutes, and then he left.

Here it comes, Matty thought. He knew he was getting ready to get another beating.

But it didn't happen, at least not immediately.

Their mother prepared dinner like nothing was wrong.

Matty didn't sleep at all that night, waiting for their mother to whoop him and wear his butt out with that punishment strap, in his underwear no less.

She never did.

Matty was up and dressed extra early the next morning. The thought of seeing Stephanie made his heart beat faster. In fact Matty was late to class that morning for running around the entire school looking for her.

Matty then went to the principal's office, and asked Mrs. Cloninger, the secretary, where was Stephanie.

"Matty, you don't know?"

"Know what? She was here yesterday."

"Matty you were not in school yesterday." Mrs. Cloninger replied. "In fact, come to think of it, Stephanie was not in school yesterday either."

Matty magnanimously ignored Mrs. Cloninger's suggestion.

"Mrs. Cloninger, Stephanie!" This time Matty was a little more insistent.

"Stephanie's father took her out of school early this morning."

"What! What do you mean he took her? Took her where?"

"I am not supposed to be telling you this," she said as she was looking around to see if anybody else was in the office listening.

Mrs. Cloninger never got nervous about anything. Matty wondered if she knew what happened between him and Stephanie.

"Mrs. Cloninger, please it is very important that I talk to Stephanie!"

Her eyes were telling Matty something, but for the second time in a couple of days, Matty could not figure out what a woman was trying to tell him.

"Please," Matty begged. He didn't know if he was going to blow up or cry. He also didn't know what he was feeling. Maybe it was a mixture of both.

Finally, she blurted it out. "He put her in a private girl's school." Immediately, she put her hands over her mouth like she had just released the biggest state secret in the world.

"Where?"

"Matty, I'm sorry, but I am not allowed to divulge that information. I shouldn't have told you what I did tell you."

"Mrs. Cloninger, please."

She motioned for Matty to lean in a little closer.

"I cannot tell you where, but I will tell you it is out of the state."

Matty's heart dropped like he was on one of those drop chairs at Six Flags, except there was no laughter of sport attached to his heart dropping this time.

"What is wrong with me?" Matty asked.

Matty was so distraught that he merely went through the motions of the day. No one knew this but inside Matty's mind, there was a vacancy side hanging. Matty had completely checked out the rest of the day.

No one paid any attention to Matty's distress except…

Matty was so upset that he was totally alone even in the crowded hallways of Carmel. The bell rang, Matty got up and walked to his next class in time enough for the next bell to ring. And he did that the remainder of the day without so much as taking out a book or a writing pad.

When the last class bell rang for the day, Matty stood outside in a daze. For a moment there, it was clear he honestly did not know where he was. Then he saw his classmates coming out of the gym in their shorts. Then he knew where he was.

Matty went into the locker room without even thinking about his man boobs. He changed his clothes and went outside to join the rest of his class. The world seemed so different yesterday.

Yesterday, Matty was alive and full of life and energy. Today, he was a reject sitting on the bench because nobody wanted him.

The bell rang again and Matty walked back into the locker room without having broken a sweat, grabbed his bag, and walked to the bus, still wearing his gym clothes.

That went on for the remainder of the week.

Friday night came and went, and Matty was no better.

Then Saturday came and Matty spent all day vegetating in front of the television looking at the full line up of Saturday morning cartoons, the *Fred Kirby Show*, and *The Little Rascals*. It was nice to watch the television show since he, Fred Kirby, used to live down the street from their new house. After that was the full line up of *Godzilla* movies.

Before long it was Saturday evening and the sun was starting to go down. Matty moved outside to the front porch for the first time that day or more appropriately, evening.

"Hey Matty."

Matty just looked at him.

Shaun grabbed Matty by his shirt collar and dragged him off to a spot obviously chosen in advance by Shaun.

Matty had no fight left in him. He did exactly what Shaun told him without so much as a whimper.

Matty's steeliness made Shaun uneasy and extra cautious, but it wasn't enough to deter him completely.

This went on for the remainder of the school year. No matter where Matty found himself day or night, Shaun found him. So Matty stopped hiding.

In fact, he put himself right square in the middle of Shaun's eyesight, thinking that this would make Shaun grow tired of him.

Matty was wrong.

Shaun came after him even more often and more aggressively.

While Shaun was busy fighting to keep their secret hidden, on the other hand he was busy grabbing, rubbing, touching, and fondling Matty every chance he got.

"Matty you know I'm going to the club tonight. Make yourself available for when I get home."

"What time are you getting home?"

"What difference does it make? You just be here when I get back."

"I'm going home by 11. So if you not back by then you won't see me tonight."

Matty had some control, but he was too naïve to know it. And even if he did, he wouldn't care because he was more interested in freedom than control.

"You better be here."

"You know I hate you right?"

"You can't hate me."

"Well I do. And if you think I'm going to be here when you get home, I can show you better than I can tell you."

Shaun didn't know what to make of Matty's new found strength. So Matty had bought himself a little bit of distance from Shaun. But that wouldn't do him much good.

That was Matty's summer.

The next year, Matty was in Algebra II and so was Buddy.

"Hey Matty."

"Hey Buddy."

"Matty I need your help with Algebra."

Matty ignored Buddy's request.

"I know you not just going to ignore me?"

"Watch me."

"Why won't you help me?"

"If I agree to help you will you leave me alone?"

"Hell yea."

"Okay. Where's your book?" Matty said in that exasperated tone.

"Oh damn I brought the wrong book."

"Walk with me and we'll work on it at my house so we don't have to make two trips."

"I don't want no shit out of you Buddy."

"Man, what the f___ you talkin' 'bout?"

Matty was embarrassed at the suggestion. So he dropped it.

"Where's your sister or your parents?"

"They are all gone."

"Come on in man it's okay."

"Matty got that feeling again but he went in anyway."

"Let me go get my book."

"Okay I'll wait here in the den."

Matty was looking around the house, when Buddy came back down the hall.

"Buddy!"

"What's wrong?"

"You are…"

"Wearing a smile."

"You're naked."

"What's wrong with that?"

"Look at that thing. What do you plan on doing with that?"

"I was hoping you would have some ideas."

Matty started sniffing himself.

"What are you doing?" Buddy asked.

"I am trying to figure out if I give off some scent that makes me attractive to men like you?"

"What the hell you talking about?"

Matty jumped up to leave, but he didn't know Buddy had locked him in.

"I've got the only key. So you cannot get out until I am ready to let you out."

With that Buddy snatch Matty around and kissed him.

Matty tried to resist, but his body actually was enjoying the kiss - - Matty's first kiss with a man.

He opened his eyes to see Buddy's face. Then he realized who Buddy was. Matty pushed Buddy off him and slapped him. WAP!

"What the hell you hit me for?"

"Because I just realized where I know you from. You used to come over to JPH's house when we lived off Remus Road and both of ya'll used to try and get my pants off me."

"Man that shit only happened a couple of times."

"It happened enough that I remembered it."

"Okay I'm sorry. Is that better."

"Hell no. Why would that be better? You know what it doesn't matter. Let me go. I want to go home."

"I'm sorry Matty I don't want you to go."

"Buddy open this door!"

"I'm not. If you leave what am I going to do with this?"

"Whatever you want. Do whatever you did to get it like that."

"Touch it."

"No."

"Come on touch it. It ain't gonna hurt you."

"It looks like it might hurt somebody."

"I'm tired of this shit." And with that Buddy literally ripped Matty's pants and underwear off of him right there at the front door.

"Buddy what are you doing?"

Matty was caught up in between being upset and excited.

Then they started wrestling, but Matty was guaranteed to lose because Buddy was a bona fide athlete and he was strong as an ox even though he did have a handicap.

Buddy stuffed his pole inside of Matty, all 10-inches of him.

Matty screamed a piercing scream.

Buddy covered Matty's mouth and kept on pushing.

The smell was awful because Matty could not hold his bowels; and, even worse, the more Buddy smelled, the more he knew he was hurting Matty by plunging deep inside of him. And plunge inside Matty Buddy did.

Buddy plunged so deep inside Matty that Matty had no choice but to let him in.

Then Buddy started a rapid plunging in and out, in and out, in and out, until he thrust powerfully forward inside of Matty until he released himself inside Matty. All of him!

He was so excited he did it all over again to Matty two more times before he let him go.

Matty's clothes were covered with shit, what was left of them anyway.

Buddy gave him a pair of underwear to wear home and a pair of sweat pants that were way too big.

Matty didn't know what to say. He was stunned at the unbelievablility of it all.

"Buddy was laughing at the entire scene."

Matty walked home in total shame and disgrace, but he refused to cry. But he did keep asking himself over and over, "Why me? What have I done to deserve this?"

Even worst, Matty had to see Buddy in Algebra class every day.

Matty kept thinking about it over and over again, then he finally figured it out that Buddy was one of his gropers on the bus a few years ago.

After Matty got home, he went into the bathroom, cleaned himself up, and took a nice long hot bath that burned in him like a fire. But there was no other way to clean the stench from his body and pain from his soul except with hot cleansing water.

After he was clean, then he carefully wrapped his torn and shit-covered clothes all nice and neat in newspaper. Then he threw them all away.

After that he did his homework and went to bed without eating any dinner.

The next day on the bus Matty would not look at Buddy. Buddy pretended not to be staring at Matty, but he was actually watching Matty's every move.

When they arrived at school, Matty was walking up the long ramp to the entrance of the school, and Buddy ran up behind him and smacked him on the ass, like in football.

"Was up man?"

Matty stopped dead in his tracks and winced at the pain.

"You wanna try it again?"

After that day, Buddy literally started courting Matty like they were boyfriend and boyfriend, but no one knew it except those two.

Eventually Matty and Buddy figured out how to make sure Matty was cleaned out before he came to see Buddy, but Matty did willingly start seeing Buddy.

And when Matty refused to see Buddy, Buddy would make sure the next time they saw each other that Matty was so fully satisfied that he would never refuse him again.

Buddy learned to do all sorts of unimaginable things to make sure Matty was satisfied. The relationship became so intense that Buddy and Matty learned how to give themselves to each other. Actually Buddy taught Matty how to give himself to him until he was completely satisfied.

But the plan backfired.

Buddy became so obsessed with Matty that he learned how to give himself to Matty in the same way he had taught Matty to do.

In fact, Buddy was so consumed with Matty that he used to sneak out of his bedroom window, on Friday nights, in particular, so that he could be with Matty at their secret rendezvous spot on a regular basis.

Although Matty's mother was strict in every sense of the word, Buddy's mother was even more strict, probably because Buddy had proven himself to be an untrustworthy child, except when it came to Matty.

In fact, during the school day, Buddy would find ways to meet Matty on the stairs when no one was around just to kiss Matty. Buddy would carry that hard on the remainder of the day so that by the time they got home Buddy was damn near animalistic.

That one shitty moment, grew into a long relationship to the point where Matty started having feelings for Buddy as if Buddy was his long-term, rough love.

Matty learned how to give himself to Buddy like Stephanie gave herself to him. And Buddy taught Matty how to take him and to enjoy every bit of him. They were truly secret lovers.

But Matty could not forget about Shaun primarily because Shaun would not let him forget. When Matty was not available for Shaun, Shaun would wait around until Matty returned. And then he would punish Matty by trying to hurt him physically while he made Matty perform rough fellatio on him.

Matty made sure that Buddy and Shaun never knew about the other because both of them were insanely jealous over Matty although neither one of them was in love with Matty.

This dual love life went on for more than three years and the longer it went on the more intense it became. Matty and Buddy started doing homework together and having sex while doing it. It wasn't easy but they managed to do it.

Buddy started making A's and Matty was making O's, multiple O's.

Then without any forewarning, Buddy dropped out of school and moved away. Matty was crushed again by love.

A few weeks after Buddy's disappearance, a song came on the radio.

*Here we are, the two of us together*
*Taking this crazy chance to be all alone*
*We both know that we should not be together*
*'Cause if they found out, it could mess up*
*Both our happy homes*

*I hate to think about us all meeting up together*
*'Cause soon as I looked at you, it would show on my face, yeah*
*Then they'll know that we've been loving each other*
*We can never no, no, no, no, we can't leave a trace*

*Sittin' at home I do nothing all day*
*But think about you and hope that you're okay*
*Hoping you'll call before anyone gets home*
*I'll wait anxiously alone by the phone*

*How could something so wrong be so right?*
*I wish we didn't have to keep our love out of sight, yeah*
*Living two lives, just ain't easy at all*
*But we gotta hang on and after fall*

*Secret lovers, yeah that's what we are*
*Trying so hard to hide the way we feel*
*'Cause we both belong to someone else*
*But we can't let it go 'cause what we feel*
*Is, oh so real, so real, so real*

*You and me, are we fair?*
*Is this cruel or do we care?*
*Can they tell that's in our minds?*
*Maybe they've had secret love all of the time*

*In the middle of makin' love, we notice the time*
*We both get nervous 'cause it's way after nine*
*Even though we hate it, we know it's time that we go*
*We gotta be careful so that no one will know*

*Secret lovers, yeah, that's what we are*
*We shouldn't be together but we can't let it go*
*'Cause what we feel is, oh so real*
*So real, so real, so real, so real*

The song said everything Matty could not say. But that was radio - - the sounds coming from a box. Matty's heart was hurting in real life, and he wasn't sure why, including the conflictions of his conscious, let alone his manhood or boyhood in his case.

Still he didn't even have time to mourn Buddy's departure because that was another bomb dropped on him unexpectedly.

"Jacob, you did what?"

"I asked mom could Shaun spend the night with me tonight so we can watch a horror fest together and she agreed."

"Where is Claude going to sleep?"

"Claude has that military weekend this weekend so he won't be around. So I'll have the whole room to myself this weekend."

Jacob's answer didn't satisfy Matty.

"Besides Matty what do you care? You are going to be sleeping in your own room by yourself."

"Why didn't you ask me to watch the horror fest with you Jacob?"

"Because you don't like scary movies."

"So," was all Matty could come up with.

Matty stayed under his mother's dress tail that entire weekend. And all was well as they went to bed Saturday night, although Jacob and Shaun were still up watching the horror fest.

Everyone was fast asleep, including Matty, because the weekend went by without one problem.

As he rolled over in his sleep, Matty woke up with a dark shadowy figure standing over his bed. It was about two or three am when Matty woke up to this aberration from his dream come to life.

Matty started to scream, but before he could get it out a hand covered his mouth. Then Shaun pleaded with Matty not to scream. At that moment he seemed so vulnerable that Matty agreed not to scream.

Besides, Matty didn't know how he would explain all of this to his mother and brothers, and his grandpa. So he chose a coward's way out and kept silent.

"Shaun what are you doing in my bedroom?"

"What you think?"

"I don't know."

"I only spent the night so I could see you."

"What? Where is Jacob?"

"He's asleep."

"Why aren't you sleeping?"

"Because I stayed awake so that I can see you."

"What do you want?"

Shaun took off all his clothes and get in the bed beside Matty. Although Shaun wasn't necessarily known for taking bathes every day, it was clear he had cleaned himself up for that night.

With Buddy gone, Matty sort of enjoyed Shaun's company that night. In fact it was the first time that Matty actually desired being with another man.

And Shaun enjoyed Matty so much that he and Matty explored each other in ways they had never done before. Shaun did not leave Matty's bed until he was completely satisfied several times over.

But when Shaun put his clothes on and snuck back into Jacob's bedroom, he didn't know that Matty had made a decision.

That Sunday morning when Matty came out of his room, he ran right into Shaun in the hallway.

"Man get off me," Shaun said as he pushed Matty against the wall.

Shaun's actions sealed the deal for Matty.

A few weeks later, Matty went to Shaun's house to visit with his family, specifically, with his mother.

Matty had decided to come clean about his shame to Shaun's mother. He had decided that he was going to tell the whole story and he didn't care if anyone believed him or not.

And if that was the case, Matty had a secret weapon. Matty had kept a diary of every single time that Shaun had accosted him since the very first time they met on their patio doing the bump.

Matty's book was the truth without adding or taking away anything from it.

Matty walked into the house prepared to bear his soul and to be challenged by the entire family of ten. Matty wanted Shaun's mother to know in intimate detail what Shaun was doing and had done to him.

But there was no one home.

Matty couldn't recall all the details of how it happened, but before he knew it Shaun had coaxed Matty into his parents' bed with their bedroom door closed. He was lying down completely naked on his back. And there Matty was laying prostrate in between Shaun's legs - - when his sister walked in and caught them. Neither of them heard the back door open, let alone the bedroom door.

Matty was mortified!

Shaun tried to stop his sister but she was determined to tell their mother and she did.

Their mother wanted to talk to Matty, but he was so ashamed that he ran home and hid in his dog's house until it got dark and Sadie sent his brothers to find him.

Matty was sitting there crying with his dog King, while he was licking Matty all over his face. But Matty didn't care. Then he reached back to grab his book of evidence.

"It's gone!"

Then Matty really started to cry.

Matty wanted to tell his mother but he just didn't know how and he didn't have the courage to say the words. The saddest part of all, for Matty, is that everyone (at least those who know) thinks it was all his fault and his doing, but the truth is that Matty was the one being pursued and he just got so caught up in it that he didn't know how to get out.

When his mother found him in the dog house that night, Matty had already been crying for hours. His eyes were literally swollen shut.

Their mother started crying too when she saw Matty's swollen eyes.

"Matty, no matter how much it hurts honey, and no matter how much you do not want it to be true, your father is gone."

Matty wanted to tell her that was not why he was crying, but he kept his mouth closed and let his mother believe what she wanted to. And it was true that Matty had not gotten over his father's death.

When they got inside the house Matty fell to his knees in mother's lap once more. He had no more fight in him. Matty cried some more in my mother's lap until he could cry no more. He was tired of crying.

"We are all we have now," Sadie whispered in her youngest son's ear.

Her words resonated in Matty's spirit, but they also did more than that. In his mind, those words defined who he would be for the rest of his life.

"I know it is painful son. It hurts me too, and there is nothing we can do but find a way to go on living."

Matty was silent. But in truth his mother was absolutely right even though she did not know what Matty was up against.

"Your grandmother always told me that 'God don't make no mistakes.' "

"Momma you said that to me when grandma died. What does that mean," Matty asked under his crusty dried tears and swollen eyes.

"I am not sure Matty. I'm just not sure. But one day, He will let us both know. One day."

With that she put some warm compresses on his eyes to make the swelling go down and Matty went to bed.

As Matty lay there in bed thinking about everything that he had endured over the past few years, he realized that all those manhandling events made him start to see men differently than he had before. Then his thoughts turned to one of Shaun's sisters, who he was insanely jealous of but didn't know why.

After a few minutes of walking down memory lane it hit him, he was jealous of her because she had the most handsome and attentive boyfriend in the whole neighborhood. He was tall, formly and well made, had the perfect afro, was bowlegged, and he had a chiseled chest that was accented on either side by sledgehammer arms. Most importantly, he looked innocent but there was a bubbling of bad boy underneath the surface.

Matty was so jealous in fact that one day Shaun's sister gave him her little wallet to hold. Matty being the nosey, curious kid he was looked inside to see what all she had in it. There were some ID cards for both Shaun's sister and her boyfriend, some money, and both of their social security cards.

"Wow a hundred dollar bill."

Matty had never seen a hundred dollar bill before, so he pilfered the c-note and then hid the wallet in another neighbor's backyard. She didn't remember giving it to Matty so he thought he was home free.

But it was just Matty's luck, that neighbor's brother found the wallet in the backyard that same afternoon and gave it to his mother, who sent it around to Shaun's house to give to his sister. Matty was busted. So not only was he a troubled child, but now he was a thief also, and a bad one at that.

Matty fell asleep that night with that thought at the fore front of his mind. As he lay there, a song popped into his mind.

*As we lay, we forgot about tomorrow as we lay*
*As we lay, didn't think about the price we had to pay.*

"How much of me have I given up to become who everybody else wants me to be – sex or no sex? On top of that, I never knew anything about or even cared for sex until they taught me to care for sex."

Matty knew the answer even if he didn't want to know.

He had given up all of himself.

"Is there any me left inside this shell?"

The next morning was a Sunday morning. As usual, after church, at the same family church, the only church, they had ever known, Matty was in the backyard playing basketball by himself.

He managed to talk his mother out of their usual Sunday afternoon visits by insisting he was simply too tired to endure a long Sunday afternoon. His mother agreed because she knew her son was tired, but only if she knew exactly how tired he was.

As Matty was in their backyard trying to teach himself how to dribble and maneuver on the court, he spent more time concentrating on the lack of his brothers' approval he so badly craved on every level, and how he used to try and gain that approval by trying to join in on every sporting event his brothers participated in.

But the truth was that Matty didn't have the natural athletic skills his brothers possessed, but he knew he could learn if they would teach him. But Matty was a bookworm, a nerd, not because he wanted to be but because he had to be as a defense mechanism.

And as unusual, his basketball lesson was interrupted by one of his brothers' friends. Despite what Matty's brothers thought of him, their friends sought Matty's attention, away from his brother's eyes.

In fact, Matty became so popular that the friends of his older brothers stepped in and picked up where Buddy left off.

No matter how Matty tried, he could not keep the older boys from being attracted to him. The harder he tried to stay away from them, the worst things got.

Matty craved partners to play the game with but his partners were not the ones he craved. And it wasn't the game that he craved so much but the camaraderie with his brothers that was the prize for him.

But in his brothers' absence, their friends were more than willing to fill the void in Matty's life. It wasn't long before Matty had his veritable pick of any one of long list of unwanted Shauns in his life.

After that Matty was forever running through the neighborhood and it wasn't for the exercise. Those guys all had an advantage over him. They were older, bigger, and stronger. Matty was tall, but not tall enough, and he had lost some weight doing all that running, but not enough.

And he was getting a crash course in sexual intercourse that he neither wanted nor desired but that didn't matter either because it desired him.

The problem for Matty was he didn't know if *it* was the sex or those boys or a combination thereof.

Either way he was on the losing end of that stick. And the craziest part is that his brothers never knew.

But life had to go on, and that it did.

"This can't go on like this," Matty said to himself.

He had just walked into their front yard, when his brother Claude was talking to one of his friends.

Matty got the feeling that conversation with Claude was not the real reason he was there, but Matty didn't care. He kept on walking toward the door.

But before he could get that far, he heard Claude's friend say, "Man I got to go. I'll holler at you later."

Then he motioned for Matty to follow him.

Matty shook his head no, but Vaulden was having it.

If Matty was being honest with himself, he had always liked Vaulden, his brother Claude's friend, but he never would have approached Vaulden because he was freakin' gorgeous.

He was high yellow with beautiful curly black hair, tall and thin. He was the epitome of a smooth criminal because his voice was soft and strong, and he carried himself with the kind of confidence that only goes with good looks.

Matty shook his head no, but Vaulden gave him a look like no was not an option. Matty turned around and followed.

Vaulden went in the house first to make sure that it was clear. Then he came to the front door and motioned for Matty to come in. Reluctantly, Matty did.

Matty stood there looking in his beautiful green eyes. He didn't know what to do.

Vaulden took of his pants to reveal a surprising revelation.

Matty stripped.

Vaulden gave him a look of approval.

Then he slowly caressed Matty's man boobs.

Matty wanted to teach Vaulden's beautiful body but instead he stood there scared to act on what he desired to do.

"Where do you want it?" Vaulden asked Matty.

Matty laid down on Vaulden's bed, face down.

Within seconds, Vaulden was riding him furiously.

It didn't take long before Vaulden was releasing himself all over Matty, and he was moaning in total satisfaction.

"This is our secret," Vaulden stated.

Matty wanted to say, you'll ask me to keep quiet, but clearly all of you "guys" gossip like girls.

So then Matty thought, "Why haven't my brothers said anything to me or momma?"

None of it made sense.

Matty never saw Vaulden again period. It was like he disappeared.

Shortly after that rendezvous, through a series of unfortunate events, Shaun's parents separated, and half of the family moved away and the other half stayed with their dad. This turned out to be a double blessing and a triple curse for Matty.

Unfortunately, that personal family separation set off a mass exodus from the neighborhood. Once again, Matty was on the short end of the stick or at least it felt that way for Matty. So he traded one set of strangers for a new set of strangers.

## Chapter 8

One day after the house-split, Matty was visiting Shaun's sister when he heard a lot of noise and ruckus outside.

He walked over to the kitchen window expecting to see eight is enough and some more kids descending on the house.

Instead, what he saw looked like a small gang of street performers standing at the end of the driveway. Actually, they looked more like a group of clowns and Matty kept looking around to see their car with the big key on it.

Not a one had the courage to knock on the door.

Matty had to get a closer look, maybe because those kids were everything he was not. He had long ago resigned himself to the fact that he was a nerd.

The only thing that kept Matty from being a geek was the fact that he didn't have one of those plastic pen holders in his shirt pocket full of ink pens all turned the same way. But everything else, Matty had.

In his defense, he had lost everything or everyone he had ever cared about. So his brains were all he had left to nurture, and so he did just that. And in doing so, he began to look the part.

He had the big collar white dress shirts, the pants jacked up over his stomach and he wore glasses. And of course had the nickname butterball given to him by the mother of his arch nemesis, even though he no longer looked like a turkey. Still, he felt that way.

Besides, Matty decided if he could make himself look less attractive, then maybe he would be less appealing to those around him.

"What has it gotten me anyway?" A rhetorical question to which even Matty didn't know the answer.

Those kids were wearing strange garb with wild haircuts, and they spoke a completely different language. When they noticed Matty staring out the window at them, they just stared at each other for a few minutes until Matty gathered up the courage to walk outside and inspect the group up close.

It was practically a biology experiment. Actually, Matty was really more intrigued than anything else.

"I hate to say this but they all look like they are dressed in some sort of tribal garb – bright, colorful, authentically designed tribal garb," Matty whispered under his voice.

"What did you say man?" He heard one of them yell at him.

Still Matty was too intrigued to stop now.

The only thing they lacked was the painted facial markings. But then again they didn't need any.

As Matty got closer he observed something that made him laugh to the point that he could not hide it.

They were some of the absolute ugliest teenagers he had ever seen in his life. They were so ugly that he started laughing at their ugliness and they were clearly offended.

But still Matty kept walking around them in circles, not wanting to overlook one single detail of what was before his eyes.

Some of them had what looked like belts draped around their bodies similar to a sash a beauty queen would wear in bright pinks, blues, and greens. A few even had bags attached to their belts in the back like they were carrying supplies across long distances and rugged terrain.

Others had on baggy pants in various order – some short, some extra long, some mid-calf, and some that just seemed to wrap around their bodies forever on end.

But what was truly amazing was that Matty could not tell where the clothes stopped and their bodies began on anyone of them.

And to top it all off, they all were wearing Jeepers in psychedelic colors that Matty had never seen in any store. A couple of them even had on Jeepers that looked like they were hand-painted.

"Wow," Matty said.

To them it probably sounded like he was disgusted. But in actuality Matty was quite impressed.

Their shirts were no different. Some of them were so tight that the threads looked like they were going to start popping out one at a time at any moment. Others barely covered their chests, let alone their stomachs. One even looked like he was wearing an actual corset as his shirt.

And their haircuts, man, they were as colorful as their garb. They looked like mathematical shapes straight out of

Geometry. If Matty had studied their haircuts before his final exam a few years ago he might have made a B instead of a D+.

The best way to describe this group is to say that they all looked just like characters out of *Michael Jackson's Thriller* video before *Thriller* ever existed. That is no exaggeration.

As Matty was finishing his investigation, the loudest and almost ugliest of the entire group shouted, "Is Norma at home?"

Although it wasn't his house or his business, Matty responded, "Don't no Norma live here," with the same attitude that had been presented to him.

This was a new Matty. They didn't know him and he wasn't interested in knowing them.

All they saw was this semi-thin kid wearing glasses, a pink Izod shirt, and a pair of beige khaki shirts with some penny loafers.

They didn't know Matty had a sorted history.

As Matty prepared to walk back into the house, he looked up to see this kid, this one lone guy, standing away from the crowd, sort of attempting to be incognito like he was purposefully trying to separate himself from them and not be seen at the same time.

But he was clearly watching what was going on, and now Matty was watching him.

He was freaking gorgeous!

Matty tried to pretend not to notice but he was not good at pretending.

This guy was completely black, not just black, but pitch black, blacker than Shaun.

"Damn," Matty said. "I didn't know they made them that black."

But it was a beautiful black, like a black pearl. He also had beautifully toned black skin, completely even and unblemished, again just like a pearl, and it looked as smooth too. His teeth were white, incandescently white without the hint of a flaw.

His face was in stark contrast to his teeth in that it screamed danger, intrigue, and lust.

Matty was attracted without trying to be and without knowing what attraction truly meant, on this level.

Worse yet, Matty didn't have a soul that he could ask about the meaning of attraction. His only two confidants were gone before they had a chance to give him any life lessons as an adult.

Darryl, was the black guy's name. He also had the perfect afro – not too long, not too short, perfectly round and it too was jet black. It was the perfect mix of black on black.

The only obvious drawback, not that anyone cared what Matty thought, was that he was much shorter than Matty was. Darryl was about 5'5."

But his small frame was completed by beautiful hairless bowlegs, not too big, but strong and shapely.

This was all in contrast to Matty because even though he was no longer as fat, he was tall - - big and tall.

Then Matty noticed the most unnatural sight.

Darryl was wearing a full-on leather jacket - in the summer!

Matty walked over to him, and said, "What the hell are you doing with a leather jacket on in the middle of summer?"

His posse burst into laughter and so did he. Matty didn't mean to cause such a stir and meanwhile he was standing there feeling stupid.

"None of your damn business man," Darryl finally replied after the hearty laughter.

By that point Matty was no longer interested and turned to walk away.

"Hey," he yelled after Matty.

Matty kept walking.

"Hey boy, what's your name?"

Matty turned around, walked back over to him, and got close enough to give him a kiss. But instead Matty whispered in his ear, "You don't impress with all of your friends around to make you look like a bad ass."

For the second time, Matty turned to walk away. Still Darryl yelled out, "You still didn't answer my question."

Although Matty tried to resist this personal intrusion, his body was not nearly as strong.

"Matty."

"What?"

"My name is Matty."

Matty could not help but to have disdain in his voice because he was angry that his body responded to this intrusion so easily. But the intrusion didn't stop there.

"Hey Matty, can I get your number?"

Those words made it feel like the summer heat melted the pavement right where Matty stood. And his sneakers were bronzed into the tar like the baby boots he never had.

Matty stood there unable to move or maybe he didn't want to move. He wasn't sure.

But, when his mind became unstuck, then and only then could he walk away from the open, but unrequited request.

Over the next few weeks, Matty saw black beauty more often than he would have liked. The only problem with this fact was that Matty's mind told him one thing, but his body told him something else.

However, it was odd that before a few weeks ago they didn't know each other existed, and suddenly Matty couldn't stop seeing him.

But Darryl wasn't coming to the neighborhood to see Matty, or at least that's what he said.

Yet, despite Matty's mental objections, he felt his body betraying him more and more each time he saw him.

If you were to ask Matty, he would not be able to tell you the day he gave in to that original request or even why he did, but he did.

The good news was because of that decision he at least had something to do for the summer. It wasn't a Gonzales-type family vacation but something was better than nothing. And Matty had had enough of nothing for long enough.

However, there was some good news in the midst of all the chaos.

Matty used to be jealous of his wealthy friends who lived in the suburbs, particularly Gonzales.

Matty never knew his first name. It wasn't important at the time.

But Gonzales was this scrawny kid with this wild, curly, black hair that flopped every time he moved and hung down in his eyes, just like a sheep dog.

And what first caught Matty's eye, even though he didn't understand why, was that Gonzales used to wear the tightest old jeans that looked like he was going to burst out of them at any moment; and, they were high-waters! But they gripped his ass like a girl.

He looked poor as hell.

Yet Matty was fascinated by Gonzales.

Then one day Mrs. Sweet, their 6th grade teacher, Matty's favorite teacher ever, asked everyone to tell the class what they were going to do that summer.

This was going to be their final summer as elementary kids before they started junior high school.

Incidentally, that day was the last time Matty was going to see Gonzales because they had been assigned to new separate, rival schools for the 7th grade, schools that just happened to be each other's arch rivals.

When it was Gonzales' turn, Matty was stunned at what he was hearing.

But Gonzales' words just rolled off his lips so matter-of-factly that Matty knew it was true.

But at the same time, it was clear to Matty that Gonzales didn't really want to tell the class his summer plans. He seemed to be genuinely embarrassed by it all.

Nonetheless, his summer vacation plans became the standard by which Matty judged all summer vacations.

That summer, Gonzales' parents had planned a different two week trip for each month of the three-month summer.

The other weeks would be spent with the nanny taking them to the movies, the library, and other stuff like that, as Gonzales put it.

Although Matty would never see Gonzales again, he changed Matty's life forever.

Matty could never decide exactly why he was jealous. Was it the trips, his parents, or the fact that he carried his family's wealth so well that no one would have ever thought for one second they were rolling in dough?

Years later, Matty was still jealous of Gonzales.

Darryl was no Gonzales but still he had something that was his and his alone, something that he didn't share with anyone.

At the same time, Darryl was separate from the rest of Matty's life – separate from his school and from his family.

And the only thing it cost Matty was the telephone.

Day, night, late night, and early morning – Matty was on the telephone talking to Darryl, which was black beauty's name. He went to bed with him and he woke up with him - - on the phone.

But this relationship was a one way street of Matty's choosing.

"I can't have no man calling my house without raising all kinds of questions from my brothers or my mother."

Worse yet, Matty had no idea what the hell he was doing anyway so he damn sure didn't have any answers to unwanted questions.

But despite all of these obstacles, Matty was happier than he had been in quite a while.

Yet, all he kept hearing was, "Damn, get off the phone. Momma, make Matty get off the phone so someone else could use it! Man, you ain't got nothin' better to do than talk on the phone all day like a girl?"

Everyone was complaining except for their mother.

Since the complaints were not coming from their mother, Matty didn't care and he didn't understand. He thought they all wanted him to be happy and focused on a regular activity that would keep him out of trouble and out of their way.

All Matty could hear was their mother forever saying, "You need to find something for you to do to keep you out of trouble."

Well Matty had done just that and since he had started talking to Darryl he was staying out of trouble. So Matty honestly didn't understand why everyone was complaining.

For the first summer ever since their grandmother died, Matty had a regularly scheduled activity that happened to be fun and it brought him great joy. And best of all, it didn't cost anything.

Besides that before Matty started using the telephone every single day to talk to Darryl for hours on end, Matty could not recall anyone in their house ever using the telephone before he started talking on it.

"Hell, the phone was gathering dust before I started using it because it rang so little, if ever."

"Matty, don't make me come in there and handle that mouth for you," their mother used to yell from her favorite spot in the den.

It was a chance that Matty was willing to take because he had at least fifteen years' worth of stored up talk to let out, and he had found somebody who was willing to listen to him for a change, and without all the subterfuge.

So despite all of their protests Matty was laying in the floor in the bathroom for some privacy on the phone. Stretching the cord to the limits in the backyard to spend time with his other best friend, their German shepherd, King, Matty was on the phone. Hiding under his mother's bed, Matty was on the phone. Wherever he could find privacy he was on the telephone with Darryl.

And the real beauty was that no one knew who Matty was talking to the entire time.

But from the very beginning Matty always thought it was strange that after he dialed those familiar digits a different voice answered every single time.

"Hello!" The person on the other end always screamed at Matty like he was interrupting something. Matty was undeterred.

"May I speak to Darryl?"

"Who?" Matty heard that every single time without fail.

But instead of someone hanging up the telephone, Matty would hear a lot of commotion in the background.

Next, someone would yell out, "Sista."

"Hello."

"Hello."

"Who is Sista?" Matty asked Darryl.

"Where the hell you been man?"

"Hello to you to. You didn't answer my question."

"What question?"

"Who is Sista?"

"Nothin' man. Ain't no big deal."

"I wanted to come see you."

"Why?"

"I missed seeing you."

"You didn't act like it when you hung up on me."

"I know."

"I outta kick your ass."

Matty started laughing.

"Ain't shit funny man."

"Why can't you just say you like me like a normal person."

"Cuz man. You comin' over or what?"

"Yes. I'll see you soon."

The only thing that was left was for Matty to get his allowance from his mother. Now that would take some real work.

Within the hour, Matty was on the bus. But Matty was concerned if his mother was feeling okay because he got his allowance within lightning speed compared to her normal timing.

The bus ride, allowance, and everything that came with the two were regular occurrences in Matty's life after he met Darryl.

The phone calls, the strange names, and dialogues were all new additions and welcome distractions into Matty's otherwise drab life.

But it didn't just all happen overnight. It was a long, drawn out process that took months of work to accomplish.

Matty's first trip to Darryl's was a complete surprise to both of them.

Matty had spent weeks secretly checking and rechecking the directions, but he had no exact day when he was going to put his plan into action.

Then one day he wasn't on the phone.

"I guess they aren't complaining today," Matty said. He was talking about his brothers.

Sadie lifted one of Matty's many restrictions and he got this crazy idea about the same time.

Their mother wasn't very good at counting days when it came to punishments and she wasn't very good at being reminded either. Reminding her of the days only made the days longer not shorter. So Matty just had to wait. But she wasn't Matty's problem.

The problem was of a different matter. But it was still a problem that slowed Matty down, temporarily, but it did not stop his planning. In fact, Matty didn't think about it again until…

Even though he knew it was going to take three different buses to get to the other side of town, the longer he rode the more he wondered why.

Although Matty was riding inside the bus, he could feel the rotation of every single tire taking him closer to a world he had never known or knew existed until a few months ago.

"But how different could it be?" Matty asked.

Still this was not like his bus rides to South Charlotte, which he had occasion to ride a few times, outside of his obligatory rides to school.

The bus ride to South Charlotte was like being on a luxury tourist ride compared to the bus ride he had purposefully and secretly chosen to take that day.

What Matty didn't know at the time he made that decision was that it was one of the most dangerous decisions he could ever make.

Anyway, the buses going to South Charlotte would meander in and out of beautiful tree-lined neighborhoods with huge oak trees that covered the streets and houses like shaded canopies.

Manicured lawns, polished cars, mothers walking children in strollers, others jogging along the sidewalk, and houses that proudly stood up as the buses passed by that appeared to be smiling to show off their uniqueness, those were all staples of those neighborhoods during the South Charlotte bus ride or tour of homes as it were.

Even though Matty was less than a temporary resident of all and none of those neighborhoods, he could not help but feel a part of them while he was on that bus. Except that South Charlotte residents didn't ride the bus, back then anyway.

Even the streets were different on the South Charlotte bus ride as compared to that bus ride across town.

They were smoother without any potholes whatsoever and were freshly painted. The asphalt even looked newer, blacker, almost unused at all.

And the bus was different too. The buses going into South Charlotte were clean, freshly washed, and had no graffiti on them. And there were no torn or tattered seat cushions. Their cushions were soft, plush, and firm that almost gripped your butt purposefully.

That South Charlotte bus ride would have been a picturesque window, except for one minor detail - - all the riders were black middle-aged women wearing maid uniforms.

They had the finest ride to the job Matty hated most in the whole wide world for one particular reason.

The pride Matty felt was the same pride that was used to try and destroy those beautiful black women with care-worn hands, beautiful crowns of hair, and soft but strong faces that masked their anger better than any plastic mask ever could.

Matty saw his mother in those women, women that raised white kids to be proper children far better than their own parents ever could.

Nonetheless that was not Matty's new bus ride.

The ride to Darryl's was different but Matty looked forward to it more than he did the ride to South Charlotte.

He didn't care that he was riding on a crowded, dirty bus with graffiti written all over the walls, and torn seats with the stuffing coming out of the cushions.

He didn't even care that the driver seemed to be hitting every single pothole on every street on the route.

He was excited about this bus ride. Hell, he was almost giddy.

It was a true tale of two cities and Matty was the common denominator that was clearly not a citizen of either one.

He was too poor to be a member of South Charlotte and he was too rich to be a member of North Charlotte. Once again Matty was caught in the middle. He had a brief flash of the closet fiasco, but he dismissed it.

Matty remembered what his mother always told him, "God protects babies and fools."

Well baby, Matty must have been a fool and God was protecting him because he had no idea what he had committed to doing until it was too late.

The first part of the trip was not that bad, and not much different than his last bus ride. But the further away he got from downtown, the more things were different.

"Oh my God. I had no idea."

Matty's face was plastered to the window because he was stunned by the squalor of it all.

"How could people be made to live in such abysmal conditions?"

Matty was completely shocked by what he was seeing.

When he finally realized how bad things really were, he started praying.

No sooner was the thought out of his mind, he heard a voice, clear as day say, "That's what you should have done first before you started planning this little jaunt."

Matty whipped his head around immediately to see who was whispering those words in his ear. There was no one there.

Then he felt a warmth come over him but it wasn't a scary kind of warmth. He had only felt it once before.

He had the urge to jump up and start screaming like they do on the cartoons to distract people. And when the bus driver stopped the bus, Matty would jump off and run back home. The only problem with that plan was that he didn't know his way back home without being on the bus.

The more he rode, the more terror griped him. But the more the terror wanted to rise in his spirit, the more the warmth flooded his body until he was at a place of total peace.

The bus was stopping and starting, and people were getting on and off.

Matty was sure he looked stupid as he tried to understand what was happening around him and inside of him.

But that was probably a good thing, because it made him fit right in with the crowd. He was a little sweaty, but still he was at peace.

And the more the engine revved up and down, the closer Matty came to the for real deep in da' hood, sho' nuf roughest part of the Queen city. And despite all the internal turmoil, Matty was happy to do it.

Now if that ain't a fool?

It was too late for him to come to his senses now.

Besides, he had come this far and spent the last of his weekly allowance to get there, so he figured he might as well go the rest of the way and see what he shouldn't see.

As he looked out the window with great anticipation, he recognized the marker that the operator had given him on the phone, a granite carved archway that served as the gateway to North Charlotte.

It was a remarkable piece of architectural beauty against the backdrop of destitute surroundings, which made Matty realize that he had reached the end of the line – the bus line for his trip.

The rest of the way was up to him.

When the bus got to the final stop, Matty pulled the cord, and the driver let him off at the next designated stop.

Matty almost said, "See you later," before he realized this was not a defined relationship like he had with his school bus driver.

He had learned how to pull the cord to stop the bus by watching all the people who got off the bus before him pull the overhead cord when they were ready for the bus driver to stop at their particular location.

And there were a lot of people who had gotten off before Matty.

That is one of the reasons why the ride took so long and the bus was still not empty by the time he got off.

The rest of the trip was easy, with the exception of the end result still looming.

Nevertheless, things had gone just the way Matty had planned, according to the map he had committed to memory, per the instructions given to him over the phone by the bus operator.

When he got off the city bus, he walked about two or three city blocks, turned left, and walked about another block or two. The house was down on the right on Woodside Drive.

As he continued deeper into the neighborhood he noticed that the few stores in the area all had bars on the windows.

"Wow," Matty said taking in the scene.

But even stranger than his surroundings was the fact that he felt no fear even though he was completely out of his element.

The neighborhood was so neglected that it almost looked like a shanty town but the bare bones of the neighborhood said to Matty that this was once an affluent area.

But today the houses were all falling apart, literally.

The porches were all broken down and missing boards and steps. The handrails, where those few were still standing, were all broken. The doors were hanging off the hinges. There were broken windows in every house and plastic window coverings were the neighborhood's standard decor. Most of the houses did not even have screen doors, and the few that did have them, the screens were all torn and hanging out everywhere. And there was barely any grass growing in any of the yards. But there were lots of children playing happily everywhere Matty looked.

This was clearly a far different experience from anything he had ever seen. Before he reached the house, he had not paid attention to the scouting party that had alerted Darryl to his presence.

In a way, they actually did Matty a favor.

But the first thing he noticed about the house was not the structure, but it was the yard.

The structure was similar to all the others in the neighborhood. The yard was almost completely covered in red clay dirt - the exact red dirt that his mother used to whop his ass for playing in on Sunday afternoons in his church clothes.

But he could not turn around now. He had come too far.

The worst was still yet to come.

Finally, Matty took his first unsure step onto that front porch. A few more and he would be at the door.

Before he could utter one word, he was greeted by a very unhappy Darryl, black as ever with a heavy towel draped around his neck almost to his stomach.

"What the fuck you doing here, man?"

Matty was stunned, truly stunned by Darryl's words but he tried not to let it show how hurt he was.

But how can one not let such words impact your spirit?

It took Matty a little while before he gathered his thoughts enough to respond to the question.

"I came to see you. I thought it would be a good surprise. But, if you don't want to see me I will leave." Matty turned to walk off the porch.

"Wait a minute man," his voice was much softer now.

Matty didn't say anything. He just decided not to take that final step off the porch.

While he was waiting, Matty had attracted a small gathering.

There was a whole host of little kids standing around his legs looking up at him, smiling and welcoming him to the neighborhood.

They were happier to see Matty than Darryl was.

And their happiness made Matty smile.

They started laughing and talking as if they were all old friends.

One little girl in particular was so dirty that she looked as if she had not had a bath in weeks. She was wearing a pink dress that was faded and worn out, and the lace was almost torn from the dress around the fringe and the sleeves.

She had a thick head of hair that was loosely platted in pigtails all over her head; and, her head was full of lint, like you would find on a dark sweater that had been washed incorrectly.

But there was something remarkable about that little girl.

Underneath the dirt, grime, and torn clothing was this beautiful little girl with the happiest smile Matty had ever seen, and she had a head of hair that any woman would be happy to wear as her crown and glory.

This little girl made Matty forget everything else that had just happened.

Matty never saw her again but he also never forgot her truly happy face in the midst of the worst surroundings. That was a lesson worth remembering.

"Come on in man," Darryl's words startled Matty and the kids.

For that split second, Matty had completely forgotten about him and his surroundings.

As he started back up the steps, he looked back at his little fan base, particularly his dirty little raggedy Ann doll.

They waved goodbye and so did Matty, but with a heavy heart.

Just as quick as they were there, they were all gone.

"We entertain angels unaware." His grandmother's words popped into his head.

He walked into the living room and took a seat very near the front door, trying not to be surprised by his sparse surroundings.

As he sat there taking it all in, he wasn't the only one taking things in.

When he finally took his eyes off his surroundings and started to focus on the people, he realized that there was a whole other group of people checking him out as well, like he was some sort of alien.

Matty didn't understand it.

He was clean. He had on a pair of khakis and a turquoise, button-down, collar shirt, clean socks, and a pair of penny loafers. But they were still staring.

Matty started looking at his attire to see if something was wrong.

He didn't see anything that looked out of place.

When he looked up again, he noticed there were three or four people peeping from around the kitchen corner staring into the living room at him.

He tried to pretend not to notice, but every time he started to turn his head towards the tiny hallway he could not help but here the bumbling noise of people scrambling to not be seen.

Then he noticed that there was a second group also staring.

The second group of two or three more people was peeping from the opposite side of the hallway from around the bedroom corner.

He whispered, "How many people live in this house?"

Then he started at laughing at the thought of it all.

As best he could tell there were only two bedrooms.

So he was really confused but he shouldn't have been because they used to live six to a two bedroom apartment that was smaller than that house.

Then when Darryl came into the room, everybody on both sides of the hallway jumped back as if they had not been staring at all.

"What the hell ya'll doing? Damn! Ya'll act like ya'll ain't never seen nobody before." Darryl barked like he was the one in charge.

Matty couldn't help but laugh.

He tried to see if any of the people staring at him were part of his original cast of characters from the day of their meeting, but he wasn't sure.

Maybe this was a whole other group that knew of Matty because they had heard his name so many times on the telephone.

Darryl and Matty walked outside only to walk around to the small back porch, in the shade.

Why didn't we just go down the hallway and through the kitchen, I could see it from where I was sitting, Matty thought. But he dared not ask the question.

Compared to Darryl's family, the Pottishear's were rich.

"Isn't it funny how only a few degrees of separation divides us all, mentally, that is."

"What you say man?"

"Nothing," Matty replied.

If they only knew? Matty thought.

Then Matty had to ask the question that was burning in his mouth. "Who was that pretty little girl in the yard?"

"What girl?" Darryl asked.

"Are you always so damn gruff?" Matty shouted back at him.

"Whacha you talkin' bout man?"

"I'm talking about the nasty attitude you have every time I ask you a question. Listen if it bothers you that much that I came over here I can go home because you are not the person I have been talking to on the telephone for the last few weeks. That is the person I came to see."

"Man shut the hell up and sit down."

"I'm going home."

"You ain't going nowhere. Sit your ass down."

Despite how he said it, there was a great deal of passion behind those words. It actually sounded like a plea for Matty to stay. So he relented, started smiling, and sat back down.

"So are you going to tell me?"

"Tell you what?"

"The little girl's name."

"Man what little girl you talking about?" His words were softer now.

"The little girl that was wearing the pink dress when I first got here."

"I don't know."

The tension between them eased considerably after that little exchange. They sat there and laughed and talked for hours until the shade moved to the front porch. Meanwhile, the telephone inside the house was ringing off the hook.

Each time the telephone stopped ringing Matty heard different voices say the same thing, "She ain't here!"

Click."

Every now then Matty and Darryl would lock eyes with each other with a longing to touch one another that was so thick you could cut it like a piece of cake, but they couldn't.

They were still being watched by the guards inside the house, who only took a break to answer the telephone, a telephone, which by the way, appeared to be more of a nuisance or intrusion, at least while Matty was there.

Matty heard somebody in the house say, "He talks strange."

But Matty didn't take offense because he knew what they meant. They meant that Matty used proper English instead of talking in the street vernacular they were accustomed to hearing.

"What made you ask me for my phone number that first day I saw you?"

"Damn, man you sho' nuf nosey."

"Darryl, if I didn't know any better I would swear you were blushing."

They both started laughing so hard that Matty almost peed in his clothes.

It was so funny because Darryl was so black that you couldn't see him blushing even if he wanted you to.

Yet, as strange as it sounded, there was an expression on his face that still seemed to indicate that he was blushing.

They started laughing again.

"It's okay. You don't have to tell me that you like me. I can see it all over your black ass face."

Matty didn't know how or why but for whatever reason he had catapulted to the top of Darryl's notch-on-a-belt list, except that they had not done the deed.

Matty wasn't sure how they were supposed to do the deed. Frankly he didn't care about the deed, based on his past experiences.

As much as Matty liked Darryl, he had no interest in sex. He just wanted some companionship.

Anyway, they were having such a good time that both of them had forgotten about the time. It was starting to get dark.

Matty jumped up. "I've got to go home."

"I know. Hold on and I'll walk you to the bus stop."

When Darryl came back outside they started walking toward the bus stop.

It was almost romantic, like boyfriend and girlfriend.

Only thing is that Matty couldn't figure who was which.

Out of the blue Matty heard laughter behind them. He turned around to see a small contingency walking behind them.

"Do you always have a posse with you everywhere you go?"

"Shut up man," Darryl was smiling while he said it.

"Are you trying to hold my hand?"

"Shut up man."

They walked hand in hand for as long as the darkness shielded their identities. This was all helped by the several street lamps that were out until they got closer to the main street.

Before they reached the very end of the darkness, Darryl jerked Matty so hard that his body spun around to face him.

And without the slightest notice he did it.

He stood on his tiptoes and kissed Matty square in the mouth. But this kiss was not like kissing Buddy. It was soft like kissing Stephanie.

There was no time to talk about it because somebody in the posse, the posse that had gone from being a security team to being an advance party yelled, "Here comes the bus."

Matty sprinted to the bus stop not to miss it. He barely made it.

The lights on the bus were extremely bright compared to the nighttime darkness.

Matty tried to rush to pay his fare and find a seat so he could look out the window and wave at Darryl for as long as possible before he disappeared from his eyesight.

But it was too late.

By the time Matty got into his seat Darryl was already out of sight.

Matty had never seen the city like this before, at night that is.

It was the most adventurous day he had ever had.

It was a good day.

The bus ride home was sort of the icing on the cake.

Matty enjoyed looking out the window and seeing all the various lights of the city.

It reminded him of Christmas. It was beautiful and exciting to see.

This was all so totally different from the boring life Matty was living in the near-suburban-type subdivision they were living in.

And the bus was full of people that reminded Matty of characters from a television show.

There was a guy sneaking drinks from a brown paper bag. Several older ladies wearing maid uniforms were sitting together. Some kids were sitting near him laughing loudly and playing music on a boom box.

The bus driver told them to cut the noise several times.

There were even a few white guys on the bus.

It was all so exciting and this was only the first bus ride! There were two more buses to go.

When they arrived back downtown to what Matty learned was the square, the center of downtown, it was busier then he would have ever imagined.

It reminded him of a scene from a book they were reading last year in advanced English but the name escaped him for the moment.

People were coming and going from all four corners of the square – north, south, east, and west.

And they were of every kind, shape, size, and type of person imaginable. It was a veritable smorgasbord of people.

Matty was having such a wonderful time people watching that he almost missed his second bus connection.

Then, the farther away they got from downtown the sadder Matty became because he was returning to his boring sort-of-suburban life that had no excitement and no flashing lights.

Although people were still coming and going, the remainder of the ride home was more of the same - - boring.

Matty was wondering what he would do with himself for the next week, until he got his next allowance.

Then somewhere near the middle of the week, their mother dropped a bombshell on all the boys.

"Matty, I want you to stay around the house this entire weekend. I am going out Friday night and I don't want you going anywhere. Your brothers are going to be here to babysit you. And to make sure you all do what I say, no one is getting their allowance until Monday."

"Why can't I go on Saturday?"

"Because we have church on Sunday, and you are hard enough to get out of bed without having any extracurricular activities to distract you."

And that was that.

When their mother spoke they all listened and there was no changing her mind - - ever.

It didn't matter to her that they all moped around the house the remainder of the week. Sadie was completely oblivious to that kind of behavior.

"So you coming over here this weekend?"

It took Matty a long time to answer.

"No." That's all he said.

Darryl hung up on him.

Matty waited for him to call me back. He never did.

"That's pretty awkward for a guy who didn't want me to come to house because he never invited me, now he expects to see me every weekend. I guess me deciding to give him my phone number after months of him begging wasn't enough."

Friday night came and Matty and all his brothers were all supposed to hang around the house but none of them did.

Actually it looked like they were having a block party down the street and Matty went down for a minute or two to see what was going on.

But he didn't feel much like dancing after that. So he made his way through the crowd and walked home. Nobody even noticed he was gone.

When he got home, he was all alone.

So Matty turned on their 12-foot stereo that had these disco lights on each end that blinked according to the beat of the music.

*Play that funky music*
*white boy.*

*Play that funky music*
*right.*

*Play that funky music*
*white boy.*

*Lay down and boogey*
*and play that funky music 'til you*
*die.*

Matty remembered that was the song they were playing on the bus when the driver told them to turn down the music a few days ago.

So Matty was dancing through the house, singing, and thinking 'bout Darryl when the door opened.

He didn't pay much attention until he was pent down on the living room sofa.

Shaun had followed Matty home.

Matty looked Shaun square in the eye.

He did exactly what Shaun wanted him to do without a fight.

It lasted for more than an hour.

Shaun held Matty's nose and his mouth so he couldn't breathe until…

To add insult to injury, after he was finished, Shaun said to Matty, "It's about time you start to enjoy me like I enjoy you."

Matty steadied his face.

"What did you do with my book?" Matty blurted it out.

"What book?"

"The book that proves everything you have done to me."

Shaun back handed Matty so hard that it knocked Matty back on the living room sofa.

"If you ever tell anyone about this I will kill you."

Matty didn't have to respond. He was already dead inside to Shaun.

After that happened Matty made it his business to see Darryl practically every weekend after that for almost a year, with a few exceptions like getting in trouble in school or other family engagements, which there were a lot of those.

The Minwhites were about as large as the Pottishears. They were not as rich as the Pottishears but they were much happier than his father's side of the family. And they loved Sadie and her handsome boys.

In fact, Matty still had to run around hiding from all his girl cousins.

One time, Matty was running from his cousins and he ran into the house.

The sight made him stop dead in his tracks.

Matty was so intrigued, in fact, that he took a seat in the kitchen. His presence went undetected because Aunt Roseanna was hard of hearing, so he thought.

"Matty, I see you sitting over there starring at your old Aunt Roseanna."

Matty's mouth fell open.

"Close your mouth baby before you swallow a fly."

For that moment, Matty thought he was sitting on the back porch with his grandma, which made sense, because Aunt Roseanna was his grandmother's oldest living sister and the last one of the original family on her grandma's side.

His great grandfather, Aunt Roseanna's father, had died a few years back from cancer.

He and Matty had a heart to heart before he died, but the most memorable part of that conversation still sticks in Matty's mind today.

In fact, they were at a family reunion when his great-grandpa decided to have a conversation with him.

"Grandpa, why won't you have the surgery to remove the cancer?" Matty asked.

"Can't do that son."

"Why not grandpa?"

"Matty if I let them cut me, the air will hit that cancer and it will spread like wildfire. I have a much better chance not letting them cut me."

His great grandpa lived about another seven years after he and Matty had that conversation.

"But I digress," Matty said to himself.

Aunt Roseanna kept right on cooking, which was the amazing reason why Matty stooped in the first place. Aunt Roseanna was cooking with a magnifying glass.

Matty sat right there the rest of the afternoon talking to Aunt Roseanna.

They talked about everything under the sun. And she kept right on cooking an entire feast for over 50 people using that magnifying glass.

"Aunt Roseanna why won't you let everybody buy you some glasses?"

"Matty baby that don't make no sense when I'm getting ready to die."

Matty's big brown eyes widened and filled with water, like a pool.

"Come here baby. You don't have to be sad. Its' okay."

"It's not okay Aunt Roseanna. You said you were going to die."

"Matty everybody has to die. And dying is okay after you have lived a full life because we get to go see God and Jesus."

"Is that where grandma, daddy, and great grandpa went?"

"They sure did baby. So don't you cry because you will see them all again someday."

"But I miss them so much."

"Matty your grandma and daddy talk to you all the time, so does Jesus."

Aunt Roseanna pointed right to Matty's broken heart.

'They are always right here inside of you."

Matty was so happy he gave Aunt Roseanna the biggest kiss ever.

He got ready to run outside and play. But he remembered one thing.

"Aunt Roseanna, if you die will you come into my heart too?"

"If I'm there now baby, I will be there then too."

"You got a deal."

They smiled and Matty went back outside to let his cousins chase him some more.

After that day, Matty made it a point to never be alone again.

As for Darryl, Matty loved hanging out with him because sex was not a part of their relationship and that was fine with Matty.

Matty wasn't ready for sex although he had been having it for many years, except for Buddy.

So they never did the deed.

Matty was glad they didn't because from what he had seen sex only came with shame and abuse, and he was the one on the receiving end of both.

It was two more weeks before Matty could see Darryl because of other commitments made by his mother. But as soon as he could get on that bus heading north, he was on it.

While he was sitting on the bus trying to figure out what's life all about, he remembered this quote from English Literature that he never understood until that day.

It was written by this guy named Pascal. He said, "All of our reasoning ends in surrender to feeling."

Out of nowhere, Matty heard this couple arguing and before any of the riders knew it, she smacked the shit of him right there on the bus.

Then she said, "Now pull yourself together so you can get this job and start taking care of me and this baby. You wanted me now you got me. This was your doing so you are gonna' do right by me."

That's when Matty realized that living wouldn't be so hard if it wasn't for the day to day minutia that gets in the way. But that girl was living proof that Pascal was right.

He couldn't help but think that entire show was all meant for him to see for some reason.

But for now Matty was happy to be ignorant and he was glad that Darryl didn't need him in his life that way.

"Damn, I ain't got no problems compared to Terrell." Terrell was the guy who got smacked on the bus that day.

"I hope that is as interesting as my bus ride gets today."

Within two hours, after riding three different buses, Matty was turning the left corner at Woodside. And as it had happened every day since the first day he visited, there was somebody watching to see when he turned that corner to see what he had on.

Matty never could figure out why that was important.

But he had decided that today was going to be different. And it was.

When they saw each other there was this awkward silence between them for the first time.

Matty didn't know if he was happy, sad, or angry at Darryl.

It was equally clear from his expression that Darryl was having the same sort of conversation in his head, but Matty knew he would never verbalize it.

Matty was so caught up in Darryl's facial expressions that he had almost forgotten about the leather jacket until it made its reappearance that day.

Then Matty had a mental bookmark. Why did Darryl always wear a towel around his neck?

"You're smiling," Matty said.

"Shut up man."

"Happy to see me."

"C'mon man."

Matty needed to know but he wouldn't dare tell that to Darryl.

"If you are so excited to see me, why is it so hard for you to tell me that?"

"Why do I have to tell you what you already know man?"

One thing lead to another and before anyone knew it, they were having a full-fledge argument.

They spent most of the early part of the day just sitting across from each other staring past each other.

In truth, they really were staring at each other but neither one of them would dare admit it.

"This is not how I had envisioned things going."

"So why did you hang up on me?"

Matty just looked at him with a smrown - that's a half smile and half frown.

"I started to jump on the bus and come over there and kick your ass."

"I would have done it sooner if I had known that's what it took to get you to come and visit me."

"Don't try to play me man. Answer my damn question."

"My mother told me to never start something you can't finish."

"What the hell does that mean?"

"It means that I should not have started coming over here if I didn't have the money to keep doing it."

"Man that shit you talk don't make no sense," Darryl said as he jumped to his feet and made his way toward Matty.

Matty steadied his mind to defend himself.

"What the hell you jumpin' for?" Darryl was laughing.

"Man sit yo ass back down. I'm goin' to get me somethin' to drink." He kept on laughing.

"You thought I was going to hit you didn't you?"

Matty just looked at him.

"Good."

"Why good?"

"Cause I got your ass scared of me."

"Don't let my kindness fool you."

"Shut the hell up man and finish telling me why you hung up on me."

"First of all let's be clear. You hung up on me. Secondly. I just didn't have the money and I was ashamed to tell you that because my mother always said you shouldn't start something you can't finish. And I started coming over here but I couldn't keep it up. There. You satisfied!"

"Man that is so stupid. Why didn't yo dumb ass just tell me you didn't have the money?"

"Is that how you negotiate?"

"What the hell are you talkin' 'bout now?"

"Is that how you get answers, by insulting people?"

Knock. Knock. Knock.

Their conversation was interrupted.

Before anyone could answer, the front door opened from the outside without anyone offering an invitation to enter.

Once the door opened, in stepped this indescribably big girl with a small head and beautifully painted face.

Painted Face weighed 350, 400, or maybe even 500 pounds.

She had a soft childlike voice. But she was no child. She was purposefully alluring.

If anyone knew the meaning of accentuating the positive it was that big girl - - Painted Face.

Without the slightest exaggeration, she was big and jolly.

It was as if being big did not bother her. Hell, she was so happy she could have been Mrs. Santa Claus.

"Hey everybody," she said.

The house was immediately filled with jovial laughter. Everyone was clearly happy to see her.

"Hey Sista."

"Bitch, whatcha u talkin' 'bout," Darryl responded.

"Oops, I meant to say hey Darryl." They both started laughing.

Matty's mouth was still open from the shock of Painted Face's initial entry. But from the outsight it was quite clear that she and Darryl had a strange bond that almost made Matty jealous.

Then her tiny head, compared to her big body, noticed Matty was in the room.

"Who is this?" She started smiling like a serpent who had just discovered her very next prey. Her mouth curled up on both sides like a smile but it was something far more evil than a smile.

Matty tried to back up, but there was nowhere left for him to go.

"Why?" Darryl responded like Matty's protector.

"What's your name?" She said with an extended hand.

Being a polite Southern boy, Matty stood up. "My name is Matty." Matty shook her soft hand, but it felt slimy like a snake's skin, not a woman's hand.

Matty looked at her hand, but he didn't see her hand, he saw the truth of what was underneath.

"Matty? My name is Debbie," she said massaging Matty's inner palm before he snatched it away from her.

"Fat Debbie," Darryl said jumping to his feet.

"Let go of his hand bitch," he continued to say to Debbie while separating their hands.

Matty snatched his hand back.

Debbie did not take her eyes off of Matty.

Matty honestly felt like a piece of meat and Debbie kept looking at him like he was a chicken wang.

"Don't' make me snatch that towel from around your neck," Debbie responded to Darryl without ever taking her eyes off Matty for one second.

That statement caused Matty to be even more intrigued by the towel or what was underneath the towel.

"Something's really not right here," Matty said quietly.

Minutes later they were all laughing and talking as if nothing had happened. But this was not just a regular conversation.

They were talking like they were girlfriend and boyfriend – still. Not that Matty knew whether they were girlfriend and boyfriend before. And at the rate the conversation was going Matty was not going to get the chance to ask.

"AAARRRGGGHHH!!!" Matty screamed.

Everyone looked at him like he was crazy.

"I just had to let that out."

Matty wished he could start over from that day he gave Darryl his phone number. Here he was a complete outsider all over again.

"So ya'll used to date?" Matty blurted out in the middle of the conversation.

The house drew a total hush as everybody looked at him. Then they all burst into a unanimous laughter.

Matty turned pure red.

"I wouldn't date that bitch," Debbie said.

"You would if I would give it to you," Darryl responded.

So Matty figured it was now or never.

"What is the deal with the towel and the leather jacket?"

"Oooooooooooo," was all that could be heard throughout the house. Matty didn't know where it was coming from.

"You see what you done started!" Darryl had this charming way of asking without asking, meaning without meaning, and showing without showing.

"You gonna answer the man?" Debbie asked.

"When I get ready."

Darryl was a smooth as they came. Before Matty knew it, he had been sucked into the crowd, and was laughing, talking, and playing cards along with everyone else the remainder of the afternoon and into the evening.

It was the first time Darryl's family had included Matty in any of their activities.

"I guess I should be grateful to Fat Debbie for this," Matty said to Darryl.

But truth be told Matty wasn't grateful.

As time started creepin' up for Matty to leave, he kept hoping that Fat Debbie would leave before him so that he would get a few minutes alone with Darryl.

"Bitch when you goin' home?" Darryl blurted out like he was reading Matty's mind.

"As soon as Matty leaves."

Darryl cut his eyes at me.

"You better not go home with this bitch."

"I don't even know her. Why would I go home with her?"

"No offense." Matty turned and said to Fat Debbie.

"None taken Punk," she purposefully said a little softer but loud enough for those at the card table to hear.

The clock struck 9 pm.

"I've got to go. I'm already going to be late."

"Me too," Fat Debbie jumped up behind Matty.

"Wait a minute man. I'll walk you to the bus stop," Darryl said.

By the time they all finally started walking there was a small entourage of about 10 people or so walking Matty and Fat Debbie to the bus stop.

"Listen to me. You take your ass straight home and call me when you get there so that I'll know you made it."

"Fat Debbie, you better leave my man alone if you know what's good for you."

Fat Debbie just stood there smiling.

Matty just stood there. He wasn't sure he was shocked by Darryl's statement or by the mere fact that he actually confessed his feelings for Matty openly.

Either way Matty was stunned.

That night there was no kiss goodnight from Darryl but he did stand there and watch until the bus was completely out of his sight. Matty knew because he was watching Darryl watch him.

Matty went to the very back of the bus so that he could be alone.

Fat Debbie followed.

Matty was hemmed in.

Fat Debbie was on his left. The window was on his right.

She started touching Matty's left thigh. Matty was as jumpy as a virgin at a prison rodeo.

She had an amazingly gentile touch. To his own surprise, Matty started to relax.

"Am I under a spell?" Were the words his mind flashed in front of his eyes like a cue card?

"Relax baby. I promise I won't hurt you." Her words sounded sincere enough but they cut into Matty's soul like venom.

He kept looking into Jackie's eyes. He was powerless to do otherwise. She was a modern day Medusa because he was completely helpless to defend himself against her words, her eyes, or her touch.

A little while longer and he would be able to leave her behind after they transferred buses.

Boy was Matty wrong.

"Are you following me?" Matty asked her.

"No."

"But you are headed in my direction."

"So it seems."

"Then you are following me."

"No I am not. Get on the bus before he leaves without us."

When they stepped on the second bus, it was crowded with all kinds of people. All Matty could focus on was their eyes. Then he became embarrassed.

They were all staring at him and Fat Debbie, like they were some sort of couple.

As bad as Matty hated to admit it to himself, he was embarrassed to be seen with Fat Debbie. Then he was sad, then he became angry.

"That's the same way people used to look at me when I was fat. Hell, who am I kidding? They still look at me that way and I am not fat, at least right now."

Matty had this entire conversation with himself.

"Come on Fat Debbie," Matty said leading the way to the back of the bus.

Fat Debbie followed like a puppy but what Matty didn't know was that he had just played the final card directly into Fat Debbie's hand.

When they took their seats, Fat Debbie picked up right where she left off. This time she was more aggressive.

Matty immediately knew that he had been played like a million dollar fiddle. It didn't matter how priceless it was, he was still being played.

The time came for him to get off the bus to catch his last connection home.

"Do you have to go?"

"I do," Matty said as he started to get up.

"Come on. Stay with me a little while longer."

"No Debbie, I can't. I got to go."

"Because of what Sista' said to you?"

She had Matty's attention.

"Speaking of which, why do you and everybody else keep calling Darryl 'Sista'?"

"Everybody like who?"

"You, his family, and other people."

"That is not my business to tell."

"What business?"

"You have to ask Sista'…I mean Darryl about all of that."

The bus jerked and Matty fell into Jackie's lap. She caught him like a frying pan catching a flap jack in mid-air.

"You forgot to get off."

"You might as well come on home with me for a little while."

"What the hell. What have I got to lose?"

They rode the bus a little farther. Then they got off and started walking. It wasn't a long walk, but it was just enough to have Fat Debbie winded.

Just as they stepped up to the back door and Jackie put her key in to turn the lock, Matty realized that he was back in…....

"This is Brookhill," Matty said just as Fat Debbie snatched him into the house and locked the door.

He tried to fight her to get out of the house.

There was no way he was going to win that fight.

Her body completely covered the doorway and as she made her way toward him, she cut off any chance of him getting around her on either side.

Matty kept backing up farther and farther until he backed himself right into a seat on the sofa.

"If you want this key there is only one way to get it." She put the key in her brazier.

Matty started playfully wrestling Fat Debbie for the key. He even managed to laugh out loud a little bit.

Then in a split second...

Fat Debbie had thrown him on the bed and snatched his pants and his drawers completely down to his ankles.

Then she licked her lips and plopped all of her weight on his pole.

All of this would have been hilariously funny if it wasn't Matty on the bottom.

It felt like a ton of bricks had fallen on him.

"Debbie, I can't breathe! I can't breathe!" Matty screamed.

"You promise to do what I say?"

"Yea. Just get the hell off of me!"

It took Matty a good minute to recover from the loss of air and the claustrophobia, let alone the crushing of his bones.

"Lay down on top of me and put that thing in."

Matty was light-headed so he didn't have time to think about what she was saying. He just did it.

He was surprised that even with all of her body weight that his dick would still be long enough to get inside of her.

"It's my turn," Matty boasted

He bumped and grinded inside of her until her big ass body was convulsing and shivering all over the place. A few more strokes and ahhhhhhhhhhhhh…..

The phone rang.

"Hello," she was out of breath.

"Debbie?"

It's was Darryl and he was madder than hell.

"Is Matty over there?"

"Yea." She didn't even try to hide it. It was like she wanted him to know that he was there.

"Let me speak to him."

"Man, I'm gonna kick your ass when I see you for real this time."

"How are you going to threaten me about sleeping with a girl?"

"What!!!!!!"

"You mean to tell me that you fucked that fat bitch?"

Matty was embarrassed into silence.

"Oh hell….. Now you done gone and did it."

CLICK!

While Fat Debbie was still trying to gather her thoughts, Matty snatched the key that he had been eyeing and ran out the front door, butt-ass-naked.

He fell on in the wet grass because his drawers and pants were still down around his ankle. But he was outside and there was no way that Fat Debbie was going to catch up to him.

He pulled his clothes up on him and started walking.

He didn't know the exact way home but he knew the general direction; and, he knew that it was not that far away, at least if he were driving.

He heard a lot of noise, cars rushing. It was the highway.

Matty knew the highway ran similar to longitude and latitude. Since longitude is similar to north and south, Matty knew that he needed to head south to get home.

He walked down toward the highway and then walked the highway the rest of the way home.

There were cars blowing horns and screeching tires all the way home. Those noises kept him alert and they let him know he wasn't in the world alone, even if he was in a lonely place.

By the time he got home he was soaking wet from his head to his toes.

He tried to catch his breath before putting his key in the lock. But he was still panting very hard and very loud.

It didn't matter.

He didn't need his key.

His mother was waiting for him. She opened the door.

"Matty, do you have any idea what time it is?"

"11:30." Matty said panting and still trying to catch his breath.

"Try 1 am."

"Where have you been and why are you soaking wet?"

"I missed my bus and I ran home."

"Do you have any idea of how worried I have been about you?"

"You are grounded for the rest of the summer. You better not put so much as a toe on that street or I am going to beat your ass until you ain't black no more."

"Now get in that room and take off those wet clothes."

Even if Matty thought he had an opportunity to change his mother's mind he didn't have the energy to try. He was completely crestfallen. He went to his room as told.

He took his time taking off his clothes.

It had been a terrible night.

He had finally gotten down to just his underwear, which he just realized Debbie had torn. That was his last bit of energy.

"AAAAAGH." Matty screamed.

His mother had burst into his room and was whoopin' the shit out of him with her punishment strap.

"AAAAAAAGH."

"Mommma, I'm sorry." Matty was trying to protect his naked body from more punishment.

"Pleasssssssse." He was screaming, crying, and jumping all over that tight room.

But his mother was relentless. She was striking brutal blows of anger and worry.

"AAAAAAAGH."

"Momma, I'm sorry." Matty was pleading.

Sadie wasn't hearing none of it.

The more he pleaded the harder she hit him.

She was furious and he felt it. Her strikes were coming faster than the tire rotations on the bus.

"Mommmmmmmma," Matty screamed a piercing scream and then she stopped.

She turned to walk away and did not even turn around to see how that whoppin' impacted him. She was just that mad.

Matty was whimpering like a puppy.

He tried to get in his top bunk but he was too tired and he was in too much pain.

He pulled the covers off his bed and slept in the floor.

Normally, when he hit the bed, he fall asleep immediately. But that night he was asleep before his head hit the pillow.

Matty didn't even know morning had come.

He was still whimpering when he woke up.

His body was hurting all over. He just sat there looking at his legs, his arms, his stomach, his chest, and his thighs.

He couldn't see his back but that sting told him it matched his front. Matty had welts everywhere.

His mind wanted to replay that last scene but he refused. He pressed the delete button in his mind. Matty never wanted to see that movie again.

He managed to put on some old sweats, washed his face, and went into the kitchen for breakfast.

You would have thought Matty had the plague.

He was at the table alone.

None of his brothers wanted to be seen near him.

Matty was so embarrassed that he was too ashamed to look his mother in her face.

"Here is some ointment to put on your welts so that they won't be so soar."

"Am I going to have marks all over my body?"

"The only permanent marks you'll have will be on your pride and your willingness to so easily stray from the specific instructions I give you."

Matty couldn't say anything. It was clear that his mother was trying to teach him far more than a simple lesson about last night.

"Your body will recover completely. But if you have to have marks, I prefer you to have marks than to be dead and I be left here by myself to try and figure out what my son was doing that got him killed."

"Touché." His mother won.

"No mother wants to beat her child. But any mother who loves her child would beat him if it keeps him alive."

Matty didn't want anything for breakfast. He had eaten enough crow for breakfast, lunch, and dinner to last a while.

Matty didn't see Darryl the remainder of that summer.

It was the fall of the year by the time he saw him again.

By then Matty was a different guy. All of that walking and running must have activated his metabolism in a good way.

Somewhere during their absence, Matty woke up with a mustache and a few more muscles.

His turkey cheeks were gone, his chest was sticking out more, and he could actually see even more of his feet. Matty was amazed!

And what was left of those man tiddies were now man pecs. They were still a little larger than normal, but there was no longer the prerequisite of a pre-teenage girl's chest protector.

And to top it all off, Matty had grown a few inches also, in more places than one.

The metamorphosis appeared to finally be complete.

The next time Matty saw Darryl, their family had moved closer to the south side of town.

That was about two years or so into their relationship.

After that last bus ride, Matty was glad to no longer have to ride the bus to see him. And he never saw Fat Debbie again, by choice.

Matty could walk to Darryl's new house, although it took about one-half hour. That was a walk Matty gladly accepted.

He walked over to his house every day after school and early on Saturday mornings. He didn't see him on Sundays because they had to go to church.

The sweetest thing of all about their move was that Darryl had to wait so long to see Matty that he was giddy like a girl the next time Matty saw him at their new house.

Late one Friday night, the house was exceptionally quiet, no one was stirring and it was quite early for them.

Matty didn't exactly know how it happened but the next thing he knew his pants and underwear where on the floor and he was lying face down on the bed.

Then he was moaning and groaning with Darryl on top of him.

That went on for another three or four months.

Then one day Matty was over visiting and he just happened to pull back the curtains in Darryl's brother's room downstairs, and he saw a green pickle lying on the window sill.

Immediately Matty knew.

It was like scales fell off his eyes and he could clearly see the truth.

Matty's head immediately turned into that of a jackass and he began braying like the complete ass he was, again, like on the cartoons.

Matty was ashamed, embarrassed, and downright mad.

"Now it all makes sense - - the towels and jackets were hiding her breasts for all those years; not letting me touch his/her penis was to keep me from discovering this damn pickle; and, the name Sista was no nickname. It was to identify the fact that she is the only girl in the family!"

"How could I be so stupid!"

Matty didn't say anything he immediately.

He took the pickle and stuck it in his sock and played the game the rest of the day.

As night fell, the house got quiet. Matty walked upstairs into the bedroom as if nothing was wrong.

Once they were in the bedroom alone, Matty pulled out the pickle and backhanded Sista. While she was dazed, he snatched all of her clothes off and completely had his way with her.

While they were laying there in the bed as man and woman, Matty asked, "Why?"

"Why what man?"

"Why did you do all that to me?"

"I dunno. Shit you were so book smart and so street dumb, it just made it all so easy."

Matty didn't know what to say.

"Hell man, I been doing it so long that it was easy to keep on doing it."

Matty still didn't say anything.

"Come on man."

"Come on what?"

"You know what. Come on."

With that Matty brutally penetrated Sista with no remorse for any potential damage. But to his surprise Sista gave herself to him even more.

Matty didn't see Sista for a few weeks after the confrontation.

But he didn't leave him(her) either. And the stupid thing is that Matty didn't know why he didn't leave him but he didn't.

"When you coming back over man?"

"I don't know."

"Damn man, how many times I got to tell you I'm sorry?"

"You must have apologized to someone else because you certainly haven't apologized to me."

"Okay man, I'm sorry."

"How many damn people have you been playing for a fool?"

"Man let that shit go and come on over."

That song popped into Matty's head.

*Everybody plays the fool*

*Sometime.*

*There's no exception to the rule.*

*Listen baby.*

*It maybe factual it may be cruel.*

The next time Matty saw Sista she was laughing.

The problem was that Matty didn't know if she was laughing at him or with him, except that Matty wasn't laughing.

In short order, it was quite clear that everybody that knew about Darryl and Matty also knew about Darryl and his pickle - - everybody that is except for Matty and her parents.

Matty was the laughing stock for weeks, not to mention they had been laughing behind his back for far longer.

It was no consolation to Matty that he wasn't the only one being duped by Sista.

There were several others, but one in particular. Her name was Rivian.

She was a cat-fighting, hair-pulling, dumb, ghetto bitch (which is how Sista described her to Matty) who was madly in love with Darryl.

Matty tried to find Rivian to tell her the truth. He never found her, but it didn't matter. Sometime later he did hear that Rivian found out that Darryl was a girl and she became even more obsessed.

"So now that I know you've decided to tell the truth?"

"You are the only one I care about."

Matty was stunned by the admission, but it was several years too late.

"So that means you have been fucking only God knows who else since we have been together, and I have been riding two hours on three buses to be with you?"

"Man shut up."

"You shut up you lying bitch!"

Matty smacked Sista.

She started crying.

But Matty's heart was frozen over.

Matty kept replaying everything over and over in his mind, including those really big cupcakes under all of those towels and jackets for all that time.

The more the story played, the more Matty felt like a true jack ass like in those *Porky Pig* cartoons, except this was no cartoon.

Suddenly it all made sense all over again. And Matty was an even bigger jackass this time than he was at the first reveal of those sorted details of dual personalities.

"Nobody would ever believe this shit if I told them. Hell I don't even believe it and I'm in it."

Matty just sat there thinking.

"Hell, I would be too embarrassed to tell anyway that I was so damn dumb - - the lack of touching in certain areas; no male prowess; and, being forced to lie face down on the bed before sex."

But still Matty couldn't get Sista out of his system.

Long after the truth came out and they had swapped positions, and it was real sex as a man and woman - - Matty discovered yet something else Sista was hiding from him.

Sista was like four years older than Matty. So the sex was not man and woman, it was more like boy and a woman. She had dropped out of school when she was in the seventh or eighth grade.

Matty was in the tenth grade, but he clearly still didn't have any common sense, which is why his mother was still trying to beat some into his head. But she wasn't having much success. So his body was growing, changing, and maturing, but his brain was not fairing so well.

Still Matty could not help but to continue torturing himself by replaying their entire history in his mind over and over again.

No matter day or night, in school or out of school, Matty just couldn't let it go that he and Sista used to pretend to have sex as two men, rather a man and a boy, and now they were having sex as a boy and woman.

And that very first night he found out about the green pickle, he had her legs in the air screamin', hollerin', and moaning like a bitch in heat.

"Stephanie," Matty said. Sista reminded Matty of Stephanie.

Matty's back was so scratched up that night after they finished having sex for about three hours that Sista had to put salve on Matty's back for a while before the pain started to subside, pain that he did not feel when they were in the heat of passion.

Matty would never admit it to anyone, but he knew it was revenge. The problem was that he didn't know if it was revenge for the pickle, Shaun, the man tiddies, or just the overwhelming disappointment of his stolen manhood.

Whatever it was, it fueled their passion for more than seven long months, four times per week, and all night on Friday and Saturday nights.

"Nothing is going to give it back to me," Matty was talking to himself about his manhood or lack thereof.

But even he was confused.

There were moments when he was the epitome of a man and there were others, far more others, when he was simply at the bottom of the heap, literally and figuratively.

But the worst thing of all is that Matty had not even realized that he had fallen in love with Sista, probably because he didn't know what love was.

*In my life there's been heartache and pain*
*I don't know if I can face it again*
*Can't stop now, I've traveled so far*
*To change this lonely life*

*I wanna know what love is*
*I want you to show me*
*I wanna feel what love is*
*I know you can show me*
*Aaaah woah-oh-ooh*

Matty was a fool in love and it didn't make any sense to anyone, let alone him.

The craziest thing is that Matty's life had turned into snippets of songs, including Tina Turner's *Fool in Love*.

"Matty I want you to stop seeing this girl you been seeing."

His mother didn't say another word at that point. But Matty knew that her want was actually a demand. And if that demand wasn't met in a reasonable time period, pressure would be applied until that demand was met.

Matty didn't know what to say or do in response to his mother's demand. Now his heart was really torn.

"Can I think about it momma?"

She didn't respond, which meant she didn't like it but she was going to give him a little time to comply.

Matty had never defied his mother before, so he was left with no response and no options.

"May I go now?"

"Where are you going today?"

No response.

Sadie had her answer.

"I want you home by midnight, and not a minute later."

Matty jumped up.

"Just for that make it 11pm, and if you continue acting like a spoiled brat I will cut it far shorter."

"Yes ma'am."

The entire walk over to Sista's house that day was like a sentence, a jail sentence. It was the longest walk ever.

When Matty finally reached Sista's place he was exhausted, not from walking, but thinking.

"What's wrong with you man?"

Matty didn't have an answer for her either.

They made some small talk, but Sista had finally been around Matty enough to know when something was wrong.

"Matty there is something wrong with you and I want you to tell me what it is."

After much pushing, Matty finally decided to let Sista in on his secret.

"My mother told me I had to stop seeing you or else."

"You can't stop seeing me."

Matty was back to being silent.

"You can't stop seeing me Matty. Did you hear me!"

Sista grabbed his face and forced him to look at her.

"I'm pregnant."

Matty fainted right there in their dining room. It shook the whole first floor.

Everyone ran into the dining room to see what was going on.

"What the hell is going on in here Sista?" Her mother asked in front of the entire family.

Sista didn't tell a single soul their secret.

"Carry him over to the couch ya'll." Her mother said to her brothers and her husband. "Sista go get some cold rags."

When Matty finally came to, all he could see where all these crazy looking faces staring down at him, up close and personal.

"Damn man, I thought you had died," Sista said right there in front of everybody.

Matty picked up right where they left off.

"When did you find out you were pregnant?"

"Pregnant?"

Matty's word set off a firestorm. There was chattering, cussing, screaming, yelling, tears, and more going on in that house at that moment.

Everyone was trying to get answers from Sista, but Sista was trying to find out if Matty was going to leave her.

"Look ya'll, I'll talk to ya'll later. Right now I need to talk to Matty."

They left and went for a walk in the park a few blocks away.

"Anything you want to know man?"

"Hell yea, but I don't even know where to begin?"

They sat there for a little while.

"When did you find out you were pregnant?"

"I went to the doctor two days ago."

"Why did you wait until now to tell me?"

"Because I am getting ready to start showing."

"Is it my baby?"

"I don't know."

Sista paused a while.

"I don't think so."

Matty should have been relieved but he wasn't. He was jealous.

"So what do we do now?"

"I don't know man."

"So then tell me this. Why are you telling me and not the baby's daddy? And for once be honest with me."

"Because you'll be a good daddy. You smart, you going somewhere, and you'll love my baby."

"Let's go," Matty said.

"Where you going?"

"I'm going to walk you home, then I'm going home."

"What's wrong? You don't want me tonight?"

"I can't have you tonight."

"What's stopping you?"

"I have to be home by 11 pm."

"Matty it's barely 6:30."

"I know but I have a lot on my mind."

"I hate to say it man, but you are right."

Matty was so torn that he didn't see Sista again for a couple of weeks.

"Shit, things were simpler when Sista was Darryl."

During their hiatus, the time came for them to go school shopping.

Matty had been secretly stashing money from his mother and from Sista. Although he wasn't necessarily in the mood for shopping, especially with his mother and his brothers, it was a welcomed diversion.

As usual, Matty was wandering alone when he stumbled upon the most unique pair of shoes he had ever seen in his short, long life.

He pulled out his own $120.00 and gave it to the salesman.

When he got back to his family, "What did you buy Matty?" His mother was curious. His brothers were stunned.

"Where did you get money boy?"

"I saved it like most people do, you dumb…"

"You better not say it," his mother said.

A few short weeks after their shopping spree, school was set to begin.

It took a little while, but as soon as the chance presented itself, Matty broke out his new shoes. They were the talk of the school. Hell, they were the talk of the neighborhood.

When Matty got back home from school that day, he reshined his shoes, wrapped them neatly, and put them back in the box.

Although he and Sista were having conversations on the telephone, Matty still had not seen her in more than a month.

"What you gonna do man?"

"Sista stop asking me that. This is some crazy shit I am dealing with, and I am not sure what I should be doing."

A few more weeks passed.

Knock. Knock. Knock.

Someone was rapping at Matty's front door.

It was the middle of the week and Matty just happened to be walking down the hall into the living room.

When Matty opened the front door he started laughing.

There was this strange fat kid standing at their front door, about Matty's age.

"We don't want any kid."

Matty got ready to shut the door.

"Hey. What you talking about? I'm not selling anything."

Matty stopped and gave *Humpty Dumpty* a few more seconds to explain himself.

"So then what do you want fat boy?"

"I'm not fat. I'm just short for my age."

"Okay short fat kid, what do you want?"

"Are you the kid that has those glass slippers?"

Oddly enough Matty said, "Yea."

Then he paused.

"I don't know you. You don't go to my school. So how do you know I have those shoes?"

He said, "My friend Gail saw you wearing them and she told me about them. I decided that I wanted to see for myself."

He went on to say, "I have been hearing about some new kid that wears bad ass clothes that had moved into the neighborhood."

Matty was standing there amazed at the fact that someone was talking about him in a positive way, notwithstanding the fact that they were paying attention to his clothes.

For more than a brief minute Matty completely forgot that this fat kid was at their door. He sounded like *Charlie Brown's* teacher, "Waa-waa, waa-waa, waa-waa."

He was so far out of Matty's mind that he had started to close the door a second time when he shouted out, "Wait, I'm not finished!"

That shout brought Matty back to the present and to him, the kid at the front door.

Matty thought he was going to ask him where he purchased the shoes but he didn't.

So again Matty didn't think much more about it and was getting ready to shut the door for a third time.

Then he blurted out, "Can I borrow your glass heel shoes?" like he and Matty were friends and had been friends for years.

Now he had Matty's undivided attention.

"You shittin' me."

But fat kid was serious.

"You really think I am going to let your fat ass borrow my black patent leather glass-heeled dress shoes with the ace of spade card in the glass heel, and I've only worn the shoes one time?"

The fat kid just stood there.

"On top of that I don't even know your fat ass."

"I'm not fat. I'm just short for my age. And to answer your first question, yes."

"Yea. I want to borrow your Cinderella slippers. You have already worn them to the ball right?"

Matty stated laughing.

"You must be out of your mind. I saved up my allowances to buy those shoes and I have only worn them to school one time."

So Matty started to shut door for a fourth time.

He said, "Wait. I'm serious."

Matty looked at him. He was clearly serious.

Then Matty looked down at his feet and his shoes were all creeled over, worn out, and the heels were completely gone. He had these really fat feet and he walked on the sides of his feet so he wore the outside of his shoes down first.

Matty thought about telling him to get his fat ass off their porch and closing the door without another thought. But then completely out of the blue, Matty did the dumbest thing.

He agreed to his request.

How dumb was that?

Matty took a liking to that fat kid because he had spunk – something Matty didn't have, and he was funny.

Immediately they became friends.

Before long Matty was walking around to Paris' house several times a week after school and almost every Friday because they had a basement where they could have some privacy.

They had their own *Wayne's World* effect going on way in advance of the show becoming a mega hit.

Every time Matty saw Paris, he asked, "When are you going to give me my shoes back?"

Paris always had some reason why he couldn't give them back – there was something special going on at school and he had to wear them, or he had a particular ensemble he was going to wear and the shoes were a necessary part of it.

The bottom line was that Matty was never going to see his shoes again.

But what Paris didn't know is that he served as a diversion for Matty and his problems with Sista, and her pregnancy.

Meanwhile, every time Matty visited Paris, he made it a point to keep those shoes out of Matty's eyesight.

"What do you tell people when they ask you where you got those shoes?"

"It just depends on who's asking. It really ain't none of their business."

"Well what made it your business to ask me about my shoes?"

"All you could say was yes or no."

"So why won't you give me my shoes back?"

"Because you have a whole wardrobe full of clothes and shoes you can wear. You don't need those shoes. Hell you probably don't even miss them. They probably were stuck in a box in the back of your closet."

"Paris you may be a little quick on your feet, but you are a terrible liar."

Later Matty learned that Paris wore those shoes to school every single day after he got them from Matty until the aces were gone, and then the heels, and for a little while after that.

But Matty did learn a very important lesson from Paris. He learned to never lend his clothes out to anyone ever again.

Yet Matty knew that the day he lent Paris his shoes, he knew that he would never see them again after he looked down at those fat feet.

He knew, without ever seeing those shoes again, that they were all worn out, wrinkled with deep creases in them, and all the sheen was gone.

Those shoes were probably screaming for Matty to come to their rescue but it was much too late the day he agreed to Paris' unusually bold request.

Paris' big feet were much, much wider than Matty's feet.

He had to squeeze his big feet in them from the beginning, but Matty lent them to him anyway.

The shoes just didn't seem that important anymore. So Matty didn't see any reason to get worked up about them. Especially since he loved hanging out with Paris.

But Matty never told his mother what happened to those shoes, considering what they cost in his allowance.

One Saturday afternoon, without any notice or any forewarning, Matty got off the phone with Sista, packed his little suitcase and he headed for the front door.

It was a Saturday afternoon, his mother was in the den on the telephone, and the front door was wide open.

It was the perfect opportunity to escape.

But Matty didn't know his older brother Junior was watching his every move.

As soon as Matty made his move toward the front door Junior yelled out to their mother in the den, "Momma, Matty got his suitcase and trying to run away."

Matty kept walking - down the porch, across the front yard, and down the street.

He kept looking back over his shoulder to see if his mother was sending his brothers to come and get him.

No one came.

He was home free.

Matty had walked down the hill and was near the end of the street when their mother came roaring up behind him in her new, fresh off the showroom floor, dark green Cutlass Supreme.

Matty turned around just in time enough to jump out of the way of his mother who was careening directly toward him.

She was furious and she was crying.

She said, "I can't believe you are running away from home. Why?" She asked.

Matty didn't know it then but he didn't have a good answer.

He was so stunned that mother tried to kill him with her car that he ran into the Nelson's yard at the end of the street, dropped his suitcase, and ran.

"If you want to run away you are not taking anything with you that I paid for." She was crying more.

Then she said, "I'm going to go get my gun."

Matty turned around.

He knew his mother. She meant what she said.

Matty had to book it out of there.

By the time he got to Sista's he was exhausted from running five or six miles to her house.

Matty stayed at her house all day.

"Matty your mother has to be home sick with worry. You have to go home."

Sista kept telling him to go home too, but this whole thing was her idea.

So about midnight, her mother said, "Matty, go home."

The entire time he was walking home he kept thinking how he had messed up his home for nothing.

He had more than enough time to think about it because he had five or six miles ahead of him.

Matty had really messed up and he didn't care that he was walking home alone in the dark.

When he finally got home and went into his same bedroom, there was his suitcase sitting on the floor near that old floor model television.

When he went down the hall to see his mother, she turned her back to him.

Later on his mother's sister told him that his mother turned over and cried in her pillow that night because she said Matty was breaking her heart.

The next morning their mother was standing at the kitchen sink when Matty came in the kitchen, she started crying.

Matty knew he really hurt her and that he broke her heart.

Matty started crying too.

His mother kept asking "Why would you want to run away, Matty?"

"Momma, I'm sorry."

Matty kept saying it over and over.

"I promise I will never do that again."

His mother was right, she was as good as she could be to him and his brothers, if not better, after their daddy went off and left them the way he did.

It took them several months to get past that little stunt of Matty's.

But his mother was winning.

Matty cut back his time with Sista but he never stopped seeing her completely.

He did learn how to hide this fact from his family.

Part of this reasoning was that he could never explain how he could justify his need to be with someone who had lied, mistreated, betrayed, and berated him as a man and as a human being. Matty couldn't explain it, but he knew something was wrong. But he didn't know or couldn't see that all the shit he had endured was weighing on his head and impacting his decisions in life.

But Matty couldn't help but torturing himself. He kept recalling the details of Darryl's admission that he was a she.

While Matty was in school all day, Sista was getting banged by several different guys on a regular basis. And worse, the man party continued way after she and Matty switched positions.

She was pregnant and did not know who the father was.

"You dumbass," Matty told himself.

He knew something wasn't right when there was milk coming out of her breasts when he used to make love to her, but he didn't have any experience from which to draw upon.

"I was naïve enough to think she was enjoying being with me but in actuality she was out getting screwed while I was in school. I was simply a small toy in her much bigger toy box."

But Matty still didn't stop seeing her probably because he was already so accustomed to being abused.

Foolish Matty, he became more committed to her and to a baby that may or may not have been his, although the latter seemed more likely to be the truth than the former.

Before he knew it, Matty was a teenage father who was unsure about fatherhood or the skills necessary to achieve such a status.

He was going to school by day and in the afternoons he was rushing to see a beautiful baby girl that he did and did not want to be responsible for.

Instead of using his allowance to ride buses across town and buy junk food and clothes, he was now buying diaper bags, pampers, food, clothes, and anything else Sista told him to buy.

In the meantime, he was preparing to tell his mother the news about Sista and the baby. Hiding all the stuff he was buying had become to challenging.

Six months into this new role, Sista had yet another surprise for him.

It was a Friday night and Matty was sitting on Sista's bed holding his daughter.

"Man I got something to tell you."

"Okay," Matty said without taking his eyes off the baby.

"She's not your baby."

Matty still kept looking at the baby.

She was on her way to sleep like she always was when she was in Matty's arms. He waited until she was sleep and then he put her in her crib that he had also paid for.

As soon as Matty put her down he walked over to Sista and backhanded her with a force that through her across the room.

It was a dangerous move because he was on her turf and because he had seen her fight before and Sista could give him a run for his money.

But she looked into Matty's eyes and his eyes told her that today was not the day to attempt such a feat.

"Take your clothes off."

Sista did what Matty told her to do.

"Lay down on the bed. Face down."

Sista was scared, but she did it.

"Whatcha you gonna do man?"

Matty mercilessly entered Sista from behind with hatred, thrust, and forcefulness that could not be repelled no matter how hard she tried.

She started crying.

Matty thrust harder.

Then he grabbed her mouth so that no one would come to her rescue and so that she would not wake the baby.

No one heard the rumbling upstairs because they were too busy downstairs having one of their usual Friday night parties that ended up in dramatic knock down drag out fights that included cast iron frying pans and Matty hiding in a closet on more than one occasion.

When Matty was done, after several hours, Sista didn't move. She just laid there on bed whimpering, while she starred at Matty.

Matty was completely unapologetic. He was furious and he was prepared for a fight that night no matter what.

"Haven't you done enough shit to me?"

She didn't say a word.

"Answer me!" Matty screamed.

The baby woke up crying.

Matty picked her up and held her in his arms. It was the only thing that kept him from killing Sista that night with his bare hands.

"She's hungry. Get your ass over here so you can feed her."

Sista' got up, slowly walked over, and sat down beside Matty on the bed. She started breastfeeding the baby while he held her in his arms.

Matty turned to look Sista straight in her eyes. "I wish I knew what kind of hold you have on me so that I could quit your ass."

She took the baby out of his arms and put her in her crib.

Then she gave herself to Matty as violently as he demanded and in any way he desired. Something she had never done before.

Matty was happy to return the favor.

Matty didn't see Sista for another month or so, though they talked on the phone almost every day.

Matty was more confused now than he was when she was a he.

"So child talk to me," Paris said.

Matty wasn't sure what he was talking about but he was just glad to not have to be dealing with some of Sista's shit.

It was a refreshing feeling to be able to let his guard down. It was also completely different from everything Matty had grown up with.

"Matty where the hell is your mind? You are not paying me any attention," Paris said.

"Sorry Paris what did you say?"

The more they talked, the less Matty understood what he was saying.

There was something else different about Paris too, but Matty couldn't put his finger on it. Still he didn't care.

Paris was fun-loving, care-free, and most of all he was genuine. He was completely different from anyone Matty had ever met, and he loved that about him.

Matty was so relaxed around Paris, unlike anyone else he was around. They spent hours on end talking and laughing about everything. They just enjoyed each other, chilled together, and the sweetest part of all is that it was completely unforced.

Matty felt more freedom with Paris than he did with his own family.

Hell, Matty felt more freedom with him than he did with himself.

That alone was worth the price of those shoes.

Without even trying Paris taught Matty how to be more confident.

Maybe those shoes did have some sort of *Cinderella* effect because Matty was being transformed right before his own eyes.

"You know anybody in the neighborhood yet?"

"A few people."

"Haven't ya'll been living here about six or seven years?"

"Yea, but I'm not good at making friends."

"Why?"

"I don't know Paris. I guess I just don't trust a lot of people. So I stay to myself."

"There's something you are not telling me."

"You don't know the half of it," and Matty left it there.

"Damn Matty. You are good looking and you can hang out with anyone you want to."

"Well, I guess I don't want to."

"So is that why you stay stuck up in the house all the time?"

"I don't stay stuck up in the house all the time. I'm around here with your fat ass two or three times a week."

They both started laughing.

"I'm not fat. I'm just short for my size."

They laughed even harder.

One Friday night while Matty was on hiatus from Sista, Paris pulled another first.

Paris pulled out this little gold bag and some white flimsy papers. Then he started rolling what looked like a cigarette.

"You roll your own cigarettes?" Matty asked. "Your mother lets you smoke?" Matty continued.

"You are really green as hell. You know that?" Paris said. "You've never smoked before?"

"Cigarettes?"

"You are being serious aren't you?"

"Yea. I have no idea what you are talking about."

"Reefer. I am talking about reefer. You've never smoked reefer before?"

"Hell no."

"Have you ever seen reefer before?"

Matty didn't answer.

"Damn," was all Paris said.

What Matty didn't tell Paris was that he had seen a big bag of reefer his mother pulled out of his brother Claude's drawer. But of course, Matty wouldn't tell that because it would violate the family privacy policy.

Still, Matty was too curious, so he meticulously watched every step of this intricate and detailed process. He even practiced on a couple of joints, as Paris called them.

Within a few minutes Matty was an expert reefer roller.

But he refused to smoke it. That was too much for Matty to handle.

So he became a bystander but his clothes smelt like he was a major participant.

When he got home from Paris' house that night he was practically naked when he came through the door because he had to get those smelly clothes off and into the laundry before that scent permeated the entire house.

Then one day, after several months of offers, Matty decided to see what the big deal was all about.

Paris started smoking and so did Matty.

Actually, Matty was choking, coughing, and turning green, then yellow, then red.

"Damn Matty you look like a rainbow." Paris was laughing.

"Paris, I don't feel so good." Matty was so sick that he turned as purple as that little girl in *Willy Wonka* who ate the dinner gum and turned into a blueberry.

"I'm going home."

"You dumbass. You can't go home. You are high as a Georgia pine and your mother already doesn't like me. If you go home she would tell my momma and then I would be dead. You want that on your conscious?"

"How do you know my mother doesn't like you?" Matty was stumbling, laughing, and searching for his words all at the same time.

He knew his mother didn't like Paris, but she would never say that to Matty or Paris. That wasn't her style.

By the same token, if his mother didn't like something or someone, it would be obvious on her face. But Matty's mother wasn't the problem.

Paris' father never liked Matty from their first meeting.

He literally growled at Matty like a dog the first time Paris introduced them. And his disposition toward Matty never changed from that first day.

Matty never understood the disdain Paris' father had for him, especially considering all of the errands he used to run on behalf of his family because it was the decent thing to do. Still…

"You really are a dumb blonde. That's obvious. Now lay your dumb ass down until you come down off that shit."

They were laughing so hard they were crying.

Matty was already lying down on the big sofa Paris' had in the basement, and he was so relaxed that his entire body was limp. Thank goodness he didn't have to pee because he wasn't sure if he had enough awareness to make sure that he didn't pee all over himself.

"Okay Matty, tell me the truth. Tell me the real reason you stay stuck up in the house."

"Ouch," Matty moaned.

It felt just like he had been punched in the gut.

Matty just laid there staring up at the panes in the ceiling. Not even that potent reefer could make him give up all of that baggage he had been holding onto despite the fact that he really wanted to let it all go.

Matty just wasn't there yet.

During his hiatus from Sista and in between his learning how to get high with Paris, Matty passed driver's education at school and got his learner's permit turned into a real license.

But the next task was going to be more formidable than any he had attempted thus far in his life.

Matty was going to attempt to talk his mother into letting him drive her brand new car. That was a feat that not one of his brothers had accomplished.

It took a good bit of doing over the course of a few days, but Matty did it.

And as his mother was giving him her final instructions he was already kissing her on the cheek and grabbing the keys.

It was a flawless drive but he couldn't think of anywhere to go.

He ended up going to Sista's house.

He pulled into the driveway without any fanfare. They didn't even know he was there until he knocked on the door.

"Man, whose car is that you are driving?"

"My mother's."

"That's a bad ass car man."

"Come on, let's go for a ride."

Matty wasn't sure it was a good idea, but he couldn't say no to Sista.

But still he let Sista, a few of her brothers, and a couple more friends pile all up into his mother's brand new car, despite his better judgment.

Matty slowly started to back out of the driveway.

Sista's family lived on a busy corridor in the southwest part of the city, so it was impossible to backup and go the way he wanted to go.

"I don't know why I didn't park in the big church's parking lot across the street," Matty kept saying out loud.

Actually, he was doing quite well.

He had safely backed into the street and was preparing to cut his wheel left when this huge old car, made of steel, came careening down the Boulevard.

Matty thought for sure he was going to stop or slow down, but the old man speeded up. And there was so much commotion going on in the car that Matty could not concentrate.

He was almost home free when he heard this CRASH!

That old man with the steel car purposefully hit Matty's mother's right front end.

It didn't do any damage to the old man's car whatsoever.

It ripped the entire front off Matty's mother's car.

And before the police came, everybody who was in the car with Matty scattered like cockroaches.

He was standing there alone holding the bag. And he had moved the car.

Everything his mother was trying to teach him suddenly sunk in.

Matty was so ashamed of what he had done that when he saw his mother's face he could not look her in her eyes.

His mother walked over to him, reached out her care-worn and loving hand, lifted up his chin, and said, "It will be alright."

She vanquished all enemies and challenges to her authority forever in that one moment. And the beauty of it was that she wasn't trying to do it.

She was simply loving her son through yet another crisis of his own making.

To Matty, that was remarkable, absolutely remarkable.

He finally had gotten the lesson but at what cost to his mother.

But those cockroaches had sealed the permanent breach between him and Sista.

Finally it was completely clear to Matty that she was no good for him.

Matty finally understood the beauty of the song *The Spinners* made, *Love Don't Love Nobody*.

The lyrics said "*It takes a fool to learn that love don't love nobody. It takes a fool to learn that love don't love no one.*"

Matty was the fool that had finally learned the lesson.

But learn it he did.

## Chapter 9

Now that the distractions of Sista was out of his way, Matty turned back into Sadie's loving, happy, gentle child.

His relationship with Paris grew to the point where Matty was living a double life.

His life outside of school was quickly becoming more interesting than his life in school. But it was an emotional separation and it didn't involve the chaos that Matty was used to having with Sista and her family.

In school he started to calm down and became more organized, open, and care-free.

He was happier than he had ever been which was aided by the fact that he had grown taller and was much thinner than ever before.

Matty used to be so happy on the bus ride home, after all of the bullying ended and he entered the post-Sista era of his life, he would be downright giddy come Friday.

Then something happened in school that made him tell Paris what he didn't want him to know, at least part of it anyway.

They had the radio playing the Friday night jams and they had enough money between the two of them to purchase reefer and the necessary requisite snacks.

"Paris, before we start smoking or doing anything else I need to tell you something while I have the courage to do it."

"Oh shit, this sounds serious." He sat the plastic bag down.

They had graduated from the gold bag to the larger plastic bag.

Paris grabbed his cigarettes, which he always did when he was nervous or upset.

Matty sat there that night and told Paris some of what JPH had done to him.

"Okay, here is what I don't understand. I have been asking you this for months. So why are you telling me this now?"

"A few weeks ago JPH and his old sidekick were both transferred to my high school. His former sidekick was not that bad. And not bad looking either. I actually liked him and he was cordial. But JPH ignored me and acted like he had never met me before."

The other day I was walking down the hall and he yelled out, "Fag," although there was no one around but me and him.

"That fat-ass, perverted, slob, who I hear is now a drug addict, had the nerve to call me names."

Paris looked at me for a while. "Wow child. No wonder you are so confused. I know you wanted to come out the closet, but damn I did not mean literally."

They started laughing.

"Look Matty, the only reason he is saying that shit to you is because you remind him of what he is. And the problem with that is that he is scared you would tell somebody else what he did so he is trying to get an advantage on you before you do."

Then Paris floated off into a completely different language that left Matty with no idea what he was talking about. But that night it was okay. Besides, Matty had said enough real talk for the both of them.

They both just sat there the remainder of the night.

Neither one of them wanted to talk very much anymore.

That was fine by Matty.

So they started getting high, higher than Matty had ever gotten before.

Suddenly he needed to get high, Matty told himself.

Matty didn't see Paris for a couple of weeks after that. Frankly, he was too embarrassed to face him.

That's when Paris got up the nerve to start calling Matty at home, which eventually helped him win over his mother - - some.

"Listen child. I think it is time you get out of this funk you are in. Let's go to the club Friday night."

"Club?"

"Yea the club. You have heard of a nightclub before?"

"What kind of club?" Matty was whispering because he didn't want his mother to hear.

"A dance club."

"We aren't old enough to get into a club."

"You let me worry about that."

"Okay. It's decided, we are going to the club on Friday. You are going and don't wear any of your preppy, school-boy clothes. Wear something relaxing and cool."

"Cool?"

"Hip Matty, in style, like the glass heels."

"You mean the ones I don't have anymore?"

Before Matty could say another word, he heard a dial tone.

Matty was nervous the whole week. It took him until midweek to build up the nerve to finally ask his mother if he could hang out a little later on Friday night.

His mother was never one to give a quick answer.

So Matty had to brace himself for an unbelievably long wait.

He asked her right after breakfast, as soon as had brothers headed out to do only God-knows-what. That way he didn't have to deal with any outside voices from the gallery trying to influence her decision just to spite him, although their mother was always independent and made up her own mind.

"Damn, why didn't I have my mother's strength?" Matty asked heaven.

But she surprised him and came back with a quick and positive response.

Matty didn't dare ask why.

He kissed her on the cheek, something she hated, and ran into his bedroom to try and find something cool to wear out to his first club adventure.

"Don't make this a habit and you better be home by 2 am, and not a moment later."

Friday night came and Matty walked around to Paris' house after he got dressed.

"2 am Matty," was the last thing he heard his mother say.

When he got to Paris' house there was an air of excitement about the night. Matty had dreaded this all week, but now he was actually looking forward to it.

Paris took one look at what he was wearing, and said "We can't all start out with a perfect ensemble. We can't do anything about that now."

Matty looked just like a confused puppy with his head slightly cocked to the right and he was staring at Paris for answers.

"Okay. Let's go."

Matty thought they were going to get in a car.

They didn't. They set out walking.

"We are going to walk to the club?"

Paris started laughing. "I keep forgetting I have to teach you everything."

They walked about three or four blocks to another house in the back hole (common name to residents for back part of the neighborhood) to another street where Matty had never been before.

Matty wanted to ask questions, but it just didn't seem like questions were welcomed.

So he kept his mouth shut – yet again – and went along with the plan.

"Paris you do realize that I don't like surprises right?"

"Hey Gail."

Paris said to the girl who answered the door.

It was Matty's first time ever meeting or seeing her.

"You ready?" Paris asked her.

"Not yet child. I am still trying to convince my mother to let my father take us to the club."

She spoke so fast Matty heard absolutely nothing in the middle of her sentence. All he heard were the bookends, the first word and the last word.

No sooner were the words out of her mouth had Paris jumped into action.

First he introduced everybody to Matty.

He actually told them a little more than Matty would have preferred, such as he was the new kid in the neighborhood, he stayed stuck up in the house all the time, he didn't know no body, this was his first time ever going to a club, and that he needed to go out to learn how to be more sociable.

And he said it all in one breath without even coming up for air.

Gail's parents started laughing.

And then he went into this elaborate sales pitch.

Within minutes they were in the backseat of Gail's father's car – on their way to the club – the Disco 9000. But Gail's parents called it, "The Disco Nine Hundred."

Matty had no idea what he had gotten himself into.

When they got to the club, Matty's first surprise was that it was so close to their neighborhood.

They really could have walked if they had to. But apparently it wasn't cool to arrive at the club walking.

But Matty still couldn't help but try to figure out how cool it was to be dropped off at the front door and then for your ride to drive away, if you weren't riding in a limousine. And although Gail's parents had a nice car, it was no limousine.

Anyway, when Matty saw the building, he immediately remembered passing that building many times on the school bus and in the car with his mother.

It was such a nondescript building sitting in such an obvious location that made it the perfect spot for a nightclub. Others clearly thought the same thing because the parking lot was completely full.

In fact cars were double and triple parked. And there were more cars parked as far as the eye could see on every side street within a four-block radius.

Matty didn't know how Gail did it, but once they got to the front door, the check-in clerk let them in without them having to pay a dime, which was a good thing for Matty, at least, because he had not thought about needing money not once the entire week.

Then came the obligatory "feel you up" as Paris described it with a smile.

Each one had to be patted down by this guy who was blocking the final entry into the club.

Paris quickly jumped in front of Matty and Gail with a devilish grin.

When Matty's turn came, he was too busy looking around to notice that it was both his turn to be felt up and that he was taking a little longer to pat him down than he did with the rest of the entourage.

But when Matty stopped looking around like a tourist, the glaring lights hit his face just enough for Matty to see his patter-upper clearly for a moment.

He was already staring into Matty's face. Then he smiled when they were finally focused on each other.

The crowd behind Matty was getting restless to get into the club, and he actually felt someone push him on through the door.

Once inside the club, Matty didn't know what to think.

There was this elevated dance floor in the middle of the club. It was a glass floor with lights flashing underneath the glass. There was no room for another single person on the floor but people were steadily streaming to the floor. So too was Paris and Gail.

What Matty heard in the background was, *"You can ring my bell, ring my bell, my bell. Ding. Dong. Ding."*

Matty couldn't help but stare at everything and everyone while the music was blasting in the background. It was an experience beyond compare.

People were drinking, smoking, laughing, hugging, and kissing. Matty was totally amazed.

As loud as the music was blasting a person could still hear the rancor of the crowd over the music, and there Matty was looking completely out of place, soaking it all in like a sponge.

There was every kind of person imaginable in that place - tall women, short women, fat women, skinny women, and every kind in between.

There was no lack of the male species either. Suits that looked like some of the suits he saw in church on last Sunday along with hats, canes, jeans, some short and some long, and almost any other kind of fashion imaginable was also on display in the club that night.

Ten songs later, Paris and Gail were still on the dance floor.

Matty was smiling because it was nice to know that fat people had rhythm too, and staying power, at least on the dance floor. And Paris had all of that and then some.

In the meantime, while they were still dancing, older women were offering Matty drinks and older men were trying to corner him to whisper things in his ear he had never heard before, even with his experiences.

Despite his militant attempts to fight off these temptations, his body was excited by the prospects.

But he wasn't completely stupid, he knew that he was only enjoying the attention, even if it was fleeting and for all the wrong reasons. Still it was nice to be the apple of someone's eye, even if both the apple and the eye were flawed.

Then suddenly, out of nowhere, a strange hand grabbed Matty's and was dragging him down a short but secluded hallway into the back of the club.

But there was no fear attached.

This stranger led Matty into a surprisingly quiet office. He could feel the vibrations of the beat, but the sound was muted.

It was the guy who had patted him down on entry into the club.

"Alfred," he said with an extended hand.

"Matty," he said shaking this welcoming hand that was twice as big as his and twice as strong.

"Matty." He said with this beautifully captivating smile. "You look too smart to be hanging out on a Friday night."

"You don't want to know," Matty said looking around the office.

"This is your first time in a club isn't it?"

"Is it that obvious? It's interesting and all, but I am not sure I want to repeat the experience."

They were both laughing. Then it happened.

Right in the middle of their laughter, Alfred kissed Matty.

Although every muscle in Matty's body fought hard to resist Alfred, he just didn't want him to stop.

Matty had no choice but to stand on his tiptoes in order to wrap his arms around his neck, and give in to the desire.

If Alfred was forbidden fruit, Matty had just bitten off a huge chunk. And worse yet, his kiss, this kiss, tasted like sweet nectar.

But as quickly as Matty gave in to him – this masculine, well-built, fully formed man –his body became as stiff as a board.

That's the funny thing about desire, once you give in to the lust of it, it is immediately followed with guilt.

Matty pushed Alfred away just as the door opened.

"Breaks over man."

No words were necessary between him and Alfred because they had shared more than words could ever say.

But Matty's body was screaming inside for him to say or do something.

"Where have you been?" Paris asked as he approached Matty walking back down the hallway through the fog, mostly in his brain, although there was a fog machine running in the club also.

"Nowhere," Matty said trying to turn the conversation. "Ya'll are soaking wet."

He had to change the subject because he didn't know how to lie, and he didn't really know Gail well enough to tell the truth.

"I know. The club is hot tonight," Paris said.

"What time is it?"

"It's 1:30."

"Shit, ya'll I've got to go."

"Okay, we've got time for one more dance."

"*Love-ove-ove, tau-au-au-ght me, who was, who was, who was the boss*," were the words blasting across the club.

Then as quickly as it all started, it was all over.

The music had turned into slow-dancing tunes. The lights weren't flashing so fast now. People were headed for the door. Matty's heart was racing.

He pounced on Paris as soon as he and Gail got off the dance floor.

"How are we going to get home?"

"Child, you worry too damn much. Bring your ass on," Paris replied.

They walked out the doors like it was no big deal.

Matty was prepared to start walking the short trek.

They walked over to a shiny, black, two-door, T-top Trans-Am. The door was open.

Matty looked at Paris.

He looked at Matty and said, "So whatcha you gone do just stand there?"

That was all the push Matty needed.

He crawled across the back seat to take his place behind the driver's seat. It was tight, but who was he to complain.

Paris was beside him. Gail was in the front.

They just sat there for a few minutes.

Then the driver's side door opened. Matty's mouth and heart dropped.

"Sorry about that," Alfred said.

Gail was smiling like a chess cat and so was Paris.

All Matty wanted to do was get out of this car. It felt like the car was closing in on him.

"Who goes home first?"

Matty shouted, "Me."

Alfred cut his eyes at Matty in the rearview mirror and reached around and grabbed his left leg with his left hand and he would not let go.

"Yea, that's cool take him home first," Gail said.

Paris grabbed Matty's right hand like he didn't want him to go. This time the puppy was gone. Matty knew exactly what he wanted.

This was all too much for Matty.

He was confused all over again.

When they pulled into Matty's driveway at exactly 2 am, Alfred reluctantly opened the door to let him out.

It was a two-door car, so as he was moving the seat, he managed to kiss Matty on his right cheek, without being seen, as he crawled out of his backside position.

Matty tried to pretend it didn't happen but Alfred was too irresistible to ignore.

Still, he refused to look back. They set in the driveway for a good three or four minutes after Matty closed the back door before they pulled off.

"Matty?"

He knew he was going to get a beating. He did not even try to offer his mother an explanation.

He just prepared himself for the inevitable.

"Just in the nick of time."

That, he was not expecting.

The next morning at breakfast his mother dropped the hammer.

"Don't ask me again about going out that late anytime again soon. That experiment worried me too much."

What she didn't know is that was fine with Matty because he was already tired of that experiment.

His brother's just looked at him and shook their heads.

Matty just kept eating his oatmeal so that he could go and watch Saturday morning cartoons.

There were about two weeks left in school and then it would be summer.

"It's going to be a boring summer," Matty said.

A few days later he was at his second neighborhood hangout. Partly because it was the only place his mother would let him go, and in part, it was the only place where he wasn't embarrassed to be seen.

In truth, it was a place Matty also hated to visit because it was such a happy place, the complete opposite of their house. No matter when anyone would go to this house laughter greeted them at the door, notwithstanding the fact that there were twice as many children and adults in their house.

Yea, anyone who knew Matty knew he was jealous.

But he loved every single one of them.

He loved them all so much he made himself a total nuisance.

If they were gingerbread cookies, Matty would have eaten them all up in one sitting.

Yet somehow he was able to forge a special bond with every single member of the household. And though he hated going to their house because it was so happy, once he got there, he would stay all day long.

In fact, their mom used to have to force him to go home.

Anyway, this particular day, Matty was surprised when he got there because there was no one at home but their mom. This had never happened before.

Even though it was shocking, at the time he did not think much about it. He just enjoyed the fact that he had her all to himself. He especially loved her.

She was a tall, light-walnut complexioned, beautiful woman, inside and out.

She was young, young-spirited, mentally astute, and had the most inviting personality. Matty had never in his life met a woman who had it together in every single way possible, outside of his mother.

But Banya was different from his mother. Matty couldn't put his finger on it but they were just different.

Since Banya rarely had time to herself, if ever, though she never seemed to mind – Matty asked her, "Do you want me to go home?"

"No," she said. "You can stay."

Matty was so happy because Banya was the closest woman to a second mother, if ever he had one. He was closer to her than he was to many of his own family members.

It was wonderful to be in her presence and not have to have forced conversation.

Matty could not recall quite how the subject came up but they started talking about religion.

And Matty asked her about a specific group, a group that many have seen knocking on doors in their own neighborhoods, especially on Saturday mornings.

"I remember how it started," Matty said.

Matty asked Banya about this strange building in the neighborhood that a lot of people who did not live in the neighborhood visited quite often.

"That's the hall," She said.

"Hall?"

"Yes. The meeting place for Jehovah's Witnesses."

She went on to explain the group and their beliefs to Matty in some detail. In truth Matty was less enthused by the story but more enthusiastic about the storyteller.

Banya made everything seem so interesting.

Then she told him the most unexpected detail of all – she used to be a member of the group.

"Used to be? What happened?"

"I just realized that there are some things that they teach that I don't quite agree with."

Matty just looked at Banya, and she knew that he did not understand.

"Let's just say that there are some things I am not quite sure about, and so I stopped attending."

As Matty sat there trying to understand what Banya said, he asked her, "Banya, what do you think it will be like to grow old?"

Without a moment's hesitation, Banya said, "I don't want to get old," in a very strong voice.

"Why!" He exclaimed.

"Because I don't want someone to have to take care of me and help me around. The idea of someone having to change my diaper really does not appeal to me. I just don't want to grow old and have to depend on someone else. I don't see anything good in growing old."

Matty never forgot those words.

Not too long after that he was back hanging around Paris' house in their basement.

"You have a secret admirer."

Matty's heart sank because he thought Paris knew about Alfred.

"He told me he has been watching you walk here for quite some time."

"Paris, I am not interested in anyone in that way. I have just had enough of bad encounters. I cannot even call them relationships because those encounters were never like any relationship I ever imagined."

Then Matty's brain caught up with his mouth.

"Paris did you say he has been watching me walking around here?"

"Yea why?"

"No reason." Matty knew that Paris or Gail did not know about Alfred.

"Matty you are a good looking guy and you are almost seventeen years old."

"What's wrong with being a virgin?" Matty asked.

"There are at least two things wrong with that statement. First, you are not technically a virgin based on everything you have told me. Second, it is just not natural for a good looking boy like you to not have sex."

"Paris, why are you pressuring me to have sex?"

"Matty, I have known you what, a year or more? I have seen you in public and private. Your mouth says no but your body says yes. Like it or not it's the truth."

"How do you know that I have not had sex already?"

"Well if you have, it has not been very good or it has not satisfied that need."

"That's the problem."

"What are you talking about?"

"I started having sex long before my mind was ready and now it is trying to catch up to my body so I am all out of sync. You see my mind and body used to work together all the time that is no longer the case. I have urgings and longings that I can't explain and don't know what to do about any of it."

"Where are you going?"

"I'm going home. I don't feel much like partying."

For several weeks after that each time Matty saw Paris they had the same general conversation and Paris had a new detail about this secret admirer.

About mid-summer, before they had time to discuss the situation again, Matty's home phone rang late one night, maybe about midnight.

His mother was asleep. His brothers were not home yet. The house was actually quite peaceful.

"Hello," Matty said in a pensive voice.

"Matty?"

"Yea, who is this?"

"It's Lee."

"Lee who?"

"I am the one Paris told you about."

"How did you get this number? Let me guess, Paris."

"Yea."

"Hey, can you walk around here so that I can talk to you for a minute?"

"Do you realize what time it is and what you are asking me to do?"

"Yea. I know, but I just got home from work, took a shower, and got all cleaned up."

"So. And cleaned up for what?"

Much to his own surprise, Matty started to get that tingling feeling.

"I'm studying," and Matty hung up the telephone.

"That was dumb, it's summer."

The very next day Matty couldn't wait to go around Paris' house to discuss the situation.

"Man I ought to beat your ass! Where the hell you get off giving a stranger my phone number?"

"Calm down child. It's not that big of a deal."

"Paris, you just don't get it. You are selling me out just like everybody else has done."

"Matty, you are gay and you can't keep hiding behind what other people have done to you so that you don't have to make a decision."

"I am not gay!"

"You don't even believe that statement yourself. How do you expect anyone else to believe it?"

"Here, smoke this and shut up."

While Matty was smoking, the word kept rattling around in his mind.

"Matty, it is about time you start seeing somebody."

Matty could not focus on what Paris was saying because he was still focused on the word gay. It was the first time he had an identity, even if it was one he wouldn't have chosen for himself.

"Maybe they all knew before I knew," Matty said.

"Child, you talking to yourself again? Give me that shit, you already too high."

Matty abruptly changed the conversation.

"Paris I have been seeing somebody, I just didn't tell you about it."

"Why not? Give me details."

"It's too embarrassing."

"You know what?"

"No what?"

"I got an idea."

They didn't discuss it anymore that night. The following Tuesday, Paris called Matty early that morning.

"Get your ass around here right now."

"But," was all Matty got out before he heard CLICK.

He barely had time to shower and make it around there.

Matty thought something was wrong. They were in the basement as usual getting high, when the phone rang upstairs.

Thump! Thump! Thump!

"Matty," he heard Paris utter his name in shear excitement.

Then he heard foot stomping!

"Matty. Get your ass up here! Hurry up!"

Matty could not help but jump to his feet and rush up the stairs. He was so high and scared that he was falling and stumbling the entire way.

It was really funny, at least it was at the time.

"Paris what the hell is going on?"

"Come on. We don't have much time."

"What?" Matty was really scared now.

"Do you need to go to the bathroom?"

"No. What is going on?"

Knock. Knock. Knock.

They both stopped and starred at the front door.

"Just a minute," Paris yelled out.

"Come on," he said dragging Matty down the hallway.

They rushed into Paris' parent's bedroom.

"Get in here," he said shoving Matty into the closet.

Knock. Knock. Knock.

"Okay. Okay. I'm coming."

"Matty listen. Stay in here. Be quiet. Do not make a sound."

Matty had no idea what was going on. He thought they were being robbed. His heart was beating so fast that he thought it was going to beat out of his chest.

"Paris?"

"Shh. Be quiet. Remember, not a sound!"

Knock. Knock. Knock.

Then Matty heard two voices instead of one.

Then he said, "When do robbers knock?"

They were coming down the hallway.

They were headed directly toward Matty.

He didn't know what to do. He was ready to jump out of that closet at any minute.

He was beyond being scared.

"Shit," Matty said in the dark.

"Fuck. How did I get back in the damn closet of silence again?"

Matty tried to focus on his surroundings, but it was too dark.

The smell of worn shoes mixed in the air with his mother's sweet perfume.

Matty's wandering was interrupted by what he thought was a belt buckle being unfastened.

Matty got curious and slightly opened the closet door shutters so that he could see what was going on.

He saw this long black thing sticking straight out near the shutter.

Matty feel back at the shock of it. Thank goodness there were blankets behind him to soften the blow.

"What was that?" He heard somebody say.

"I didn't hear anything," Paris said.

Matty eased closer to the door a second time.

"Oh my," Matty dared not utter the name in such a situation.

But now Matty was too intrigued to turn away.

"That's a dick! What the hell is going on?" Matty whispered.

He was mesmerized by the physique attached to that black club.

He couldn't see his face very well but he wasn't interested in his face either, at least not yet.

He was standing perpendicular to Matty and the closet. So all he could see was his profile.

"Wow," that was all Matty could say. He had never seen 11-inches before, stiff as an iron pole that he used to ram his bike into to stop when he first learned how to ride.

"Damn, what am I thinking? I have never seen another one before period, not like this."

Matty was good with math after struggling through Algebra II. Well maybe not that good, but at least he knew a straight line and how to measure lengths.

He had to admit that he had a pretty good side view.

He had a flat stomach with a soul patch that extended up his stomach and ended just below the base of his ribs. There were just a few beads of water trickling down the center of his chest rolling toward his soul patch.

From the side view it looked like a miniature waterfall and when the sun hit it, his bare stomach almost sparkled. And he had nice obliques, or at least the one Matty could see.

His white tee-shirt covered up his chest. But Matty got the feeling that his upper half was as good as his lower half.

Matty had a beautiful view. He could not have purchased front-row tickets that would have given him any better view, and he didn't need any buttered popcorn either.

This beautiful, dark chocolate, well-formed stranger was wearing some red bikini underwear that gripped his firm ass like the perfect glove.

Those red underwear were a beautiful contrast to his smooth, dark skin, his slightly protruding ass, and his muscled, well-formed legs.

But Matty's primary focus was on that miniature baseball bat with a big red knob on the end that was displayed for all to see - - at least for Matty to see. The red underwear were underneath the bat supporting it like a flagpole.

"That's beautiful," Matty whispered.

Matty was thankful for it all. Intrigued and very thankful.

Then Matty found himself gagging.

He was imitating what he saw Paris doing and he got choked on his own saliva.

Matty could not hold it in.

He was choking.

"Cough." Small cough.

"Cough, cough." Bigger cough.

Then Matty was coughing so hard from trying not to cough that he fell out of the closet, which knocked the stranger on the bed.

Matty didn't want him to see his face.

But when he saw the stranger's he said, "Damn."

Matty couldn't believe it.

He was lying back on the bed, his pants down around his knees, and his woody was standing tall like a lighthouse.

But Matty was still focused on his face.

Matty looked at him and then at Paris, then back at him.

"Damn," he said a second time.

By this time, the stranger was rushing to put his clothes on and was hurrying to get out of Paris' parents' bedroom and their house.

"Paris, who the hell was that ugly ass boy?"

He told Matty his name.

Matty said to Paris, "Well he sho' does work hard to live up to his name."

They both started laughing so hard that Matty's side was hurting.

"Once again you have managed to make my problems seem very small, at least for a little while."

Paris did a little curtsy, "Well I do what I can do."

"Oh, before you go I need to tell you something."

"What?"

"You fan club is becoming anxious. He has been pressing me to set up a meeting between you two. I think he really likes you."

"What are you talking about?"

"Would you be willing to talk to him in person?"

"I can't answer that right now. Besides, what would make you think I need you to set up dates for me?"

"Calm down child," he said to Matty.

"Paris, I don't know. I just don't need any more headaches right here at the start of school. Why would an older guy be interested in me," Matty asked.

"Why not Matty?"

"Does he look like yours?" Matty asked.

"Child please."

"What does that mean?"

"It means a big hell no."

Paris went on to tell Matty once again, "He's been watching you walk throughout the neighborhood and when he saw me and you together he asked me about you. He is a friend of my older sister and he used to be a friend of mine."

"What does that mean?"

"That means just what you think it means."

I said, "I've got to go."

"There you go again."

"What?"

"Trying to deny what you naturally feel."

"Whatever." Matty didn't know what else to say.

"Okay, let's change the subject."

"Agreed."

"Then do you wanna go to the club this Friday?"

"Hell no. I don't want to spend the rest of my summer all cooped up in the house to hang out with people I don't even know for a couple of hours, and in the dark the whole time."

"Okay. I'll call you."

Matty had to smile. Paris was not one to take no for an answer in a helpful non-threatening way.

Matty didn't see Paris for a couple of weeks because he had to go work at a summer camp, but he thought about everything he said the entire time he was gone. When Matty got back, the conversation picked up right where it left off.

But before Matty left for summer camp, he went to his first gay nightclub. It was called the Odyssey. Matty was barely

17 years old at the time, but a friend of a friend pulled strings to get him in the club.

The entrance to the club was a glass staircase that overlooked downtown.

Matty was so caught up with the sights of downtown to the point that he didn't even realize that he was the hottest new sight inside the club.

The line was unbelievably long because the Odyssey was the place to be and to be seen in according to everything Matty had been told.

Actually, Matty was rather reluctant to go after his Disco 9000 experience, but he agreed after several weeks of begging and prodding by Paris and the crew.

As they slowly made their way up the stairs, this tall, rather handsome white guy approached Matty and struck up a conversation.

"I've never seen you here before."

"That's because I've never been here before."

"You look a little young to be out here."

"I'm old enough," Matty replied as he prepared to go into the club.

"Why don't you come with me?"

"I don't know you."

"I insist."

"No." Matty was too late, the stranger had already grabbed his hand and was dragging an unwilling Matty through the club.

Everybody was staring at them with widened eyes.

Matty was getting a little scared because he didn't know what was going on.

They went into a private room that was dimly lit, and then the guy closed the door.

"I'm Steve."

Matty still didn't say anything.

"I own this club."

Matty was caught between surprise, shock, and fear of arrest.

"Why didn't you tell me that at the very beginning?"

"I wanted your honest response, not one that was influenced by me."

Matty's demeanor softened a little.

They talked for quite a while more.

"Are you ever going to tell me your name?"

"It's Matty."

"Matty, tell me the truth, how old are you?"

"Seventeen."

"Matty don't you know I could lose my liquor license for you being here?"

"Nobody knows that Steve but me and you," Matty said as he pulled out his fake.

"What's even worse is that I am physically attracted to you."

"Well, if we are being honest, I am attracted to you to, especially your wide hips."

Steve was blushing.

He walked over to Matty and put Matty's hands on his hips.

"You do like my hips," Steve said looking down at Matty's manhood.

"What can we do about that?"

Before Steve could get his kiss in, the door opened.

"Steve, we have a problem out here?"

"What's wrong David?"

"You need to see for yourself."

"Stay here Matty."

David and Matty had locked eyes.

"David, bring your ass on."

They closed the door.

They weren't gone two minutes between Matty was out the door.

The next time Steve saw Matty he was hemmed in a corner by David Baker.

"You know that he is young and wild. Don't make him feel guilty about being young."

Steve smiled at his old friend and let Matty stay and have a good time, even though that good time didn't include him.

Even though Matty was captivated by David, Matty had learned enough to know that he was just another notch on the belt. But David reminded Matty of a drawing that Matty saw one time done by this guy called Tom. Matty never knew his last name but he did remember that he was from Finland. Matty was glad to be a notch on David's belt.

David was a cowboy without the hat. He had striking, dark male features including a dark mustache. He had those wide-gap legs that held up his torso that was purposefully formed to entice Matty-types. And he was not big and not small by any standard, but he was extremely well made.

He had a black man's ass and a bodybuilder's torso. But for Matty, the most enticing part of David was that he had this little twitch in his walk that was more like a girl. So the contrast of hard body and tenderness so captivated Matty that David became his new play toy, at least for the month leading up to summer camp.

David had a loft apartment over the garage of some very wealthy benefactors that was way back in the woods. The woods offered them shelter from the world and it let them roam the area near the lake in the buff.

Although Matty never went back to that club, there was not a need to, David would go home and sleep a little after his work at the club, then pick Matty up around 8 am and keep him all day until it was time to go to work at night again.

To Matty's surprise, David was as tender in bed as he was hardcore looking out of bed.

"Do you treat all guys like this or just me?"

"Only the young ones," David replied.

When it came time for Matty to leave for summer camp, he knew he would never see David okay, but he also knew that he would never forget David either.

"Matty what are you doing?"

"Ruining you for anyone that comes after me."

"Well you're doing a good job."

David didn't go to work that final night. And neither one of them had any sleep.

Matty needed summer camp just so that he could recoup from the lure of David.

By the time Matty returned from summer camp, he had David out of his system and was full of energy and renewed spirit.

"How was summer camp?"

"You're not interested, so don't pretend."

"Okay. Listen Lee has been worrying me to death about you and when you were coming back."

"Paris, how old is he?"

"I don't know. 25 or 26, 27, 28. I'm not sure." Paris had this kiddy look of innocence. But it was naughty.

"Paris, I appreciate your interest in my personal life. But you have missed a few steps."

"Whatcha you talkin' about?"

"First of all shouldn't I be the one to decide when it is time for me to see someone? And shouldn't I be the one to decide who that person is? And what about me seeing someone my age?"

"Child, have you seen the boys our age? They are well-formed but have shit for brains and are immature."

"Paris. I don't even know that I am gay. I have had sex with a few men before but it didn't have any feelings attached to it. Well maybe with one guy."

"Yea, but do you want to?"

"Why do I feel like I am in the Garden of Eden and you are a serpent talking me into something I am going to regret?"

"So what harm will it do for you to at least talk to him?" Paris continued.

"I don't know Paris. I just have so many questions. The one thing I do know is that I want love. I want the love that momma had/has for my daddy. The kind of love that lasts long after death has lost its sting."

"Who doesn't? But that does not mean you stop living until you find the answer to every question."

"Matty, let me be serious here for one moment. Sometimes the answers come while you are on the journey. But you want answers while you are standing still, without ever going on the journey. What kind of life is that?"

"You know you are pretty smart sometimes to be a fat kid."

"Bitch I told you that I am not fat. I am just short for my age."

"Alright. Well it's 10:30 so I better get going. I'll talk to you tomorrow."

Matty purposefully left early so that he could take his time walking home and think about what Paris said.

Not long after he left Paris' house he noticed headlights behind him.

Matty kept walking pretending not to notice the car.

He slowed down to give the car an opportunity to pass him. Then the car slowed down even more. Then the car pulled next to him.

"Matty?"

He turned around. He didn't know the car or driver.

"Matty? It's me. Lee."

Matty just stood there looking.

He put the Volkswagen in park and stepped out of the car.

Matty's mouth dropped open.

He took all of him in in one instant.

He had a fresh cut and was wearing a black, tight-fitting tee-shirt that only covered his torso down to his navel.

Then Matty saw the most enticing thing of it all.

He was wearing some jean shorts! Daisy Dukes that looked like a skirt they were so short. And he was rock solid hard, all of him!

Paris was right. Matty's body was clearly excited by the sight.

"Shit," Matty said out loud. "You are better than eye candy."

Then Matty rushed to put his hand over his mouth as if he clearly didn't mean to say that, at least out loud.

"I was hoping you would like it."

"How did you know it was me walking?"

"I live right there."

It all started to make sense.

"You mean to tell me that you have been watching me walking around to Paris' all this time."

"Yea, whenever I was at home."

"Is this what you did to bribe Paris into giving you my phone number?"

"No, I did all this specifically for you. And by the looks of it, it is working," Lee said looking down at my own gentleman.

Matty couldn't say a word. He was completely naked before him, so to speak.

"You like me enough to come over for a few minutes?"

It took Matty a few seconds to gather his thoughts because he was freakin' gorgeous, even if he didn't tell him.

"No. This is my first time ever seeing you and you think I am going to come over to your house? Are you crazy?"

"I must be to go through all of this for you."

"For me? How old are you?"

"Yes for you. 28."

"You are almost eleven years older than me."

"And?"

"Doesn't that bother you?"

"No. Does it bother you?"

"To tell you the truth I'm not sure. It should but I'm not sure."

"Well at least get in the car and let me take you home."

"Lee. I am not getting in the car with you. My legs work just fine."

"I promise I will take you straight home."

"Promise?"

"Promise. Please don't make me beg. But if you want me to get on my knees for you I will."

After adjusting the seat, Matty got in the car.

"Damn. This bug is spotless. Do you ever let anybody ride in it?"

"I can count them all on one hand without using all my fingers."

"Wow," Matty said trying to pretend to be interested in the conversation.

"Am I distracting you?" He asked showing off his perfect white teeth that sparkled under the moonlight.

"Wasn't that your goal?"

"Not quite. I wanted a whole lot more."

"Like what?" Matty asked.

"Do I really have to tell you?"

"Yes, you really do."

Then Lee did something that repulsed, shocked, and excited Matty all at the same time.

He took Matty's hand and put it on his smooth, dark brown, muscled thigh. His touch sent chills up and down Matty's spine, to the point that Matty's underwear were wet. If that wasn't enough, he opened his legs wider and Matty's hand fell in between his legs.

"This is a skirt."

"No. I just ripped the inside seam to give you easier access. That is if you want it."

Matty was torn between his body and his mind. They were like identical twins with completely different attitudes and styles forced to share a room.

Like twins, he could not tell if his body and mind hated or loved each other.

But at that moment, Matty's body was definitely loving the feel and his mind was lovin' the view.

"So we agree for once," Matty accidentally said out loud.

"So you agree we should see each other again?"

"Uh? What?"

Before Matty could get his thoughts together, Lee took his finger and put it a spot Matty never knew existed on a man.

He put his finger in a warm, soft, plush spot that was warm, wet, and tight. It reminded Matty of Sista. It could not be!

Then Matty was totally flabbergasted by what Lee did next.

He stood up on his tiptoes while he was sitting there driving.

Matty saw it, he didn't understand it. And he wouldn't have believed it if he didn't see it with his own eyes.

As his finger slide deeper inside of Lee without any effort, his Johnson was throbbing so hard inside his pants that it was visible.

"May I touch it?"

Matty stared Lee directly in his eyes.

"I take that as a yes."

Matty still didn't blink once.

They continued to stare in each other's eyes. Matty's eyes widen at Lee's touch.

"You're wet," Matty heard him say.

Matty could resist no longer.

Matty rushed to kiss him.

He was so hot at that point that he didn't realize the force with which he used to pounce on him.

Lee lost his footing in his seat. Matty's body weight thrust him against the door and his head hit the glass really hard.

"I'm sorry," Matty said as he continued to kiss and bite his lips to the point of near bloodletting.

Lee did not resist.

In fact, somehow, he had managed to get his legs in the air and he had started to pull Matty's pants down.

Matty didn't know what happened in the next few minutes, but he was inside of Lee, in that warm spot and he was thrusting hard and harder.

Lee, this masculine beautiful, chocolate beauty of a man was underneath Matty moaning and writhing like a girl. It turned Matty on even more.

The sight of it all made him more ferocious and conflicted inside.

Matty took Lee's legs and pinned them further over the back of his head against the door. But Lee was a willing participant.

Matty thrust harder. Lee opened up even more. His hole was warmer, softer, and more inviting than Sista.

"Oh shit, I'm going to cum."

Matty tried to pull out.

Lee held him in.

They locked eyes again.

"Don't."

The base of Matty's shift was hitting his ass harder and harder and harder.

"AAAAAHHHHHHH."

Matty looked up and realized where they were.

He jumped up and out of the car and ran into the house.

The next morning at breakfast his brother Jacob shouted out, "What the heck was wrong with you last night?"

"Huh?"

"I heard you tossing and turning all night next door. Then you started moaning like a girl."

Matty turned as red as a new born baby who's ass was just slapped by the doctor. Everybody at the breakfast table was staring at him.

Matty looked at their mother to see what her response would be. She pretended to ignore us, but Matty knew she was clearly aware of it all.

As soon as she walked out of the kitchen, his oldest brother Junior said, "Sounds like you had a wet dream."

They all started laughing.

"What's a wet dream?" Matty asked.

"Man you ain't never had a wet dream?" Claude asked.

"No. I don't even know what that is."

They all got up from the table and left Matty sitting there alone.

It took Matty a while but he knew he had been played.

Lee trapped him into wanting him to the point that he would do almost anything he asked.

Despite being played, Matty couldn't get Lee off his mind.

But then again, Lee didn't give Matty enough room to breathe to get him out of his mind.

"Hey Matty."

"Hey Lee."

"Whatcha you doin'?"

"Studying."

"You think you can stop long enough to come see me for a few?"

That conversation went on for months, three or four times a week.

Matty was living more a double life now.

By day, he was a mild mannered junior in high school.

By night, he was the secret lover of the most secretive guy in the neighborhood.

Although Matty didn't want to admit it to himself, he was enjoying being Lee's whatever, in private.

As the relationship went on, they started seeing each other on Saturday afternoons and Sundays, after church.

Not only did the frequency of the meetings grow, but so too did the intensity. Matty and Lee were exploring each other's bodies deeply and regularly.

Matty was so fulfilled he stopped seeing almost everyone he knew outside of his family, including Paris.

They were having sex in every room of Lee's home - - the kitchen, the living room, the hallway, the bathroom, the den, and the cold storage room. They were engaged in every room of the house except for Lee's bedroom.

"Hello."

"Hey."

"Hey."

Matty realized that his feelings were now wrapped up in Lee. They had been secret lovers for more than a year at that point.

"Would you do something for me?"

"Sure."

Matty got dressed and put on his jogging clothes. Then he walked around to Lee's house in the dark of night.

He was excited at the prospect and also apprehensive about it.

Matty walked past the house, then circled back, and came through the backyard.

Then Matty stood at the outside at the bottom of the Lee's bedroom window.

The window opened. Matty jumped up and climbed through.

His prize was a beautifully sculpted body standing in nothing but some perfect tighty whitties in the dark, waiting to be had by Matty in any way he desired.

When they were done, they lay in each other's arms completely soaked in sweat, drenching sweat.

And they had made love underneath the stars. The room was completely dark and the windows were open so that all they could see was each other's eyes and white teeth. But then again, they knew each other's bodies so well, they didn't need any additional light.

After that night, Lee and Matty both knew that Lee had Matty.

Then Lee's manipulation over Matty kicked in and Matty was completely helpless to deny him.

He started putting Matty off until Matty was so horny that he would do almost anything Lee asked just so that he could be with him.

Matty was whipped although he didn't know it at the time.

Then Lee really taught him how to creep.

Matty learned how to sneak around to see Lee without ever getting caught.

He used to sit by the phone late at night just waiting for him to call, and somehow Matty knew that Lee knew he was sitting by the phone waiting for him to call.

Matty desired Lee so much that he learned how to sneak out of the house and back in, and no one was the wiser.

He used to effortlessly climb through Lee's bedroom window like he was shemming up a tree and Lee would be waiting - - sometimes naked, sometimes in underwear, sometimes in a tee-shirt - - it just depended on his mood.

Matty truly loved being with him because he was so interesting, not to dismiss the fact that he was the consummate black beauty.

By the time that Matty realized that Lee had him wrapped around his phallus, it was too late.

"Hey. You want to see me?"

Matty didn't say a word. He just sat on the phone and listened to Lee.

Then Matty did something that even surprised him.

He hung up on Lee.

Before Matty could take the phone off the hook, Lee called right back.

"Okay, okay I'm sorry. Please come see me."

Matty hung up a second time. But he could not resist.

He got dressed, but he tried to do it as slowly as he possibly could, but he could not help himself.

Within minutes, Matty was climbing through Lee's bedroom window.

But that night was different.

As soon as Matty came through the window, Lee closed the window and the blinds, and then he pulled the curtains closed.

Then he turned on the lights. Lee was fully dressed.

Matty didn't understand.

"Take off your clothes."

Matty did as he was told to do.

Then Lee pulled out his this small green tube, it looked like a makeup jar.

He sat down on the bed beside Matty and kissed him.

Then he opened up the jar. It was full of white powder.

Lee scooped up a bit and put it in his nose.

"Watch me," Lee told Matty.

Then he scooped up some more and put it up his second nostril.

"Now you do what I just did."

Lee scooped up a fingernail full and put one, then two up Matty's nostrils.

Then as the drug started to take effect on Matty, Lee stood up and started to undress. It looked like he was giving Matty a lap dance.

Matty was engrossed in every inch of Lee's body.

"Stick your tongue out."

Matty stuck his tongue out.

There was nothing else for Lee to take off but his underwear.

While Matty had his tongue sticking out, Lee turned around, pulled his underwear down, spread his ass, and told Matty, "Stick your tongue in my hole."

Matty did it. Lee's ass smelled like strawberries and cocoa butter. It was intoxicating for Matty.

"Now eat it."

Matty was so high that he could not resist doing exactly what Lee told him.

The remainder of the night, Lee continued to feed Matty that white powder, as he spread his ass wide open on his knees for Matty to eat him for hours nonstop.

They did not end the night until the sun was almost up.

It was a good thing for Matty that the next day was Saturday because he slept all day long.

That night changed their relationship once again.

A few days later Matty had to tell someone and there was no one else to tell but Paris.

"You did what?"

"I did. And I hate to admit it Paris but I enjoyed him in a different way."

"Of course you did. Matty, child, Lee gave you cocaine. So of course you would do what he wanted you to do and enjoy every minute of it."

During his walk home, that's when it hit Matty that Lee was a pervert and so Matty figured he was going to have to get away from him.

"Damn you Paris."

Matty took a few more steps.

"It's my own fault for letting myself be talked into doing something I thought was wrong from the beginning."

That entire week during school Matty could not concentrate on any of his work for thinking about Lee.

Uncharacteristically, during the middle of the week, the phone rang just after midnight.

Matty knew who it was.

"I'll just have to be firm."

He answered the phone.

"Hello."

"Hey." Lee sounded almost happy.

"Yea."

"I want to see you."

"It's a school night."

"I won't keep you all night. I promise."

Matty was thinking about it, despite his attempts to fight back his feelings.

"Please. Don't you want to come around here and play in your black hole for a little while?"

"See you in a few."

Sure enough when Matty arrived Lee was prepared to start feeding him more cocaine.

He was also standing there butt naked with a rock hard Johnson.

Matty was so far gone now that there was no way for him to turn back because Lee knew he was a willing participate to his perversion.

Matty was trapped in Lee's spider's web.

And he loved making love to Lee's body, every inch of it. And Matty thought Lee loved making love to him as well.

Their sex became so consuming that they started having sex all night on Friday nights and sometime all day on Saturdays.

It wasn't easy for Matty to keep coming up with school activities to be involved in, but whatever it took for him to be with Lee, Matty did it.

This went on well into Matty's senior year.

Then one night Matty came through Lee's bedroom window and he was wearing his jean skirt again. The same skirt he was wearing the first time they meet.

But this time he was different.

While Matty was half way in the window Lee walked over and turned his beautiful, black muscled ass into Matty's face.

"Stick your tongue out."

Matty did as he was told to do.

Lee lifted his skirt and put his asshole square on Matty's tongue.

It was wild, he was wild, they were wild.

Then he slowly led Matty into his bedroom by slowly walking forward with his ass still fully planted on Matty's tongue.

Once Matty was completely in the bedroom, Lee slowly undressed him, pushed him down on the bed, pulled his skirt up again, and sat down of Matty's phallus until he was completely inside of him.

"Don't you move."

Lee rode Matty like he was a horse until Matty could no longer hold it.

All the while he was feeding Matty cocaine.

Matty's thrusts become harder and more rapidly.

Matty tried to push Lee off of him but Lee was too strong.

"Please, I can't hold it."

Lee held Matty down and forced him to cum inside of him. And as he was cumming Lee spread his ass wider to take it all in.

While Matty was lying there with Lee on top of him and totally spent, they started getting higher with the cocaine.

Matty started to grow inside of Lee again.

That lasted for three more hours.

"Sniff," Lee said.

First Matty's left nostril than his right nostril.

Matty was immediately hooked.

Then he rode Matty's rising phallus again, this time even harder, and harder, and harder.

The last time Matty came it was so loud that Lee had to cover his mouth with his hands.

Lee held his hands over Matty's mouth, but he said, "Don't stop."

Lee looked right into Matty's eyes as he came, almost enticing him to release even harder.

When they were done Lee smiled, which was his way of telling Matty he approved - - that Matty had done a good job.

A few weeks later was spring break.

Matty and Lee had sex every single night for 10 days straight.

By the time it was time for Matty to go back to school, he was completely exhausted.

Matty slept in class, on the bus, at home and that whole weekend.

But as soon as he recovered Lee called.

Despite all of Matty's protests, he and Lee were in absolute sync with each other and maybe Lee more than Matty.

Nonetheless, when Lee called Matty ran to him.

"I wonder what he has in store for me this time?"

Matty simply could not resist the intrigue of Lee and they were both animalistically attracted to each other.

In spite of the fact that Lee had taught Matty how to do cocaine at the age of 16, Matty was completely satisfied with this almost thirty-something man.

His physique and his physical prowess were all the nectar Matty needed, despite the fact that there was enough shame attached that Matty would never want anyone to find out.

"Even if they did, I am not going to stop seeing him."

This particular Friday night, Matty was already in the mood to do anything and everything that Lee wanted. It wouldn't take very much coaxing on Lee's part, but Matty was going to try and not appear anxious, except that Matty had not had his Lee fix in more than a week because of exams.

When Matty arrived Lee was already higher than he had ever seen him before. As usual Matty stated out eating Lee's ass, then in the blink of an eye, Lee had jumped on Matty's back and was violently riding him.

Matty bucked back like a wild horse.

That went on for a couple more hours.

After three for four orgasms between the two of them, Lee had come down off his high a little bit.

Matty was prepared to put on his clothes and leave.

"Where are you going?"

"I thought you were done."

"I'm not finished with you. You finished with me?"

Matty took his clothes back off.

Lee pulled out his famous green coke bowl and started to feed Matty.

Matty was more than receptive.

"This is a little different than what you are used to."

Matty stared at Lee with wanting eyes waiting for the other shoe to drop.

Lee stuck his dick in Matty's mouth and shoveled more product up his nostrils.

"This is cocaine and heroin mixed."

Matty didn't bat an eye. He was just that deep under Lee's spell.

"Good boy," Lee said.

When he released himself, he bent down and kissed Matty in the mouth. Yea, they shared Lee's juice.

This was a first and it was the final hook in Matty's nose.

Matty completely cut off everyone else after that.

He only went to school and came home.

Lee did the same thing.

He only went to work and came home.

He had Matty so trained that Matty would be waiting for Lee when he pulled into the driveway.

Sometimes Lee would be naked by the time he got home and he would give himself to Matty right there in the driveway, which was no easy task in the beetle.

Other times, Matty would perform fellatio on Lee's sweaty work body before they ever went in the house.

They would shower together, get high, shower some more, and then make passionate love in and out of the shower, and anywhere else that Lee desired.

By the time their second or third anniversary rolled around, Matty and Lee spent New Year's Eve, New Year's Day, and two more days thereafter getting high on cocaine and heroin, and having ridiculous sex together.

They were both raw at the end of those four and half days.

When Matty came home, he slept for the remainder of his Christmas break. But he was fully satisfied in every imaginable.

About two weeks later, Matty got that Lee itch again.

Sure enough, that Monday night the phone rang.

They got high and had sex.

Then the phone rang Tuesday night.

They got high and had sex.

Then the phone rang Wednesday night.

They got high and had sex.

Then the phone rang Thursday night.

They got high and had sex.

"I want you around here at 8 o'clock tomorrow night. I'm getting off from work early so I can spend all night with you."

"I had plan on going out tomorrow night with Paris."

"Cancel them."

Matty wanted to say no, but he simply couldn't tell Lee no.

"Whatever you say."

Sure enough the next night, Matty was at Lee's house at 7:59 on the dot.

Lee was sitting there waiting and looking at his watch, in his tee-shirt and some tighty whitties.

"Damn he looks so fetching."

"You want me don't you?"

It was as if Lee could read Matty's mind.

"Come and get me."

Although this secret relationship had been going on for about three or four years, the sex and the intensity had not diminished one iota. In fact it had increased exponentially.

Matty even started including Lee in his nightly daven.

"You ripped my underwear Matty," Lee said after he had finished giving himself to Matty.

He gently grabbed Matty's hand and they walked down the hall to Lee's room.

Matty was stunned.

Lee's room looked like a movie studio.

"I've got a new toy and I want to try it out on you...us."

Lee had set up a brand new video camera and lights and everything.

For a multitude of reasons, Matty got up to leave refusing to be videotaped for a million reasons.

But Lee physically forced him back down on the bed.

Matty got up to leave a second time.

Lee smacked him, really hard, and made him sit back down on the bed.

Stunned at the turn of events, Matty was still holding his right cheek, when Lee kissed him.

He kissed Matty deeply, so deep in fact that it went beyond passion.

He kissed Matty so good, so long and so hard that Matty completely forgave that he just hit him.

While he was kissing Matty he started shoveling his product mixture of cocaine and heroin in his nose and Matty didn't dare refuse him again.

"I want to videotape you eating my ass so that I can look at it anytime I want to."

Matty thought to himself why is that necessary since I am here practically every day. But he would not dare say that to Lee.

Without delay, Lee turned on the camera and slowly pulled what was left of his tight white Hanes underwear down to reveal his beautiful ass like it was an apple to be eaten.

Then he slowly got on the bed, first his left knee, then his right knee, and spread his legs to reveal his open and twitching hole.

"Look at the camera."

Matty did it.

"Stick your tongue out."

Matty did it.

Then while staring at the camera the entire time, Lee slowly slid his hole onto Matty's tongue, again and again.

Once again Lee had taken ownership of Matty.

The camera was rolling, so was Lee and so was Matty's head.

In that instant Matty realized that he had made his first porn. The thought of it still haunts Matty today.

But still Matty refused to leave Lee in spite of the fact that Lee had turned him into a drug-using, gay porn actor.

Matty continued seeing Lee well past his first year in college.

One Saturday night, there was an unexpected knock at Matty's front door.

He knew the guy's face but he didn't really know him.

"Matty?"

"Yea."

"I'm Negar."

Matty remained motionless.

"Can I talk to you for a moment?"

Matty opened the door and stepped outside.

They sat down on the porch and started talking.

Matty noticed the biggest knot in Negar's pants that he had ever seen. Then it hit him what this was all about.

"Let's cut the chase. You want me to perform fellatio on you, right?"

"Yes and no."

"I'm listening."

"I want you to eat my ass like I saw you do in that video with Lee. The one where you looked like you were eating an apple pie, you were eating his ass so good."

Matty was furious.

"Come on."

Matty lead Negar to his own secret spot and he did everything to Negar that he did for Lee.

Without warning, Matty entered Negar and Negar was too engrossed to respond. He let Matty have his way with him. But Matty didn't just leave him hanging.

When Negar was finished being satisfied by Matty, he was convulsing and whimpering like a puppy.

Matty pulled up his clothes, "Don't ever knock on my door again."

After that Matty realized that Lee was sleeping with several others in the neighborhood and that he was one of many concubines that Lee owned. Or did he only own Matty.

"But when does he have the time or energy to sleep with someone else? Hell he is always with me."

Matty started distancing himself from Lee.

That difficult task was made easier when Matty found out that Lee was showing his videotape to as many people as he could find, which was quite easy for Lee since he had such a crowded bed.

Not long after Matty's encounter with Negar, Lee called.

Matty went.

He creeped out the house as usual, went around to Lee's place, and came through his window like he always did.

But this time it was different.

Lee was sitting there with another person.

Matty almost shitted in his pants right there.

"I was stunned, hurt, and embarrassed," Matty told Paris.

And the worst of it all, the other person was a drag queen!

Matty could not believe his eyes.

"What's wrong?"

"What's wrong?" Matty screamed.

"Keep your voice down."

Lee continued.

"I want him to eat your ass while you eat mine."

"Hell no!"

Matty crawled right back out of that window and went back home. But he was furious because he badly wanted Lee that night, but that was not going to happen.

Matty was irritable for several weeks because he had an urge that he didn't know how to get fixed.

Then terror hit Matty because he started realizing that his secret rendezvouses with Lee was no longer secret.

"If the video is out, what else is out?"

A cloud descended on Matty - - a cloud of fear, shame, and exposure.

Matty was glad he had graduated because he didn't know what he would do if that news got out around school.

It didn't bother himself so much about the neighborhood because he never cared for most of the people in the neighborhood anyway.

But none of that changed the fact that Matty was in love with Lee.

But for him, Matty was just another dumb punk to be used. Matty was a fool, a fool in foolish love with no love to call his own.

Matty started to see himself as being tainted.

*Soft Cell* made this song called *Tainted Love* and that song became Matty's mantra.

All the time Matty was with Lee, he kept him separate from school. He kept school separate from Sista, and he kept Sista separate from Paris. And they were all separate from his family.

Although Matty was in the middle of the circle, he didn't seem to truly belong anywhere in his own life.

"Who do I have to blame for the whore I have become, me, JPH, Lee, Buddy?"

And therein lay the conundrum that Matty has lived with all his life.

# Chapter 10

Although Matty was in community college, it still was not enough for him. Matty had dreams, grand dreams that didn't include community college, but Lee had taken all of that away from him.

In truth Matty could not get over the idea of losing Lee. However, he also could not abide by the idea of being one of many sexual partners.

Matty kept replaying all of the voices from his friends' plans after senior year. Those plans included college and school, traveling to Europe, and going to work in some prestigious jobs.

Matty didn't have any plans.

"I have never really thought much about it all. I don't think I ever had time to think about what I wanted to do when I grew up. I was too busy responding to life instead of creating opportunities for my life," Matty was looking in the mirror.

Matty graduated at the top of his class.

But graduation didn't happen that easily. Matty had several issues that demanded his attention prior to graduation.

Near the beginning of his senior year, Matty had gotten his first job with Ivey's department store.

He never told his mother why, but the truth was that he needed to find a way to break away from Lee.

"Momma, I want to save money to buy my own car."

Reluctantly, his mother agreed to his incessant pleas for a job.

"But if your grades start to drop so much as one digit, you and that job will be parting ways."

Matty was good at the job and the job was good for Matty. Although he never stopped seeing Lee, he still started to improve overall and become more responsible. But he had to schedule his work around Lee's desires in the beginning.

Anyway, things were going really well, until that day.

It was only the second time that Matty had ever seen a hundred dollar bill in his whole life.

Then, sure enough, before that day was over, Matty had gathered three of those gems. He marveled at the bills.

Matty put all the money in his cash drawer as he was required and went back to work, never thinking about the money any more.

Closing time and it was time for Matty to cash out his drawer, after he had shut down the men's floor.

As Matty started counting the money, he got the ridiculous notion to take one of the bills.

"Hell, why take just one? Let's take two."

Matty continued his cashout duties.

"Don't do this," he heard a voice say.

Matty continued working.

" They'll never know that I took this one."

He locked the cash drawers, turned in his receipts, and went outside to wait for his mother to pick him up.

Matty pilfered one of the three, one hundred dollar bills.

He was off for the next three days and would not be back at work until the following Saturday morning. He figured by then it would all be forgotten.

As usual Matty spent that Friday night with Lee and got up the next morning and went to work at Ivey's. He had actually forgotten about taking the money.

The hundred dollar bill was more of an art piece than anything else.

Matty never spent the hundred dollars.

Not even an hour into his shift, Matty was approached by two gentlemen wearing suits, cheap suits, but still suits.

"Matty?"

"Yes."

The gentlemen announced their names and positions but Matty had tuned them out because he was still reeling from being up all night giving himself to Lee and vice versa.

He was sore all over and he had bruises to boot. Lee pulled out all stops last night - - putting hickies all over Matty's body, drinking his man juice several times, for the first time ever.

Matty remembered telling Lee, "You really missed me huh?"

That made Lee pound Matty harder.

When Matty got ready to leave, "You ain't going nowhere. We just gettin' started."

Lee flooded Matty's heads with drugs and then rode Matty like a horse for four more hours."

"We need to talk to you for a moment. Will you please come with us?"

Matty was in another world.

"Matty," the men in black exclaimed.

"Huh?"

"We need you to come with us."

"Oh, okay," Matty blindly followed their orders.

Together the three of them walked to a room at the back of the store, a room that Matty had never seen before, nor did he know existed.

They began asking Matty all kinds of questions, but none of them seemed of any importance. They asked him about school, working, his family, and the job.

"Matty do you remember working last Wednesday?"

"Should I?"

"Anything happen or particular problems?"

"No."

This dialogue went on for a while longer.

Meanwhile, they were losing Matty because he was floating in and out of last night. Matty remembered Diana Ross made this song that said, "I've got the sweetest hangover I don't wanna get over." That was exactly how Matty felt and therefore he was not paying his host very much attention.

"Well Matty we have a problem."

Matty said nothing.

"You see we cannot understand why your cash bag was short $100?"

"100?" Matty said.

Now they had his attention - - his undivided attention.

He tried not to look shocked or confused, but he was not good at hiding or lying. Still he said nothing.

Then the gentle conversation turned into a full press. And the men where now taking turns asking Matty questions all at the same time.

After more than two hours of interrogation, Matty confessed that he took the hundred dollar bill.

He was scared and wanted to cry, but he didn't. Instead, he just sat there waiting for whatever came next.

The scent of Lee was all over him because he didn't have a chance to take a proper shower; and, every which way he moved, he felt Lee.

They left Matty in the room by himself for a long time. They never told him he could call his mother, they never told him he could leave, and they never told him he didn't have to answer any of their questions.

After that long intermission, during which Matty was never feed any food or given any water, the men came back in and had Matty sign some papers.

Matty got up and was ready to leave.

"Sit back down you thief. We are waiting for the police to come pick you up."

Now Matty was neither interested in or attempting to hide his shock. It was in full blown discovery.

Matty sat back down and waited quietly until the police arrived.

One of the men told the officer, "You don't have to cuff him he won't be any problems."

And sure enough the officer didn't put the shackles on Matty.

They walked quietly to the car, and Matty got in the backseat, and they drove off to downtown.

The officer was talking to Matty but his mind could not focus on what he was saying because his brain was all over the place.

But Matty did hear the officer say, "Crime doesn't pay."

It only took Matty a few seconds to realize that he would be a terrible criminal.

"Son you don't even look like a criminal."

The next time the officer had Matty's undivided attention, they were pulling in the underground garage at the police station, which again, Matty didn't even know existed.

When they got out of the car, the officer walked Matty up to a glass cage where he was buzzed into the station.

Then after they were buzzed into several more doors, they gave Matty a placard with is his name and a number on it and made him hold it in front of him while they took his pictures, front, side, and profile.

Then they were getting ready to go into another room, and another officer yelled, "Wait. You can't put that kid in there with them, they will eat him alive."

"What do you want me to do with him?"

"Let him sit out here until his mother comes to get him."

"Mother!" When Matty realized that she was going to have to come get him, he turned pure green, green eggs and ham green.

"Call you mother son."

Matty wanted to run, but there was nowhere to run.

"Good thing I am at the police station. She can't kill me in front of all these people."

As Matty dialed each number, his mother's words rang out in his ears like bells going off in a church steeple.

"If you ever go to jail, do not call me because I know you did it and I am not coming down there to get you because you know better."

Matty could not get those words out of his mind.

"Claude, is momma home?"

"No, Matty, why?"

"Tell momma I am down at the police station." CLICK. Matty hung up the phone.

One hour went by. Then two. Matty figured his mother was not coming to get him and so he prepared himself to be stripped and taken back to where the real criminals were being held.

Then he started turning colors.

"Look! That kid is turning purple!"

"Is he sick?"

"Check his breathing."

By the time Sadie arrived, the police had Matty laying prostate on a bench and giving him oxygen.

She had one of those if looks could kill looks on her face. But that changed when she saw Matty being pumped with oxygen.

"Oh God, Matty! What's wrong with my baby?"

No one knew that Matty was sick at the thought of his bruised covered body being discovered or uncovered.

Once everything was complete, she dragged Matty out of there by his ear lobe, almost removing it single handily from his head.

"This is too big for a whoppin'. You are punished until I say when."

School and back home was all Matty could do. He couldn't even go outside, and for the first three weeks he could not even watch television.

It wasn't easy, but one thing was sure, Matty was not going to stop seeing Lee that is until that ultimate test of fidelity or infidelity.

But the worst of it came when Matty had to go to school and tell his advisor, Mrs. Beal what he had done. You see Matty was the district president of DECA.

Mrs. Beal, in a completely non-judgemental way, went and told Mr. Shutzky.

Mr. Shutzky pulled Matty into his office.

"Matty if you tell me the truth I will help you, but if you lie to me, you are on your own, and I will have your presidency pulled from you."

Matty confessed his complete sin to Mr. Shutzky.

Mr. Shutzky protected Matty the entire way and so too did Mrs. Beal.

They made sure Matty's indiscretion never got out. And Matty was so grateful he never stole again, at least until….

They went to court several times over the course of the school year, but it kept getting pushed back because Ivey's would never show up.

In the meantime, the attorney that Matty's mother's friend hired had Matty take a polygraph test.

Matty passed with flying colors.

The last time they went to court the judge said that he was not going to delay it anymore. He set a sentencing date.

Before they could return to court, a new judge was appointed. According to the attorney, "This is a mean man and very strict."

They were all in a panic mode.

The night before the sentencing date, Matty's mother and her friend left out very late that night and they were gone for more than a few hours. They didn't know that Matty was wide awake when they left and when they returned.

The next morning as everyone was getting up to get ready for school and work, Matty's mother came into his room and put some kind of powdery sand-type of mix in his left pocket.

"Don't touch it."

Off everybody went their separate ways.

"You not going to court with me?"

"No," is all his mother said. But what Matty didn't know is that his mother was too scared to go to court with him.

When they got to the court, Matty and his mother's friend, the judge was handing down some extremely harsh sentences. People were screaming, yelling, and cussin', as the bailiff was dragging them out of court.

Matty's turn came to face the judge.

His attorney pleaded, "Nolo contendre."

The judge looked at Matty, down at the papers, and back at Matty.

He shook his head as if he was not buying it.

Then he said, "The court agrees. But son let me tell you this. If I ever see your name down here again for so much as a speeding ticket I am going to charge you with the old and the new. Do you understand me?"

Matty's mouth was desert dry with fear.

The attorney had to tell him, "Answer the judge."

Matty managed to eek out a barely audible, "Yes sir."

They left the court room and Matty was jumping up and down. He couldn't wait to get to school to tell his mother. She had taken a job at the school as a cafeteria worker to watch over Matty to keep him out of trouble. And all his teachers knew she was there, so Matty straightened up.

Matty thought it was her way of not having to send him to military school.

What he didn't know is that his mother went back to work to try and help him pay for college, since he was the only one of his brothers that had ever talked about going to college.

While all this was going on Matty had also been approached by an agent to become a male model. It took a lot of prodding but eventually, his mother agreed to the agent's pleas.

Immediately, Matty started attending the TRIM school of modeling. Overnight, Matty underwent a metamorphosis.

His clothes, his posture, his language, his walk, and his attitude all changed.

Somehow, through his misfit crew of friends, it got out everywhere they went that Matty was not only smart, genius by their standards, but that he was good looking and a model.

They were more than proud to be seen with Matty.

As it was, one night they were all at the club partying, one of the few nights that Lee let him go out with his friends.

This fairly good looking guy named Eleaf came up to Matty and started inquiring about his background, his modeling work, school, and everything else.

Matty being the naïve ass that he was, gladly told Eleaf everything he wanted to know, thinking that Eleaf was interested in him. Matty didn't know that Eleaf was insanely jealous of him.

Eleaf never called Matty once and he never talked to Matty again at the club. Rumors had it that Eleaf was extremely jealous of Matty.

Matty was more than a head turner, and Eleaf did everything he could to covet that same attention.

A few weeks before graduation, there was a knock at Matty's front door.

"Hey Matty."

"Eleaf?"

"Yea, I came by to see you."

Gullible Matty sat on the front porch and talked to Eleaf for about an hour.

"Matty I need your help."

"Okay what can I do for you?"

"I hear you are really smart."

"They say so."

"I need your help in writing a paper so I can graduate. Without an A on this paper I will not graduate."

"Okay I will help. Show me what you have."

"I'll call you in a couple of days."

"Sure," Matty said.

When Matty read what Eleaf had given him he was stunned by what he was reading. It was on a $7^{th}$ grade level.

Matty took the paper and rewrote it completely in a matter of hours.

The next time he saw Eleaf on his front porch, he was giving him a product that Eleaf could have never produced on his own.

Eleaf never came over to Matty's house again.

A few weeks later Matty saw Eleaf at the club. He was with a group. Matty walked right up to Eleaf, "So what grade did you get on your paper?"

Eleaf's group was stunned that Matty was even talking to Eleaf.

"Oh hey Matty, I didn't see you over there."

Matty didn't say a word, he just stood there waiting on an answer as he was being oogled by everyone single member of Eleaf's group.

Matty ignored them all because he never they would never have a chance with him in their wildest dreams.

"I got an A."

Matty was satisfied and walked off.

Eleaf graduated which made him hate Matty all the more.

Matty also helped Paris study for his history exam so that he too could graduate.

Neither thanked him for his work.

Yet despite Matty's work, he spent his graduation night sitting on the corner by himself drinking and smoking until he fell out.

"I used the $10 my grandfather gave me to score."

It was the first thing he had ever given Matty, besides that lecture about defending himself when he was being bullied.

A few months later Matty was sitting in his College Trigonometry class, in the middle of the lecture he got up and walked out of class.

He was so serious that he walked down to the recruiter's office, which was only about 10 or 12 blocks from school.

He went to the Army first.

"I can't do this," Matty said.

Then he went to the Marines.

"Oh hell no. They are worse than the Army," with that Matty turned around before he ever crossed the threshold.

The Air Force was next.

"I've never flown before. I'm not sure that I want to fly around the world for thirty years."

"There's nothing left but the Navy."

Matty walked in and signed up immediately. That was in May of 1982.

Matty could not wait for his mother to get home from work so he could tell her his good news. As soon as she walked into the house, he showed her his papers.

"You signed up for the Navy?"

"Matty, what are you thinking?"

"Momma, I am not doing anything else with my life. I cannot afford college. I blew all of my scholarship opportunities. It is either this or be a bum."

"When do you leave," she asked with her head hanging down.

"45 days."

It was Sadie's turn to be silent.

"Momma, I don't have any other way to help you. And nobody else is trying to help us."

"Matty, honey, what can you do?"

"Momma, I can at least try! That is more than any of my brothers are trying to do!"

"Matty…"

"Momma, we are poor. You may have known this for a long time, but I just found out."

The matter was never discussed again.

Matty spent those next 44 days partying, like he had never partied before. He was on the verge of being out of control again.

But the truth was that Matty had not felt so alive in a really long time. It was a shame that it took booze and other stuff to make him feel that way.

The first Friday night after his announcement, Paris and Sheila wanted to take him bowling.

Matty was not a bowler, but it was the first time that either one of them had ever agreed to pay for anything, so he was not about to turn them down.

When they got to the bowling alley, the evening started off just fine.

They were all laughing, missing the pins, and having a wonderful time.

Matty left the group for a moment to go to the bathroom.

When he got ready to exit the stall, there he was standing right there in the doorway. Henri, Sheila's boyfriend, had followed Matty to the bathroom.

Matty tried to step around him, but he just moved to block whatever direction Matty was trying to go in. So Matty stopped moving and just stood there looking at him.

Henri was in his mid-thirties, and Matty was only 19.

He was also built like a brick house and was twice as big as Matty. He didn't know what was about to happen, but he tried not to look Henri in his eyes. But Henri would not let him look anywhere but in his eyes.

"I heard you're leaving for the military."

"Yea, in about 40 days."

"I probably won't ever get a chance to see you again."

"Probably not, but why is that important?"

He mumbled something under his breath.

"I didn't hear you. What did you say?"

"I said that I like you."

And before Matty could respond, he did it. Henri gave Matty the most passionate kiss that he had ever had, second only to none from his past - - male or female.

And as much as Matty wanted not to, he could not help but kiss Henri back.

When he finally came to his senses and pushed back from Henri, Matty told him, "Man, this is wrong on so many levels."

"I know. I have told myself that same thing a hundred times, but I can't get you out of my mind. I have been thinking about you since the first time I saw you. What am I supposed to do?"

"You asking me?"

They both just sat there taking turns looking at each and at the outdated, green, tile floor.

"Okay, look this is too much for me to handle right now," Matty said as he jumped off the sink and headed for the door.

"Right now we need to get ourselves together and get back out to the alley before they start to miss us."

Matty tried to adjust himself to walk out of the bathroom and pretend that nothing happened.

He heard Henri say, "Damn, you can't hide that."

Matty thought about what he said for a moment. "You go ahead, I will be out in a minute."

Before they parted, he kissed Matty again, and touched Matty in a way that made his body ache.

Matty was already straining against his jeans, but now there was no way to conceal it. Henri was Matty's first touch since he left Lee because of Matty's military commitment.

When he finally did come out of the bathroom, it was not easy pretending nothing happened. And he hated feeling like he had lied to or betrayed a friend, maybe she more than him.

When it came time to leave, Henri tried to take Sheila and Paris home first, but Matty refused. Henri got so mad, he started speeding through town, purposely.

He had a top-of-the-line, two-door hotrod, Camaro Z-28, grey with black stripes.

Matty was sitting in the back seat, on the passenger's side. He was sick and claustrophobic from the speed, the motion, the alcohol, and being cramped into that tight spot.

"I was literally terrified!"

The walls were closing in, and Matty was about ready to scream, when they heard the loudest CRASH!

The next time Matty saw Henri, he was waking up in the hospital, three days later from a coma.

Henri never left Matty's bedside the entire time, so Matty was told.

When Matty finally did wake up and started to look around, he realized they must have been telling him the truth because he was hooked up to all of these machines.

Somebody was rubbing his head, and Matty strained to see who that was.

But the touch was too familiar.

"Momma."

"Hey Matty. We thought we had lost you there for a while."

"I was lost momma, but God don't want me."

"God uses the foolish things to confound the wise Matty."

The doctor came in and started doing a lot of talking.

Matty wasn't paying him any attention, as he turned his head to look back at Henri.

As Matty's eyes began to focus, his monitor started going crazy, and everybody was rushing around trying to figure out what was going on.

His heart rate and blood pressure had shot up through the roof, for no apparent cause.

Matty could not lift his arm, but his finger was pointing, yet no one was paying attention.

Henri stood up and backed away from the bed.

Matty's eyes were big and he was still pointing.

Matty's mother rushed over to Henri and whispered something in his ear.

Henri took his shirt off.

Matty calmed down.

"The blood on Henri's clothes made Matty remember the accident," Sadie said, like only a mother would know.

There was not a single scratch on Henri.

Everyone in the room was now staring at Henri's remarkable physique. It was superb and still that was not a sufficient description.

Matty had never seen Henri this way before.

He had a perfect caramel color complexion. His chest looked like it had been chiseled out of marble.

You could tell his chest was hard as a rock, not to big, not too small. Each pec was a mountain big enough to climb, but small enough for Matty to rest his head on.

His nipples were so beautiful that they would make anybody lick their lips, as evidenced by both of Matty's nurses.

Henri's chest sat atop washboard abs unlike any seen before, at least that Matty had seen anyway.

If Lee was handsome, Henri was the statue David and then some.

Henri was naturally hairless, until your eyes landed just above the lip of his jeans, and just below his navel. It was an inny. Together, his torso formed the perfect V.

His arms, were the perfect book ends to this masterpiece of a man. They were hard enough to snap a neck, but firm enough to hold - - Matty.

These were the arms of a hard working farm hand, which Henri was, on his father's million dollar farm.

But Matty was so exhausted that he fell back off to sleep.

Matty was in and out for at least another week. Then the time came for them to take the tube out of Matty's mouth. But his eyes asked Henri what was going on.

The reparatory therapist was yelling instructions at Matty underneath the anesthesia. Matty was responding appropriately. Then as the second phase of the removal began, Matty woke up very agitated. His eyes were stretched wide and he was scaring Henri.

"He's choking," Henri said.

"No sir he's not. He's okay. Just keep him calm."

"I'm glad that's over. Those were the roughest twenty minutes of my entire life," Henri told Matty after the tube was out.

But Matty had no idea what Henri was saying because he was still out of it. The next time Matty woke up, he had absolutely no idea what had transpired the past couple of weeks.

"Hey good looking."

"Matty smiled."

Henri helped Matty get cleaned up and brushed his teeth.

Then he kissed Matty again.

"I'm glad you are happy to see me."

Matty's throat was sore from the tube so he still couldn't talk very much, but he saw the extra bed and his eyes were inquisitive.

"Your mother had them bring an extra bed in here for me to sleep."

Then Henri bent down and whispered something into Matty's ear.

"No one knows that I have been sleeping in the bed with you every night."

Matty smiled at the thought.

Matty didn't know what Henri did to gain his mother's trust, which was not an easy task even under normal circumstances, but he did.

After Henri told Matty that, Matty used to watch the clock with baited breath because his nurse made her final round at midnight.

As soon as the door would close, Matty would secretly watch Henri get undressed before he got in the bed. It was like having his own private dancer every night.

Matty never did figure out how Henri managed to keep the nurses out, but he did.

He did everything for Matty.

Once the tube was finally taken out of Matty's throat, Henri feed him, bathed him, walked him, and went to therapy with him until he was released, and even after.

Henri literally nursed Matty back to health. And he never asked for anything in return.

If Matty wanted to talk, they talked, if he didn't, they didn't.

He never made one single demand on Matty.

"Matty, I never had the chance to tell you how sorry I was for what I did to us."

'Us,' Matty said.

Matty didn't blame Henri for what happened. No one knows why. But Matty still had all kinds of questions about himself, that night, he and Henri, and the Navy that he could not answer.

Then it dawned on Matty, Henri was committed to him for….

"It's a beautiful day outside. Let's go for a walk."

"Didn't you hear what I said?"

Matty looked into Henri's gray eyes and surprised himself.

Matty could fight it no more. Matty kissed him the way he kissed Matty the first time. But this time Matty was in no hurry to pull away from him. It felt so natural.

"I forgive you."

"Let's forget the walk. I have a better idea."

His face begged Matty to give in to his request.

Matty smiled.

They deliberately took their time undressing and caressing each other.

Matty finally had his opportunity to touch Henri's beautifully chiseled, warm, naked body. Henri's soft skin covered his rock hard physique like cold ice cream baked inside a hard outer shell. In both cases you can't wait to get to the treat inside.

And although Matty's own thoughts betrayed him, Matty refused to stop. He was completely open to Henri and so was he in return.

Matty equally enjoyed Henri exploring his body with obvious pleasure for both of them.

Although Matty had a much smaller frame, it was well made – firm, tight, and well defined under his bronze colored skin, including his small man tiddies that had started to return.

Henri loved all of Matty, including his man tiddies. Matty would cream just from Henri caressing his tiddies.

They gave themselves to each other completely, holding nothing back.

Their bodies were not their own.

Individually, they were two compatible instruments that when combined made the most beautiful melodies Matty had ever heard.

It started out with an intricate but delicate verse that repeated itself several times before it climbed to a pre-chorus, which crescendoed into an emotional chorus of blended voices.

Then there was a brief interlude before a new song began that was just as passionate.

The first song was soft and gentile, like a ballad.

The second was hard and rough, suitable for pent up frustration.

Neither song lacked anything, each of them taking their turn at leading.

After he woke up, Matty spent a total of thirty-five additional days in the hospital.

To his own surprise, he didn't have any other visitors while he was in there, but somehow he didn't care.

But Henri told him that there were gobs of people there while he was in the coma.

Of course Matty's mother was there every day, before work and after work.

She said very little but Matty knew her too well.

"Momma what's wrong?"

She didn't say anything.

"What are you worried about?"

She still didn't say anything.

"Mrs. Pottishear, if you are worried about the medical bills, don't. Between my car insurance and my parents, we are going to pay every single thing it takes to get Matty back up on his feet, and you too for that matter."

When it came time for Matty to leave the hospital, Henri brought Matty's mother to the hospital to sign the release papers.

It was the only time he was away from Matty during that entire period.

"Nurse, these papers state my son has a zero balance."

"Yes ma'am, your son's balance has been paid in full."

Sadie didn't say another word.

"Mrs. Pottishear, it was my fault that this all happened. My father has also agreed to give you an extra $40,000 for all the trouble I caused," Henri said handing Matty's mother a certified check.

"Henri, you do not have to try and bribe us. We are not looking for anything, and we are not trying to sue your family."

"There is more where that came from Mrs. Pottishear if you should need any more."

Sadie walked out to the nurse's station for a moment.

Henri knelt down beside Matty's wheelchair.

"I know your family has been struggling and I just want to help ease your mind so that I can have all of your attention."

"But you don't have to buy my love Henri."

"I thought I had your love before I gave your mother the check?"

"Checkmate," Matty said.

As the attendant rolled Matty down the hallway toward the elevator, Matty's heart rate started to go up again.

"I have another surprise for you Matty."

The elevator ride was the longest ride ever and was eerily silent. Matty didn't know how he was going to be able to ride home in that Camaro.

When they got to the patient departure area, Matty didn't see the car.

"Henri, where is the car?"

"You are looking at it."

"This is a jeep."

"I know. I bought it a few days ago when I found out you would be getting out of the hospital."

"But how, when you were with me the whole time?"

"I have my ways."

Henri drove really slow.

"Momma, I would like to go and stay with Henri at his parent's farm until I leave. I think it will be good for me to get away for a while."

"Okay," she said without a second thought.

Something was happening to Matty's mother and he didn't understand it, but now was not the time to try and figure all of that out.

After Henri got Matty settled into the guest house on the farm at the back of their property near a beautiful stream, Henri basically became Matty's servant.

"You are not going to wait on me hand and foot Henri because if you do I will never get stronger and better."

"So what do you plan on doing?"

"I plan on following you around like a puppy dog and trying to learn how a farm works. Meanwhile, it might also help me to build a body like yours."

"You own me and this body. I am completely at your disposal."

Even though they had to be extremely gentle, Henri meant every word he said, and he proved it to Matty every day before they started work and every evening after they were done, and sometimes in between.

Meanwhile, Matty opened up and told Henri his entire sorted past without leaving anything out.

Matty was amazed.

Instead of Henri being as repulsed as Matty was, Henri seemed to be falling deeper in love with Matty.

Henri had Matty completely to himself and it didn't require any drugs or subterfuge.

Matty never knew that making love could be so intense and so intensely satisfying, but it was in every way.

Whatever Matty had given to Lee, he gave to Henri a thousand times more, in part because he was in his right mind, and more importantly because he was completely in love with Henri.

In the haystack, behind the barn, in the open field at their private picnic, on the banks of the stream, in the back of the work truck, and everywhere else in between.

And Matty did learn how to do some work around the farm, but mostly he just played with the animals and he did what errands Henri told him to do.

"Henri maybe I should go do something else. I am slowing you down tremendously."

"Do you hear me complaining?" Henri would say in that deep cowboy drawl.

"Now give me a kiss," Henri would say as he patted Matty's ass.

And that kiss always turned into much more, mutually more.

"It's a good thing that your parents don't depend on you for production purposes around here."

"To tell you the truth Matty, I wasn't very focused until you came here. I just didn't see the value in being so far out here away from everything and working so hard with nothing to show for it."

"Are you kidding? I would trade our city existence for this in a heartbeat. The freedom to roam for as long and as often as you want to, to do an honest day's work to go to bed tired from work than tired from worry, not to mention the body you have developed."

Henri started laughing.

"You see how good you are for me."

They were in their bedroom and Henri was wearing a pair of black bikinis, just for Matty.

"I would have never worn a pair of these before I met you."

"I would have never wanted a man to wear a pair before I met you."

"I guess that makes us even?"

"Not really. I think I got the better part of the deal," Matty said.

"Let's see."

They stayed up all night long that night making love. Matty gave himself to Henry over and over that night.

"I want you to be too exhausted to work tomorrow."

"Do you realize what you are asking for?"

"Yes."

"Your wish is my command."

By the next morning, Matty was completely awash in Henri's juices.

But Matty was the one exhausted.

He did, however, manage to see Henri put on some form fitting boxers as he was leaving.

"Where are you going? I thought we could sleep in this morning?"

"I'm going to pick up some hay. I'll be back in about hour. Then I am all yours for however long you want."

"You promise."

"I promise."

"I love you."

"I love you too. Oh by the way I left something for you in the bathroom."

Matty went ahead and got out of bed because there was no use in being there without Henri.

Matty got up, completely soar, but smiling none the less, and walked into the bathroom.

There was a small box on the counter.

Matty opened the box, he started crying.

Henri had given him a diamond studded wedding band with an engraving inside that read, "Saddled for Henri."

The ring was a perfect fit.

After Matty got out of his hot bath that soaked his swollen…which was completely covered with love bruises, there was a knock at the door.

"Mr. Legamon."

"Matty, may I come in?"

"Yes sir. Absolutely."

"Matty, let me get right to the point. I do not approve of what you have done to my son."

Matty didn't say anything, although in his mind he corrected Mr. Legamon - - your son did it to me.

"Still I know my son loves you and I have never seen him as happy and focused in my life. But I would be lying if I said that me and my wife didn't want grandchildren."

"Mr. Legamon, Henri and I have talked about having several children."

Before they could continue the conversation, the telephone rang.

Matty dropped the telephone and ran out of the house.

"Matty what's wrong," Henri's father yelled.

"Henri was in an accident."

"Come on. Let's get Sal so we can head to the hospital."

Matty was a wreck, and so were Henri's parents.

Everyone was crying except for Henri's dad.

By the time they got to the hospital, Henri was in critical care.

"Henri!" Matty's wailing.

His tears covered Henri's face. Matty was wiping them away, but he couldn't wipe them away fast enough.

"I love you. Sorry for everything."

"That's okay Henri. I love you too. There is nothing for you to be sorry about."

Henri's parents were standing on the other side of the bed.

They saw the ring for the first time.

Henri started smiling.

Matty kissed him in front of his parents.

Henri died in the middle of their kiss.

Matty was screaming and hollering to the point they had to give him several sedatives and still he wasn't calm.

Matty stayed with Henri and held him in his arms until they had to almost tear Henri's body from Matty's arms.

When they got back to the farm, Matty started packing to leave.

"Where are you going Matty?" Mrs. Sally, Henri's mother asked.

"I figured you guys didn't want me around here no more."

"No. This is your home, stay. Henri would be too upset with me if you left."

Matty fell to his knees holding Henri's shirt.

It was the complete smell of Henri and he had worn it so much it was shaped like his body.

It took several days before Matty could begin making arrangements with Henri's parents for the funeral.

Matty wanted Henri buried under the big oak tree behind their cottage so he could visit him always.

But that didn't satisfy the ache in Matty's heart and his arms to hold Henri again.

And Matty didn't know what to do or how to feel about the drunk driver that killed Henri so he let Henri's parents deal with all that.

But he did go to the final sentencing.

When the judge asked if the family wanted to say anything, Matty stood up to speak. Both of Henri's parents were crying.

"Although I want to hate you for taking the love of my life away from me, I have to forgive you because Henri would want me to since I had to forgive him."

Matty walked away clearly dejected along with Henri's parents. As they walked out the door, they heard the judge give him 40 years. Henri wasn't his first victim.

Matty slept on Henri's grave for more than two weeks.

Every night, Henri's mother would bring a blanket and put on him.

Then one night Matty had a dream, but when he woke up he could feel Henri's touch on his body.

"That was no dream," Matty said.

But the year and half he spent with Henri was over, and as hard as it was at first, Matty had peace that it was time to move on.

"I only regret that we didn't have those kids so that I could raise my own Henri junior."

Matty left the farm.

"Matty where are you going to go?"

"Mrs. Legamon, I am going to finish what I started and join the Navy. I've been a vagabond my whole life so the Navy seems as good a place as any to continue."

"What do you mean Matty?"

"I have lived out of bags my whole life. My life just seems to keep me moving from place to place like a nomad, so

I might as well go into the military. At least I can travel and see the world, now that Henri has told me I can go."

"What happened at Henri's gravesite last night Matty?" Mr. Legamon asked.

"I'm not sure I can explain it sir."

"Try, please."

"Okay."

"I had a dream, but it wasn't a dream because I know that I actually saw Henri. He was wearing all white with a white cowboy hat and he had a new body, an incandescent body. He didn't say anything. He just smiled at me with a smile of pure happiness."

Henri's mother had clasped her hands around her mouth. She was in such awe.

"But then something happened that let me know it was not a dream and that it was really Henri."

"What was that Matty?" Henri's father said.

"Henri reached out his hand and touched my heart. I could feel my heart healing immediately under his touch. My hurt and pain were immediately gone."

Their eyes said that was an incredulous story but Matty didn't care. He knew it had happened to him, and it healed his broken heart. And that's all that mattered.

"I have lost both my sons this day," Mrs. Sally told Matty, although Henri had several other brothers and sisters.

"No you haven't. We will never stop seeing, writing, or loving each other until the day I die."

Matty didn't hesitate to set things in motion to leave as soon as possible. But he still had to wait a couple of weeks.

So Matty took that opportunity to reconnect with his friends, whom he had not seen since Henri's funeral. They talked a little at the funeral, but Matty was not interested in any of their bullshit at that time.

He had not missed them although he would not dare hurt their feelings and tell them so.

"So what happened to all you bitches signing up with me to go into the Navy?"

Practically in unison they all said, "Child I ain't going into no military. We would not make it."

That's when Matty realized that if he didn't leave his friends, he would forever be stuck in a hole his entire life, although he was in a big enough hole as it where, so to speak.

"Hey Matty, you remember those guys from the club the other night?"

"Not particularly."

"Well they remember you and they have invited us all to a pool party tonight."

"Sammie I am not particularly interested in attending a pool party tonight."

"Matty this is your next to last weekend with us here. The least you can do is hang out with us a little while."

The guilt had Matty in agreement.

The party was in full force by the time Matty and his crew arrived.

Although Matty was clearly the center of attention, it didn't stop his competition from doing their best to be noticed above him.

By the way his competition was his own crew, although there was no competition, except for Sammie.

But what none of them knew, even though they should have known was that Matty was not remotely interested in anyone, regardless of who they were.

Not long after their arrival, they were all at the pool -- smoking pot and drinking.

Everybody was in the pool except for Matty and Charles.

Then without any notice, Matty stepped off into the pool.

He sank to the bottom of the pool.

Within seconds, Matty was jumping up out of the water as if he was drowning.

"Paris, you are closest, save him. He is drowning."

Paris didn't move. He was glued to the edge of the pool gagging at the sight of it all.

Sammie swam over and pushed Matty to the edge of the pool.

"Bitch what were you thinking?"

Matty was still coughing up water.

"I thought the number said 6 feet."

"You dumbass, you were looking at the numbers upside down."

"And she's drunk child," Paris shouted.

That was their last outing before Matty left for the Navy.

On the final night before Matty was to leave, his crew was once again gathered at their usual watering hole.

Despite all of their coaxing, when they all said their byes, Matty came home early and sober.

Matty spent the remainder of that night with him and his mother watching television together.

Never a word was uttered.

When it came time for bed, Matty kissed his mother on the forehead, something she hated immensely.

The next morning, Matty got up early, packed the few things he was allowed to bring, according to the list they had been given, walked into his mother's room, kissed her cheek, and left.

His mother did not even open her eyes to see him leave.

But Matty could see a teardrop roll down the side of her face and fall on the pillow.

As he got into Sammie's car, Matty refused to look back, because if he did that would mean that he was leaving forever.

All Matty wanted was a way to make his mother's life better than it was.

Sammie tried to talk to the entire ride, but it was hard to have a conversation alone.

"You don't have anything to say about what you are doing?"

"Nope." Matty just kept looking out the window at the frosty air.

As they pulled into station, all Matty heard was "bye," as he closed the door behind him.

Once, he got inside, he started walking slowly as he tried to take in all the activity happening around him.

"Where are you supposed to be recruit?"

"What?"

"Don't what me boy! This is the U. S. Navy. You address me as sir."

"So I ask you again. Where are you supposed to be recruit?"

"I don't know, sir."

"Oh, I see how this is going to work. You are one of those punks that is going to have to learn things the hard way."

Matty was thrown into a room with the rest of the new recruits.

"Strip."

Everybody in the room started looking at each other.

"You heard me STRIP!"

Matty and every other new recruit in that room started taking off their clothes.

His man tiddies had started to come back and so did his shame, so Matty crisscrossed his arms to cover his chest.

Out of his peripheral view, Matty noticed that he was not alone in his desire to hide his chest. But that was a fleeting affinity.

"Bend over and spread your cheeks ladies!"

There was actually a guy who came down the line up and checked everybody's butthole.

Twelve hours later, Matty and the other Navy recruits were boarding a plane for their trip to basic training in Orlando, Florida.

It was Matty's first plane ride ever, but he refused to panic.

In fact, Matty was the calmest of all the recruits on the plane. Panic was written all over their faces.

As for the plane ride, it was quite calm as plane rides go.

After the plane ride, the rest of Matty's stay in Orlando was rather straight forward.

In fact, Matty loved being in the military. The hard work, shining shoes, making beds, going to bed at 8 o'clock, having military drills at 3 am, and then being up at 6 am for physical training, were all adventures to Matty.

"Hey momma."

"Hey Matty."

"How are you?"

"Momma, I am having a wonderful time. This is the best time I have ever had in my life."

Sadie was stunned.

She was expecting her baby son to call her depressed, crying, and complaining.

Matty was happy.

Every time, every phone call went the exact same way.

Sadie was relieved that Matty was happy and doing well.

Additionally, Matty was sending every penny of his money home to his mother, except for what he absolutely needed.

The only problem Matty had in basic training is that he almost drowned a second time.

He let his pride get the better of his decision making and when asked who could not swim, Matty did not want to be included in that group.

He let his pride led him into jumping off the diving board into 12 feet of water. While there were safety divers in the pool to protect them all, when Matty jumped into the pool and could not recover, he heard one of the safety divers say, "I ought to let you drown for telling me a lie that you knew how to swim."

After that Matty quickly learned not to let his pride make any more decisions for him.

But that same diver saved Matty's life and taught him how to swim before he left basic training.

The only problem was that his touch was both hypnotizing and softer than it should have been.

Matty thought, "Oh Lord here we go again."

Even though this Navy seal had the ability and the skills necessary to snap Matty's neck in an instant, his touch said something completely different to Matty, a touch that was all too familiar to Matty.

The saving grace for Matty was that they never had even the remotest possibility of ever being alone. And that was completely okay with Matty.

The second most thrilling thing for Matty was that he had the chance to spend a whole two days at the happiest place on earth just outside of Orlando, Florida. Matty earned the free two day pass for not only passing every single test with flying colors, but for also tutoring half of his recruit class so that they could pass all of their retests and graduate as standout recruits.

Their group was originally labeled misfits but they turned out to prove they were perfectly suited for the Navy or the Navy was perfectly suited for them.

This same concept applied equally to Matty. The Navy suited Matty and vice versa. There was no hiding from anyone, no perverted sex movies to be made, and no JPHs or Shauns to get away from.

Matty was free to be Matty.

From Orlando Matty was transferred to Meridian, Mississippi, a place he had never heard of before.

But that was okay with Matty because he figured most of his time would be spent on the base so that he would never have to interact with any potential Klansmen, although the bus ride from Orlando to Mississippi took them through some potentially dangerous areas.

But again, when Matty arrived at the base, got checked in, and settled in, he adapted to his surroundings with absolute ease.

His most difficult test was passing the typing test. It took him almost seventeen days to pass that test. But finally he passed it.

The test was required in order for Matty to graduate upstairs to begin the remainder of his training to become a yeoman. But it was not Matty's original choice of job.

Matty originally want to be a cryptologist but he made the mistake of letting one of the interviewers corner him into admitting that he was gay, which was a disqualifying factor for both the Navy and for the job position of his choice.

"But instead of putting you out of the Navy, I am simply going to change your job position. Since you scored so high, you can do anything you would like to do, pretty much, so what would that be?"

Matty was tired of school so he chose the yeoman billet because it would not require a great deal of additional schooling.

But it was not lost on Matty that he had truly dodged a bullet.

Anyway, Matty graduated upstairs to true yeoman training. He was an absolute whiz. He was doing in hours what others were doing in weeks.

He was so focused on his studies that he didn't realize that he had an admirer.

His name was Harry. He was a little shorter than Matty, with a chocolate fudge complexion.

It was almost the second week of "A" school training, which is specialized on the job training for different jobs.

Actually Matty spotted him staring at him during class on the very first day, but he ignored him.

That didn't stop Harry.

He kept on staring at Matty more and more and walking past his desk, which was on the opposite side of the room from his desk, so that Matty could see his physique.

His body wasn't like Lee's or Henri's, but Harry was still solid. He was a short, muscular running back type of build.

Anyway, one day Harry caught Matty off guard and smiled at him. He had the most beautiful, perfectly straight white teeth that Matty had ever seen, including television.

Matty could not help but smile and shake his head.

Normally Matty stayed late in class so that Harry would already be gone by the time he got ready to leave.

But on this particular day Matty left early for some reason.

He was almost to his barracks when Harry ran up behind him and through him on the ground and put all of his weight on his chest so that Matty could not get up.

No one said anything because it looked like they were rough-housing it. But then again they were on the backside of a hill so neither of them knew if anyone actually saw them.

All of this was in Meridian, Mississippi at the time.

After that Harry started walking Matty home every afternoon.

But nothing ever came of it because Matty just wasn't sure how he was supposed to handle being gay in the military. So he had decided prior to going into service that he was not going to entertain that notion; and, with that Matty shut down.

Then a few days later out of the blue, Harry showed up at Matty's room for lunch.

No one is sure why Matty was in his room for lunch but he was.

Matty, against his better judgment, let him in.

"Why won't you give me the time of day?"

"What am I to you, your latest conquest?"

"I haven't f…."

Matty's facial expression told Harry that he better not say that around him, regardless of the fact that they were in the Navy.

"I haven't been with anyone since I arrived here."

"How long has that been?" Matty asked.

"A few weeks longer than you," Harry replied.

And he just kept going on and on.

"Hmm, now that I think about it, Harry was begging," Matty muttered

Before he knew it, Matty had blurted out, "Take your clothes off."

Harry was shocked and so was Matty.

But after the words were uttered Matty didn't change his mind.

"Right now," Harry side with wide eyes.

"Right now."

Harry started to walk toward the door.

Matty thought it was all over.

But it wasn't.

Harry went to the door so he could lock it.

Then he came back and gave Matty the most sultry striptease he had ever had without any music. Actually, it is the only striptease Matty had ever had.

When he took his shirt off, he had on a pure white tee-shirt that looked like it was wet because it clung to his body in form fitting fashion.

Then he slowly slipped the tee-shirt above his waist, than his chest, and finally over his head.

Matty almost creamed in his pants as he watched him gyrate his waist like a man on a mission - - slow and easy.

"Damn that's hot," Matty had to admit.

Then he slowly began to unbuckle his belt and unzip his pants taking time to make sure that Matty was clearly watching.

And he was.

Matty just sat on the top of his room refrigerator watching every inch of this beautiful body.

"Then I thought I was seeing color," Matty said.

But Harry was not yet ready to reveal himself to Matty just yet.

He slowly turned around and let his pants drop to the floor, planned, but made to look unexpected.

Matty tried to hide his excitement but it was beyond difficult now because Harry was wearing a pair of form fitting purple bikinis.

Not only were they against regulation, they accented his firm ass like…

That purple against his fudge chocolate skin was worth biting into.

Then he turned around and Matty was done. You could have stuck him with a fork.

Although Matty may not have been in love with Harry, he certainly was in love with how he pursued him - to have him.

So anyway, Harry didn't stop there.

He pursued Matty even more furiously after that day, and despite his protest, Matty didn't have much resistance left in him.

So one Friday night Matty waited until everyone was gone and he walked over to Harry's barracks. His roommate was gone, and Harry wasn't expecting Matty.

He was getting ready to go out but when he saw Matty, he immediately undressed.

And it started from there.

Harry explored every inch of Matty's body, and Matty happily returned the favor, all night long.

Then it happened.

Matty gave himself to Harry, emphasis on gave.

The song on the radio was softly playing:

*You are the sun*

*You are the rain*

*That makes my life this foolish game.*

*You need to know*

*I love you so*

*And I'll do it all again and again*

*Whoa, whoa, whoa, yea, yea, yeahhhh*

When they were done Matty was happy to lay his head on Harry's chest.

"I felt so safe, warm, and loved at that very moment."

And Matty got up to leave before Harry's roommate returned. Harry had a different plan.

He refused to let Matty leave and he made his roommate go sleep in another friend's barrack.

Anyway, after that Matty spent the next few days going to Harry's basketball games as his personal cheerleader, in private of course; and, Harry took Matty to the officer club a couple of times so that they could just about rape each other under the table in between pool games.

But there love was not meant to be.

A few days later, Matty received orders to leave Meridian.

They thought they had about six or seven more weeks left but they had barely more than 36 hours.

So they made an agreement that they would spend the last night together and that Harry would take Matty to the train station the next day.

They never made love but that once.

Harry didn't show up that last night and he left Matty stranded in his room waiting for the train.

Matty had to take a cab.

"I cried my eyes out all the way home."

Matty stood on that train track until the very last minute hoping, praying and wishing Harry would come rushing in and unbreak his heart and say he loved Matty again.

When it came time for Matty to finally get on the train or get left Matty knew that Harry's love for him was counterfeit.

Matty came home for the Christmas holidays before he was to meet up with his battalion in Okinawa, Japan.

Although they wrote each other every week after that, Matty realized that Harry was gone.

He had to let him go because for Harry it was about the pursuit and once he had Matty, then Matty was no longer any good.

Harry broke his heart and if you talk to Matty today, he will tell you that his heart still has that scar from that stab wound.

It took Matty the entire Christmas break to get over Harry enough, at least enough to function when he left home to go to his new duty station, Gulfport, Mississippi, on the coast, near Biloxi.

Matty checked in at Gulfport, got all of his requisite 21-overseas vaccinations, and then he was free to roam until it was time for him to leave for his first international flight.

While he was waiting for his transfer overseas, Matty took his first jaunt over to New Orleans.

By day, Matty slept, undisturbed, unafraid, and untouched.

By night, Matty wandered the streets of New Orleans as a complete neophyte, willingly getting lost and giving himself over into the hands of the creatures of the nights. Then something happened.

Matty discovered the French Quarter, then Bourbon Street, and then…Matty stumbled upon the back streets and Titi's.

Matty was both appalled and intrigued by the curious place. It was in a non-descript building that sat at the edge of the quarter, near the back.

"How apropos," Matty said.

Still he had to go inside to see what the club offered. It was a maze – a cold, concrete and brick maze that had a few lights strategically placed. It was filled with more shadows than people and smelled of sex - - old, new, hot, and sweaty sex – "Filled with reckless abandon," Matty added.

"$10," said the door attendant.

Matty handed over the money.

Then the attendant laid a towel on the counter.

Matty looked at him.

"Your clothes."

Matty kept looking at him.

"If you want to go in you have to strip."

Matty looked around. Everybody behind him was already stripping.

Matty joined in, reluctantly, but still a willing participate.

He wraps the towel around his waist and follows the crowd into the narrowing doorway that leads to the maze.

The tangles of all our lives are left at the door. There was nothing inside the maze but bodies and towels, and even fewer of the latter.

They were free. They were all sinfully free and having unrequited sex. They didn't want answers. They only wanted another body.

Big, little, young, old, fat, thin, black, white, and every color in between was having sex. Matty wanted to leave, and prepared to do as much, when a new shadow stepped from around a dark corner into Matty's pathway.

He stepped right up to Matty and began whispering something into Matty's ear. Matty thought, "This has to be how the devil whispers into my ear. With such a lustfulness that I do not want to refuse him."

Matty shook his head and tried to walk away a second time. But this stranger, dropped his towel. As he did, the dim light hit his face for a brief moment, and Matty said, "David, David Baker."

Matty was hooked. His towel fell, and the stranger had no chance at escape. He had beaten off far more than he could chew.

Despite the confliction in Matty's heart, his body refused to turn back. And Matty unleashed a torrid of pent up frustration and wantonness on his prey. They ended up staying in that same room for two days straight.

When Monday morning came, Matty got up and left without so much as a glance back.

But he couldn't help but wonder, who really won? "How much did I lose?"

When Matty returned to Gulfport, he spent what was left of those two weeks in Gulfport, hanging out every night partying and sleeping all day, except for his obligatory physical training that was conveniently scheduled for mid-afternoons.

Back in Gulfport, Matty had no lack of suitors both on and off the base. Still Matty was not interested in anyone or anything.

He was going out drinking and partying because it was the easiest way to keep himself from crying every night about Harry, considering that he was back in Mississippi.

But to Matty's dismay, he had to break up several fights at the local gay bar. Apparently, Matty had upset the status quo by refusing the attention of several local stars to talk to a relatively new and unknown curly haired white boy, who was otherwise non-descript, in the backseat of his rental car, on more than one occasion.

The good thing for Matty, that no one knew, was that he was going to be leaving in a few weeks, and they would be left to sort out that whole mess on their own.

But Matty didn't care.

"What has caring got me this far in life? So I am only thinking about me."

This was contrary to Matty's personality, but his heart was really broken. He just couldn't admit to anyone, especially to himself.

And what they all didn't know including Matty was that his orders had already arrived and were awaiting his final security clearance. The next day he was on an airplane headed to Okinawa. He flew for more than 36 hours straight.

Matty left them holding the bag and trying to figure out where he was and who to fight over next. As devious as it was, Matty was enjoying the irony of it all. The irony of it all carried Matty all the way to the Pacific Rim.

Within days of his arrival in Okinawa, Matty started noticing a spot on his left leg. The spot started getting bigger by the day. In Matty's mind it was getting bigger by the minute.

Matty was so distracted by the spot on his leg that he had not even taken the time to notice that he had become the freshest piece of new meat to all of the construction men he worked around.

When he arrived in Okinawa, he had a stack of mail waiting for him. All of the letters were from Harry.

Matty looked at the letters long and hard, rubbing the envelopes, smelling them, and almost opening them before putting them aside yet again. He did this every day for several weeks before he actually decided to read them.

Meanwhile the Matty that Harry knew was long gone.

He wrote Harry several Dear John letters. And he tore every one of them up before he ever mailed the first letter confessing his heart and hurt.

In Matty's mind, although not completely untrue, Matty was changing into an ugly duckling just as his pheromones were attracting every kind of man imaginable to his room, without him having to do anything.

Matty practically had a room to himself because one roommate never came home, and the other roommate when he did come home, would wake Matty up early in the morning masturbating.

One morning Matty rolled over and as he opened his eyes, he realized that McConnell was masturbating. Matty was stunned at the openness of what he was doing, and he was stunned at the size of his primary object of attention at 4 am.

As Matty watched, he got the impression that McConnell was putting on a show for him. And perform for Matty he did, right up to the climatic ending.

After that Matty tried to get a transfer to a new room, but every request was denied. And McConnell masturbated even more.

In between being forced to deal with a chronic late night/early morning masturbator, Matty would come home to find a veritable smorgasbord of men in his bed, literally.

"Where the hell is McConnell?"

Matty find out later that McConnell had been paid to go to the petty officer's club and drink himself into a nightly stupor, which was an easy thing to do because the booze was so cheap.

Matty had his pick of men of every type, except that he wasn't interested in anyone because he was having too many problems with his skin to be interested in sex.

But that did not stop his suitors from being interested in sex with him.

"Believe me, some of them were hard to turn down," and sometimes Matty didn't turn them down.

There was not a bad body in the bunch because they were construction workers - - hard working, brick laying, pipe-fitting, hole digging construction workers. Some of their faces, however, were a different story. They reminded Matty of Paris' friend from the closet. But their hearts were a different matter altogether.

But Matty had reached a point of no refusal. He could no longer fight the feeling or the guys any longer.

One night he gave in to his desires to the most unlikely of candidates. He was a tall Asian. Dayodang was his name. Matty gave in to him, "Probably because he was the most convenient recipient I could find."

To Matty's complete surprise Dayodang long-dicked Matty all night long. After that Matty could not get rid of Dayodang, and Matty had every type of unimaginably handsome guys waiting for him when he got home, without exaggeration.

"That damn Dayodang!" Matty said.

They all said the same thing to Matty. "Don't tell anybody."

Clearly they were the ones talking because how else did it get out.

But the greatest surprise came when they started giving themselves to Matty.

"I bet they not telling this to anybody," Matty chuckled to himself.

Matty used to always say, "I would rather have an ugly man with a great body than a good looking man because the good looking man is never going to treat you right because he will be so vain."

After he returned from Okinawa, he was never heard making that statement again.

As for the sex, it was not nearly as good as Matty would have liked because his heart was never in it. Couldn't be in it because he had very little heart left.

He could never figure out how they were getting into his room, and how many others knew about what was going on.

The entire time Matty was in Okinawa, the suitors, the unexpected visits, and the sex never stopped, no matter how hard Matty protested.

But in spite of everything going on, Matty would go to bed alone and wake up early just so that he could take a shower alone because his man tiddies had returned in a big way and his once-flawless skin was changing right before his very eyes - - becoming black and blotchy.

None of this closed Matty's brothel. They loved his gynecomastia and they fucked in the dark.

Somehow things that Matty hated about his body, his suitors loved and showed their affection every chance Matty would let them.

Between the endless suitors, who sometimes cornered Matty, even in his office, kissing him and practically raping him, and his ugly body that was getting uglier by the day, Matty was at his wit's end by the time they were ready to leave.

One Friday night Matty was so disgusted with everything that was going wrong in his life that he didn't go home. Instead, he changed clothes at the office and went into town.

Since he had never been into town at night, let alone being alone, he ended up in the Red Light District by mistake.

When Matty's green ass was spotted by the locals, he was literally snatched into a strip joint.

There were several Asian women dancing on different stages in high heel shoes and the skimpiest bathing suits possible.

As soon as Matty had gotten used to the sights, a different lady walked out on stage into total darkness.

When the lights came back up, she was completely nude except for her high heels.

She started her routine and twenty minutes into the routine, she pulled out a banana and played with it for a little while, in her mouth and other orifices.

Then she peeled the banana and slid the entire banana into her vagina.

But that was not the amazing part.

The amazing part is that she would push a small piece of the banana out and cut it with her vagina, completely hands free.

And even more shocking, was the fact that a few military men, actually ate the banana off the stage that had fallen directly from the human cutter.

Matty had seen enough. He was ready to go.

"Damn," Matty said as he also saw one of his unwanted suitors he had repeatedly refused an audience.

Matty left quickly trying to avoid being seen.

He didn't know he was being followed.

Not far from the brothel, Matty was grabbed by five sailors and marines and gang raped that night, at the rear of the base near the ocean - - repeatedly.

He never told a soul about what happened. By the time the battalion was ready to leave Okinawa, Matty was an absolute emotional wreck.

When it came time for Matty to get on the plane, there were very few seats left. Matty had his choice between sitting in the middle of the cess pool of suitors or he could sit by Big Red, who was a giant of man, but had the most gentle soul, and he liked Matty and protected him like a little brother.

Matty slept on Big Red's left shoulder the entire ride home. No one said a word.

But when they arrived back in Gulfport things got worse.

Matty was given his own room and he was housed in the middle of the construction workers, which was unusual because normally all administrative workers bunked together.

Matty had a virtually revolving door of visitors seeking him for money, sex, or both.

Despite his refusals, the number of partners and demands increased incessantly.

Bobby T was his first.

He was a bad boy with a bad attitude, and a body that was soft and supple like a girl, with hips that spread like a girl's hips, in private, anyway.

Bobby was also thief.

Once while Matty was away on a training mission, Bobby removed the hinges from Matty's locked closets and robbed him blind. He even took some of Matty's underwear.

He didn't get the ring Henri had given Matty because it was locked away in a secret location that only Matty knew existed.

To get even Matty took it out of Bobby's hide in his late night visits to Matty's bed.

After that first night, Bobby never stopped coming to see Matty or spreading his hips for him, which was quite surprising since Bobby was in and out of the brig as often as he was in Matty's bed.

In fact, he bragged so to his other friends, he had to because Matty started getting even more suitors.

It seemed the uglier Matty became, the more those men wanted him. And the more he gave them or took from them, the more they sought him out - - during morning physical training, at night when they were all supposed to be asleep, in the shower, in the woods, and in the tents when they went out on training exercises.

Things got so bad for Matty that he tried to commit suicide and was taken into the psychiatric ward at the hospital of the Kessler Air Force base.

They kept Matty in a strait jacket for three days, and he spent another week or so in the psych ward after the jacket was removed.

When he was first taken in, Matty kept saying, "They made me do it. They made me do it."

The doctors had no idea what Matty was speaking of.

"Do we need to contact the police?"

Matty kept saying that over and over for the first twenty-four hours he was in the unit. After that he went to sleep for two days, without being drugged.

Then he went silent. Matty did not utter a single word, until he met Checkers. He got his name because that's all he did, every day.

Checkers was a really big fat guy who no one wanted to be around. But to Matty, he looked like a big kid. Matty took to Checkers and he to Matty.

No one ever knew what Checkers said to Matty, but whatever it was, it got Matty back on track. And Checkers lost his only friend shortly after that.

When he got out of the psychiatric ward, after agreeing to continued future counseling, and that he would never try to kill himself again, which was a lie, Matty went back to the battalion. Nothing had changed in his absence. In fact it had only gotten worse while he was gone.

After Matty was released from the crazy ward, Roger and Fat Louie invited him to go out drinking with them.

"Come on Matty. We'll pay for everything and it won't cost you nothing."

It was a boring Friday night in Gulfport, Mississippi.

"What the hell I got to lose?"

They met up with two older women that Fat Louie knew, so they were drinking and having a good time at a country western bar.

Then one of the women said, "Let's go to the bike club."

When they got to the biker's club, Matty said, "Roger we can't go in there."

"Whatcha mean we cannot go in the club?"

"Roger this is a white biker's club. They don't like me in there."

"Come on y'all, let's go in."

When they walked into the club, the place was full of big burly white bikers, and the entire club went hush when Matty walked in last. Although Matty was light-skinned, he was not light enough to be white.

The girls apparently knew almost everyone in the club so that let Matty come on and sit down for a drink.

Fat Louie gave Matty a twenty dollar bill, "Go buy us a round of drinks."

Matty walked over to the bar and placed his order.

Then this tall, really tall, dark haired guy with a huge mustache walked over to Matty wearing skin tight jeans, a form fitting shirt, and a leather jacket, and tapped Matty on the shoulder.

When Matty turned around, the guy said, "We don't like your kind in here. You need to go."

Matty said, "We'll be leaving in a minute after we have a drink or two."

"No, we don't like your kind in here," and then he pulled his vest back to reveal a long silver six shooter that was hidden under his vest.

Matty forgot the drinks and went back over to the table and told everybody what happened.

Nobody believed him.

When Matty looked back at the bar, his friend had gathered a small following, and it was getting bigger.

Matty immediately walked toward the door alone and left, after the blockade parted down the middle and let him leave.

He started walking back toward the base. He was scared but he had to do it.

The place was deep in the woods of Gulfport, in a part of town that Matty didn't even know existed.

Matty had been walking for about twenty minutes when he had almost reached the end of the street where there were street lights to light his path.

Then he heard a loud car roaring up behind him. Matty thought they had changed their mind and was coming to get him and kill him.

He had started running into the woods he was so scared.

But the car careened past him and kept going.

Matty started running toward the street lights.

It took him more than two hours, but he finally made his way back to the base.

After he made his way back to the base, Roger came in much later and told him the entire story.

"Matty I'm sorry. We should have believed you and left when you told us to."

"Why what happened?"

"After you left, Louie went to the bathroom and they cornered him in the bathroom and kicked him and beat him until they had broken his nose, his wrist, his arm, and four ribs. We rushed past you because he was bleeding everywhere and we thought he was going to die."

Matty didn't know what to say.

"They told Louie they didn't appreciate him bringing a…"

"Say it Roger."

"They didn't appreciate him bringing a Niger into their joint."

"We took him to the hospital."

"Is he going to be alright?"

"Yea they say he is going to be alright but he will have to be in the hospital for a few weeks."

"Wow, was all Matty could say. I told you they were going to kill me."

"I know. I'm sorry."

Fat Louie didn't make the trip to Puerto Rico.

But in a way Matty felt justified. But there was no time to gloat because he had to prepare the office for transfer to San Juan, Puerto Rico.

No one ever knew that Matty almost died at the hands of white supremacist in the back woods at a club in Gulfport, Mississippi. And Matty didn't want them to know.

Matty had endured so much pain in his life that he just went on as if nothing had happened.

But, if things were bad in Gulfport, they were tripled worse in the heat and alcohol of San Juan.

Before the battalion left Gulfport, Matty was selected to be the Captain's Yeoman, which meant that he worked directly for the Captain and his Executive Officer.

This put Matty in the highest visibility position possible. Anyone who didn't know his name suddenly knew Matty's name and where he worked.

Matty became a highly sought-after prized commodity.

Again, as they settled into their new home at Roosevelt Roads, Puerto Rico, Matty became popular in spite of his own desires to not be popular.

Not long after their arrival, Matty started having nightly visitors, and this time they were not taking no for answer.

What Matty would not give they would take. If that didn't work, blackmail was next up on the list.

Matty was defeated.

He gave in.

At the same time Matty gave up, his skin disease was getting worse, rapidly worse.

Actually Matty knew that he had psoriasis before they left Gulfport, although he didn't know how to treat it or what it was. All Matty could do was think of Job. And he didn't know if he was being tested or if he was being punished.

All Matty could do was cry.

He had spent his entire life trying to do the right thing and no matter how hard he tried he always ended up doing the wrong thing with the wrong guys. He was at his wits end.

All he could do was cry some more.

"I am no Job but maybe sometimes even when you are doing the right thing the storms of life will come. I don't know if this is how Job felt but I certainly can identify with some of his physical pain." Matty was crying and scratching his skin all at the same time.

After repeated visits to the on-base clinic with no resolution and continued refusals by the hospital corpsman to allow Matty to see the medical doctor, Matty made an appointment to see a private dermatologist in Gulfport on his own.

A few days before they were to leave for Puerto Rico, the dermatologist called and gave Matty the results of the biopsy. It was psoriasis.

Although Matty turned the information over to the medical staff, it was too late for them to do anything about it, and therefore off to Puerto Rico he went.

They flew into Guantanamo Bay, Cuba first.

Although Matty was surrounded with the beauty, the heat, and the history of Cuba, he could not enjoy one moment of it all because he was depressed, although he didn't know what it was at the time.

And his depression didn't stop there.

This depression was bad for Matty but it was good for his midnight visitors because that meant Matty was more amenable to their requests, although they didn't immediately understand why.

But what Matty didn't know was that his suitors were not after him but the power he welded in his new job position. However, that boy was so naïve that he had no idea that he was being sought after for his power.

He did think it strange that anything he wanted in bed he got, and he got it from some of the most unlikely participants imaginable.

As Matty skin problems grew worse, he worked later to try and take his mind off things, since he didn't have anything else to do.

In return, his suitors started seeking him at his office, after they realized that he was not in his hut, as he was supposed to be.

And just like that Matty started having sex in both the Captain's and the XO's offices on a regular basis.

His favorite suitors included enlisted men, officers, and at least one marine that enjoyed wearing daisy dukes after hours or maybe only when he planned on seeing Matty.

The truth is Matty had more sex than he could have ever desired, and at the same time he had no interest in sex whatsoever.

That's when Matty realized that he had been having sex with someone he didn't even like - - himself.

"How can they love me and I don't even love me?"

After one of his clandestine meetings, Matty asked his marine suitor, why him.

"Matty don't ask me shit like that."

"Either you tell me or we stop seeing each other. Besides, I have seen parts of you that your wife doesn't even know exist, you might as well tell me why you enjoy being in my bed."

That smart alec comment earned Matty a backhand that knocked him clearly across the desk. Papers were flying everywhere and Matty was screaming as he tried to brace himself when he hit the floor.

"Matty I'm sorry. I'm really sorry."

Matty knew he could bring him up on charges, and then he could finally tell his story, except that he didn't keep a black book like he did with Shaun, so he didn't have any evidence even though he still had dates and details.

The officer rushed and got some ice to put on Matty's check immediately.

"Matty, listen. I have never been with another man before until I met you. I don't know why you have gotten in my head, but you have and now it is not as easy as I thought to let you go."

Matty was in pain.

"When you asked me to verbalize all of this I was embarrassed and angry."

"Who am I going to tell? This is between me and you because I wanted to know what you see in me."

He kissed Matty.

"Let's forget this ever happened and you can slip my daisy dukes down, as you call them."

"What do you mean as I call them, I can see your underwear, when you wear underwear, and when you don't I can see your butt cheeks, your white butt checks. That makes those jeans daisy dukes."

"You complaining?"

"No, not at all. But forgive me if I'm not in the mood for any more sex right now. I'm tired and I would like to go to bed now."

"Okay, let me help you up so we can straighten up some of this mess before we leave."

They did all of that and then some despite Matty's protest otherwise.

"Can I see you tomorrow?"

"We will see."

Matty walked off.

On his way home that night, Matty bumped into Rodney.

"Hey Matty, what the hell happened to you?"

Matty looked up. He hadn't even noticed Rodney was standing near him because he was in so much pain.

"Oh, hey Rodney."

"What happened to you?"

"Oh I got into a little altercation."

"With who?"

"It doesn't matter. You can't do anything about it. So let it go."

Matty continued walking and he fell.

Rodney rushed over to help.

"Come on man, let me help you back to your quad."

After Rodney got Matty situated he left for a moment.

"Drink this."

Rodney shoved a bottle into Matty's face.

Matty refused.

"This will help kill the pain so you can sleep tonight. If you don't I'm going to go tell the chief somebody beat your ass."

"Okay, sit down and shut up."

Rodney sat down and Matty started drinking.

"What is this Rodney?"

"It's Jack Daniels."

"Damn this is strong."

"I know. That's why I drink it."

Matty got up to try and take his clothes off.

He was so drunk that he fell back onto Rodney.

They were laying on Matty's bed and starring into each other's eyes.

After a long awkward silence, they kissed each other.

"You taste like Jack Daniels Matty."

"It's your fault Rodney."

Matty fell asleep right in the middle of their kiss.

When he woke up the next morning, he had a slight hangover, was completely naked, and he had a sore jaw.

As he made his way to the shower room at 4:30 am, it took him a lot longer to get it together that day.

"Damn," Matty said when he recognized the huge bruise on his right jaw.

"There is no way to hide this."

Matty got dressed and went to work early so that he could get the mess cleaned up from last night's altercation before the captain or the XO arrived.

"Petty Officer Pottishear what happened to your face?" The XO asked.

Matty hemmed and hawed.

"So you don't want to tell me."

"All due respect sir, I do not want to tell you."

"Tell me this. Are you having a problem with anyone that I should know about?"

"I promise you sir if I cannot handle it I will come and tell you."

"If I ever see another bruise on you I am going to put you in jail until you tell me the truth. Do you understand me?"

"Yes sir."

"Go home and don't come back here until your face is clear. I don't want the Captain seeing you. I will tell him you are sick."

"But sir."

"No buts. I will get the master chief to send over a replacement for a few days."

As Matty was walking back to his barracks he kept replaying what had happened in his mind. He had never seen the XO show any personal interest like that in him before.

"Then again, I have never come in the office all bruised up before either."

But Matty welcomed the uninterrupted rest.

While everyone was at work during the day, Matty slept in total peace without thought, concern, or fear of being accosted.

But it also angered all those around him. There was green in everyone's eyes when it came to Matty.

At night, Matty was nowhere to be found and this increased those already angry with Matty, not to mention their tension levels.

Rodney used to steal Matty away every night, sometimes for only a few hours, and at other times, all night long.

Unexpectedly, during one of their nightly trysts Matty told Rodney, "Rodney you have to stop talking to me."

"Why, what's wrong?"

"Because people are getting mad and I don't want you getting in any trouble."

Rodney was a simple guy. He didn't ask Matty any more questions.

"Okay," Rodney said.

To Matty's surprise, Rodney started coming to see him even later at night and they would share Matty's twin bed every night.

"I don't know how we never got caught," Matty often said.

Matty had never looked at Rodney 'in that way' before but after Rodney started sleeping with Matty, Matty noticed that Rodney would wake up every morning with a brick.

"Rodney do you have a girlfriend?"

"Why do you ask?"

"Because you have been spending so much time with me that you have not had any time to take care of your personal needs."

"Maybe I don't need a girlfriend."

Matty dropped the conversation right there on the spot.

Matty was tall, Rodney was shorter. He looked scruffy by day and like a surf-boarder by night. He had soft brown hair and he was white.

But when they were in bed beside each other none of that mattered.

Matty didn't see Rodney for two weeks because they had to go out on a temporary construction project.

It was two weeks of living hell for Matty.

He had no peace during that time period, which left Matty thinking that someone was watching him and Rodney.

And several guys told Matty pretty much just that.

When Rodney returned, Matty told him exactly that.

"Well hell, since they all know, ain't no need in hiding no more. Besides they won't tell because they are scared you will tell on them."

"What about you Rodney?"

"I can take care of myself."

Rodney got in bed with Matty that night as usual, except that he got completely undressed that night.

Matty recognized that Rodney's club was hitting him in his chest not long after they went to bed.

Matty was not willing that Rodney should suffer any more. Rodney woke up to pure pleasure.

Matty had to cover his mouth he was moaning and writhing so loudly, before, doing, and after.

By the time they were finished Matty had willing drank Rodney's Kool-Aid, not like when he drank Shaun's and several others by force.

Rodney was the only partner Matty willingly gave himself to like that since Henri.

Those two became thick as thieves.

Then one night Rodney showed up with a little surprise.

"Close your eyes."

When Matty heard Rodney sniff, he knew immediately what was Rodney's surprise.

"Rodney, we can't do this. What if you get popped for a drug test? Besides you don't need that to impress me."

Rodney got completely undressed. Matty followed suit.

They got high all night long and had incredible sex. Matty was starting to truly enjoy Rodney and his steel pole.

And somehow Rodney did not mind that Matty's skin was no longer smooth and flawless.

But Matty never got over the fact that they had done drugs together. He started counting, in his head.

One day went by, no drug test.

Two days went by, no drug test.

Then the third day was almost over, when Rodney's name was called. Matty didn't know this at the time it happened.

They continued seeing each other and Rodney never told Matty about the drug test.

On Wednesday afternoon three weeks later, Matty was getting ready for Captain's Mast and he saw Rodney standing in front of him waiting to be seen by the XO for sentencing.

Matty's mouth dropped.

Rodney shook his head, telling Matty not to acknowledge him or his presence.

Matty jumped up ready to go to the XO and speak on Rodney's behalf. Matty was going to cash in that one chip he had with his good relationship with the XO to save Rodney.

Rodney snapped Matty by the arm and said, "Don't you do!"

Matty had forgotten that Rodney was a scrapper, and that he had seen him in action a couple of times. He was little, but he was a powerhouse, in and out of bed.

But Matty was determined to help Rodney.

"Matty no."

The XO's door opened and it was Rodney's turn to go in.

Rodney was standing at attention.

But his eyes were talking fast and they were not asking Matty, they were telling Matty what to do.

Rodney went in without Matty.

Matty was no good at work the rest of that afternoon. He spent the entire afternoon looking at his watch.

When 5 o'clock hit Matty was gone for the first time ever.

He went looking for Rodney to find out what happened.

Rodney was nowhere to be found.

Matty was going stir crazy but there was nothing he could do. He accepted that fact and went back to his room and sat on pins and needles until Rodney decided to make himself known.

"Rodney where have you been?"

Rodney could not respond.

"You're drunk."

"Yep."

Rodney was so drunk that he started babbling and telling Matty, "I love you."

"Rodney you are drunk. Lay down here and get some sleep."

Rodney started wrestling with Matty. Initially, they were really wrestling. Then it turned into passionate love making.

It was the first time that Matty went to that place with Rodney. He gave the most intimate part of himself to Rodney, and Rodney could not be satisfied after that until it was mid-morning.

Matty had no idea what he had done until it came time for him to take a shower. Rodney was bone dry when he got up.

They had just enough time to talk.

"I have been sentenced to the brig for two weeks, a loss of one pay grade, and loss of one week's pay."

Matty walked over to his secret place and pulled out a wad of cash.

"Here take this."

"Matty this is a $1,000 bucks."

"I know what it is."

'You are giving this to me?"

"I just did. But you have to hide it because you are not supposed to have money in the brig."

"Damn Matty, why are you doing this?"

"Rodney, let's not go there. Just take the money."

"I'm not taking a dime until you tell me why you are giving it to me."

"Then give me money back."

Rodney handed Matty the money.

They locked eyes.

"You thinking what I'm thinking," Rodney asked.

"It's almost time for everyone else to get up," Matty replied.

"Then we'd better hurry."

They didn't know how to hurry, but they tried.

Matty was in pain.

"You want me to stop," Rodney asked while he and Matty looked directly into each other's eyes.

"No please don't. I love you Rodney." Matty was holding on to Rodney's smooth strong back.

"I know you do."

"They started laughing."

They never stopped stroking during their entire conversation.

But Rodney's strokes started coming longer and harder. "I love you too Matty."

They both released at the same time.

It was truly orgasmic!

Rodney went to jail completely satisfied and with more money than even he could have imagined.

Rodney had been gone barely two days when Matty's health took a turn for the worse.

Matty laid down one night and woke up the next morning looking like a snake. He had several layers of white flaky, scaly skin from his neck down to his ankles. And his bed has so much skin in it that when he took his sheets outside to shake it off, it looked like snow was falling.

As soon as sick bay opened, Matty went to see the doctor.

He was in tears and he was hyperventilating.

Dr. Hopper prescribed Matty almost every single topical steroid imaginable in addition to tubes of lubricants.

Nothing helped.

Dr. Hooper knew that Matty was beyond his ability to treat him, but the Captain and the XO believed that Matty was too valuable to release him.

To Matty's pure surprise, a few of his suitors built him a sun tanning box facing the ocean on the beach, once they heard about his sickness.

Dr. Hooper had convinced the Captain and the XO that since they would not allow Matty to leave, that the sun should help Matty's condition. So they allowed him to sunbathe on the beach for two hours every day at the peak heat of the day.

That created even more trouble for Matty.

When he used to go to the mess hall to eat, he was mistreated by everyone from the mess hall staff down to the last construction worker in the open eating area.

"Captain's pet. Hey fellas, look who's decided to grace us with his presence, the Captain's fair-headed girl."

Matty tried to ignore all the comments, but it was a practical impossibility.

"Punk, dick-sucker, snake, AIDS."

The comments only got nastier and nastier as Matty went to the mess hall.

It got so bad that Matty started skipping meals. Within days Matty had lost 5, 10, 17, then 24 pounds.

He was so frail after that he actually looked like he had AIDS. Even worse for Matty, every step he took he left a pile of skin.

His clothes used to fit him perfectly and he wore tight underwear and tee-shirts tucked down into this underwear so that they would catch all the skin that fell from his torso. And because they wore fatigues, his pants were tucked into his boots so that the skin from his legs gathered inside his pants' legs.

At the end of the day when Matty would get undressed, he would stand in one place so that he could sweep up the piles of skin that gathered.

No one believed that Matty was really sick, until a group of spies caught him laying naked one day in his box.

"What the fuck you freak?"

They took buckets of cold water and threw on Matty along with a bucket of salt.

Matty's skin burned and bleed for days.

Someone told the Captain and the XO what happened, and those who did it were punished severely.

Their punishments ranged from the brig to loss of pay to demotions, and any combination thereof.

Matty was given a few days off to get himself together, and the mess hall was ordered to start preparing Matty special boxed meals to eat in his room. Matty never ate the meals because he was never sure they had not been tampered with extra protein, if you know what I mean, or worse.

None of this was helped by the fact that Matty had several meritorious promotions do him for all his outstanding work prior to joining the battalion.

So although Matty had only been with the battalion a little over nine months, he went from an E1 to an E4, practically overnight.

It didn't matter to outsiders that it all came from his hard work and efforts. To them it just looked like another benefit for the Captain's pet.

In the midst of all of this, there was another yeoman who had become so jealousy of Matty, the attention he garnered, and all the power he welded, including driving the Captain's car anytime he wanted to, that Duran called the Naval Investigative Service and said that Matty had made sexual advances toward him.

If you saw Duran, you would immediately know that Matty would never make an advance toward this guy - - EVER. He was literally a hairy, sweaty, nasty, pig, who chain smoked, and he had yellow teeth.

Duran even started following Matty around trying to catch him doing something wrong.

Dr. Hooper knew he had to do something for Matty because he was headed for another nervous breakdown.

After several meetings with the Captain and the XO, Dr. Hooper was able to convince them to let Matty leave, temporarily, for treatment at the Naval Hospital Bethesda, Maryland.

Under the negotiated deal, Matty was to go to Bethesda for six weeks of treatments and then return.

Two days before Matty was to leave, Dr. Hooper came to him and told him, "Pack all of your things. You will not be coming back."

"Dr. Hooper?"

"Don't ask any questions Matty. Just do what I tell you and do not say a word to anyone about this conversation. Now, the Medevac plane will be here to pick you up on Thursday morning."

Matty packed his things.

There was only thing left to do.

Matty did everything he could to make himself attractive, although he couldn't hide the weight loss and his skin, he tried his best to make himself as presentable as possible for Rodney's return.

Matty didn't care about anything or anyone at that time. He just wanted to see Rodney before he left. This was a Wednesday night.

6 pm came and went.

7 pm came and went.

8 pm came and went.

9, 10, finally Rodney showed up at 10:30.

Matty was so happy to see him that he couldn't help but hug and hold him.

And to Matty's surprise, Rodney kissed him.

"What the hell have you been up to since I've been gone?"

"You wouldn't believe what has been happening since you left."

"Yes I can. I heard all about it."

"Everything?"

"Everything. So we don't even have to talk about it. I'm just sorry I wasn't here to help protect you."

"To tell you the truth I was glad you weren't here because I didn't want you to get singled out for being around me."

"I keep telling you I can handle myself."

Then Matty blurted out, "I'm leaving in the morning."

"What?"

"Dr. Hopper had made all the arrangements for me to go to the Naval Hospital Bethesda, Maryland to be treated."

"When are you coming back?"

"I'm not, but nobody knows that."

While Rodney was still talking, Matty started undressing him.

"I need to take a shower. I'm all sweaty and dirty."

"I don't care. This is our last night together. You can take a shower tomorrow when I am gone."

At that point Rodney was naked and so too was Matty.

One, two, three, four, five…after five they stopped counting.

Matty did not sleep one moment that last night, and he refused to let Rodney sleep either.

"I forgot to tell you that I arranged for you to have tomorrow and Friday off."

"Matty you didn't."

"I did it because I knew you would be exhausted."

Rodney gave Matty one of his rare smiles.

Matty gave Rodney everything he had and then some.

"I need to tell you that I took care of Duran for you."

"How did you know about that?"

"I have my ways too you know."

When Matty got up to get dressed in time enough for his escort to take him to the airstrip, Rodney still desired his attention.

Matty was late to catch his ride. But there was nothing anyone could do but wait. They did make it to the airstrip just as the plane was taxing down the runway.

Matty slept the entire ride from Puerto Rico to Maryland although the plane ride was one of the worst he had ever experienced.

Since it was a medical flight, there were several patients on the brightly lit aircraft that had absolutely no creature comforts.

But the rough flight did serve to remind Matty of last night's events, so that Rodney was on his mind the entire flight.

Matty spent the next seven months in the hospital being treated in the dermatology clinic for the most "severe case of psoriasis" his doctors said they had ever seen.

Matty was treated with every kind of imaginable psoriasis treatment available. Initially nothing worked. The nurses had to change his bed and sweep his room from all the dead skin three times a day.

Then Matty started taking UVB light therapy three times per day. Essentially, he had to stand inside of a box similar to an upright tanning bed and let the intense radiation light bore into his skin. He started at 2 minutes and eventually worked up to 20 minutes per day, three times per day.

But Matty was never allowed to leave the hospital during that seven month period.

By the fifth month, Matty was going stir crazy and his skin looked better than it did before he got sick. Matty had a beautiful golden bronze hue to his skin.

Matty snuck out of the hospital one Friday night with nothing but his overcoat, a pair of sweat pants, his bedroom shoes, and his hospital gown still on.

He hitchhiked from the hospital almost to Virginia Beach and back to the hospital without anyone ever knowing he was gone. He had no money, no food, and nothing else but his wits and his body - - his beautiful, new body.

Matty used the tools he had to work with.

Additionally, Matty had to depend on the kindness of strangers the entire trip, and kind they were.

When Matty got back, he was calm enough to settle in for the remainder of his stay in the hospital, and no one was the wiser.

It was strange, but the first time in his life Matty was totally relaxed, and he felt like he was living a normal life, although he was confined to the hospital.

"Something is wrong. My life is going much too smoothly."

No one knows if Matty spoke his own demise into existence or whether the decision was already preplanned.

But shortly after his return from his little jaunt, Matty received orders to go to Greece to be a yeoman on the Admiral's flag ship.

The day after that he received notice that he was being discharged from the Navy for medical reasons.

His career was over before it ever began.

Matty was discharged from the hospital shortly after that awaiting final orders to go home.

So while he had to remain in D.C. he threw himself into the temporary work he was assigned to.

His job was putting people out of the Navy and managing the Navy brig at Quantico, Virginia.

Matty became so good at the job that he received another promotion from an E4 to an E5, and he became the office supervisor over a trained staff that had been in the office for several years prior to his arrival.

So by day, Matty was a mild-mannered office worker, and by night he tried to maintain that same mild-mannered quality. However, it wasn't too long before Matty got the eye of a whole host of men on and off the base.

He became a regular at the night club and at La Cage Aux Follies, in between the regular knocks on his dorm room door, which was right next to the showers.

Matty did keep up with the battalion and they with him. That's when Matty found out that Duran walked around the base for several weeks after Matty left with two black eyes, and they said they were real black eyes.

"Thank you Rodney."

Soon after that Matty was discharged, and it was just in the nick of time, because there were rumors that the NIS had picked up that investigation again and were preparing to interview Matty firsthand for evidence against him.

## Chapter 11

Just like that Matty was back at home, back at that same house in that same neighborhood he hated so much, in the same old room.

Even his old crew was still intact.

Little, if any had changed while he was gone.

Once again, Matty was floundering because he had no idea what he was going to do with himself.

Then he decided to go to college.

He was good at school, terrible at love.

Matty's heart was cold and callous this time around. He had the biggest black book ever and still he wasn't satisfied. That went on four years.

One night, the old crew invited Matty out to party. It was supposed to be a simple night out.

No sooner had they walked into the club did Matty start receiving drinks - - Jack Daniels with a splash of Coke.

"Who keeps sending me these drinks?" Matty asked the waiter.

Matty was stunned when the waiter pointed out Matty's secret admirer.

"Hey kid, what's your name?"

"I'm not a kid. I'm probably older than you, and my name is Darryl."

"Oh Lord not another one of you."

"What does that mean?"

"I mean that I used to know a guy named Darryl and he was more than a pain in my ass. He cost me a lot of time, money, heartache, and pain. I don't need another Darryl in my life," Matty prepared to walk off.

No matter what Matty said, Darryl followed him around the club that whole night like a puppy dog.

After that night, Darryl started calling Matty practically every day and showing up at every event Matty attended.

"Paris."

"How much did Darryl pay you to get my phone number and to start hanging out with you? And why would you take that boy's money?"

"Child if you don't take it someone else will."

"You just don't have any scruples do you?"

"I don't even know what scruples are."

"Exactly my point."

Although Matty grew to like Darryl a little bit, it was more pity.

"Matty why don't you like me?"

"Darryl you are okay to hang out with but I don't want to have sex with you."

"Hell but I want sex with you. What will it take for me to get you to take me to bed?"

"Darryl look. You are a nice guy, but you are just not my type. I have been through this before and…"

"Because I have a slightly deformed head, I'm short, and I don't have the perfect body."

"Darryl, come on man…"

"I'm rich."

"What do I look like a prostitute?"

"I just figured…"

"You just figured because you can buy Paris you can buy me too?"

"Well yes."

"You should stop hanging with Paris, because he doesn't me nearly as well as he has made you believe he does. And you should get your money back."

"How much?"

"Darryl, if you would stop being so pushy and stop trying to buy me, you might get what you want. And just to sit the record straight, I am not hooked up on looks. A truthful heart is more beautiful to me than any man any day."

Darryl started to back up a little and tried to take it slow. In return Matty warmed up to him a little more.

A few months into their strange relationship, there was a huge party that everybody who was anybody had been invited to.

"Matty are you going to the party?"

"I guess so Darryl."

"May I meet you there?"

"Sure you may."

Matty was notoriously late for any and everything.

When they did finally arrive Matty went looking for Darryl. In between being stopped by every Tom, Dick, and Harry, Matty kept looking for Darryl.

Finally Jonathan told him that Darryl had been upstairs in the private lounge. The one place Matty didn't check because he didn't know anything about the lounge.

"So where is he now?"

"He left the party with some guy that was in the lounge?"

"Who? What guy?"

"I don't know. He was somebody I didn't know."

Matty didn't have a good time the rest of the night, and Darryl never returned to the party.

Matty didn't have a number or an address for Darryl so he had no way of contacting him. Darryl wanted it that way.

So all Matty could do was wait for Darryl to contact him.

It was late February.

Matty's birthday was the end of the month, and on his birthday the telephone rang.

Matty was devastated by the news.

The guy that Darryl had left the party with robbed Darryl that night after he probably talked Darryl into believing that he was sexually interested in him.

Then he cut and stabbed Darryl, and threw him in a ditch left him for dead. They found Darryl's body and his car several days after the murder.

Matty never forgave himself for causing Darryl's murder.

The next few months meant very little to Matty. In fact, Matty spent the next several months locked away in his old bedroom, and he had very little contact with the outside world.

Winter came and went. Spring came and went. Summer came and went. By the time the Fall rolled in, Matty had started to break out of his depression a little bit.

All Matty could think about was the Brothers Johnson song, *I'll Be Good to You*.

"How ironic."

It was a cold rainy day in early November, there was a knock at the back door.

Knock. Knock. Knock.

Matty looked out the back door to see who was knocking.

There was no one there.

It was raining cats and dogs that day so Matty didn't think much of it.

He went back into his bedroom and turned the stereo up again.

BAM. BAM. BAM.

This time Matty heard it for sure.

He ran down into the den to answer the door. He was in a panic because he thought something was wrong.

"What the hell you doing banging on our back door like you are crazy?"

Sammie pushed Matty aside and came on in without waiting for an invitation. He was crying.

Matty's heart dropped.

"Matty, I am in trouble," Sammie blurted out.

Matty just looked at him without uttering a word. He was waiting for the real news, because with Sammie you never knew what you were getting until you had agreed to purchase a lemon.

Sammie proceeded to tell Matty the entire story.

"See last night, Charles and I went out riding to smoke a couple. We were bored and you or the other girls (guys) were not around. So we went to the club, nothing was happening. We rode around and smoked one or two, and then we ended up at David's bookstore."

Matty still hadn't said a word yet. He wanted to know what he was committing to before he said anything.

"So, I saw this guy. Damn why didn't I listen to Charles?"

Now Matty needed to speak. "Listen to Charles about what?" he screamed in a clear panic.

"Charles told me he went to school with this guy and that he was bad news and I should leave him alone. But I just thought he was being typical Charles so I started talking to him anyway."

"Oh my Lord," Matty exclaimed. He knew something really bad was coming.

"Anyway, we smoked another one, the three of us, and then Charles said he wanted to go home. So we took him home."

"We!" Matty yelled.

"Then on the way back to the bookstore he said that he was going to rob a bank tomorrow and that I was going to drive his getaway car. I thought he was kidding so I started laughing. He said I am not kidding. So I got really scared and I drove home."

"What did you do with the boy?" Matty asked.

"That's the crazy part. I took him home with me."

"You dumbass," Matty jumped up and yelled down at him.

"Sammie, damn every time I turn around ya'll are always getting into some of the dumbest shit that I can't even imagine, and then you come to me to fix shit I wasn't even a part of. You and Paris!"

"I'm not finished," Sammie said.

Matty sat back down to brace himself. All the while the rain was coming down even harder.

"While we were sitting in the driveway he told me that if I didn't help him rob the bank that he would come to my house and kill my mother."

"Why didn't you call the police?" Matty asked.

"I didn't know his name, where he lived, or anything else about him. So I didn't know what to do."

"Sammie please don't tell me what I think you are about to tell me," Matty interjected.

"I picked him up at…"

"Wait, where did you take him last night? Why couldn't you call the police after you dropped him off?"

"I dropped him off in some neighborhood off Brookshire Freeway."

"At what address?"

"No address. Just a corner."

"Damn," Matty said. All he could do was hang his head in his hands.

"I picked him up at the same place this morning and we drove over to Nations Bank off Freedom Drive. He told me to park in the back of the bank and to keep the car running. A few minutes later he came back to the car and I drove off."

"Oh my God." Matty was stunned.

"I didn't know he had robbed a bank. He didn't have a bag or anything in his hands and he wasn't running or rushing."

"So where is he now? And what is his name?'

"I think his name was Mike. And when he got back in the car he told me to get on I-85 to go to Gastonia."

"So where is he now?"

"When we got to Gastonia he gave me $2,000, jumped out of my car near the mall, and told me not to try and find him."

"Where's the money?"

"I spent it."

"You are really a piece of work. You know that? And what really pisses me off is that you always come to me after you have gotten into fucking trouble and expect me to clean up your mess! What the hell did I ever do to deserve a friend like you? Shit Sammie!"

Matty sat back down and tried to gather his thoughts.

"What did you spend $2,000 on this early in the morning on a rainy Thursday?"

"Clothes."

"What?"

"I spent the money on clothes. I went to the mall…"

"What mall?"

"Gastonia mall."

"You mean to tell me that you went to the Gastonia mall at 9:30 in the morning and spent $2,000 on clothes?"

"No."

"Good. Finally you did something right."

"I spent $1,400 on clothes. Here is the other $600," he said as he reached Matty a roll of 20's.

"You need to go get that money back so you can turn it in," Matty said to Sammie.

Needless to say, Sammie went to jail and after that his life spiraled out of control.

"But I couldn't just turn my back on him because we did have some history together. We did sleep together once or twice, if you can call it that. My mother caught him hiding in the closet one time and sent him home, and he did save me from drowning."

So Matty felt like he owed it to Sammie to help him.

Although Sammie's problems were not Matty's only problems, friends with problems that is.

Don't forget that Matty had problems of his own. He had continuous health problems the entire four years after he got out of the Navy. And to make matters worse, Matty had in his mind that he could regain the golden bronze tan that he had while he was in the hospital at Bethesda. Not for the lack of trying, Matty never reached that goal again.

He spent so much time in the dermatologist's office and arranging insurance payments that he could have run a doctor's office.

Bottom line, Matty's skin gave him pure hell during that period!

Up and down, up and down. The doctors could never get his skin to settle down and ease out, but Matty never gave up.

Sure as the pattern of his life went, the uglier Matty felt, the more he was appealing to other men and women.

And every time Matty gave in to the desire for sex, it was at one of his lowest period, physically and mentally. And each time he had to find a way to hide the gobs of dead skin that would fall off his body, enough dead skin to full a dust pan to overflow three times.

And despite all of this, Matty had a black book that was damn near as thick as the yellow pages. In fact, Matty was so good at what he did and at hiding his flaws, he had guys that would rob to give him money to do whatever it was he desired, as long as he gave them what they wanted - - him in bed.

Matty was the best and ugliest gigolo walking, but he lacked for nothing, and he never worked a day and he drove a brand new Volkswagen Fox.

He was flying around the country for free, shopping in Philadelphia, sightseeing in Tennessee, hanging out at the Mardi Gras, bumping and grinding in Hotlanta, and partying in New Jersey, New York and Washington, DC almost every single weekend, all with a different boyfriend.

By force, Matty also became a makeup artist, a superior makeup artist. He took all of his modeling experience from TRIM and learned how to apply his makeup flawlessly to cover up.

The only thing is that Matty didn't use any makeup on his face. He used it all over his body.

He bought the absolute best makeup on the market at the time and learned how to meticulously apply Golden Brown Chroma cover crème to hide all of his bodily imperfections, when his skin was in remission that is.

Then he would apply Warm Safron setting powder in such a blended perfection that absolutely no one knew that he had on makeup, even his own, "too live crew."

When he got home from the club, he would use the Nettoyant remover to meticulously remove every bit of makeup and reveal the true Matty.

And yes, when it came to sex, Matty's makeup would come off on his partner's bodies, but Matty's talents were so in demand that his partners never brought it up for fear that Matty would cut them off.

One time Matty was in bed with a long-sought love interest, and it happened to be, of course, during one of Matty's most violently active outbreaks. They were in the complete dark.

Unbeknownst to Matty, Rodney's lover came in, turned the light on, and exposed Matty's secret. Matty was so devastated that he ran out of the house butt-ass-naked, leaving dead skin his entire path.

Still that didn't stop Matty's suitors.

Matty was barely healed when that same love interest came back again, despite Matty's beastly appearance.

In fact, some of his partners got close enough to Matty that he actually gave them the privilege of going makeup shopping with him. Of course, they paid for the makeup, which not a single one refused.

As for Sammie, by the time Matty finished college, Sammie was also out of jail and in college.

About a year after his graduation, Matty got a job offer to go work for the Navy as a civilian.

When he told Sammie, Sammie said, "I'm going with you."

Matty said, "Okay," because he thought it would be nice to take a little piece of Charlotte with him, and he thought Sammie would have a better opportunity of getting past his checkered past in a new city.

A couple of weeks prior to their departure, Sadie took out a loan so that she could purchase new furniture for the apartment, and Matty would have some starting money that was supposed to carry him until he received his first paycheck.

In addition to that, Sammie ran into one of their old high school classmates - - Bernard.

No one is exactly sure how it happened, but Bernard and Matty became quasi-lovers, and the next thing everybody knew, he was on his way to Washington, DC along with Matty and Sammie.

On the day of their departure, Sammie and Bernard were in a hurry to leave before Matty and his brothers were to leave with the U-Haul full of furniture.

Matty had purchased a rather large package of cocaine for them to break in their new apartment with once everyone left.

But by the time that Matty and his brothers arrived, the cocaine was completely gone, Bernard was nowhere to be found, and Sammie was out clubbing.

"Then it hit me that I had made a mistake allowing Sammie and Bernard to come with me to DC. Sammie had never been trustworthy with anything up to that point and he remained true to form. We even had to wait for Sammie to come home from the club before we got into the apartment because he had the only key, although my name was the only name on the lease."

That was day one.

Matty's brothers left the next day and Bernard didn't come home until that next night.

That was day two.

"Bernard was supposed to be my lover I guess, except that he wasn't really gay. He was just going along for the ride so that he could try and start over also." A carefully concealed fact.

So Matty was the only one with a job supporting three grown men.

And they took turns sleeping in Matty's bed since they only had one bedroom.

Every day and every night Sammie was out partying and bringing home a different stranger every single night.

So they were already arguing over the closet, the bathroom, and Matty's bed; and, they hadn't been in the apartment one good month.

"You guys, I think we should get a two bedroom."

"We can't afford a two bedroom," Sammie and Bernard said in unison.

"Well I am tired of sharing my bed and my bedroom when my name is the only name on the lease. And I am also tired of stepping over all of your stray dogs every morning Sammie."

What Matty should have done was told them to go back to Charlotte, but he didn't.

Anyway, Matty went ahead and got the two bedroom. And he had to move the entire apartment, every single piece of furniture, by himself, from the one bedroom to the two bedroom that was up on the hill. Sammie and Bernard refused to help move the furniture since they were against the idea from the very beginning.

"Well I am only going to pay what I have been paying," Sammie said, which was very little. And when he did pay it was late because he had to wait on his mother to send him the money to pay his portion of the bills.

Again Matty let it slide.

After they moved into the new apartment things only got worse.

Bernard got a job as a graphic designer and had to use Matty's car to go to work and come home but Matty picked up all the expenses, including Bernard's extravagant lunches while Matty took bag lunches to work to save money.

Bernard and Sammie started giving Matty even less because they were both too busy partying on the weekend while Matty was keeping them all afloat.

And do you think either one of them ever offered to take Matty out with them on their dime one time?

Hell no!

And Sammie was working sporadically here and there.

Then the shit really hit the fan.

Bernard and Matty weren't having sex at all because come to find out Bernard was having sex with a crack head who didn't live far from them.

That is also when Matty found out about Bernard's crack head past, and that he was having sex with the same crack head he met the first night they moved to Alexandria.

Shortly after that, he stole all of the rent money out of Matty's briefcase while on one of his binges.

Matty went searching and found out where the girl lived and went around to her house to get his money back.

They laughed at him and threatened to call the police if he didn't leave.

A few days later, Bernard stole Matty's car.

Matty had to practically beg Sammie to take him to the girl's house to get the car.

"Bernard, you can come get your stuff tomorrow, and don't worry about your key because I will have the locks changed by then."

"You're putting me out?"

"You are damn right and you and that stank bitch can have each other."

"Who you calling a bitch?"

"You! Now if you want some of me, come on. I will put my foot up your stanken ass, you nasty ass bitch."

Then Matty spit on her and dared her or Bernard to do anything.

Then Bernard begged Matty to come back and told him he was going to change, so Matty being a sucker for a good sob story took him back.

Bernard was okay for a few weeks, then he was gone again.

This time he stole the car and hid it.

And Sammie didn't even want to help Matty find his car.

"I was so hurt I didn't know what to do."

Well Matty did find the car and he also found out that Bernard was on parole and was not supposed to be out of the state of North Carolina.

Matty walked boldly up to the girl's house where she lived in her parent's basement.

BAM! BAM! BAM!

"Give me my car keys right now."

Bernard reluctantly gave Matty his keys.

"Hey Matty come on. You been wanting to have sex with me, so come on you can fuck me while I fuck her."

"Are you out of your damn mind? I wouldn't fuck you if I had to, you weak ass facsimile of a man!"

"You think you better than me."

"You damn right I am better than you because I used to smoke crack and I straightened myself out, you weak minded pussy."

"Fuck you man."

"You wish. Let's see how you do when your parole officer finds out you are up here!"

Bernard could have shit bricks right there.

"Let's go Sammie."

The next morning Matty called Bernard's parole officer and told her everything.

He came running back to their apartment pleading with Matty, but it was too late.

"Your home is in that dank, dark basement with your crack head whore."

She even came to the apartment and begged Matty not to turn Bernard in, and then she had the nerve to offer Matty some of her tainted pussy.

Matty laughed at her right there in her face before he her them both out.

Then Bernard came back later, pulled his pants down and spread his ass, "Here man."

Matty walked right past him as if he didn't even exist.

"Who's laughing now bitch?"

Matty did exactly what he said he would do.

He called Bernard's parole officer and gave her his current address and every sordid detail of their non-relations relationship.

He came to Matty crying like a girl and begging him not to do it.

"It's already done. There's no turning back."

He continued crying.

"I am not going to be made out to be the bad guy in all this."

The last time Matty saw Bernard he was clean and dressed up in a grey suit looking back at him crying as he got on a Greyhound bus headed back to Charlotte.

Matty was smiling on the outside and crying on the inside.

Then after that it came Sammie's turn to act up.

He stopped paying bills altogether because basically no one would hire him.

"I am not your mother and you are not going to lay around here on me, eating, sleeping, shitin', and bringing every damn dog you can find home to lay up in my house. So you are either going to get a job or go home!"

So Sammie came home to Charlotte and brought all of his bedroom furniture back to the two bedroom apartment that he wasn't paying any bills in.

Matty started laughing.

"My mother used to always say lay down with dogs and get up with fleas. I never thought I would see that in real life until now."

Anyway Sammie went to work for a temporary agency and the agency finally found him a lucrative position with the FBI.

He had a choice to tell them the truth about his past or tell a lie.

Matty told him not to take the job.

"Matty, this job pays almost $30 an hour."

"Then if you plan on taking the job, you need to tell them the truth."

Sammie took the job and about three days later he came home and told me he had been fired and a national alert was attached to his name.

"What the hell? Why were you fired?"

He was eating in the FBI cafeteria with his normal flamboyant self and he was recognized by one of the agents who worked his arrest case in Charlotte. The agent told the chain of command. But that is not why they fired him. They fired him for lying on his application. After that he could not get a job anywhere.

So he lay around all day while Matty was at work and he partied every night with every mutt he could find.

Then Matty had to go to Hawaii to work for about 45 days. So he wrote out checks for every signal bill, a little over $2,000.

Matty had an absolute ball in Honolulu and he only went to a gay club one time. But he didn't need to because he was having a different kind of fun in Hawaii.

One of his co-workers, Ed, immediately took a liking to Matty because he found out that Matty was a cool cat who was not a snitch or as uptight as he appeared to be. So Ed started taking Matty along with him at night to his favorite spots.

Every night for more than a month Ed took Matty to the most extravagant male strip clubs, tiddy bars, where they regular guests in the back room of every club. Later Matty found out that Ed was dropping more than a $1,000 per night on girls and champagne, and he never asked Matty for one red cent.

Matty was having an absolute ball because no one was making any demands on him at work or at play. The novelty of it all was whimsical to Matty, and he was just fine with being a casual observer - - in  total silence.

When he came back home, on his birthday, he had to catch a cab from the airport because Sammie wouldn't pick him up.

Matty came home to a filthy apartment.

It was spotless when he left because he had cleaned it from top to bottom.

Sammie had let some strangers sleep in Matty's bed several nights with their shoes on. His white pristine sheets were as black as the tar on the street.

Then he told Matty that he didn't have any money so he cashed all of the checks Matty had written for him to pay the bills, and partied on Matty's money and did not pay a single bill.

Matty went ballistic.

He had to cash in all of his bonds and stocks to keep them from being out on the street.

The only reason they didn't drive his car is because Matty had the keys with him in Hawaii.

"I talked with Sammie almost every day I was in Hawaii, and he never gave me any indication of what was truly going on."

After Matty spent all afternoon going around gathering up money to pay the bills, he wanted to go out to celebrate his birthday and party a little bit.

They all went to a strip club and had a ball.

Matty drove.

After the club Sammie and his most regular boyfriend Ronald, a Marine, started fighting because Sammie got missing with another guy at the club.

They were throwing serious blows on the way home and Matty was trying to stop them from fighting.

In the midst of trying to stop them Matty wrecked his car.

He hit a median in the road, but they were so busy fighting and he was so busy being hit that not one of them noticed until they almost got home.

Then the car stopped and they had to walk home.

The car was ruined and had to be towed in.

Matty was so busy taking care of Sammie and Bernard's issues that he had forgotten to pay his car insurance. The car was totaled.

As Matty lay in his bed, on his fresh, clean sheets, his mind could not help but wander back through all the piles of shit Sammie had laid at his door over the years of their friendship.

"File number 1,452," Matty's mind told him to stop and pull out the file.

Inside that file was the story of Matty walking 20 miles on a dark cold night - - again because of Sammie.

Matty had been given two free tickets to one of the first professional football games to ever be played in the Charlotte area, except that the game was not being played in Charlotte. The game was going to be played in Columbia, SC.

Matty couldn't drive to Columbia because his driver's license had been revoked.

"Different file number," Matty said.

Anyway, the only other person of their sorry crew that had a driver's license and a car was Sammie.

So Matty invited Sammie to the game.

"You know I need some candy to drive way down there and stay up all night."

"What, shit, you don't even have a job and you stay up all night anyway, you greedy bitch."

Still Matty relented and gave Sammie the money to pick up some candy.

True to form, Sammie was late picking Matty up for the game and when he did finally get to Matty, he had snorted almost all of Matty's candy.

"Let's just go."

They made it to the stadium in time enough for the start of the half time events.

The game spiked their interest.

"Let's go to the Candy Shop," Sammie said.

"Okay. I don't want no shit out of you. If you leave me down here you know you got an ass whoppin' comin'!"

Sammie's eyes got big because he knew Matty went that with an exclamation point.

"Okay."

When they arrived at the club, it was rather quiet.

Ten minutes later, the club was "on and poppin'" as they say.

Twenty minutes after that Matty was in his date for the night, and Sammy was in a car in the parking lot doing who knows what.

One hour went by. Two hours, and then three hours later, Matty's date said to him, "Dayum, don't you ever get tired?"

"I warned you about this when you first started cruisin' me didn't I?"

"Yea but I didn't know you meant that shit. Most nigga's be bluffin' and puffin' hot air."

"So you thought I was one of them?"

"Hell yea."

"So what, you want me to stop?"

"Shit nigga' it's too late for that now. You done tore my shit up so you might as well go on and finish. I didn't go through all of this to not get to the finish."

And finish Matty did!

"Nigga' I don't ever want to see you again."

"Don't worry you won't."

"I can't handle what you dishin' out on a regular basis."

Matty walked off, unfazed by the comments, and laughing at the same time.

It took him a while to stroll through the parking lot until he found Sammie.

Rap. Rap. Rap.

Matty knocked on the window.

"Let's go. I'm exhausted."

"We are not finished."

"Yes you are too."

Matty opened the door and pulled Sammie's naked ass out of that backseat.

"Matty!"

"Put your clothes on. It's been more than three hours. Hell if I can do it in three, you damn sure can."

"Man what the hell you doing?"

"Who is this clown trying to talk to me?" Matty said to Sammie.

"Oh this is…"

Before Sammie could finish, Matty interrupted. "What gives you the impression I want to know who that jiggy boo is?"

"Man I will…"

"You'll do what!" Matty exclaimed.

And with that he kicked the guy so hard in his chest that it knocked all of the breath out of him.

Matty dragged Sammie off to their car wearing nothing but his underwear, homeward bound.

Matty had to keep smacking Sammie to make him stay awake and stop weaving. It was no easy task.

They had almost made it to the Carowinds exit. They had only about four more exits to go.

Blue lights!

"Damn Matty, I'm going to jail."

"Don't tell my momma. Tell her a lie."

Sure enough the officer pulled Sammie over and read him the routine.

"Sir do you know why I am stopping you?"

"No sir I don't."

"You have been weaving for more than three exits."

While he was interrogating Sammie, Matty noticed there were baggies on the dashboard.

"Damn, this dumb bitch is gonna cause me to go to jail with him," Matty said as he waited for the baggies to be spotted.

"Turn around sir."

And with that Officer-who-gives-a-shit slapped the cuffs on Sammie.

After he put Sammie in his squad car, he walked back up to the car.

"Sir do you have a driver's license?"

"Yes."

"May I see it?"

Matty paused a long time.

"Well?"

"Well what?"

"May I see your driver's license?"

"I don't have it."

"Why not?"

"Because it has been temporarily revoked."

The officer reached inside and took the keys.

Matty was sitting in a useless car on a major highway -- alone!

"Sir you will have to walk."

"Why can't you give me a ride at least to the state line?"

"Because we are not a limousine service."

After Matty had gotten over the shock of it all, he started walking.

It took Matty almost five hours to walk twenty miles. The sun was completely up and everybody had gone to work by the time Matty got back home.

He was exhausted.

As he was preparing to go to sleep, the phone rang.

It was Sammie's mother.

"Matty what happened?"

Matty didn't immediately say a word.

Sammie's mother continued to talk.

Matty was no snitch.

But then it happened.

Sammie's mother said, "Sammie said the police pulled you over for drunk driving and both of ya'll had to go to jail. So why are you out and Sammie's still in jail?"

That sealed it.

"No ma'am, let me tell you exactly what happened so you will know what you need to do to get Sammie out of jail."

Matty sang like a canary that day. And he didn't care that time.

It cost Sammie's mother more than $4,000 to get Sammie out of jail that day.

As Matty was drifting off to sleep, full of anger and self-disappointment with his agreement to let Sammie invade his life once again, his bedroom door opened.

It was Ronald, standing in Matty's doorway wearing nothing but his underwear.

"Sammie kicked me out of the bedroom."

"Shit, come on."

Ronald slept with Matty that night on his clean sheets.

"Welcome home, Matty?" Matty said out loud.

"What did you say Matty?" Ronald asked.

"Never mind. It's not important."

Ronald walked over to the bed, took his underwear off, and slide his ass right up underneath Matty. He had gotten Matty's attention and his manhood's too.

File number 1,452 was burning in Matty's brain.

Without the slightest hesitation or concern, Matty pulled out a box of magnums, slipped on one, and furiously pounded Ronald.

Ronald never once refused Matty.

That went on all night long. When one condom was full, Matty pulled it off threw it on the floor and put on another one. His Johnson never went down, and neither did his anger.

It was daybreak Saturday morning when they were finished.

Ronald was bleeding profusely, like a bitch in heat.

Matty used two boxes of magnums that night.

"Flea protection," Matty called it.

That's when Matty realized that his bed was crowded, just as Shakespeare said.

Matty slept the rest of that day away and on into the night.

For the next few months Matty had to use public transportation back and forth to work.

Sammie, who still wasn't working, took his friend Ronald to work and picked him up every day. They would drive right past Matty standing at the bus stop and not even wave.

November and Thanksgiving were coming up.

Matty rented a car to come home. He didn't tell a soul about everything that had been going on.

Sammie came home too, but Matty refused to see him the entire time they were home.

Once Matty got home, his mother told him that JPH was in the hospital sick and that they were not expecting him to live.

Matty showed not one single emotion.

A few days into the vacation they got the phone call that JPH had died.

Several old classmates came to Matty and told him that JPH had gotten hooked on shooting up cocaine in his veins.

"Matty do you want to go to the funeral?" His mother asked.

"Momma, I have to think about it for a few days."

Then he started to tell his mother some of the story. He also got the notion to admit his homosexuality to his mother.

He couldn't bring himself to tell her either.

"You know what momma, yea, I want to go to the funeral."

"I want to go see him in that casket," Matty said with clear hatred in his voice.

"Matty what's wrong?"

Matty refused to answer his mother for the first time ever.

"Sorry momma, you are only thirty years too late," Matty said under his voice.

Matty didn't have one bit of remorse seeing him in that casket or seeing his family crying.

In fact it only made him madder because they were crying for someone who they never truly knew.

"I looked at him in that casket and I knew that he had died of AIDS. Then I looked at his momma to my left crying. I felt nothing for her and her pain. I stood there at that casket by myself, not afraid, just looking at him. I wanted to turn that casket over, but the only reason I didn't is because it would have embarrassed my mother."

Then Matty snapped. Without notice or forewarning, Matty spit in JPH's face right there in the funeral home.

Then as quickly as he snapped Matty was back in realty and he was ready to leave. He left that wake that night without saying a word to JPH's family. But he did go to the funeral.

"Good riddance," Matty said when it was all over.

Matty went back to DC and went back to his life, if you could call it that.

After Thanksgiving vacation, Matty and Sammie went out, after Matty had calmed down a little bit.

They got into a huge argument because Sammie wanted to dump Matty so that he could take a stranger back to their apartment.

When they got home they started fighting and Sammie was jumping all over Matty's furniture.

Matty blew his lid and lunged at Sammie in the most violent way.

Sammie ran into his room and locked the bedroom door.

"You better not come out of that room the rest of the night, and if you need to piss you better piss in his hands."

The next morning, Matty told Sammie that he had had it and it was time for him to go home.

Sammie didn't believe Matty.

Matty called Sammie's mother while he was standing right there and told her everything and that Sammie had to come home. He was unapologetic about the whole matter. He was understandably exhausted.

By the middle of the week Sammie was gone. And he was mad at Matty for sending him home.

After he left Matty was left with a pile of bills that he had to struggle to pay for all of the shit that Bernard and Sammie had put him through.

Matty tried to go back to a smaller apartment but the apartment manager would not budge. So he started looking for cheaper apartments.

There was nothing around that would fit into Matty's budget except for cockroach infested buildings.

So Matty didn't know what he was going to do.

Then an old high school friend, Annie, called him and offered him the opportunity to move in with her, into her studio apartment.

So it was either that or go home to Charlotte defeated.

Once again, Matty was stuck with emptying out an apartment all by himself and moving into a studio apartment, alone.

Matty accepted her offer and started emptying out his apartment of all the new furniture he and his mother had paid for.

He gave several pieces away and the rest he put in storage. After a while he sold his storage unit and everything within it because he didn't think he was going to be able to do anything with it for a while.

Matty moved every single piece of furniture in that entire apartment by himself, loaded and unloaded it into the moving truck, and cleaned the entire apartment alone.

The day he moved into Annie's apartment, he had four things: his personal cosmetics bag, which included jars and jars of creams and topical steroids to treat his psoriasis; his briefcase; his one and only overcoat; and a large traveler's trunk that carried his entire life inside of it, a trunk by the way, that was large enough to carry a full grown man inside of it.

And in his pocket Matty carried his driver's license, his metro card, his door keys, and the list. Nothing more was necessary.

He didn't have a wallet during those years because he had no money.

But nothing was more important to him than that list. It completely ruled Matty's life and dictated his every move.

However, Matty's survival was not the only matter at stake.

Others were counting on him to succeed. In fact, others needed him to succeed.

So for the first time in Matty's life he was learning how to succeed by developing the ability to think in practical terms.

In the midst of his pain and disgrace, Matty finally realized and admitted to himself that he had made a record number of bad financial moves.

Even though he did not know how to fix all his problems, he kept every last one of his mistakes on his list because he promised himself that one day he would make good on all his obligations.

As a matter of fact, Matty became consumed with being debt free and worry free, and no sacrifice was too great for him to achieve that one goal.

Matty was also happy because that list had served its purpose of forcing him to make real financial choices unlike those previous decisions that lead to his own, personal wilderness experience that left him wandering in his own desert of sorts.

In his efforts to survive, Matty cut back, downsized, right-sized, and basically turned into a hermit in order to reach his goal of paying off all his debt, which included all of his mother's debt, and living debt free from that point forward.

He also had been brow beaten, beaten up, beat down, and kicked to the curb.

He had given up his independence and moved into a cramped studio apartment where he was treated more like an imprisoned child than an adult.

Matty had no privacy, no voice, and nowhere else to go.

For more than three years, Matty slept on the new sofa he and his mother had purchased for his initial move to D.C., while Annie slept in her bed.

She refused to share her bed, and Matty didn't want to share her bed.

So Matty got dressed in the dark in the mornings for work, and he had to learn how to sleep through Annie's noise when she got home at midnight or so from work.

He did absolutely everything he could to not be an inconvenience to her or to upset her life in any sort of way.

Outside of paying all of his bills on the list, purchasing a bi-weekly metro card to go back and forth to work, and getting his hair cut every two weeks, Matty gave practically every single penny he had left to Annie for rent, laundry, and food.

He did not purchase one single new piece of clothes during that entire three year period, including any new underwear. His wardrobe remained unchanged for those three years and longer.

Whatever Matty had packed into that trunk was all Matty had to work with.

His weekends were spent walking the streets of Foggy Bottom, and being jealous of all the others who could financially enjoy the amenities, the shopping, and fine dining experiences in the area where they lived while all Matty was able to barely afford was a dream of a better future.

Although Matty had a full-time job making more than $60,000.00 per year as a young urban professional, the truth is that he was flat broke! Actually, Matty had to have money to be broke.

Matty was less than broke.

Annie took Matty's money every month and then refused to buy any food.

It was as if she was purposefully trying to starve him to death while she was going out and eating all kinds of lavish meals behind his back.

In school Annie was always known as being a nasty bitch, but she became much worse than that while they lived together.

To try and escape his despair that was closing in around him after the first year, Matty enrolled in the Master of Public Administration program at George Washington University.

Matty also started saving up money and rebuilding his credit.

Meanwhile Matty's skin was doing cartwheels in that apartment, in part because it was so filthy.

It was a dirty, old building that was smelly and had rats running around the garbage. There were cockroaches throughout the building; and, the parquet floor, at least in their apartment, was torn up and so badly splintered that Matty could never get it clean.

It was an absolute mess, despite Matty's efforts to incessantly keep it clean. He was the only one who cleaned the apartment.

Matty's skin forever itched and stayed broken out for months at a time.

But despite all of these challenges, Matty never stopped paying his debts and he never quit school.

He paid Annie without fail every single month, and the more he gave her the more she wanted.

He even did their laundry every two weeks without fail, including washing Annie's big girl panties and bras.

Never did Matty complain, not to one single soul.

He cleaned and did everything he could do to be as invisible as possible.

She worked second shift. Matty worked first.

Then without provocation, Annie turned against him.

And instead of talking about it so that they could solve the problem, her undeserved animosity against Matty only beget his animosity in return.

On more than one occasion, he came in and heard Annie sitting on the toilet, which was where she lived, with the bathroom door closed telling her mother and or her sister how she "was sick of Matty."

She lied and told her family that he "don't do nothing. I have to do all the laundry, pay all the bills, and cook all the food," none of which was true.

Matty tried to overlook it all, but it was not easy.

Then without giving Matty any notice, her mother and sister came for a visit.

When Matty walked in and realized they were there, he tried to be his happy cordial self. But they were blatantly rude and nasty toward Matty.

He was stunned at the openness of their dislike, although he knew it was all based on lies.

Matty was so mad that he could have eaten nails and not have missed a beat.

He prepared himself to have to sleep on the steps that night.

"I've got to do something better than this."

If that wasn't bad enough, when she had company, male company, she would put Matty out of the apartment.

Even though sometimes she would give him a little money to party with, Matty had to pay her back, and he had to go to the club and hang out with people he would have rather not spent time with.

Matty had to resort to skills he would have rather not ever had to use again, with every kind of stranger imaginable, just so that he would have a place to lay his head down on those nights that Annie put him out.

And when all of that failed, Matty had to sleep on the stairs in the lobby of their roach and rat infested building because Annie would take his key and lock him out until her company left.

On top of all of that since she would never buy any groceries, if it wasn't for their mutual friend Val, who worked at a convenience store, Matty would have completely starved -- short of eating out of the trash can of some of their neighbors who ate on top of the hog.

"I hated using Val like that, but I simply didn't have any other choice, and Val understood that."

Things got so bad that Matty would go drinking after church on Sunday afternoons, and once he got caught by the members of the choir.

Matty was angry.

"Shit. I am sick and tired of trying to be everything everyone else wants me to be. I want to be me for me, good, bad, or otherwise."

So Matty's meals consisted of stolen moments alone in restaurants, leftovers from the trash cans of the really rich that threw out really good leftovers because they lived in Foggy Bottom, and convenience store meals stolen from Val's employer.

There were a few, a very few good moments while Matty lived with Annie, one of which included Matty screwing Annie's cousin who was built like a dark chocolate brickhouse.

The problem is that Matty made the mistake of getting attached and her cousin broke it off.

But before Matty moved away from Annie, he took her cousin against his will.

One Saturday night while Matty and Annie were sitting there looking at television, not talking to each other, her cousin came over to visit.

"He looked so fetching."

Matty snatched her cousin, whose name Matty will not divulge, into her bathroom, snatched his pants down, and proceeded to ride him while he forced his face against the wall in the prone position.

Her cousin had nowhere to go and no way to do so with Matty so deep inside of him.

It wasn't long before Matty realized that he didn't want Matty to stop, and they ended up having one of the most passionate, intense twenty minutes of sex either one of them had ever experienced. (Side note, Matty was not normally good at or willing to experience quickies.)

"There is an exception to every rule," Matty would say.

Then one day Matty had had enough.

He started working on a plan, a private plan.

Matty focused his efforts on purchasing new furniture and putting it in storage. Then he started cleaning up his credit so that he could find his own apartment.

Matty completely threw himself into learning everything he possibly could about credit - - how to use it, how to gain it, and how to keep it.

Once everything was in place, after about six months of hard work, Matty woke up on a Friday morning, his day off, slide his trunk out the door, gathered up his few remaining items, and moved out while Annie was still asleep.

When he closed the door behind him that Friday morning, he closed the door on that part of his life and Annie.

"It may not have been the most mature thing to do, but I have never looked back on that decision, not once."

Matty left so much skin in that apartment that they probably still haven't cleaned it all up yet. The only way to truly clean it up would be to bomb the building and start over.

"Although it was beyond nerve-wracking, I am so grateful to my former friend now because her unconventional help broke my pride but not my spirit. She backed me so far into a corner that I had to succeed. I was forced to succeed! There were no other options."

# Chapter 12

Finally, Matty was in his own one bedroom apartment, and he was a completely different person.

It was a dream come true and even though he was living it, he still dared not believe it.

Matty had spent the better part of the past five years working toward this goal and consumed with reaching that very moment.

Those were five of the absolute roughest financial years of Matty's life.

But he did not care, he knew it was worth every scar.

So when it finally mentally registered that all his hard work had brought him the financial success he had drooled over for so long, all Matty could do was sit down in his own new apartment and shed a few tears.

It was the first private moment he had had in more than five years.

Think about that for a moment.

Matty was so happy to actually be in his own place that he didn't mind walking, riding the metro, or taking a taxi cab everywhere he needed to go.

It didn't even bother him that he was once mugged in a Hispanic neighborhood on his way to pay his Rent-A-Center bill for the television he bought, which was the only way he could purchase it at that time.

He kept his wits about him because he was surrounded by a crowd of Latin-men who again told Matty, "We don't appreciate your kind around here," in a thick accent.

Matty wanted to respond, but he had to accept it because he was alone. But it wasn't enough to keep Matty from walking down to that neighborhood every week to pay his bill.

And when the small crowd saw that he was not going to stop, they no longer bothered him. Additionally, Matty had picked up a little protection so that if he was forced to defend himself he would be able to do so with some reasonable success.

After Matty paid all of his moving bills off he thought that maybe it was time to get a new car.

His credit was so good that he qualified for a $35,000 signature loan in 1994.

"I don't need that much money," Matty told his banker.

"Take this letter and go find whatever car you want and we'll take it from there."

Within days Matty was driving the first Mazda Millennia in the D.C. area - - burgundy with gold trim accents. And the company installed a car phone in the vehicle at absolutely no cost to Matty for the first year.

Matty was rolling.

Matty tried to keep a level head about all of his success, but he could not help but be proud to show off his new vehicle.

And he had no lack of dates.

In fact, Matty had devised a new way to meet quality men.

On his days off, he would hang out around K Street and Massachusetts Avenue - - bankers and diplomats.

Matty had gobs of business cards that he carried everywhere he went.

He would step on the business cards and make them look worn and tethered from being walked on on the sidewalk.

When he would see a guy that interested him, he would walk up to them.

"Excuse me, but you have a business card stuck underneath your shoe."

Sure enough they would have one of Matty's business cards under their shoe.

"Oh wow, that is my card."

Dinner, date, and pillow talk. It became as easy as pie.

One night the favor was returned on Matty.

He had agreed to go out with one of his suitors, although it was really Matty controlling the situation.

Anyway, while they were sitting at dinner, at one of the most coveted spots in Georgetown, Matty looked at his date's suit pocket, and sure enough a cockroach crawled out of his pocket right there at the dinner table.

Matty didn't make a scene because it would have reflected on him also.

Matty stood up.

"You have a cockroach in your breast pocket."

Without giving his date a chance to respond, Matty walked out and threw all of his business cards away.

After that, the credit cards started arriving in the mail by the groves. Each one had a $5,000 or $10,000 credit limit.

Matty had been duped.

He went on a shopping spree. Hell he went on several shopping sprees, for himself, his family, and his friends.

He was also now on the A-list for the best of the best of all shopping spots in town.

The only problem was that Matty was not prepared for managing this kind of success.

Although in Matty's defense he was never taught how to use money or credit. They were poor and although he didn't know they were poor because they were a happy family, his parents were fare better money managers with far less to manage than Matty could have ever hoped for, with so much more available to him.

Part of this came from the fact that when Matty was a child his parents did not believe in using credit.

In truth, his parents probably did not use credit because they could not obtain any credit - - so everything was cash or no carry.

Needless to say, their family did not have access to many nice little pleasures that most people live for and, without which, consider life not worth living.

In addition to that, Matty never once heard his parents talk about money, ever - - period.

So no one knows where Matty got the idea that he had to have so many "things" to be happy, especially after seeing so many of his friends' families with so many things live such unhappy lives.

And just like that Matty was in financial trouble again. But this time it was much worse than anyone could have ever imagined.

Literally, Matty laid down one night financially okay and awoke the next morning to find himself drowning in debt.

He had dug himself in so deeply that bankruptcy looked like the only way out.

Matty's demise reminded him of the story of Joseph.

Despite the fact that he was deceived by his brothers, thrown into a pit, twice sold into slavery, scorned of a woman, falsely accused, thrown into prison, and still became ruler over all, Joseph never changed! His character was obedient and intact no matter where he found himself geographically.

The difficulty of Joseph's everyday life prepared him to be successful under any circumstances, even as the ruler over all of Egypt – as a Hebrew.

Matty, on the other hand, was not prepared. He was trying to resolve situations and moments, but he had completely forgotten about his character.

So when his character was tested, he failed the test because in all his getting, he failed to get understanding.

Matty was so focused on becoming rich that he did not think about how that would change him, or what to do with money once he had complete control over it.

Although it had taken him more than five years to reach that pinnacle, his fall happened before he ever had the chance to plant his feet on the ground.

By this time Matty was locked in his room (apartment) as Otis Redding put it. This time he was pondering his future with far greater consequences than even he could have imagined.

Matty's success was no fluke. It was genuine, but his ability to handle it was a different matter.

By the time he realized that his success in life was attached to both his character and responsibility, not just his selfish indulgences, he was standing in front of a bankruptcy judge.

Bankruptcy was the irrevocable final solution to Matty's long line of big money mistakes.

By now Matty was finally ready to get off that financial rollercoaster, and start over again the right way. But that was easier said than done.

Although Matty was a working professional with a Bachelor of Science degree in Finance, and he was in the most serious financial trouble of his young life, he could not recall a course in Financial Recovery 101.

But the embarrassment hadn't hit him - - yet.

Matty had a couple of important business dinners he was hosting that week.

He rushed out to the grocery store for a rare weekly visit.

After spending two hours walking around that store making his selections, he finally got up to the register where the total rang up to be $204.32.

Matty swiped his Visa check card and had started to leave with his groceries when his card declined just as he picked up his bags.

Then he swiped a different card and it declined also.

Meanwhile, the line behind Matty was growing, both in size and agitation.

He then swiped a third and then a fourth card.

Matty was struggling to be calm and not embarrassed. Then he started all over again.

Finally, Matty accepted his fate and walked out of the store without any groceries and a bag full of shame that he had to carry all over his face.

Matty was a thirty-something who had fallen into a credit hole with no way out.

He stood in the window and watched as the repossesser drove up to his apartment with his trailer to take back that which once was possessed by Matty, at least temporarily.

Matty stayed in the window the entire time as they prepared to drive his former burgundy Mazda Millennia up on to its resting place as it was to be driven away from Matty's life.

And once again Matty was back on the metro, which he gladly rode in financial peace.

But Matty's spirit was unsettled.

"Is this what I am supposed to be doing with my life?"

Matty's soul was searching for something but he could not find it no matter where he looked.

After months of searching and talking to everyone he trusted, Matty decided to leave his lucrative job position to go to seminary in Tulsa, Oklahoma.

Matty truly believed he had been called of God to preach. He had so many prophecies spoken over him in church that he honestly believed it was the right thing to do.

Sadly no one could give him a real reason to help understand that he didn't have to leave his job to serve God. But their cries fell upon deaf ears.

"Actually I don't think I had one single friend who would stand toe to toe with me and chastise me so that I would not leave such a good job."

In the absence of any reason not to go, Matty set his plan in motion.

"Not even my own mother would tell me not to leave my job."

She said, "It is not for me to tell you how to live your life. You have to make your own decisions."

Matty left his job around Thanksgiving 1996, drove from D.C. to North Carolina in his older model white, Ford

Taurus with its dangling rear bumper that had started falling off two days after Matty purchased the car.

And from there he drove west across the Mississippi River to the land of Oklahoma, where he made his home for two years.

Although Matty succeeded in school, he was met with much opposition by those around him.

Matty willingly accepted a vow of celibacy and held fast to every other rule of the honor code, but that was not good enough for some.

The first year of seminary was a breeze for Matty, since this was his second masters level program.

He had money, good grades, focus, and most importantly, Matty had his own space that he did not have to share with anyone. And, he didn't have to run or hide from any men or women.

For the first time in recent memory Matty was drug free and sex free.

Yep, Matty was celibate.

But there was one small problem.

Matty wasn't feeling inspired.

School was just school.

By the time the next school year rolled around Matty began thinking about his future and what he would do once he graduated.

Matty had become so depressed he thought of becoming a monk and joining a group of monks in a faraway, secluded monastery.

"I can't do that. It would break momma's heart. Hell, it would break my heart."

Matty remembered how hurt his mother was when he tried to run away. He scratched that idea and went back to the drawing board.

The second year rolled around and nothing changed, except that he caught the attention of one of his classmates, Mike.

But it was not the normal attention that Matty was used to receiving.

About midway into the semester, Mike cornered Matty in a classroom, alone.

"What's going on Mike?"

"Look Matty."

From there Mike literally tried to force Matty into admitting that he was gay so that he could have Matty kicked out of school.

When Matty refused, Mike established a vendetta against Matty, which was not helped by the fact that Matty was personally chosen by the Assistant Dean of the school to be his graduate teaching assistant.

Mike was jealous of Matty.

Matty became hated for doing no more than trying to be an honest student of the Word of God.

Still Matty never quit.

In fact, Matty excelled so that he passed several classes for the Master of Divinity degree, which he sought, by testing out of those classes completely.

But his success did not come easily.

Shortly after that Matty became deathly ill. He was stricken with shingles on the left side of his face.

Immediately after that Matty had the most severe outbreak of psoriasis he had ever experienced. He was covered from his scalp to the soles of his feet with psoriasis.

His skin again became horribly deformed while in Tulsa.

In fact, his skin was so bad that Matty started breaking out every day, until it got so bad that Matty woke up in bed one night to find that he was completely covered in ants!

They were eating all of the dead skin that had accumulated in his bed from the psoriasis in just one night.

He jumped up smacking those ants and trying to knock them off, but his body was covered with them.

There were just too damn many.

Ants were hanging on Matty like they were gathered on a tree limb.

He had forgotten that he was naked.

Immediately, he ran to the shower to wash them off, and the hot water was scolding his already bruised and bleeding skin, but at that very moment Matty did not care.

He looked down at the tub as he was stepping out of the shower to see that the tub was full of dead skin and ants still eating at the pieces of skin that looked like rotten, broken pieces of crepes.

Still Matty didn't quit, despite all his challenges.

Although Matty had fallen significantly behind because of his bout with psoriasis, and despite the fact that he looked more and more like a leper, he refused to give up. And this despite the fact that he was isolated and alone.

In order to make up all the lost work he had missed, Matty completed an exhaustive list of reading assignments and writing papers for each assignment while he recovered from his leprosy episode, which took more than four months.

But by then Matty was so far behind there appeared to be no way for Matty to ever catch up.

However, Matty was no quitter.

Matty petitioned the school to let him take several classes by examination.

And in Matty-fashion, he passed each and every examination with flying colors.

Finally, Matty was on track to graduate from seminary with his Masters of Divinity.

"Matty."

"Hey momma."

"Matty."

Pause.

"Momma, what's wrong? Matty's heart was about to beat out of his chest.

"Why are you crying?" Matty was frantic.

"There's been a fire."

Matty immediately interrupted his mother.

"Are you okay momma?"

"Yes."

"Everybody else okay?"

"Yea, everybody is fine."

"So why are you crying?"

"I can't get the insurance company to fix my house."

Without the slightest hesitation Matty said, "I'll be right there."

She was the only person that Matty had ever been true to outside of Henri and Harry. Matty was not even true to himself.

Matty would never refuse his mother no matter what was going on in his life.

Sadie had come to that boy's rescue so many times that Matty knew in his heart he could never repay her. And even if he could, he would never tell her no.

Anyone that knew Matty when he was a child knew that anytime he came home crying that Sadie would immediately go wherever she needed to go to quash the problem.

They used to laugh in the neighborhood barbershop about how Sadie would go to the Bethlehem Center often, every day if necessary, to find out what happened to Sadie's baby, Matty, anytime that boy came home crying.

So with that memory intact, Matty laughed as he prepared to immediately dismantle his household and head back home to Charlotte with only the basic necessities.

But Matty was used to rebuilding himself. So this was no different.

1. Call a furniture dealer
2. Ship the files
3. Pack the car
4. Develop travel plan
5. Stop in Knoxville, Tennessee (rekindle fire or prove fire is out?)
6. Arrive in Charlotte refreshed
7. Hit ground running

He went back to the dean and explained his circumstance and asked if he could take one final examination.

Except there was a catch.

Matty wanted to take the test at home in Charlotte because he needed to leave school asap in order to get back home to his mother and their family home, a home he has hated since the day they moved in.

The dean agreed to Matty's request with the understanding that Matty would still be honor-code bound during the entire time he was at home until the examination had been completed and returned to the dean by mail.

Despite all his past travails, Matty was a truly honest person, in part because his mother trained him to be that way by beating his ass every time he told a lie and because he learned in Sunday school that God loves a honest soul.

But when Matty got back home repairing his family's homestead was not the only repairs that were needed.

It was then that Matty also realized that his own life needed much repair.

There was nowhere else for Matty to run to.

He had left with the intention of never coming back. That failed.

He went to college, twice, and ended up homeless and basically prostituting at no cost to his clients.

Therefore since Matty was never able to study and take the exam properly, without cheating, Matty never opened the envelope that contained the exam.

He wanted to preach but he was no good at delivering the Word, at least in the same fashion that he was accustomed to hearing in the AME Zion church that had been in their family for over 100 years, the same church his great grandfather started.

"And I've squandered all of my job prospects and talents by hoping around the country chasing dreams being unsettled, unfocused, and trying to hide from myself and the world."

In the end, Matty was in his same old room looking up at those faded blinds that had been a resident of that same room for as long as or longer than he had been.

"I guess this means that Harvard, my dual PhD, and law degree are gone."

The words stuck in Matty's throat for days because he had no time to swallow or digest the bitter words.

RING. RING.

"Hey Matty."

"Hey Grandpa."

"I want you to come down here boy so I can talk to you."

"Okay Grandpa. When you want me to come?"

"Come now boy. Why would I call you if I don't want you to come now?"

His grandpa chuckled.

"Grandpa?"

Matty didn't want to go immediately because he wanted to sulk about the loss he just recognized by his own admission.

"Boy you better not Grandpa me again."

"Yes sir. I'll be right there."

Before Matty got in his car and headed toward his favorite place in the world, he realized that he had spent his entire life trying to run away from his past or doing things to try and make sure people liked him.

But the problem is that Matty spent so much time trying to get others to like him, he never got around to liking himself.

"And there's no time to think about all of that now either," Matty said.

True to his word, Matty showed up within his grandfather's allotted time limit he had given Matty to arrive.

Although his grandfather never said a word about a timeframe, Matty knew his grandfather's unspoken rules of response time to his demands.

"You just made it boy."

"Hey Grandpa."

As expected Matty's grandfather was looking at his watch when Matty walked through the door.

"You were almost late son."

Matty chuckled.

"Grandpa, how was I almost late when I have another 30 minutes by my watch?"

"Come on Matty, walk with an old man."

As they separated from the long bear hug his grandpa always gave him, they walked out of the living room and back out onto the front porch.

No matter when Matty visited that little white house, he was the same six-year-old standing there watching them take his grandmother away.

Matty's grandfather saw the sadness in his eyes, the same sadness that had been there for more than thirty-five years. And it was still there today. It was hard for Matty's grandfather to see him sometimes because he was a constant reminder of what they had all lost that day so many years ago.

He didn't say a word to Matty. And Matty responded in kind.

The place didn't look the same anymore.

Matty's grandfather was a tight wad and an even worse, downright terrible housekeeper.

That once pristine living room that was both beautiful and stylish, not to mention spotless, was now overtaken with riggety pieces of furniture handed down to Matty's grandfather from anybody and everybody.

Secondly, the living room was also taken over by piles of heating wood that his grandfather had chopped for the larger wood-burning stove that replaced the smaller more demure stove that once sat in its place before Matty's grandmother died.

"You coming boy?"

That was Matty's grandfather's way of letting him know that he understood his pain.

"Yes sir."

"Matty, there are some things I need to tell you."

They walked over to the farthest left corner of the property.

"This is where our property line begins."

They started walking that line.

"You gettin' this Matty?"

"Yes sir."

And Matty wasn't lying. He was paying particular attention to every step of the way.

As they got to the creek bed that was once Matty's private swimming pool, his grandfather stopped.

"Matty, your granddaddy has cancer."

Matty didn't say a word.

"It's serious."

Matty could hold back his tears no longer.

"Now listen son. Everybody dies."

Matty cried harder.

"Matty stop crying son. I'm not dying tomorrow."

"How long?"

"We got a while to go. The doctor said he caught it in time."

"So why you telling me? And why now?"

"Because there are things you need to know about and do while I'm still in my right mind."

"What are you telling me…that you are going to lose your mind?"

Matty was screaming, but it didn't matter, there was nobody around to hear them.

That was the beauty of that place.

"I don't know Matty. What I do know is that you are in charge and you can't tell anyone."

"Why must I bear this burden alone?"

His grandfather turned him around and looked Matty straight in his eyes.

"Because you are the strongest and smartest of all your brothers. You always have been, but you had to find that out on your own."

"Why didn't you say something years ago?"

"If I or anyone else had told you that you would not have believed us, and it would only make it worse for you. So you had to find out in your own way, in your own time."

Matty started walking again.

"Where are you going boy?"

"I'm walking the property line. Isn't that what you wanted me to see?"

"How do you know where the property line is?"

"I saw a property map a long time ago laying around in the old trailer after you had it attached to the back of the house."

"You see."

"See what?"

"You are smarter than you brothers."

Once upon time that might have meant something to Matty but not anymore.

As they continued walking to the back of the property, his grandfather said, "There's more."

"Like what Grandpa?"

"Boy, who you talkin' to?"

"Sorry, granddaddy. I didn't mean it the way it came out. But you do have to admit this is an awful lot to take in…on top of everything else."

"What else? Your momma okay?"

"Yes sir."

But, Matty whispered under his breath, "I'm not okay grandpa, I'm not okay."

By this time they had reached the top of the hill at the very back of the property.

"Damn."

"Matty what did you say?"

"I said granddaddy look at all that sh____"

"You better not say it or I while spank your ass right here in these woods. I don't care how old you are."

Matty didn't want that because he knew what his granddaddy's whoppings looked like.

Once they were all sitting in the living room and a snake came crawling across the floor out of nowhere. Without a thought or a concern, his granddad picked the snake up with his bare hand and squeezed the snake's head until it popped like a balloon. All in a matter of seconds.

And this was just a few years ago before Matty went to Tulsa.

Matty sat down on a log and his granddaddy beside him.

"Matty, I'm not your paternal grandfather."

"Look, granddaddy."

"Matty did you hear me boi?"

"It looks like Fred Sanford's place, only worse."

"Oh, I get it. You trying to pretend I didn't say what I said."

Matty was waiting for the other shoe to drop.

"You see Matty, I married your grandmother when your momma was a little girl. I met your grandma shortly after I stopped seeing your Uncle June's mother."

Matty's eyes had so many questions.

"Yea Matty, your Uncle June and your Aunt Sue were not your mother's natural brother and sister."

"But…." Matty tried to interject.

"Yea, your Uncle June loved your mother and protected her above anybody and everybody, including his own mother and his sister. She was his favorite."

"Grandpa, you are the only grandpa I have ever known."

"You actually met your real grandpa…."

"YOU are my real grandpa."

"Don't interrupt me boy."

"Now like I was saying, you met your real grandpa once before your grandmother died."

"I don't remember that."

"Once he came to visit ya'll when you lived off Remus in that apartment. He came to visit your mother and he was drunk and made your momma cry."

"I remember that man. Daddy was so upset with that man that he grabbed him by his shirt and jacked him up off the floor. Then he told him that if he ever came around again that he would kill him."

"That was your grandpa."

"That was just a man. You are my grandpa."

"Okay Matty, have it your way."

"Daddy, look at the house down there."

"Yea, what about it?"

"It looks worse than Fred Sanford's place. At least he made money off his junk."

"Let's finish walking the property line," his grandfather responded.

They continued walking the property line and came down on the other side of the property, on the right side.

"Now you know the entire property line to this land so that if you need to sell it you will know exactly what it is worth."

"Granddaddy we didn't have to do all of this. I told you that I already saw the map."

"Well, humor me. I like to do things the old fashioned way. Do you know when we were slaves the only land we could claim after we got our freedom was the land that we walked with our own feet?"

"No sir. I didn't know that."

"Now you know."

His grandpa kept on walking to his old wooden shed that stood at the back of the property near the back porch.

"You know your daddy cheated on your mother several times while they were married."

Matty didn't know what to say.

"Your daddy, his brother, and one of his nephews used to chase women like they was water."

"Grandpa, I'm not going in that old place. I know it's full of snakes."

His grandpa didn't say a thing. He knew Matty was playing the denial game again.

"Maybe I have told you too much in one day," his grandpa said.

"That's okay. I don't want them," his granddaddy said about the snakes as he kept on walking into the shed while Matty stood in the door way.

His grandfather went deep into the shed, moved some old mattresses, opened the doors to a cabinet, pulled out the bottom of the cabinet, moved some dirt, and pulled out a little tin box.

"Boy I didn't raise you to be afraid of life," his grandfather said once he met Matty back at the front door.

"Granddaddy you know I ain't never liked snakes every since I was little."

"Don't nobody like snakes Matty but you can't stop living because they are in your way."

That argument made so much profound sense to Matty that day although its application was years past.

"What's in the tin can?"

His granddaddy wiped the dirt off the beautiful can that looked like it was an old antique.

"Matty inside this tin can is $10,000 that I have saved up. Much like your grandma did for your mother."

Matty was confused.

"Get your momma to tell you the story sometime."

Pause.

"Pick your bottom lip up boi before it falls off."

"$10,000 Granddaddy? How did you save $10,000?"

"Matty you can do anything you want to do if you put your mind to it."

"Now you tell me."

"Where were you when I was trying to get rid of JPH and Shaun?" Matty whispered.

Then Matty thought to himself, I wonder how granddaddy would feel if he knew I was gay?

"Matty this $10,000 is for my funeral."

"FUNERAL! You said you were not getting ready to die!"

"I'm not Matty, but someday I will and I want to know that you know where the money is."

"Well don't put it back in there or else you won't be getting buried."

His grandfather chuckled.

"I'm giving it to you for you to take care of."

"Why?"

"I trust you Matty. But it is not enough for a headstone. You are going to have to buy your old grandpa a headstone yourself."

Matty was in full blown tears.

"Granddaddy explain it to me again why you are charging me with all of this important work."

"You are going to force me to say things I don't want to say."

"No disrespect Granddaddy but you owe me that much."

"Okay Matty. The truth is that I had given your Aunt Sue all the information to take care of everything. But after she died I didn't have anybody I could trust to get this all right."

"What's wrong with my momma?"

"Matty, your mother is too inpatient to handle these details. And since she dropped out of school around the 9th grade, your mother is not going to know how to navigate all of this stuff."

"What stuff?"

"When the time comes you will see."

One year went by.

Two years.

Three years.

Four years.

By the end of the fourth year, Matty was taking care of all of his grandfather's matters including his medical appointments.

One day, his grandfather had to have a surgical procedure regarding his prostate cancer and Matty had to help him get undressed to get ready for the procedure.

"Damn granddaddy," Matty said out loud before he caught himself.

"Now I know why grandma loved you so much when everybody used to call you short and ugly. They didn't understand why grandma, who had model looks, stayed with you for 25 years or more."

Matty had an entire conversation all by himself.

After that Matty's grandfather started going down more and more.

"Granddaddy you shouldn't be living by yourself anymore."

"Matty if I leave this house I will go down like the Titanic. So I'm not leaving this house."

It wasn't long after that Matty's grandfather had a house fire because he went to sleep while cooking and the pot burned up on the stove.

"Granddaddy, you can't stay here alone anymore."

"I'm not leaving here."

"Granddaddy, please don't do this to me. Now if you die in a fire, momma will never forgive me. I don't have a choice. You have to go live with momma."

So by day Matty took care of his mother and grandfather. By night he worked long hours.

Matty was dead on his feet.

"Momma, I hate to tell you this, but we don't have a choice any more. We are going to have to put granddaddy into a managed care facility. He has developed dementia and he requires around the clock medical care."

"I know Matty. I know. I knew the time was coming but I didn't want to have to admit it to myself, but I know the time has come."

With that Matty started researching nursing homes, shortly after which Matty located a suitable, medically equipped, clean, and well-served nursing facility.

His grandfather improved for two years strong, so strong in fact that his grandfather became the rooster of his own henhouse.

Then one night, Matty got that phone call at work. They had rushed his grandfather to the hospital.

Matty rushed home, picked up his mother and they rushed over to the hospital.

The two of them nervously waited in the waiting room.

"Mr. Pottishear?" The doctor called his name.

"Yes sir." Matty jumped up, along with his mother.

"Sir, I'm sorry to tell you."

Matty would not let the doctor complete his sentence.

"My grandfather's dead isn't he?"

"I'm afraid so."

"I want to see him."

"Let me have him cleaned up and then you can see him."

Matty calmly waited. He was staring at his mother. She was an orphan now. In so many ways, Matty could see that little girl his granddaddy was trying to tell him about years ago.

When the time came, the nurses came and got Matty.

He reached his hand out for his mother.

She shook her head no. She wasn't going to go see him.

Matty walked back into the examination room, with no fear in his heart or bones whatsoever, so that he could see his grandfather.

When he walked into the room, his grandfather was lying in the fetal position on his left hand side.

"We'll give you a minute alone with him."

There was no one in the room but Matty and his grandfather.

Matty walked up to his grandfather, kissed his forehead, and said, "It's finished granddaddy. I will do everything I said I will do. And I will make sure momma's gets her money for the property. I won't break your trust."

And he did, every single thing he was required to do, down to the very last detail.

Matty went to the court and found out that his grandfather never took the property to probate when his grandmother died over thirty-five years ago. So Matty single-handedly went back and gathered every single piece of data necessary to properly transfer the title of the property from his grandparent's names to his mother's name.

That was a difficult process for a trained attorney, let alone a layman like Matty. But Matty, the layman, thoroughly completed that entire detailed process by himself and he did it flawlessly.

Then after that, Matty started cleaning up the property with his own money because now that his grandfather was dead, the people around him wanted that eyesore cleaned up or they were going to take the property.

And cleaned it up he did.

Matty had the property approximately 90% clean.

Then one night Matty was sitting at home alone, and in that moment he became overwhelmed.

Without uttering a word, Matty pulled a package out of his coat pocket that he had been carrying around for a couple of weeks.

Life had beaten Matty down to his last ounce of fight.

There was no more left in him.

Through his bloodshot eyes and his sorrows drowned in his tears, Matty began to snort huge amounts of powder.

And snort. And snort. And snort.

Matty snorted more cocaine in a few minutes than most junkies ever snorted in their entire life.

He was ready.

"Lord forgive me for what I do."

Matty got up and walked to the bathroom and he fell down.

The life began to drain from his body and Matty was prepared to let it drain.

Suddenly, a fight came in his spirit and he began to reject death.

"No. No. No. No," Matty screamed.

"I refuse to give up and be defeated like this after everything I have been through."

"No Jesus. We cannot die like this."

It was just Matty and Jesus in that room.

Jesus lifted Matty up so that he could see his face in the mirror.

God had saved Matty's life yet again.

Matty washed his face, fell to his knees thanking God, and he flushed the remaining cocaine down the toilet. It was enough to fill a sugar bowl.

Then Matty went to bed and slept for the next two days. He had already turned all the telephones off.

When he recovered he went back to the homestead, picking up right where he left off.

There was nothing left but the structures - - the house, the shed, the outhouse, and the garage.

Since Matty was paying for all of this work out of his own pocket, because he had spent the entire $10,000 his grandfather gave him on his funeral, Matty didn't have the money to pay a demolition crew to demolish all of those buildings.

Matty got the idea to call the local fire department to see if they wanted to burn the structures down as part of a training exercise.

The fire department was ecstatic at the offer of having a controlled burn to help train its men.

At the set date and time, Matty took a night off from work and showed up at the one constant that had been in his life since the day he was born.

Matty took one last walk through the entire house that his mother had arranged to be emptied weeks before by the men of the family.

The furniture was gone, so too was the infamous double-decker cast iron stove, the wash tub that was Matty's bath tub, and every other staple that was part of their lives. It was all gone.

But not one single emotion involving the place was gone. Matty held onto those emotions and feelings deep in his soul like they were more important than pure gold. And to Matty they were.

After that long walk around, Matty walked back outside and watched as the fire men lit the house on fire and started their training.

As the fire got hotter and hotter, the flames went from yellow to blue, Matty looked into the fire to see all of his memories rising up in the flames and rising up to heaven. His whole history was rising higher in the flames.

But they weren't just his memories. The entire memories of his whole family was going up in flames.

Matty could literally see their smiling faces as they rose to heaven inside of the flames - - his grandmother, his father, his aunts, his great grandfather, and his entire present family, all their happiest of days were going up in blue flames.

He could not help but cry.

He wanted to stop the fire, but it was far, far too late.

As Matty stayed and watched, and the fire got down near the ground, there were pits full of snakes all around the property that were trying to escape the fire, but to no avail.

There were hundreds, if not thousands of snakes that were burned up that day and the next day, and so on. Some of them stood straight up in the fire and everyone could see their mouths open as if they were screaming.

It was a dramatic sight to be held.

That fire burned for three solid days. And Matty visited that fire every single day for several hours, until it was all gone.

His life had come full circle.

It just wasn't the circle that Matty had envisioned.

There was just nothing left for Matty to do or give.

Matty went home and crawled into bed.

Before he went to sleep, his grandfather's sister, Aunt Naomi called him and told him, "You know your grandfather had more money than that. You burned up your granddaddy's money in that house. Maybe a hundred thousand or more."

"Aunt Naomi, if that is true, then I rather it be burned up than someone else enjoying it and spending it."

Later that the night Matty woke up.

He saw a strange new sight.

He stopped, shook his head, rubbed his eyes, and looked again.

This was no dream.

They were very much real.

Matty was staring at two, ten-feet tall, pure jet black, tamed but ferocious dogs watching over him.

At first Matty was scared.

He wanted to run, but he knew there was no way that he could out run those dogs.

He sat up.

The dogs moved their heads in response to Matty's movement.

Then as quickly as he realized what was going on, a rush of peace came over him, like a warm electric blanket.

That's when he knew that the dogs were there to protect him, not hurt him.

Matty went back to sleep in greater peace.

Then he had another dream.

He couldn't see everything but he could see all this construction going on around him but he couldn't talk to anyone or touch anything.

There were final preparations being made in heaven, for this new arrival. Inside the pearly gates, the city was buzzing about the events about to take place.

Matty wasn't sure who was the new arrival and the arrival itself was not the news. The news was the manner of this particular arrival. That was the most exciting news of all, according to all of the conversations that Matty was hearing.

"This has never happened before."

Matty was trying to see the faces of those who were talking, but he could not see any of their faces. Their faces were hidden by clouds but he could hear their voices.

It was a joyous occasion and cause for great celebration for the entire city, even though the arrival was not going to technically be a new resident. This, again, according to the conversations that Matty could hear, from the sidelines.

Matty kept walking, but it was less about walking, and more about floating.

At the far end of the city in the southern hemisphere, a structure was being built that was not two football fields long, nor was it three football fields long, but in fact it was more than five football fields long and was twice as wide as the superdome in New Orleans, one of Matty's favorite partying cities in the world, or used to be anyway.

Matty took his time and slowly walked inside this superstructure.

Having studied the law and court rooms, Matty could tell there was a gallery for more than the spectators expected to attend, a protective area for the defendant, a juror's box, and three other boxes that Matty had never seen before.

But he did recognize the largest section of all, the judge's bench, but it had this huge purple curtain that surrounded it.

Matty thought that was strange.

The workers building the structure were giants among men and were yet dwarfed by the enormous structure that was nearing completion. The building's design was more than similar to only one other ever built. There was so much gold used to decorate various parts of the structure that it would seem the earth could not contain it and enough silver to match.

The curtains were made of blue, purple, and scarlet linen woven from a single piece of cloth because Matty could not see any seams anywhere.

And there was so much acacia wood used that it would exceed the South American rain forests five times over.

It was an impossible structure built for an impossible task even in this city.

This structure was clearly expensive but for this group of builders, costs meant nothing.

As Matty listened to other conversations, he overheard that the cost of the structure exceeded $6 billion, but money meant no option in this place.

But these giant workers did care about their positions, the building's success, and the Master's approval.

They had never built such a structure like this before. Perfection, which was always Heaven's standard, and impossible by human measurements, had to show that their work cared as much as did the Master about their invited guest. A guest that was so dear to the Master's heart, which was the reason for the structure anyway, because He cared.

"So who is this invited guest? I'm in Heaven?" Matty asked himself.

In just a few human hours, timelessness in this place, there was to be a final inspection by the master builder, not one minute detail of the structure would be ignored, no one detail more important than the other, but no mistake could exist.

In an obscure dark room, quite the opposite of the bustling construction site, away from all eyes, and a world away from that scene, an equally critical task was also nearing completion.

In the very back of the room, there was a bearded gentleman who was so tall he could not stand erect in the room, which was also okay because he was tending a fire so hot that the only color in the flame was royal blue.

Sitting at a table in the center of the room was a learned gentleman crafting notes on parchment clearly more expensive then sheepskin, and using only the fire's flame as light while still one other paced the floor methodically dictating his scribe's words. A guard larger than all of them combined guarded the doorway.

*"Matthew Edward Pottishear,*

*You are hereby required to give appearance before the audience of His Majesty*

*Saturday, February 29..."*

The door opened abruptly, all work stopped, and every eye in the room addressed the unexpected guest with nonverbal reverence.

"Is it ready?"

Each worker looked at the other, none wanting to confirm the clearly obvious.

"Arcacian," offered one titan to the other, "we disagreed on the details of the invitation until a short time ago."

"The site will be inspected in less than two hours and the invitation must be ready as soon as the final inspection is approved so Herald can personally deliver it at precisely 9:07 pm."

Not another word was said. The scribe, dictator, and goldsmith all nodded in agreement at the overseer's instructions as he departed on his way to give the Master a complete update.

The matter settled, Arcacian, the overseer of the entire project, headed out for his final inspection of the construction site. The workers all jumped to attention as if they were in the army, muscles so tense and lips so tightly pierced that even their breath was constrained.

This was the moment they had all been waiting for, the moment when their work would be voted up or down. Each worker craved the affirmation not for some reward but for the satisfaction of knowing their work had met the highest standard set by the Master on the first try.

Yet, each worker fully recognized that a vote down meant they had but a few measly hours to make any directed corrections, but they were happily prepared to do so at tenacious speed because one fact would be driving their work, a delay of any kind would not be tolerated in the Master's plan.

"Arcacian."

"Gabriel-Emu."

Gabriel-Emu had come out to meet Arcacian and when the two shook hands it also shook the surrounding mountains. These warriors towered over all their workers although not one of their workers was less than nine feet tall.

Gabriel-Emu was more than eleven feet tall, weighed more than an even ton, and his face was encircled by a well-tended beard, beautiful olive toned skin, and arms as big as the sequoias in the central hills of California.

And Arcacian was even bigger than he and older looking, though not a frail warrior by any means. He was a superb combination of wisdom and strength with more than enough size to support either and honed acumen to give him a commanding edge in any battle.

"How are things in the city my dear friend?" Gabriel-Emu asked.

"Frantic, Emu, frantic" a term of endearment between the two, Arcacian responded.

Arcacian continued, "The city is especially aglow with anticipation about the unveiling and others are more concerned about the details of which they know not - - details that have not been released to anyone, not even the elders."

"Even I must admit, in spite of our many battles, we are about to face a formidable foe, which is the sole raison d'être for this ornate structure."

"Formidable in this place?" Gabriel-Emu laughed at the thought.

Arcacian did not laugh.

Gabriel-Emu recognizing the seriousness of the moment returned to the business at hand.

"Then let me not detain you any further unnecessarily. But before we begin the final walk thru, let's walk to the top of the mountain and see the fullness of our work."

Although the top of the mountain was beyond human capabilities it was but a mere hill for these seasoned veterans.

In what seemed like only a few steps, the two majestic warriors stood side by side at the top of Mt. Koreb looking down at the beautiful courthouse they had built.

Arcacian offered a vivid explanation of the sight.

"The best physical description I can provide would be the astonishingly beautiful vistas of the Wasatch Range rising behind downtown Salt Lake City. With the Master's glory shining down across pure blue skies, casting a beautiful orange hue over that portion of the mountains not hidden in the cloud-covered peaks, making the uncovered portions a symphonic reflection of his unspoken majesty."

"Gabriel-Emu, it is exquisite," Arcacian proclaimed with a rare smile that required no explanation.

The workers had exceeded even their own expectations.

The courthouse was so huge that it completely filled the valley from end to end with no room to spare, and the mountains made a superb backdrop to this picture, and would be used as secondary seating for those not able to be in the main viewing gallery.

Inside the courthouse, the workers were feverishly polishing the wood, clearing away the remaining debris, and occasionally taking a moment to also admire their work. They were tall but this structure absolutely dwarfed its builders, and it had to be because of its visitor.

"Let us go down," the two warriors, Gabriel-Emu and Arcacian said to one another.

Huge Persian guards were already posting to their positions around the perimeter of the pearl structure ready to greet every single guest for the soon to be trial that was but mere hours away, in earthly time.

The outside of the building was hewn out of a single pearl particularly chosen for this occasion. It was a pure white baroque without blemish so full in stature that it extended more than the length of the five football fields and so delicate that the slightest off-chiseled cut would destroy the entire pearl.

Therefore, the absolute best stonecutters in the city had been handpicked to carve this flawless stone into the grandiose structure appearing before their very eyes and for good reason, no other single stone was suitable for this building. Further, no other stone had adequate depth and width to meet the end purpose, fill the valley, and stand as tall as the mountains which surrounded it.

The main entrance was a massive domed entrance marked by seven columns, three on either side and one huge column in the middle, bordered on both sides by immense doors made from acacia wood with pure gold door knockers that were larger than a thirty-two-inch screen television in the middle of each door, and sparkling gold hinges to match.

The dome itself was similar in style to the Tempietto of San Pietro in Rome, Italy. It also had guards perched around its upper level.

Once inside the dome, the huge viewing gallery made an archway for those entering the courtroom, a gallery large enough to seat in excess of 10,000 oversized heavenly beings who had been specifically chosen because of their rank to view the proceedings firsthand. Each seat, large enough to hold one larger than Arcacian himself, was covered with blue cushions, so blue that eyes cannot describe its excellence, except to say that it was a blue never seen on earth.

Just beyond the gallery was a second viewing area with fewer, but immensely larger chairs for a select group, the elders, and chief advisors to the Master. Their seats were covered in a royal purple that exceeded the beauty of those in the upper viewing gallery. The only thing separating the two sides was a long, red-carpeted walkway so plush that it was like walking on pure air, and again guarded on both sides by Persian sentries who were already in position.

In front of this section, on the right-hand side was an elevated marble desk with three perfectly matching marble chairs and on the left-hand side was an even bigger red-marble table with only one chair.

On the left wall was what appeared to be a screen so big that it would dwarf any seen in the largest IMAX movie theater in Sydney, Australia.

And directly in front of it on the other side of the courtroom were the largest chairs, 12 to be exact, situated in a viewing box that nearly reached the ceiling, giving the members undisturbed viewing of the screen across the room. Their seats were covered in golden threads woven together with hints of blue, purple, and red intertwined in each.

Finally, the judge's box was the full focus and most important aspect of this architectural masterpiece. It was as large as the first seating gallery by itself with a throne centered in the exact middle of the box and the pearl, and was bigger than the base of the Statue of Liberty with a desk equally matched. To top it off, a huge opening encircled the throne in the pearl ceiling above it.

During the entire inspection, Arcacian said not a word, nor did he make any sounds while running his thick fingers along various surfaces to test their smoothness while measuring unique points of his choosing.

"Close the curtain," is all he said to Gabriel-Emu.

With that, a purple linen curtain was drawn that shielded the throne and the entire desk from the eyes of all viewers least they be consumed.

As Arcacian departed the construction site and headed for the city to make his final report, he could hear shouts of joy at his approval of their work.

Matty was ready to wake up from his beautiful dream.

Matty couldn't wake up.

www.ingramcontent.com/pod-product-compliance
Lightning Source LLC
Chambersburg PA
CBHW030211170426
43201CB00006B/54